STAGE BY STAGE

LAUGHTER AND GRANDEUR

BY THE SAME AUTHOR

Novels

The Volcano God
The Zoltans: A Trilogy
The Dark Shore
The Evening Heron
Dreams of Youth
Easter Island
Searching

Short Stories

The Devious Ways
The Beholder
The Snow
Three Exotic Tales
A Man of Taste
The Young Greek and the Creole
The Spymaster
The Young Artists

Fantasy

The Merry Communist

Plays

Prince Hamlet
Mario's Well
Black Velvet
Simon Simon
Three Off-Broadway Plays
More Off-Broadway Plays
Three Poetic Plays

Criticism

Myths of Creation
The Art of Reading the Novel
Preface to Otto Rank's *The Myth of the Birth of the Hero and Other Essays*
Preface to Kimi Gengo's *To One Who Mourns at the Death of the Emperor*
Some Notes on Tragedy
Preface to Joseph Conrad's *Lord Jim*
Stage by Stage Vol. 1: The Birth of Theatre
Stage by Stage Vol. 2: Oriental Theatre
Stage by Stage Vol. 3: Dramatis Personae – The Rise of Medieval and Renaissance Theatre

Poetry

Private Speech

Philip Freund

STAGE BY STAGE

LAUGHTER AND GRANDEUR

Theatre in the Age of Baroque

PETER OWEN
London and Chester Springs, PA, USA

PETER OWEN PUBLISHERS
73 Kenway Road, London SW5 ORE

Peter Owen books are distributed in the USA by
Dufour Editions Inc., Chester Springs, PA 19425-0007

First published in Great Britain 2008 by
Peter Owen Publishers

ISBN 978-0-7206-1298-1

A catalogue record for this book is available from the British Library

Printed and bound in Croatia by Zrinski d.d.

To Walter Glanze
who encouraged me

CONTENTS

ILLUSTRATIONS

Between pages 96 and 97

The Triumph of Love (Marivaux, 1732), McCarter Theatre, Princeton, 1991–2; directed by Stephen Wadsworth (© T. Charles Erickson)

Marie Sallé (1707–56); engraving after a portrait by Nicolas Lancret (© Mander and Mitchenson)

Jean-Georges Noverre (1727–1810); engraving by Roger after a painting by Jean-Baptiste Guérin, *c.* 1800 (© Mander and Mitchenson)

Les Plaisirs du bal, *c.* 1715–17, by Antoine Watteau (© AKG)

Marie-Anne de Cupis de Camargo (1710–70); engraving after a portrait by Nicolas Lancret (© Mander and Mitchenson)

Voltaire (a.k.a. François-Marie Arouet, 1694–1778); engraving after a portrait by Nicolas de Largillière (© Mander and Mitchenson)

Adrienne Lecouvreur (1692–1730) as Cornelia in Corneille's *Pompée* (© Mander and Mitchenson)

Pierre Augustin Caron de Beaumarchais (1732–99); engraving after a portrait by Charles Nicolas Cochin (© AKG)

The Marriage of Figaro (Mozart, after Beaumarchais, 1786) as performed at Covent Garden, London, 1949 (© Mander and Mitchenson)

The Marriage of Figaro, Act I (Beaumarchais, 1781); engraving after an illustration by Jacques Philippe Joseph de Saint-Quentin (© Bridgeman Art Library)

La Comédie Française, 1791; lithograph after an original watercolour, nineteenth-century French school (© Bridgeman Art Library)

Sir William Davenant (1606–68); seventeenth-century engraving (© AKG)

John Dryden (1631–1700); engraving after a portrait by Thomas Hudson (© Mander and Mitchenson)

Sir Thomas Betterton (1635–1710); engraving after a portrait by Sir Godfrey Kneller, 1690s (© Mander and Mitchenson)

William Wycherley (1641–1715); mezzotint by John Smith after a portrait by Sir Peter Lely, 1703 (© Mander and Mitchenson)

The Country Wife (Wycherley, 1675) performed at the Old Vic, London, 1936, with Michael Redgrave and Ruth Gordon; directed by Tyrone Guthrie (© Mander and Mitchenson)

Between pages 192 and 193

The Way of the World (Congreve, 1700) at the Lyric Theatre, Hammersmith, London, 1924, with Edith Evans as Millamant; directed by Nigel Playfair (© Mander and Mitchenson)

William Congreve, 1637–1708; engraving after a painting by Sir Godfrey Kneller, 1709 (© Mander and Mitchenson)

Love for Love (Congreve, 1695); eighteenth-century illustration (© Mander and Mitchenson)

Carlo Goldoni (1707–93); painting by Alessandro Longhi (© Mander and Mitchenson)

Eleonora Duse as Mirandolina in *The Mistress of the Inn* (Goldoni, 1753), *c.* 1850 (© Mander and Mitchenson)

Oreste (Alfieri, 1783), directed by Luchino Visconti, Teatro Quirono, Rome, 1949 (© Mander and Mitchenson)

Gotthold Ephraim Lessing (1729–81); engraving by Albert Henry Payne after a drawing by Heinrich Wilhelm Storck (© Mander and Mitchenson)

PREFACE

For the first three volumes of the *Stage by Stage* series I foraged widely to gather details and felt a moral and legal obligation to acknowledge those persons and sources from which I borrowed. Here I must do so again. My aids are largely the same – histories of theatre by my predecessors. To ease my task I am reprinting what I owned up to in the preface to a preceding volume, *Dramatis Personae – The Rise of Medieval and Renaissance Theatre*:

Properly, I should single out major sources of great help to me throughout my task, publications not critiques or biographies of this or that playwright, actor or scene designer, but of broad surveys like my own. My important predecessors – whom I have frequently consulted – include Sheldon Cheney, Allardyce Nicholl, John Gassner, Edward Quinn, George Freedley, John A. Reeves and others. I must say that some of them tell the story in elegant prose that I envy, and all possess truly awesome erudition. In addition, I have used several encyclopedias of the drama: those offered by the Oxford University Press, along with its *Oxford Companion to English Literature*; the *McGraw-Hill Encyclopedia of World Drama*; *The Penguin Dictionary of the Theatre*, edited by Bernard Sobel and John Russell Taylor; *The Dance Encyclopedia*, edited by Anatole Chujoy; the *Simon and Schuster Book of Opera*; and, on music, *Grove*; and more.

For decades I have collected articles from academic journals devoted to the theatre and the notices by drama reviewers in newspapers, most often the *New York Times* – delivered each morning to my door – but also the *New York Post*, the *New York Daily News*, the *Wall Street Journal*, the *New York Observer*, *Village Voice*, *The Times* of London, the *Observer*, the *Guardian*, the *Telegraph* and others. I have bins full from magazines: *Time*, *Newsweek*, the *New Yorker*, *America*, *New York* and so on. I have gone to the splendid New York Public Library and have had access to the stacks in university libraries.

In addition, I have found several "niche" studies helpful, such as the multi-volume *Annals of the French Stage: From Its Origin to the Death of Racine* by Fredrick Hawkins, and *Molière and the Commonwealth of Letters* by Roger Johnson, Guy T. Trail and Edith Neuman, as well as *The Influence of Molière on Restoration Comedy* by Dudley Miles; *David Garrick and His French Friends* by Franck Hedgcock; *Beaumarchais* by Frederick Grenel; *Dryden and His World* by James Anderson Winn; *Dryden to Johnson* by Roger Lonsdale; *The History of World Theatre from the English Restoration to the Present* by Felicia Hardison Londré; *The Gay Couple in Restoration Comedy* by John Harrington Smith; *Russia of the Tsars and Poets* by S.A. Wilde; *Purcell* by Maureen Duffy; *The Stream of Music* by Richard Anthony Leonard; *The Book of Opera* by Arthur Jacobs and Stanley

Sadie; *Opera* by Christopher Headington, Roy Westbrook and Terry Barfoot; *The Story of Art* by E.H. Gombrich; and *Going for Baroque* by Keith Christiansen; as well as unsigned articles by other curators published by my neighbour, the Metropolitan Museum of Art. It has been my good fortune to have lived near to that glorious repository where, as in the theatre, are preserved some of mankind's greatest achievements for our enrichment.

I am beholden to James Ryan and Antonia Owen for their editorial suggestions and to James R. Carson who has assembled the illustrations that I requested and also to Judith Haddad for help in my research and to Kim Glanze and Carolyn Steinhoff who deciphered my handwritings and prepared the manuscript for the printer.

—1—

WHAT IS BAROQUE?

This book recounts the history of theatre from the mid seventeenth century to some decades after the end of the eighteenth, the dates of the beginning and close varying from country to country. This long stretch of years is known as the Age of Baroque. It takes that tag from the pervasive decorative style that determined the façades of edifices, the adornment of rooms, the shape of sculptures and content of paintings, the sound of music, the attire of sovereigns, princes and courtiers, the ceremony accompanying everyday life that affected values and beliefs – in sum, the way in which people lived. It had certain distinctive and even unique characteristics. Here is a modest attempt to explain them.

Baroque – a difficult term to define – is a style that had its beginning in the High Renaissance with sculptor and painter Michelangelo Buonarroti (1475–1564). In his youth he was invited to live in the palace of the Medicis, the wealthy and powerful Florentine family. In their gardens was a collection of Greek and Roman statues recently unearthed; the young man, able to scrutinize them often, resolved to emulate the revered classical artists.

But his temperament led him to arrive at his own idiom. Short in stature, he apparently idealized height and largeness. With his hammer and chisel he brought to life the human images he saw imprisoned in the marble; he fashioned a world peopled by the outsized David, the symbolic figures guarding the Medici tombs, the touching God and Adam, the prophets and hooded sibyls who are portrayed in the frescoes on the ceiling and walls of the Sistine Chapel. Doubtless the ceiling's height, causing his figures to be seen at a distance, influenced his choice of a large scale, but in general his figures are exaggerated. The sculpture of David is tall and broad-shouldered, a warrior matching what one imagines he looked like. Michelangelo carves or paints mostly athletic young male nudes, their bodies muscular, supernaturally beautiful.

Further, Michelangelo's figures are not static. His statues are nearly always in motion, twisting, straining, shown from every angle in changed poses.

In his *Poetics* Aristotle says that a large art object evokes more admiration than does a small, exquisite one.

Giovanni Lorenzo Bernini (1598–1680), the son of famed sculptor Pietro Bernini, joined Michelangelo at Pope Paul IV's command to design St Peter's basilica. Michelangelo conceived plans for the basilica's colossal dome (a technical problem that no one else had solved). The basilica's front was conceived by Bernini, as was the vast, circular, colonnaded piazza traversed by worshippers to enter the great church. The circle and half-circle are familiar motifs in Baroque decoration.

Lorenzo Bernini was a master architect – as well as sculptor, painter and playwright – concerned with every facet of a building, even to have sunlight dapple its façade and have clouds shadow it. Louis IV summoned him to Paris to consult on the erection of Versailles and the Louvre. His chiselled portraits in stone are more realistic than were Michelangelo's and expressed more emotion; the gestures were broader, the hair wind-blown and the folds of garments not falling neatly but disordered, suggesting even more movement, physical strain and effort. If Michelangelo was the precursor of Baroque, Lorenzo Bernini was its mature embodiment.

Seeing the admiration and financial success these two masters enjoyed, other leading artists, including ambitious newcomers, began to emulate them. The public welcomed the change. Many commissions poured in. Studios and workshops were kept busy turning out strange and striking imagery. Ceiling and wall space were covered with dynamic, intense figures that went beyond the former placid pictures of Mary and her haloed infant son.

Soon the artists came to be called Mannerists, implying that they copied the manner of Michelangelo and Bernini, if not their spirit, insights and substance. Mannerism spread throughout Europe. It flourished in the north, especially in Catholic Flanders, where Peter Paul Rubens was its most vigorous exponent. His stupendous tapestries and allegorical paintings, alive with movement, filled with fleshy figures of overweight women, are quintessentially Mannerist. In the south, in Spain, Velázquez, Ribera and the eccentric El Greco belonged to the Mannerist school, as did Poussin in France. In Italy there were Carracci, Correggio and Salvatore Rosa. Guido Reni's canvas of the god Apollo in a chariot dashing through mist to bring the dawn on time is Mannerist, as are the tondos of Tiepolo the Elder, affording a glimpse of seemingly deep-blue skies and fleecy white clouds tipped with sunlight, permitting the worshipper gazing upward to feel that the church is open to Heaven itself.

It is in Austria and south Germany, though, where we find the largest number of Baroque churches. A feature of their decoration is flocks of tinted wood-carved or painted plaster cherubs, winged infants who hover protectively over depictions of the Holy Family and the high altar. They impart an illusion of flight that adds airy movement to what would otherwise be a static composition.

The Mannerists cast aside the aesthetic restraint society imposed in previous eras. Departing from the common subjects of Gothic and Renaissance imagery, artists often chose complex, daring innovation in their handling of light and colour. They elected to depict ugly, gruesome, violent scenes – the agony of the crucified Christ, the torments endured by martyrs, moments in which women saints experienced religious ecstasy with their features frenzied and their bulging eyes rolling hysterically upward in the sockets, the whites exposed – or they pictured drunken peasant debauchery and riotous kermesses.

Decades later, Goethe, paying his first visit to Italy, was repelled by the sensuality of the paintings. Ruskin and Henry James, too, were offended by them. Today, with looser standards of morality, we do not find them shocking, merely hot-blooded.

The Baroque sensibility put its stamp most clearly on the period's palaces and churches. Italian Renaissance architects of the fifteenth century followed their predecessors' guidelines by looking back to the Greeks and embracing them as mentors: a temple should be important but simple and perfectly symmetrical. Openings – windows and entrances – were arranged to achieve that effect. Lintels were inserted horizontally, in straight lines; vertical appendages – Doric, Ionic and Corinthian columns – rose at right angles to their base, creating an aspect of dignity and nobility, imparting to the beholder a sense of balance and calm.

Nietzsche called that type of Greek art Apollonian after the god Apollo, as a way to contrast it with rebellious, anarchic outbursts of repressed sensuality in styles evoking the spirit of the god Dionysus. In 1575, in Rome, Giacomo della Porta (1541–1604) erected a church for the Jesuits, Il Gesù, that violated sacrosanct Renaissance precepts, both outside and inside. The interior was shaped like a cross; an oblong nave faced the main altar, behind which was the apse. Small chapels lined the central aisle. Large windows allowed light to stream in and spread colour from the stained glass. Outside, atop, was a steep cupola, nothing like the pediment of a Greek temple. The façade was uneven in height and was cluttered with framing columns at either flank of the entrance, with arches over the high windows, and pilasters, scrolls, volutes and cornices added as enrichments, at the expense of austerity, plainness and balance.

Critics were divided. Conservatives deplored this odd edifice. To them it was absurd, grotesque. But the church appealed greatly to others, especially architects. By a new strange process, with time, "baroque" gradually changed from a term of derision to one implying fulsome praise. Language has scarcely any other example of change equal to this.

The Jesuits – that intellectual order employing art to enhance church interiors and lend majesty to Catholic ritual in settings of vast size and overwhelming riches – used Baroque style as an instrument of their counter-revolution. They continued and expanded a long tradition with soaring music in masses performed in a milieu of realistic sculptures of saints and disciples, the martyrs who sacrificed their lives defending their faith. Churches were given further illusion of movement by hovering winged cherubs.

The Sun King, Louis XIV of France, was a descendant of the Medicis and learned from them how to use "good taste" and a display of magnificence to show that he possessed great strength and resources, an impression helpful with diplomacy, when forming alliances with neighbouring city states and negotiating trade treaties. The incredibly lavish and costly *fêtes galantes* he and Louis XV ordered, day-long dances in which members of the royal family and their pampered, titled guests took part, were typical of the heedless extravagance of the Baroque Age, but they also had a political dimension, as did the architecture he commissioned. Versailles, his Baroque palace, served that purpose, as foreign envoys were awed by its grandeur (some would say grandiosity).

Awe was a primary aim of a Baroque artist. Monarchs throughout Europe imitated Louis XIV, creating Elsinore in Denmark, Sans Souci in Germany, the Belvidere in Vienna and the Hermitage in Russia, all palaces trying not to be outshone. Baroque is calculatedly "show-offy". Monarchs, seen as arbiters of good taste, set their subjects examples of the utmost extravagance, exaggeration, suggestion of stressful activity, and excess especially of ornamentation, another characteristic of Baroque.

Baroque triumphed in the realm of music, and Baroque music itself came about partly owing to the belated invention of at least fifty different kinds of new instruments, most of which have since vanished or are rarely available now. The most important were the organ and the clavichord. In Leonard's book *The Stream of Music* he explains how the development of multiple keys joyously invited the composer to let his fancy run free and arrive at far more complicated works, replete with intricate counterpoint and a new, fuller sound.

The development of Baroque music continued and reached a glorious apogee with Johann Sebastian Bach and his sons (he had sixteen children). This book discusses only the composers of music for the theatre during this period – Rameau, Lully, Purcell, Handel and Pergolesi. The greatest were Haydn and Mozart, but their compositions are not considered to be Baroque. Haydn wrote eleven operas, now scarcely ever heard. Mozart, needless to say, was unequalled in producing operatic scores. But the two masters are categorized as belonging to the "new generation". Their offerings are homophonic rather than polyphonic.

As John Dewey has pointed out, the public's taste is distressingly fickle; the quest for change in the arts is endless. Each succeeding generation of artists and audiences looks with disdain at the aesthetic values of its predecessors. The creative process is one of rejection of what has just prevailed or is currently dominant. More novelty counts for much. This applied when it came to Baroque music. After Bach, music of the era gradually lost its audience and was neglected and almost forgotten until Bach was rediscovered in the nineteenth century by Felix Mendelssohn, who became his zealous advocate and won him fresh acclaim.

Another century elapsed until, in the mid twentieth, Baroque music was suddenly brought back. "Early music" societies were composed of sophisticated listeners who flocked to concerts by small groups. This not only explains why Baroque composers like Telemann and Marais came into favour, but also why their music was played on seventeenth-century instruments. Romantic music was dismissed in Europe and the United States of America as only for those who were enthralled too easily by lush melodies.

★

Designating this epoch as the Age of Baroque is an oversimplification. The eighteenth century was also called the Age of Mercantilism, as well as the Age of Reason or the Enlightenment. Two different cultural climates existed and stretched parallel to the Baroque. The Age of Reason was one, in which a few men of genius, including Thomas Jefferson and James Madison, began the march to modernity. In political debates they urged the dismantling of absolute monarchies. By their courageous and clear examples they prepared the way for and envisioned democracy and caused re-evaluations among those in the British colonies in North America.

In France others, including Voltaire and Spinoza, sought to strip religion of superstition and replace it with faceless Deism. Some, like Adam Smith and John Stuart Mill, searched for principles that govern economic systems, while others, like Boyle, investigated natural phenomena and scientific theories that explained them. It was a remarkably progressive span in human history, but it had little or no impact on the fine arts, certainly not on theatre.

The second cultural climate was neoclassicism, which also infused the Baroque. Many Baroque works abounded with neoclassical elements. In the eighteenth century, in particular, educated people were fascinated with anything that had to do with ancient Greece and Rome. Prolonged excavations of the ruins of Pompeii and Herculaneum sustained and excited interest in those vanished worlds. People looked back on those past civilizations as fountainheads of wisdom, virtue and beauty and as times of great architecture, sculpture and drama.

Democracy had been attained in Athens. The Greek and Roman philosophers – Plato, Socrates, Aristotle, Epicurus, Seneca – were still unsurpassed, their intelligence dazzling. The plays of the Baroque era by Corneille, Racine, Voltaire, Dryden and Addison draw on Graeco-Roman history and mythology for subject matter. Colleges required that students learn to converse in and read Greek and Latin. English settlers in the New World wilderness named their cities Athens, Syracuse, Ithaca and Rome. Thomas Jefferson, the multi-talented president of the United States, designed his home, Monticello, in accordance with classical guidelines. So Baroque was not the only prevalent style; neoclassicism was also conspicuous everywhere.

Rococo, an offshoot of Baroque, was also a lesser movement within a movement. It was most apparent in interior decoration, but was also immortalized in the paintings of the French artists Watteau, Boucher and Fragonard. The figures in the paintings are often those of young people engaged in amorous games of pursuit. It is seen in exceedingly ornamental, dainty, intimate chairs, and sofas gilded and delicately scalloped. It exudes a spirit of gaiety and frivolity that was epitomized in the thoughtless behaviour of Marie Antoinette and her ladies-in-waiting, who dressed as milkmaids and enacted pastoral charades.

The *Oxford Dictionary* characterizes Rococo as florid, and some consider it effeminate, but many find the playfulness of the style delightful.

⋆

To what extent is the theatre of this period "Baroque"? The truth is, the drama is not a medium that lends itself easily to that mode. Stage settings, in many instances, were spectacular – painted, sliding flats artfully made use of the latest-discovered laws of perspective, to create the illusion of huge, palatial halls. The costumes, not authentic to the period of events in the play, were likely to be of rich, colourful materials that resembled the attire of the audience.

The scripts, highly melodramatic, dealt with characters seized by violent emotions. Their responses were apt to be exaggerated, as infidelity and betrayal of friendship drove them to extreme acts. The language, too, is inflated and bombastic.

In this epoch there were few major tragic poets, except Racine and Corneille in France, and in England none, unless Milton is deemed to have been a playwright. Nor was this a "people's theatre": the dramatists showed no interest in or concern about the plight of the poor or the domestic troubles of middle-class families. The drama was about and for the aristocracy. Many of the scripts, commissioned by the Master of the Revels or personally by a pleasure-loving sovereign, were staged and seen solely at court. The lives portrayed were those of rulers, courtiers and heroes, the dilemmas those of nobles involved in dynamic feuds and desperate struggles for power. For a long time, London, Paris and St Petersburg had only one public theatre; plays might be taken there for short runs.

But if there were only a handful of major tragedies, the era did bring forth many sparkling comedies. Touring companies sometimes ventured into the cities, and always the ubiquitous *commedia dell'arte* ensembles offered slapstick.

There are comic masterpieces. Indeed, the pointed exuberance of Molière's *Les Femmes savantes* and *The Rogueries of Scapin*, Marivaux's whimsical *Triumph of Love*, Beaumarchais's *Figaro*, Wycherley's wry *The Plain Dealer*, Congreve's vivacious *The Way of the World* and Sheridan's *The Rivals* are the literary equivalent of Rococo in the visual realm.

— 2 —

FRENCH NEOCLASSICISM

The Romantic effulgence that flourished in England during the Renaissance, and especially throughout the latter part of the sixteenth century, was scarcely matched in France. Prolonged civil strife, provoked by religious differences, preoccupied the country until 1594, when a Bourbon claimant, Henri IV, established his rule in Paris. His comparatively brief reign brought stability, unhappily ending with his assassination in 1610.

He liked theatre and encouraged it. At the time of his accession, and as late as 1600, the capital had only one permanent theatre, owing to a monopoly granted 200 years earlier to the Confrèrie de la Passion and stubbornly held by it ever since. At first it offered only religious works, but it had gradually turned to secular offerings and finally was permitted to stage nothing else. The Confrèrie had erected a theatre, the Hôtel de Bourgogne, in 1548; thirty years later the group ceased to function as a producer and leased its stage to others, mostly to touring companies such as the venturesome and energetic *commedia dell'arte* players. Yet as landlord it still had the final say about what could or could not be produced there.

To circumvent this monopoly during his reign, Henri IV invited various companies to his court, beyond the Confrèrie's control. His government also licensed performances at fairs, to which he enjoyed making royal visits. These outdoor *fêtes* were new. This latitude encouraged homeless travelling Italian, English and native troupes – often belonging to medical charlatans selling panaceas – to perform in particular at the Foire St Laurent and the Foire St Germain despite the Confrèrie's objections, until its monopoly became practically inoperative and then lapsed for ever in 1677.

During some years of the first two decades of the century Paris had no theatrical entertainment whatsoever. As might be expected, no playwrights of note arose. The tragedies of Étienne Jodelle (whose *Cléopatre captive* of 1552 was mentioned in an earlier book in this series) and the lesser efforts by Grévin, Garnier, Larivey and a few others are exceptions, but they are of interest only to scholars.

In 1578 the confraternity was forbidden to stage religious works; too many liberties were being taken with the sacred stories they were supposed to illustrate. Soon the members of the brotherhood ceased acting, which was all to the good since most were amateurs, and the competitive troupes that rented the premises displayed more professionalism. Two famed Italian companies, I Gelosi and the Andreinis, were among the visitors, as was a troupe from London. The rental fee was high, and the Confrèrie profited from this source of income and continued to guard its privilege jealously.

Marie de Médicis, mother of Louis XIII, was especially fond of the *commedia dell'arte* players, and they were recipients of her patronage. Though the players spoke no French, they told their stories well enough through pantomime, refining a long-lasting mime tradition.

By 1610 a French ensemble of some distinction, directed by Valleran Lecomte (or Valéran le Conte) and self-designated the King's Players, gained a foothold in Paris. They shared the premises with a farce company and flourished for a dozen years. Having trouble with the Confrèrie, Lecomte eventually had to abandon the only available theatre. It was occupied by Tabariu, Guéru and Le Grand, some native comedians who had gained an enthusiastic following in Paris and elsewhere. Rivals, the Prince of Orange's Players, in turn succeeded them in it and later moved to a new theatre, the Marais, formerly a tennis court, now adapted to a new use. (It was the third tennis court they had ingeniously converted for that purpose.)

Lecomte's troupe eventually returned to the Hôtel de Bourgogne so, though overdue, Paris finally had two good companies offering popular works.

Attached to the group was Alexandre Hardy (or Hardi; *c.* 1570–1632), its chief writer. Much as Shakespeare supplied his fellow actors with scripts, Hardy provided roles for Lecomte's company. Even more than the Bard, he is an important but shadowy figure. Very little is known for certain about him or his origin, except that his birthplace was Paris and that he received a liberal education. It is believed that he spent some months or years in Madrid, where he could have seen productions of works by Lope de Vega and absorbed from them lessons in stagecraft. A further conjecture is that back in France he was an actor for a while with a touring group. With *The Chaste and Faithful Loves of Théagène and Chariclée* (1601), produced by Lecomte, he began his long, influential career in the capital.

Paris was the scene of a heated dispute between cliques of critics and theatre spectators as to whether plays should be formally constructed as Aristotle and Horace ordained in their influential essays or could be more freely put together, disregarding classical requirements, as was the practice of Elizabethan and Jacobean dramatists across the Channel in England.

The classical guidelines, especially observance of three unities, time, place and action, had been implanted in France during the Renaissance by Jodelle and six fellow students of the Pléiades who borrowed them from Italy. That exuberant circle of young poets was dedicated to reviving the glories of the ancient days of great writers whom they revered. In England, until Ben Jonson and Dryden appeared, Aristotle's requirements for a well-made play were scarcely known.

Exacerbating the debate in Paris were two books calling for slavish adherence to Aristotle's prescription: Tomas Sebiller's *The Poetic Art* (1548) and Jean de la Taille's preface to his *Saul the Mad* (1572). Hardy for the most part opposed the classicists. He declared that he was acquainted with "the precepts of his art while preferring to follow the demands of his trade". He was concerned to offer plays that would satisfy a less literate audience, the spectators whom the practical Lecomte sought.

For his uneducated hearers Hardy borrowed ideas and styles from the popular Spanish stage, inserting scenes of violence and heroes who filled his works with fearsome, adventurous deeds. The result was a fusion very different from English tragedy, though it did anticipate the Jacobean vogue for tragicomedy introduced by Beaumont and Fletcher, a genre that Hardy is sometimes said to have invented (though actually it was forged by Euripides centuries earlier).

Also like Shakespeare and Lope de Vega, he wrote every kind of play: farces, comedies, pastorals, melodramas and tragedies. He moved his characters from city to city and country to country and presented them at different times in their lives, in violation of the unities cherished by the classicists. He sought to garner laughs, gasps, thrills and tears from the ticket-buyers. He kept Lecomte's company busy and the theatre occupied.

He did not turn away from all traditions. He retained the five-act structure. His dialogue was in verse, though as a poet he was not masterly. His lines were brief until he finally accepted the measured Alexandrine six-foot line with a caesura midway in each line, in the rhymed couplets that Jodelle used. Action counted for more than verbal exposition.

Hardy's lasting contribution was the slipshod form he introduced, which was a mixture of two conventions, classical tragedy and loose Spanish chronicle. His works are vigorously paced but lack depth and power. They often deal with passionate love affairs and by their blending of themes break from the limits imposed on his predecessors by classicists. He employed many of the devices of Greek and Roman prototypes, including ghosts, messengers and horrible moments of physical suffering that a classical dramatist would have kept offstage, indeed any ingredient that might evoke a frisson or a wince in an onlooker. His infatuated lovers kissed and embraced in scenes that were deemed shocking.

He is considered the first professional French dramatist, his output almost as prodigious as Lope de Vega's. He might compose, rehearse and stage a piece in a mere span of three days and nights. The next generation, however, looked back on him as too romantic and undisciplined and dismissed him, and so his works vanished from the repertory. Only forty-one remain, and those are little studied.

Frederick Hawkins, author of *Annals of the French Stage* (1882), is one critic who has examined Hardy's extant scripts, though from a late-nineteenth-century point of view. Judicious and tolerant, he offers a fair estimate of Hardy's place in France's literary history:

> Fortunately for the classicists, the school they warred against was soon to lose its principal support. In 1623, placed above want by the proceeds of his work, old Hardy, as he had come to be called, bade an informal farewell to the theatre, his last production being a pastoral entitled *Le Triomphe d'Amour*. By this time, according to his own count, he had put together no fewer than six hundred plays (tradition says eight hundred). Hitherto, perhaps, his importance has not been adequately recognized. He was persistently denied by those who rejected his theory; and the world at large, reluctant to believe that one who wrote so much could have written well, has adopted their estimate without troubling to ascertain how far it is borne out by facts.

> His work in general is supposed to be carelessly ordered, to abound in vulgar claptrap to the absolute exclusion of poetry, and to bear about the same relation to the best examples of the modern European drama as a gaudily coloured print of a bold buccaneer or evil-minded earl does to a picture by Raphael or Leonardo. This impression, I think, would be appreciably modified if he were studied at first hand. Bombastic and slovenly he unquestionably was; but in most of his pieces, especially those that appeared before his necessities induced him to write against time, there are many fine thoughts finely expressed, many bursts of genuine passion, many firmly drawn characters, many signs of a practical tact that any dramatist would give much to possess. At his best, however, he was not the man to attain the end he obviously proposed to himself. Nature had denied to him the genius necessary to accomplish in France a revolution in dramatic art such as England and Spain had recently witnessed. His *théâtre*, though admirably adapted to its purpose, was not of a kind to kindle enthusiasm among the literati, to uproot settled prepossessions in favour of a different sort of art, to become a law to fellow workers in the same field. In truth, only one of his innovations survived him. Down to his time the honour of having a play represented was deemed sufficient compensation to the dramatist. Hardy asked for and received three *écus* for each of his pieces; and but few of his successors failed to bear in mind the precedent he set.

In his enthusiasm for the new system, he did not entirely abandon the old, and his *théâtre* was less an imitation of the former than an attempt to blend it with the latter. That he exposed the stability of the established drama to a crucial test there can be no doubt. His writings brought fame and fortune to the theatre in the rue de la Poterie. He was saluted on nearly all hands as a *maître*.

Lecomte found it convenient to transfer his ensemble from the Hôtel de Bourgogne to the other playhouse, where, in conjunction with Marie Vernier, he increased his already high reputation.

There his resident dramatist separated a keen sense for stage effect from grandiloquence of language. The audience was too much excited by his forcible situations to observe that he fell below Garnier and Montchrétien in imagination, dignity and grace. Hawkins wrote:

> His masterpiece perhaps is *Mariamne*, the first of many theatrical adaptations of the narrative in Josephus. It appeared soon after the assassination of Henri IV, an event that Billard de Courgenay, a poetaster of the day, thought fit to commemorate in a tragedy having as one of its speaking personages, indeed its hero, that idolized monarch Louis XIII, who was at the time a mere child.
>
> From this time Hardy exhibited a change for the worse. Beset by poverty, aware that the public liked novelty for its own sake, and finding that his name – for the names of authors were now given in the bills – ensured success to anything he wrote, however trivial it might be, he

> took less and less pains with his work. He deliberately merged the poet and the artist in the playwright. He took incidents from various sources, huddled them together with no higher objective than that of carrying away his audience, and rattled them off in verse written with truly fatal facility. Most of his later pieces are said to have been composed and represented in a week. "Heaven be praised," he would exclaim, "I can subordinate all loftier aspirations to the demands of my trade." By doing so, it seems, he put money into his purse; but the liberal theory he had embraced was brought into disrepute, at least with more cultivated playgoers, by its association with such dross as that which now emanated from his pen.

Among Hardy's competitors and shortly, later, successors were the Marquis de Racan (1589–1670), praised for *The Pastoral Comedy* (*c.* 1619), and Théophile de Viaud (1590–1626), who won applause for *Pyrame et Thisbé* (1617).

Louis XIV took the throne very early; he was still a child. Two of his ancestors had married daughters of the Medicis; that family's great wealth may have made them especially attractive. From them the young King may have inherited his strong lifelong interest in painting, music, dance and plays. His boyish love of entertainment brought many artists to his palace. His guardians, first the Italian Cardinal Mazarin and then Cardinal Richelieu, saw to it that only appropriate offerings were staged at court, thus setting up a measure of censorship. Without the cardinals' approval nothing was performed there. This enforced Richelieu's ability to promote classicism. In Cardinal Richelieu the classicists had a formidable champion. An absolutist in art as in governance, he was markedly inclined to hierarchy and order in all things.

In the ballroom of his palace was a beautiful little private theatre. He convened a group of the leading playwrights and producers of the day to hear his views and suggested that a committee of five poets turn out plays, each composing one act of the same work. This was done over a stretch of two years, and three "correct" pieces resulted, including the light *The Comedy of the Tuilleries* (1638), whereupon the committee was disbanded. The Cardinal himself had literary aspirations and provided plots for this work and others he signed, though his employment of talented assistants was hardly a secret.

(Aristotle did not lay down laws that Greek playwrights had to obey; he did not have the authority to do so. Besides, the great tragedies were written before his time. He saw them re-enacted at the semi-annual religious festivals and subsequently analysed what made them so suspenseful, moving, compelling. Unquestionably the scripts fashioned as Aristotle suggests do work to very strong effect, but his guidelines do not fit all subjects – though the Cardinal seemed to think they did.)

Besides Richelieu, when Louis XIII and Louis XIV reached maturity and wielded power, they and their ministers intervened in theatrical affairs with regularity. They gave licences for performances to companies they liked and dictated what subject matter was acceptable. A certain amount of rivalry existed between sovereigns and ministers, especially between Richelieu and Louis XIII. On one occasion Louis XIII, piqued, had six actors transferred from the Marais troupe to the competition at the Hôtel de Bourgogne.

At that venue the scenic investiture still resembled that used in medieval theatre. Sometimes a bare platform sufficed, duplicating the sort employed by travelling actors who set up temporary stages at fairs.

A painted backdrop might suggest the exterior of several houses or sites, permitting the action to flow smoothly from one locality to another or even to take place in several simultaneously. Since many of the plays observed unity of place, this granted the author a broader option.

A principal scenic artist of the time was one Laurent, first name elusive; his sketches and lists of properties provide the little information available. These indicate that some canvas flats were attached to wooden frames, and there was an attempt at perspective to lend depth in painting them. These could be shifted back and forth. There might even be a room – a bedchamber, perhaps – with a missing fourth wall, exposing its contents, including furniture.

The shape of the auditorium, of the Hôtel de Bourgogne as well as at the Marais, was long and narrow. The tennis courts, covered, had balconies from which the game had been observed; hence the buildings were easily remade to serve as theatres. Candles lit them but only dimly; owing to the poor light, most performances took place in the afternoon. Benches faced the platform, and dandified courtiers and the wealthy sat in side-balconies above often quarrelsome and unruly spectators who crowded the main floor and frequently interrupted the unfolding story. Other privileged persons sat on the stage.

Young girls vended wine and fruits throughout the hall. The theatres had no front curtains, though eventually these were added.

A doorman stood guard, to keep out any who came without tickets. (One actor-proprietor who had sought too hard to demand payment from a refractory gentleman of rank was murdered, and no punishment was meted out for the crime.) When the performance began, all the candles save those on the platform were snuffed out.

Costumes were rich, in keeping with the hyper-elegant styles of the age. The acting tended to be loud in voice and excessive in gesture. This was necessary, because the audience might be noisy and inattentive, even riotous. Much testimony is preserved about the rudeness and arrogance of the nobility. Seated on the stage, they might talk among themselves and almost drown out the actors, and they also distracted from the drama by the ostentatious display of their silk-and-lace attire. Such conduct annoyed those standing in the pit, who shouted epithets at their betters, provoking numerous scuffles.

At court the audience was scarcely more polite. Attendance at a play there was an occasion for an exchange of social amenities. Usually performances were given three or four times weekly; if two troupes occupied a theatre simultaneously, each struggled to have the privilege of weekend presentations, most likely to be the best attended. Sometimes the performances started two or three hours late. From this it became customary to start the performance at five o'clock instead of two, as had been done before.

To write for such hearers was a serious challenge, and it is hard to picture Corneille, Racine and Molière directing their subtle poetic work at such spectators.

It was a former member of Lecomte's company, an actor named Guillaume Montdory, whose lasting contribution was to be the form he established, a mixture of two conventions, the classical and the loose Spanish chronicle. His works have a vigorous pace, if they lack depth or power. They often deal with love, and their admixture of themes was a break from the cold classicism of his courtly predecessors. He also held to the five-act structure and employed many of the devices of Greek and Roman prototypes, including ghosts, messengers and scenes of physical suffering. Later generations, however, looked back on him as too romantic and dismissed him; like Hardy's, his works vanished from the repertory.

After several seasons with Lecomte at the Hôtel de Bourgogne, Montdory had grown confident enough to form his own troupe and toured the provinces. He gained wide fame and the favour of the vigilant Cardinal Richelieu. What was liked at court soon got official sanction. At the order of the fastidious, erudite, cultivated Richelieu, long the virtual ruler of France, Montdory got permission, over the objections of the Confrérie, to open at the Marais, which became his permanent stage. The play that he brought to Paris with him, Pierre Corneille's adroit *Mélite*, had been popular everywhere it was performed in the provinces. Its young author was destined to be the major figure in the French drama for several decades and also the object of much controversy.

Meanwhile, as Hardy aged and got ready to retire from the fray, and his scripts became ever wilder and more slapdash, the tone of the split between his partisans and the classicists became sharper and more acrimonious. Those of the Cardinal's classical persuasion steadily gained strength and ultimately dominated.

Several young writers enjoyed momentary prominence. Most had a thin output; some were members of one clique or the other. One was Théophile Viaud, who at twenty-six had Parisians talking about his *Pyrame et Thisbé* (1617), a pastoral, but he ventured no other play. Instead he attained a considerable notoriety with some licentious verses and satiric comments aimed at the government. Though these led to his exile, he boldly continued in this vein. Parliament ultimately declared him guilty of *lèse-majesté divine* and said he should be burned at the stake in full public view. He fled again but was captured and trapped in a dungeon to await his fiery fate.

Meanwhile his effigy, cleverly fashioned of rags, was consumed by flames as a warm-up; to prolong his ordeal Parliament slowly deliberated his case once more. At last friends with powerful connections obtained a pardon for him and his punishment was reduced to exile for a season as before.

Thoroughly chastened, Viaud repented his reckless ways, returned to the Church and behaved sedately for the short time remaining to him. He died young in 1626, his life more theatrical than his only play.

Another pastoral came from the Marquis de Racan (1589–1670) whose *Les Bergeries, ou Arthénice* is summed up by Hawkins in his *Annals of the French Stage* as a "work of refinement, elegance and tenderness". Though titled, the Marquis had not been well educated; he overcame this handicap by reading Tasso and Guarini, the Italian masters of the pastoral genre, from whom he absorbed the classic rules he followed.

Jean Gombauld (1588–1666) was good-looking and talented, an unusual combination; when the Queen Marie de Médicis' husband died the alert Gombauld sent her some verses of condolence which moved and pleased her; thus he gained access to the court. There he became a rival to Racan as royal poet and playwright, but he, too, has only one script to his credit, *L'Amaranthe* (1625), a pastoral, properly classical.

Much to the strong-willed Richelieu's liking was Jean Mairet (1604–86) who astonished Parisians when at sixteen two of his plays – *Chriséide et Arimand* (1620) and *La Sylvie* (1621), both tragicomedies, the latter with pastoral touches – were successfully produced. Their precocious author, still enrolled as a boarder at Le Collège des Grassins, was of a good Roman Catholic family. He was an orphan, his parents having been lost to him during a plague.

His plays brought him invitations to the city's most brilliant and influential salons where his elders besought him to enlist in the classicists' ranks. He was fully converted and in time became an effectual leader of the conservative movement he nurtured. What is more, he was also a constant source of scripts for the actors at the city's theatres and the palace, among them a pastoral, *La Silvanire, ou la morte-vive* (1625), a comedy, *Les Galanteries du duc d'Ossone* (1627), a tragicomedy, *La Virginie* (1628), and a tragedy, *Sophonisbe* (1629). As had the English poet John Dryden he offered a *Marc-Antoine, ou la Cléopâtre*, a more "correct" version of that fatal romance as given in Shakespeare's sprawling drama (1630). In every detail it is "classic". Ambitious, too, is his tragedy *Le Grand et dernier Solyman, ou la mort de Mustapha* (1630). Two more comedies and two more tragicomedies came in rapid succession. He was now in competition with Pierre Corneille, until he recognized that he was the loser and that the classicists' cause was weakened as a result, and so he withdrew from further activity in the theatre.

The playwrights' arguments over how a story should be constructed for the stage often provoked shouting directed at the authors and helpless casts. The demonstrations disturbed the city officials.

Opportune was the arrival in the Hardy camp of nineteen-year-old Jean Rotrou (1609–50) shortly after a work by the sixteen-year-old Mairet. Young writers were welcomed on the boards. Parisians were sympathetic to the efforts of literary prodigies, who were allowed to flourish without regard to their years. In the programmes at the Hôtel de Bourgogne were a tragicomedy and a comedy, *L'Hypocondriaque, ou le mort amoureux* (1628) and *La Bague de l'oubli* (1635), both enjoyable, both written by Rotrou with skill and flair.

The youth came from Dreux where his family had long been important in the region. Though a provincial, he fitted very easily into Parisian society. He was friendly and congenial and soon became esteemed for his solid character. Despite his tendency to reject the bounds the classicists set, he earned the favour of Richelieu who chose him as one of the five poets on his advisory panel and appointed him to high posts in his native Dreux.

The young man fulfilled his duties throughout most of each year; in the off-season he hastened to Paris to oversee productions of new scripts that he composed in his spare time. They helped to keep the troupes engaged and proved that there still was a large audience for da Vega-like melodramas, comedies, tragicomedies and tragedies.

Even so the powerful, cunning Richelieu held the winning hand, and more and more Hardy's disciples lost numbers.

In Rotrou's otherwise fine character was a passion for gambling; he was arrested and imprisoned for debt. To buy his freedom he sold his script *Venceslas* (1647) for twenty pistules to a tramp eager to obtain it, and now it is ranked among his very best. (Actually it is a translation and adaptation of a Spanish play by Francisco de Roxas. Like many of his peers, Rotrou looked south to borrow material.)

While he was serving as a magistrate, the plague invaded Dreux. His associates urged Rotrou to flee the city with them, but he refused, feeling an obligation to stay with the citizens over whom he exerted a degree of governance. Within a week he was dead, a victim of the epidemic. He was forty-one.

It took two hundred years before the city of Dreux erected a monument commemorating his heroism.

Rotrou's plays consist of the mix of comedies, tragicomedies, tragedies and pastorals usual for his time: *Cléagénor et Doristée* (1630), *Ladiane* (1630), *Les Occasions perdues* (1631), *La Celimène* (1633), *L'Heureux Naufrage* (1633), *La Céliane* (1634) and over a dozen more, including one produced after his passing.

Rotrou's death was self-sacrificial, and Corneille deeply mourned him; over the years they had become close friends, standing together to ward off attacks in the ideological contest.

In Paris other young men aspired to be dramatists and see their scripts come to life on the glittering, lamp-lit stage. The companies' incessant need for short plays meant that the quality of these offerings was very uneven, as is especially likely to happen when the head of a troupe is also an actor; his choice is apt to be determined not by the quality but by whether the script has a good part for him or one of his leading performers.

Among the lesser playwrights of the day were some who were colourful and idiosyncratic. Such a one was Georges de Scudéry (1601–67), an officer of the French Guards, who came from a dignified Provençal family but whose temperament was inherently flamboyant. While still in his teens he chose the military as his vocation, perhaps because of the splendid uniform. While he cut a swathe in the capital by his lavish expenditures, buying paintings, rare coins and tulips, all collectable items befitting the discriminating tastes of a wealthy aristocrat, actually he was living far beyond his means. This prompted him to write for the stage to augment his inadequate income. That startled people, since he had spoken disdainfully of Hardy's commercialism and stated that he would never accept payment for a script.

Despite his criticism of Hardy he took his cue from that exciting showman; his first offering, *Ligdamon et Lidias* (1629), showed a talent for melodrama, and his dialogue even had poetic touches; he quickly abandoned his vow never to ask for a fee from the troupes.

His sister Madeleine was a widely recognized poet. Did he not lift felicitous phrases from her writings and did he not have his plays staged only so that he could earn royalties from their subsequent publication? Rumour had it so. On three occasions Madeleine, called "Madame Sappho", had proposals of marriage from wealthy suitors; each time her brother intervened to prevent her from accepting the offers. Did he not want to give up his supply of pretty metaphors? So it was whispered.

Gradually Madeleine quit her devotion to the Muse of Poetry and began writing romance novels that found many readers. She prospered, enabling her to lend added financial support to her "peacock" brother, whose dependence on her continued life-long. He moved away from Hardy's influence and became a favourite of the Cardinal, who tried to make use of him in his obsessive campaign to promote the Grecian format.

The classic restrictions by no means came easily to Pierre Corneille, whose temperament, like that of his busy predecessor Hardy, was exuberantly Romantic. Corneille was a Norman born in Rouen in 1606, where his father held the prestigious post of the King's Advocate. The son, too, studied and practised law there. His earliest exposure to drama was through school plays sponsored by the Jesuits, his teachers. Pious by nature, he later became very devoted to his large family.

He was twenty-three when in 1629 the Montdory troupe visited Rouen. Seeing their production of works by Hardy, he was inspired to compose a farce and submit it to them. The players, shrewd and lucky, accepted it; its success – and theirs – came quickly. It was with this script, *Mélite*, as mentioned above, that the company made a triumphal return to Paris, setting up at the Marais for a long stay.

One person of consequence not wholly pleased with the farce, however, was the watchful Cardinal. A realistic portrait of social manners, the play flouted the classically prescribed three unities so dear to that statesman's heart. Perturbed by the criticism of the loose form of *Mélite*, Corneille declared that he could easily turn out a script that met every Aristotelian demand. He attempted this in *Clitandre* (1631) and then wrote four more comedies: *The Widow* (1633), *The Palace Gallery* (1634), *The Place Royale* (1634) and *The Comic Illusion* (printed 1639). None of them accounts for his lasting fame, but all enhanced his growing reputation while he perfected his craftsmanship. In particular the last of these comedies showed a marked advance, and his superiority over his rivals was soon widely acknowledged. He also tried his hand at a "classically" shaped tragedy, *Medea* (1634–5). Even before this his exceptional talent was obvious, and he, too, was one of the panel chosen to earn his keep from His Eminence solely by his literary labours.

Though he was practical and was said to value money – indeed, he was reputed to be a bit stingy – in time he quarrelled with his churchly patron, ended a profitable association, and returned to Rouen and his law practice. He could not readily abandon playwriting, however, and composed *Le Cid*, produced in 1637, not by Montdory whose theatre was not available at the moment but by the rival company at the Hôtel de Bourgogne.

Corneille was barely into his thirties. This "heroic comedy" – so called because, though its story is mostly tragic, it concludes happily – is perhaps the most-loved play in all of French dramatic history. It is a masterpiece known to the English-speaking world mostly in summary and in that form scarcely appreciated, for its compression makes its plot sound ridiculous. Besides, its poetry is lost in translation, and its moral philosophy is largely alien to modern readers. This great play, admittedly one of the ornaments of world literature, is seldom if ever acted in English (though a year after its première it was taken to London). Today's spectator would find the appeal it had to people of its time incomprehensible.

Yet in many ways *Le Cid* sums up, with the highest eloquence, the sensibility of the age that first saw it. The subject comes from a lengthy Spanish play, *Las Mocedades del Cid* (1618) by Guillem de Castro. Corneille simplified the story and changed its chronology to fit into a time limit of twenty-four hours so it adhered to the classical rule. He also excised much of the coarseness, violence and sensationalism that marks Castro's handling of the plot. Earlier versions of *Le Cid* date back even further, to the eleventh century. (The title derives from "El Cid" or "al-Said" in Arabic, meaning "lord" or "chieftain", which was the popular name of Rodrigo Días de Vivar, *c.* 1043–99.) In the twelfth century, among a variety of other popular works, a *Poema del Cid* celebrated the exploits of this hero. Corneille therefore brought an enriching dimension to his work by drawing if not from mythical then from at least partly legendary material.

The story is that a young Spanish noble, Rodrigue, is in love with Chimène, who deeply shares his feelings. For a time, all goes well between them and their families, who are of prominent lineage and are powerful at court. But a mischance befalls the impending match: the King appoints Rodrigue's father, Don Diegue, as tutor of the royal heir Chimène. Chimène's father, Count Gomez, a bold and much-feared warrior, has been expecting the post and is angered. He and Don Diegue quarrel. The count slaps the venerable Don Diegue, who is too old to retaliate.

The precepts of honour leave the hero – the son Rodrigue – no choice but to avenge the insult to his father. When Rodrigue slays the hot-tempered, insolent Count Gomez, his beloved's father, in a duel, his emotions are sorely divided.

The same dilemma is now imposed on Chimène, who must demand Rodrigue's death, though she cherishes him above everyone else. The King's daughter, the Infanta, shares her problem, since she also loves Rodrigue. But, acknowledging her obligation to marry one of royal blood, the Infanta has encouraged the hero's suit of Chimène, hoping for their marriage, believing it might quell her desire for the young man. These parallel situations pit pure love against duty and honour, a conflict intensified by the rigid Spanish code. As the count says before receiving Rodrigue's challenge: "I can be forced to live without happiness, / But I cannot be forced to live without honor" (translation by Wallace Fowlie).

Rodrigue, appalled by his impossible situation, contemplates suicide. His father Don Diegue persuades him to choose a better way, to seek death in battle. The King, having sought to avert the duel, is distressed at its outcome and promises to summon Rodrigue before him and pass judgement on him since, as Chimène reminds him, her father had ably served the throne.

The Moors are once again advancing on Seville by sea. The count's valour will be missed at this dangerous moment. Meanwhile Don Diegue urges Rodrigue to replace the slain Count Gomez and without awaiting the King's approval head the forces swiftly gathering to oppose the African invaders. In a three-hour battle the assault is hurled back and Rodrigue returns much acclaimed, the saviour of his country, with two Moorish Kings as his prisoners.

But though he is gratefully hailed and the King pardons his killing of Count Gomez, Chimène obdurately insists that he be punished for his "criminal" deed. The King finds her attitude "oppressive"; to test her, he tells her Rodrigue is dead. She faints. When she revives, the King remarks that she still loves her "enemy". Chimène denies it, though obviously it is so.

At last she requests that her cause be taken up by a champion who will challenge Rodrigue to another duel. The King, favouring Rodrigue, is reluctant to grant this but finally consents when Rodrigue's father urges that Chimène's plea be heard, lest his son be thought cowardly. The King decrees that Chimène must wed the victor. Another of her suitors, Don Sanche, eagerly volunteers to fight on her behalf.

Rodrigue confronts Chimène and tells her that he intends to lose the duel, since he is ready to end his life to satisfy her dutiful wish for vengeance. She urges him to defend himself and his honour. But he is only more adamant when she confesses her aversion for Don Sanche. Chimène must marry the murderer of her father or the murderer of her lover.

Don Sanche appears. Chimène, assuming that he has killed Rodrigue, hysterically upbraids him. She reveals how deeply she loved Rodrigue, then learns that he is still alive; he has defeated Don Sanche but has generously spared his opponent's life. The King, pleased, assures Chimène that her honour is intact and hands her over to her valiant "foe".

The Infanta, ruefully but nobly, urges Chimène to accept this happy resolution. Rodrigue invites his beloved to strike him dead with his own sword if she wishes. When Chimène hesitates, the King decrees that the marriage be deferred a year, during which time Rodrigue shall conduct a military expedition against the Moors in Africa. Thus, tactfully, Corneille concludes a delicate situation.

Needless to say, the story, if supposed to have occurred within twenty-four hours, is preposterous. In choosing such a subject for compression into the rigid unities, Corneille assuredly made an artistic error – and clearly he limited the time only because the rules called upon him to do so. Yet within the compact, swift-moving scenes there is scarcely any mention of time, so that the spectator or reader is hardly aware of the patent absurdity. It is also true that the events dovetail so neatly that all the action is possible, however improbable. The duels are short affairs; the battle is of only three hours' duration and is fought not on a distant border but in the harbour of Seville where the Moors, attempting their surprise attack, are quickly driven off.

What makes the succession of violent events even more plausible is that they all occur offstage. As in Greek drama, they are reported, not visually enacted. Nor, in arranging a happy ending, does Corneille press the issue too far. The marriage of Chimène to the man who that very morning has slain her father is implied as an eventuality, and the audience is not affronted by having it occur before its eyes.

But if the unities of time and place are superficially observed here, the play – as was said of *Clitandre* – is not wholly successful in embodying a classical spirit. Though its popular acclaim was instantly overwhelming, a critical debate was provoked that lasted for decades and engaged some of the best minds in French literature. Rotrou, who had also drawn on Spanish sources, generously defended Corneille's treatment of the theme. Marait on the other hand, who issued a pamphlet assailing Corneille for many shortcomings, was the first prominent contemporary to find fault in print with the work. One reason for Marait's critique was an apologetic essay by Corneille himself in response to the first complaints, in which he boasted that his work was wholly original, that he owed nothing to any other playwright. He also foolhardily claimed supremacy over all his rivals. Marait asserted that, on the contrary, Corneille was a servile imitator.

A battle in pamphlets broke out. One by Georges de Scudéry severely chastised the play and its author. Another, by Chapelain, condemned *Le Cid* on grounds similar to those put forth by Scudéry. Corneille was charged with plagiarism. In response he insisted that he had acknowledged his Spanish source, at the same time that he claimed that the story was solely his and original. It was a question of definition; he had it both ways.

Georges de Scudéry declared that the play violated many rules, was weakly constructed with needlessly digressive episodes (those involving the lovelorn Infanta) and was often badly written. What virtues it had, he stated, were owed chiefly to the Spanish playwright who had treated the story earlier.

One issue argued in the pamphlets was whether a play should aim first to please or to instruct. Corneille thought a play should interest and delight before it preached a moral, though he did not intend to slight a didactic purpose. Other questions were whether a work might be deemed plausible if it did not closely observe the unities and was not in accord with the prevalent social code. In *Le Cid* Chimène persists in her love for Rodrigue, even though he has slain her father: this was improbable and shocking. Love triumphs over duty! That Rodrigue goes twice to confront Chimène in her own home after the duel that costs her father's life was also scandalous. Why had Corneille chosen such an improper subject and handled it so indecorously?

Later critics offered all sorts of suggestions. Jean Chapelain proposed that a happy ending might better have been achieved if it were suddenly disclosed that the count was still alive, or that he were not actually Chimène's father. In their wish for a play to be more "correct" and hence more "plausible", such critics proposed to make it more artificial and contrived.

To all such comments, while he lived, Corneille himself defensively replied. If the facts had historical precedent, if they had in fact occurred, that alone attested to their plausibility, he argued.

Though *Le Cid* was tactfully dedicated to Cardinal Richelieu's niece, His Eminence was among those who were not mollified. He resented Corneille's having succeeded independently and sharply objected to the dramatist's odd choice of subject. He condemned the script on the grounds that the unities were not properly observed. As recently as 1635 the Cardinal had created a national academy, the Académie Française, to regulate the French language and all forms of literature. He ordered its members to consider *Le Cid* and pass judgement on it. They did so reluctantly, condemning its transgressions with respect to the Greek model but paying tribute to the beauty of much of it. The Cardinal may have hoped for a more severe evaluation.

Richelieu contrived to have both Corneille and Georges de Scudéry named as candidates to be voted on by the Forty Immortals (the members of the Académie). The debate about their qualifications was deliberately prolonged, the uncertainty about the outcome keeping both men under stress. Finally, Corneille was denied this new, highest honour. He had to wait ten years for admission to that august body, after Richelieu's death.

Not so the foppish Georges de Scudéry who, though elected to the Académie, knew that he had been defeated in the debate over *Le Cid* since the assertions in his pamphlet had been refuted. The public paid little heed to the esoteric literary critics and rushed to see the play. Before one performance an unruly crowd, elbowing and shouting to gain entrance to the theatre, shoved and crushed two doorkeepers to death.

Soon afterwards de Scudéry became another casualty, when hostile reactions to his assault on *Le Cid* induced him to emulate Mairet and withdraw from all further participation in the world of the theatre. His defeat was absolute.

Shortly before the give-and-take in the Académie, de Scudéry had a play staged. It was greeted as less than mediocre. Richelieu had a critic declare that the author was "the greatest poet of the time". The critic, Sazzarzin, was not truly of that opinion but thought it best to comply with the Cardinal's request.

Besides, de Scudéry had other concerns. During the War of the Condé he was summoned to combat and acquitted himself well. He was appointed Governor of Notre Dame de la Garde, a fortress in Marsailles, but spent very little time there. Between brief, sporadic visits to that post, he hurried by coach back to Paris. His sister, enriched by sales of her novels, established a literary salon in the old rue de Temple where wits came almost daily and the keenest conversations of the capital took place. Her brother Georges was happiest among them. In middle age he married a wealthy young heiress, so no longer had to depend as much on the generosity of his sister and could go on living as a *grand seigneur*.

In a final contretempo, he sent an epic poem to Queen Christina of Sweden. She was pleased and proposed to give him a very costly gold chain, but first she said he must remove some lines in the poem that were a complimentary allusion to a man she disliked. The haughty de Scudéry refused, and the chain was not forthcoming.

He died at sixty-six, a dandy to the end.

The Académie's initial rejection of Corneille's membership was a public rebuke. Afterwards, however, the Cardinal maintained a façade of friendship with the erring poet. Pierre Corneille's father, the King's Advocate in Rouen, was ennobled for his long service to the crown, and few of the later critics of *Le Cid* denied that it stirred the emotions and had an inexplicable power.

Even if Corneille lacked a classical temperament and in all likelihood would have worked more happily in the free Romantic form available to Shakespeare and Webster, most of the lineaments of a typical French tragedy are perceptible in *Le Cid*. Unlike Hardy's plays, there are no comic passages. The subjects are generally historical, and the structure is five-act. The action takes place mostly offstage, while on stage the time is taken up mainly with exceedingly long speeches – the French call them *tirades* – that provide pretexts for eloquent gestures and declamation. These alternate effectively with exchanges that are epigrammatic and may become maxims. The plays are ethical debates and are primarily character studies as well.

Corneille draws human beings who are strong-willed, clear-thinking and even extraordinary – indeed, Chimène's determination to avenge her father finally evokes the impatience not only of the King but also of the spectator. Paradoxically, her strong sense of duty makes her all the more estimable and lovable in Rodrigue's eyes, as his readiness to defend his father's honour elevates him in hers. The agonizing conflict deepens their feeling for each other.

The play's language is not lyrical – Corneille writes a vigorous rhetoric, rather than poetry. He turns out many well-honed phrases, such as the lovelorn Infanta's lament: "When the sick man loves his sickness, / He will not allow any remedy to be administered", or Chimène's cry when Rodrigue offers her his sword, pleading with her to plunge it into his breast:

> What cruel fate is this that in one day
> Kills the father by the sword and his child by the sight of the sword!
> Take it away from here! I cannot bear it.

Or Rodrigue's passionate explanation of how he came to kill the count:

> I have offended you – Your beauty would have been victor,
> Had I not been convinced
> That a man without honor was unworthy of you,
> That despite the place I had in your heart
> You would hate me dishonored;
> Listening to your love and obeying its voice
> Would desecrate the choice of your love.
> Let me say it again, though it is painful,
> Let me say it until I breathe my last breath: but I had to
> In order to wipe out my shame and deserve you.

Says Don Diegue, offering half-hearted consolation to his son: "We have only one honor. There are many mistresses. / Love is but a pleasure; honor is a duty" (translations by Wallace Fowlie).

Charles Péguy has said that *Le Cid* is a poem of "honour loved with love, and love honoured with honour". But Corneille himself insisted that in his plays love takes a secondary place, though it is a noble enough passion on which to base a tragedy. Some speeches in which Rodrigue and Chimène discuss their feelings are almost brutal, and the charge is sometimes made that Corneille's heroines are not wholly feminine, they are so fierce and obstinate. What is timeless about Corneille's work is what was also the essential subject of those French playwrights of the Baroque Age who followed his lead, which is the theme of men and women tested not by a particular code of honour that might govern one era or the next but by a struggle within themselves between the real and the ideal, the eternal inner division between passion and reason in human beings. Corneille's heroes and heroines, like those of Racine after him, are torn between what they are – the sensuality and emotions to which they succumb – and what they believe they ought to be, that is, wholly rational creatures. This is a problem forever gripping human beings, that renders the Baroque tragedies still pertinent and poignant. The characters may seem almost one-dimensional in their fixed preoccupation with "honour" and "duty", and the scope of these plays oddly narrow, as well as at moments somewhat abstract, but they are lastingly vital because they treat with concerns that are particular to no one epoch or culture. In every age there is a tension between man's sensual appetite and his mind that seeks to caution or restrain him. Corneille, writing in the "Age of Reason", that neoclassical epoch in which reserve, self-discipline and rationalism were exalted, touched on what was then an imperious topic, one with which his audiences could immediately identify and to which they could wholeheartedly respond.

But even Corneille's concepts of heroism and honour are not as simple or crude as they seem at first glance. As Doubrovsky puts it, those who considered themselves to be aristocrats, of special blood, masters of the race, had to be prepared to shed their blood to prove that they valued their God-given gift above life itself. That is why the feudal-minded Don Diegue feels his son must be ready to die if need be, to protect the family's proud boast of innate superiority. This belief, held with almost religious fervour, is what allowed families like Diegue's to lead or rule others.

In spite of his defiance, Corneille did bow to censure directed against him. The furore drove him back to Rouen again, and for four years he kept silent. His next plays conform more nearly to the special requirements of French seventeenth-century classical "tragedy" and "tragicomedy". Their subject matter is largely taken from ancient Greek and Roman history or legend and deals with lofty themes, in a heroic strain, and they affirm the undying values of physical courage and moral fidelity. He considered the rules of Aristotle and Horace a hindrance, and he argued that times had changed, and the old concept of theatre should be altered. He carried on his quarrel with hostile critics in numerous prefaces and essays. Why only twenty-four hours? Why not thirty? Could he not use several places in the same city? If the academic theorists would write a few plays, they would appreciate the difficulties. But in practice he yielded to authority, and he respected the unities ever more. His concessions are to be seen in his next several "tragedies" and "tragicomedies".

Horace (1640) is a good example, and it is dedicated to Cardinal Richelieu. Language and plot have a great simplicity, the dialogue is studded with oft-quoted phrases, and if the characters are uncomplicated they are presented with admirable clarity. The spirit and tone of the work, however, are Romantic and have a bold grandeur.

The story is from Livy, and most of the characters have crucially divided loyalties. When Horace, a zealous Roman patriot, hears his sister curse her own country, he is enraged and kills her. Her denunciation of Rome arises from her love for an enemy soldier, Curiace, who perishes in a duel at her brother's hands.

Sabine, wife of the hero Horace, is Curiace's sister, hence also of foreign, hostile origin. This comes to the surface when Horace – with his two brothers and Curiace – represent their discrete causes, Roman versus Alban, in fierce combat. Horace's victory is what prompts his sister to curse Rome. In truth, she deliberately crosses him in order to provoke her death, allowing her to rejoin her betrothed. Horace is prosecuted by her rejected suitor, Valerius, and tried for his fratricidal crime but is finally pardoned by the King.

The plight of Sabine, whose husband kills her brother, is equally harsh. At one point she wishes to rush between the combatants and die, so that the men she loves will no longer be closely related to each other. She seems often about to lose her reason, but as the heroine of a Corneillian tragedy she regains her firm will and in a final scene pleads with the King on her husband's behalf. Significantly, Horace's father condones the murderous act and disowns his disloyal dead daughter.

The drama presents the faults and virtues of its genre. Many critics have found this play extraordinarily powerful. Paris gave it a warm reception.

Cinna (*c.* 1641) is set in the time of Augustus. Cinna wishes to avenge the death of his father the Emperor and so urges Emilie, whom he loves, to join a conspiracy against him. Maxime, also a conspirator, secretly loves Emilie, adding to the complications. The most unusual feature of the drama is the clemency shown by Augustus, who pardons the plotters; guided by his reason he changes from despot to considerate ruler.

The shift of interest from Cinna to Augustus midway, which somewhat mars the unity, is a possible, oft-cited fault of the play. Also, many commentators view Cinna as too base and cowardly to be a tragic hero. But at the time of the play's successful première Cinna was deemed admirable because he dared to oppose tyranny. Emilie was thought to be one of Corneille's most beautiful characterizations, and the script also had allegorical references to the recent revolt of the Fronde against the young Louis XIV, who had just inherited the sceptre.

Polyeucte (*c.* 1642) is one of the few notable French dramas with a religious theme – their scarcity is the result, perhaps, of a parliamentary decree in 1548 against mystery plays. It was daring of Corneille to approach this almost proscribed subject. A pagan Armenian, the princely Polyeucte, is converted to Christianity. His wife Pauline is the daughter of the Roman governor. The marriage is a political one, dictated by her father. Her true love is Sévère (Severus), a Roman. Pauline remains faithful to him, but she looks forward to happiness with Sévère after her husband's death.

Polyeucte acquires saintly attributes and must die for his faith. He achieves martyrdom by toppling the statues of false gods in the Roman temples. Pauline is so moved by his heroism and concern for her that she becomes a Christian in order to be able to share his faith. She invites execution, as does her father.

Much mystical feeling flows through this play, and the effect of divine grace is portrayed; but Corneille was long criticized for displaying divine love and profane human love in one work. Before the play was produced at the Hôtel de Bourgogne he read it to friends, who tried to persuade him to withdraw it. But once more the public response was overwhelmingly favourable. A question long discussed is whether Pauline loves her husband at the end or whether her feeling is still one of profound marital duty.

Many honours accrued to the dramatist. After the triumph of *Le Cid* Louis XIII ennobled Corneille's father, which was taken to be a recognition of the son's achievements. Noting the acclamation for *Cinna*, Richelieu helped his temperamental poet wed a lady of high rank. She may not have found him any more tractable than had the Cardinal, because his was a difficult personality, and he was far from handsome, though his ties with his family were as close as his piety was deep.

Following his tremendous success with *Polyeucte*, he was acknowledged everywhere as the foremost dramatist of France. But he had actually passed his peak as an artist, and his influence was already lessening. This was due to the rise of Jean Racine, who was soon to outshine him.

All the same, a stream of plays still came from the pen of the man from Rouen. *Pompée* (1642), another tragedy, is about the death of that Roman ruler. Another work of the same year is a comedy, *Le Menteur* (*The Liar*). Its plot is adapted from Alarcón's *La Verdad Sospechosa*; as treated by Corneille, it anticipates Molière in being a comedy of character. Corneille considered *Rodogune* (printed 1646) his best work, declaring much of the plot to be his original invention, but posterity has looked upon the script less enthusiastically.

He pursued his study of ancient history and myth with *Théodore* (1646), *Héraclius* (1646), *Don Sanche d'Aragon* (1649), *Andromède* (1650) and *Nicomède* (1650–51). In 1652 the bad reception of *Pertharite* prompted him to retire to Rouen once again for six or seven years. But he kept on writing indefatigably: *Oedipe* (1659), *La Toison d'or* (a spectacle play, 1660), *Sertorius* (1662), *Sophonisbe* (1663) and *Tite et Bérénice* (1671). Some of these won him renewed acclaim, notably *La Toison d'or*; however, the fervent applause for *Tite et Bérénice* on opening night came mostly from his ever-loyal partisans (it was staged in direct competition to a play by Racine on the same theme), and the eagerly awaited play was a failure.

Few of these late works added much lustre to his name. Molière, whose company produced many of these unlucky scripts, noted Corneille's loss of poetic vigour. After Corneille had another series of failures with *Othon* (1664), *Agésilas* (1666) and *Attila* (1667), and, though the critic Boileau said cruelly that Corneille should stop composing plays, the dogged dramatist kept on. *Pulchérie* (1672) and *Suréna* (1674) followed the disaster of *Tite et Bérénice*.

He was bewildered by the accumulating signs of his decline, which resulted not only from his failing powers but from the circumstance that a poet of his heroic cast of mind was not really suited to the effete new age of Louis XIV. He was too rugged for the polite culture into which France, under the aegis of the over-elegant young Sun King, was evolving.

In his last years Corneille was improvident, lost his pension for a time and ended almost penniless. When he died in 1684 close to forty years had elapsed since the short span of less than a decade in which he had enjoyed such high esteem and nationwide popularity. Nevertheless his dramas and comedies remained fully alive in France's classic repertory, and the revivals of his works are endless. He is, next to Racine, the best-known playwright in French theatre. A ringing eulogy of him was delivered at the Académie Française, most appropriately by Racine, in more ways than one his dazzling successor.

Pierre Corneille was not the only member of his family who wrote for the stage. His younger brother Thomas (1625–1704), though scarcely as gifted or famed, became a professional dramatist respected for his skill. His most esteemed script is a tragedy, *Timocrate* (1656). Though twenty years separated the Corneille brothers, they were so fond of each other that they dwelt in attached houses. Legend says a panel in the walls could be opened to give them access to each other and that when Pierre sought a rhyme and could not hit upon it the sliding door enabled him to ask his brother for help. After Pierre's death, Thomas was elected to his brother's chair in the Académie.

Jean Racine, born in 1639, was thirty-three years the junior of the formidable Pierre Corneille. In the third of a century dividing them, and especially during the time the new writer stood in the wings as a rival, the political situation greatly altered. That was also true of the social scene, which is to say life at court, in the châteaux of the aristocracy and among the wealthy upper bourgeoisie who aped the nobles. When Louis XIV ascended the throne in 1643 he was just five years old. The regents – the astute Richelieu, and after him the crafty Italian-born Cardinal Jules Mazarin, and finally Colbert – fended off the feudal lords seeking to deprive the boy heir of the sceptre. Civil strife was put down, the control of France was centralized and order was established under a smooth-running but firm autocracy. The young King finally reached an age at which he revealed a marked talent of his own for ruling. Wars raged elsewhere in Europe, and France had its share of costly military victories, but within its borders the nation enjoyed a long spell of tranquillity fostered by strong government. "*Après moi le déluge*," Louis XIV was to remark later, but he was sovereign for seventy-two years, and through most of his mature span he could also declare with confidence the oft-quoted "*L'état, c'est moi.*" During his sway France rose to its height, and culturally it dominated Europe everywhere, setting the pattern of arts and manners and criteria for architecture, painting and theatre.

Two playwrights, Racine and Molière, were the supreme embodiments of the Baroque, the one in tragedy, the other in the comedy of manners.

As has been said, to divert his restless and ambitious nobles who after the defeat of the Fronde uprising were deprived of political influence, Louis had them spend months every year in personal attendance at court. This gave him a closer watch over them and also took them a distance from their far-spread fiefs, where they might plot mischief out of sight. He built Versailles, the world's most magnificent palace, draining the wealth of France and further beggaring the hungry poor, to help the rich pass time in sybaritic indolence. The vast edifice, with its frescoed and mirrored halls and painted ceilings, flickering chandeliers and gilt furnishings, was a visible sign of France's *gloire*. In extensive formal gardens and terraces, leaping fountains were surrounded by pebbled paths laid out geometrically and bordered by clipped hedges and cunningly shaped mazes and trees. Life in this royal house and its gardens became a lavish incarnation of the Age of Reason: outwardly it was over-decorous, extravagantly mannered and accepting of a disciplined ritual.

The courtiers, at least many of them, seemed to be exemplary persons. But, human nature being what it is, their daily routine was also one of decadence, artificiality and intellectual pretension. They engaged in political rivalries, flirtations and malicious gossip. Versailles not only became the apogee of the Baroque but saw a gradual transition into the over-decorative Age of Rococo that all too soon followed it.

In the palace, Louis XIV made use of his theatre. With idle courtiers on his hands, who could be dangerous if bored, he sought to keep them pleasantly occupied from hour to hour. So, to entertain them, Italian comedians who performed the works of French writers and native acting troupes were recruited to occupy the stage. Cardinal Mazarin imported singers from Italy to put on operas. Louis XIV, who had loved to dance in his youth, along with his nobles still personally participated in pageants and *comédies-ballet* mounted on the lawns and terraces.

The King, and ministers and nobles emulating royalty, paid the artists well. For a long while the theatre became an adjunct of the court. The audience was supposedly a well-informed élite – though blue blood and swollen purses (especially if rank and wealth are merely inherited) do not always ensure sharp intelligence, wit or taste. In any event, a major determinant of what was preferred was the predilections of the three great drama patrons Louis XIV the Grand Monarch, the Italian churchman Mazarin (who had first come to Paris as papal nuncio, after which he rose to power in an alien land with Richelieu's aid) and the King's kinsman the Duc d'Anjou.

The age was by no means one that was truly civilized. Throughout his long life the King disdained cutlery and ate with his fingers. He could be generous but also cruel, and he was superstitious. Though pious, he was unfaithful, taking a succession of mistresses, and every kind of sexual deviation flourished at court. The throng of silk-attired and bewigged nobles had many appalling habits of personal hygiene and sometimes turned the royal corridors into latrines.

But though vulgar by later criteria, and heartless, heedless and often flagrantly effeminate, the exemplars of this regal society vaunted themselves on their refinement. Therefore the sensitive, erudite Racine was the playwright best equipped for them. Not that they duly cherished him; rather, they criticized and calumniated him. His beautifully polished work was decried and was at times received coldly and rudely. Much of his life was unhappy – but this was also owing to his own strange temperament.

The Jansenists were a religious cult akin to the Calvinists, with a very severe outlook that stressed man's sinful nature. Jean Racine was the son of a middle-class Jansenist family that was quite well-to-do. His father was controller of the government's salt monopoly; his mother was the daughter of a lawyer. At four years old he was orphaned and so had an austere childhood under the guidance first of his grandparents and later of a strict, pious aunt. His family was fanatically religious; several members were in the clergy, and some were nuns, members of the Port-Royal sisterhood.

Though Racine broke with his Jansenist background and rebelled against his family's moralism at times, his own personality was as split as those of the agonized heroes and heroines he was to portray. His characters were basically weak and at the mercy of their sensual instincts, however guilty they felt as they struggled vainly against temptation. Much of this seems to have been inculcated in him through his bleak early youth, as from age fifteen to eighteen he was sent to the headquarters of the cult, a monastery at Port-Royal where he received intensive instruction in Greek and Latin.

He was attracted to the plays of Sophocles and Euripides in particular and ventured to translate several of them. He also delved into such Hellenistic romances as *Aethiopica*, which his priestly teachers confiscated and burned as improper fare for one of his innocent years. He obtained another copy and memorized it, retaining its entire contents in his head before handing it over for burning, too.

But while he shocked his superiors, he also studied and won praise by excelling at theology. From the harsh precincts of Port-Royal he went on to the Collège d'Harcourt in Paris, where he took courses in philosophy and debated whether to make law or theology his career.

He shared quarters with a cousin, Nicolas Vitart, who, though also attached to Port-Royal, introduced him to theatre. The dramas fascinated young Racine.

He wrote a play and submitted it to a clever actor who called himself Molière and headed a company that travelled about the provinces. The perceptive Molière said it was not suitable for production but gave him 100 louis by way of encouragement. Abandoning all thoughts of joining the legal profession or the Church, the young man began to consider a literary career. He was also starting to behave somewhat dissolutely, drawn to not one but several young women.

Scandalized, his family ordered him to leave Paris and live with an uncle, a canon of the cathedral of the Uzès, in the southern region. Here he was to take up theology once more, with the promise of a benefice when he was ordained. Wearing a black robe, he pored over Thomas Aquinas but stole glances at Ariosto and Euripides.

He was still haunted by thoughts of women. He wrote to his friend and erstwhile fellow reveller La Fontaine that his uncle, the canon, had advised him to "be blind". At that, he confessed, he was partly a failure, but he vowed to "be mute" at least. After a year, however, the canon was no longer sure of being able to award him the promised benefice. This gave the youth a longed-for pretext to doff his black garment. He knew for certain that the Church was not his vocation. Paris and literature beckoned; he hastened back to them; he was now about twenty-four.

A published ode won him a royal grant of another hundred louis d'or. Molière staged Racine's second play, *La Thébaïde* (1664), the theme of which he suggested to his protégé. The result was not too happy: the play had only four performances. But his poetry had gained him the support of two important critics, Chapelain and Boileau. He was progressing quickly.

His relatives, however, were alarmed. His aunt, the Port-Royal nun, wrote beseeching him to give over his prodigally wicked ways, warning him that he was falling into abomination. One of his Jansenist teachers, Nicole, issued a public statement of condemnation: "Novelists and dramatists are poisonmongers who destroy not men's bodies but their souls." Stung, Racine replied angrily. (Other responses to this attack were issued by Corneille and Molière.)

After this, the rupture with Port-Royal was complete – for a while. Molière produced his third play, *Alexandre* (1665), and with typical thoughtfulness did not perform in it – the general opinion was that Molière was not a good tragic actor, and Molière was aware that Racine shared this opinion. What is more, he cast Racine's mistress, Thérèse du Parc, in the principal female role.

The play got enough applause, but Racine did not like the acting. He set up a private rehearsal by another company, the Troupe Royale, and thought his work went better there. Accordingly, he took his play away from Molière and took away Mlle du Parc as well and transferred both to the Hôtel de Bourgogne, where they scored a great success, attaining thirty performances just over two months. Enraged at such disloyalty, Molière never spoke to Racine again.

At the Hôtel de Bourgogne Racine had a more appropriate venue for his verse tragedies. His *Andromaque* was staged there in 1667. (The present version is a revision completed some five years later.) To the critic Boileau, Racine had said, "I have a surprising facility in writing my verses." The sage Boileau answered, "I wanted to teach you to write them with difficulty."

The critic applied himself to teaching the young man the precepts of Aristotle and Horace and found him to be a most intelligent pupil. That is shown in *Andromaque*, a simply plotted script whose source was both Euripides and the third book of Virgil's *Aeneid*. Racine himself claimed that when he read it to Madame Henrietta, the daughter of England's Charles I and the Duchesse d'Orléans, to whom it is dedicated, the royal lady wept aloud. When it was produced, his pre-eminence as a writer of tragedy was acknowledged at once, and he began to supersede Corneille in critical favour.

In the play, Orestes comes to Epirus as an envoy from Greece to demand from its King Pyrrhus the life of dead Hector's son Astyanax. The Greeks, lusting for vengeance, fear that the little boy when grown up might lead the defeated Trojans against them. But Orestes' true purpose in visiting Epirus is to win back Hermione, daughter of Menelaus and Helen, whom he deeply loves. She is betrothed to Pyrrhus, who has delayed their marriage because of an infatuation with Andromaque, Hector's still beautiful young widow and mother of the threatened child Astyanax. The Trojan Princess and her son are captives of Pyrrhus.

Once this exposition is unfolded, nothing physical ever occurs in the play; instead, in a succession of beautiful and impassioned tirades, the characters bare their thoughts and feelings and chiefly their waverings. Pyrrhus tells proud Andromaque that if she marries him he will protect her son from the Greeks, but she is adamantly faithful to the memory of her slain husband. In consequence Pyrrhus' affection for her turns to hatred, only to shift back to feverish desire at the least encouragement from her.

Meanwhile the spurned Hermione, whose feelings Pyrrhus has enslaved, also develops antipathy for him and seeks to use the enamoured Orestes to punish Pyrrhus for slighting her. Orestes is tempted by this chance to gain Hermione but is also frightened and repulsed at having to kill his host, who is Achilles' son and a hero of the Trojan War.

Andromaque finally consents to marry Pyrrhus, though she means to kill herself later after extracting from the King a pledge to guard her son from the Greeks and name him heir to Epirus. Hermione, cruelly spurned once more, provokes Orestes into having his men assassinate Pyrrhus at the wedding ritual. The deed is carried out, but when word of it reaches Hermione she upbraids Orestes for having acted as she herself requested and rushes to behold the body of Pyrrhus before fatally stabbing herself to death. Andromaque takes command, and Orestes goes mad. The audience must imagine this gory, violent action, as it takes place offstage.

Though the plot of *Andromaque* is more complicated than most chosen by Racine, it is far simpler than any found in the works of Corneille. The latter's theory, expounded in his *Discourse on the Three Unities*, is that the hero can undergo a succession of dangers provided that they are logically linked. While Corneille, however, packs too much action into a framework dictated by the three unities and loses plausibility, Racine avoids doing this. The simplicity of his storyline lends itself admirably to his faithful and skilful compression of time and place. He shuns digressions, never deviating from his central situation. In his preface to *Bérénice*, a later play, he was to write:

> Some people think that . . . simplicity is a sign of little inventiveness. They do not dream that it is the reverse, that inventiveness consists of making something out of nothing, and that large numbers of incidents have always been the refuge of poets who do not feel their genius is sufficiently powerful to maintain the audience's attention for five acts by means of a simple action, sustained by the violence of the passions, the beauty of the sentiments and the elegance of the utterance. [Translation by Bernard F. Dokore]

What is amazing is how a play like *Andromaque*, which has little or no physical action and consists merely of a series of monologues or almost one-sided dialogues, can hold attention and build suspense while it profoundly moves the hearer. The speeches are lucid, convincing and revealing. The play is an exploration of emotions, especially those of women torn by love, jealousy or fear or angrily defending their marital fidelity. Racine has an acuity for the psychologies of both sexes, which enables him to portray the hearts and minds of women. The title of the drama is misleading, for Hermione rather than Andromaque is the focal figure, and after her the much-troubled Pyrrhus. But all four principals in this tragedy are presented with striking conviction, and once shown in their distress they are unforgettable. Racine is credited with laying the foundations of modern psychological theatre.

The music of Racine's verse has long defied translation, depriving those who do not know French of one of the supreme pleasures of literature. His language is delicate, precise and lyrical, and his lines are chiselled, polished to perfection yet strong. Passion breaks through, given an utterance that is all the more poignant and memorable because of its precision. Yet there are passages of fury, too, and it is reported that in 1685 the actor Zacharie Jacob Montfleury, one of Molière's leading rivals, burst a blood vessel and died from acting his role with full intensity.

Most of Racine's plays are about women, and his theme is not heroism, as with Corneille, but love, which was a more popular subject in his time. A show of the utmost gallantry fitted the period. While Corneille consigned love to a secondary place as attractive but not paramount, Racine struck just the right note to entrance his audience. His women are not as firm of mind as the heroines of Corneille but are tender and confused, their inner conflict sometimes almost hidden in the unconscious from which it breaks forth to overwhelm them.

In Racine's plays tragedy and comedy are not mixed; that classical austerity he did follow. He wrote "witty and elegant" songs for his plays and excelled at translating numerous classic works. Lest anyone think that Racine lacked a sense of humour, his play *Les Plaideurs* (*The Pleaders*; 1668), which followed *Andromaque*, is proof to the contrary. Based in part on *The Wasps* of Aristophanes, it draws perhaps quite as much on his personal misadventures with the law. An amusing character in it is a judge so proud of his robes that he wears them to bed at night and another a loquacious lawyer who insists upon tracing the matter at hand back to its very inception, starting his argument by describing the Creation of the World. A witty satire on avaricious lawyers, suborned witnesses and dishonest judges, it echoes what befell the irascible author when he sued for money that he claimed was due him. The case took so long that he finally dropped it, but he vented his indignation through his play. Purportedly, he composed most of it in a tavern, not taking the script too seriously. The first audience did not laugh too heartily, but Louis XIV had it acted at court and this rapidly influenced public opinion, and *Les Plaideurs* became a solid hit. Some critics think it witty, others mediocre.

Racine went back to tragedies, at which his hand was surer, and next offered *Britannicus* (1669). But meanwhile a real-life tragedy had befallen him. Mlle du Parc, the talented actress who was his mistress, died in circumstances not easy to explain. A decade later he was to be charged with her murder. The cloud of suspicion, however, had not yet settled on him.

Britannicus is set in the decadent Rome of Nero's reign. Much of the material, apparently, is taken from Tacitus. For once, a serious play by Racine is not primarily concerned with love; indeed it is more like a Corneillian drama. The author deemed it his most thoughtful composition, and many critics agree with him in admiring it more than *Andromaque*. But the story is very unpleasant, since nearly all the characters are repulsive. Nero is unspeakably evil, and the portrayal of his tutor and counsellor Narcissus is distasteful. The title figure, Britannicus, the rightful heir to the Empire, is forever complaining and is too easily taken in by Nero's professions of friendship; and the scheming dowager Empress Agrippina is uncomfortably shrewish.

The repulsive subject notwithstanding, however, the drama is undeniably brilliant and powerful, with descriptions of exciting incidents – the poisoning of the hapless Britannicus, the flight of his beloved Juni to escape the lustful Nero's clutches in the shelter of the Vestal Virgins, the slaughter of Narcissus by an outraged mob and Nero's frustration. At the end the young Emperor is left furious, still only in the first stages of his bloody career.

Bérénice followed in 1670, originating from a single line in Suetonius that Racine expanded to five full acts. There are passages in the main character Bérénice's speeches that voice high praise and even adulation for the Roman military leader Titus as a handsome and resplendent ruler, and it is easy and logical to assume that these must have resounded pleasantly in the ears of Louis XIV, who was apt to identify himself with his distant Roman predecessor.

After Titus – son of the Emperor Vespasian – besieges Jerusalem, he falls in love with Bérénice, a Jewish Princess. She is married – in fact, for the third time – but becomes his mistress and returns with him to Rome. He succeeds to the throne at Vespasian's death and recognizes that Bérénice cannot be his empress under Roman law because she is an alien and that she therefore must be sent away.

For some time Antiochus, King of Comagena, has also been interested in her, though he has kept his feelings secret because he is a close friend and erstwhile comrade-in-arms of Titus and had been expecting the new Emperor to wed Bérénice. When the broken-hearted Titus asks Antiochus to inform her of his need to part from her, Antiochus undertakes the task, harbouring both pity for Bérénice and hope for himself.

Bérénice, however, suspects him of trickery and refuses to believe him. She hastens to Titus, who reluctantly confirms Antiochus' message. Bérénice leaves thereupon but threatens to kill herself. Antiochus pleads with the newly named Emperor to save Bérénice's life by going to her.

But Titus has been called to the senate. Though he obeys the summons of royal duty instead of love, however, his thwarted desire nearly destroys him. Duty proves as exacting as love; he enters upon both courses unaware of their cost.

Frustrated, the unhappy Antiochus, too, considers suicide. Bérénice, beholding his emotional plight and realizing that Titus loves her but as a ruler puts honour and duty above personal feelings, sees her private love as unworthy. After reconciliations and renunciations, all three sadly go their different ways. Love is denied, while other ideals – of propriety, loyalty and obligation – prevail.

The play fits neatly into the system of the three unities, and the conflict within each of the three leading characters between passion and self-discipline endows the script with a theatrical excitement that Racine's uniquely musical lines enrich and exalt; the taut, muted scenes are filled with tension and subdued anguish.

In much the same Corneillian vein are *Bajazet* (1672) and *Mithridate* (1673). The first was almost contemporary in time, though it is laid in an Oriental realm. Its heroine Roxane is another of Racine's well-drawn, passionately troubled women. *Mithridate* also has an Oriental colouring, and as always love has a dominant part in it. It was King Louis's favourite among the poet's works and was responsible for Racine's election to the Académie in 1673.

Corneille had also written a play about Mithridates, the Pontic monarch, but the palm went to the younger man's embrace of the subject, and Racine was chosen over Corneille. He was then deemed ineligible for Académie membership, however, because he would not quit the stage as an actor, a profession considered lacking in dignity.

Racine continued to derive his subjects from Euripides, basing his play *Iphigénie* of 1674 on *Iphigenia at Aulis.* Later much admired by Voltaire, *Iphigénie* was staged in the gardens of Versailles accompanied by music and was perhaps the greatest triumph of Racine's career. For the occasion, chandeliers of sparkling crystal were attached to boughs or set in the leaves of orange and pomegranate trees to illuminate the actors' features. The play was performed afterwards in Paris with equal success, having forty showings in three months. As with Racine's other works, refinement and sensibility are this script's hallmarks.

Salient contrasts abound. Innocent, delicate Iphigénie is remarkably strong in her love for Achilles and in her loyalty to her glory-hunting, weakly shifting father Agamemnon. Very different is the extroverted and completely unsubtle warrior Achilles. Agamemnon, whose ambition demands his daughter's sacrifice, is torn by fears of its consequences. His firm-willed Queen Clytemnestra opposes him throughout and makes many desperate though failed attempts to save her child's life.

This tragicomedy has a "happy ending", for Ériphile, a young girl with a pathological death wish, commits suicide, and her body provides a substitute for Iphigénie's, an offering which the prophet Calchas obligingly decides the gods will accept.

Racine should have been happy with his unfailing successes, but he was not. Corneille and his friends were jealous of the young poet's ascendancy and spread canards, especially about his personal life. Madame de Sévigné, that inveterate correspondent, wrote to her daughter in Paris: "Racine writes plays for Mlle Champmeslé [the actress], but not for posterity. If ever he grows up, and ceases to fall in love, it will be a different story. So hurrah for our old friend Corneille! Forgive him a few indifferent verses for the sublime heights to which he raises us: such master-strokes are inimitable."

Racine also had enemies at court who resented his sarcasm and arrogance. His bristly manner seemed to prove that he could not take adverse criticism. He confessed to his son: "The applause I met with often flattered me a great deal; but the smallest critical censure . . . always caused me more vexation than the pleasure given me by praise."

The "critical censure" was intense. He was charged with debasing tragic drama by concerning himself with the problems of depraved, irrational women, of stressing love too much and of ignoble sentimentality. Since the ageing Corneille was obviously no longer a match for him, his foes put forward another playwright, Nicolas Pradon, to compete with him. The feud mounted at court and in theatrical circles and went to extreme and almost incredible lengths.

When word got out that Racine, turning to Euripides again, had proposed a new version of *Hippolytus*, his enemies prompted Pradon to write a script on the same subject. They arranged for its première at the Théâtre de Guénégaud two days after Racine's play was to open at the Hôtel de Bourgogne, on New Year's Day, 1677. At first both plays bore the same title, *Phèdre et Hippolyte*, so Racine altered his to *Phèdre*.

To make sure that the Racine début would get off to a lame start with a depressing reception, his antagonists bought up a good number of the tickets and stayed away, leaving many seats vacant. The same group then gave Pradon's play a rousing welcome on its first night. Actually, both plays were well liked and enjoyed good runs, though today Racine's drama is considered one of the finest, if not the best, of all Baroque tragedies, while Pradon's is looked on as scarcely more than a historical curiosity.

In adapting Euripides' plot, Racine made many changes, and he borrowed as well from Seneca's later Roman version of the story. The synthesis resulted in a work that is rather much his own.

He was forced to alter Hippolytus' dedication to chastity; to the frivolous, loose-living courtiers at Versailles such frigidity would have been a cause for scorn and laughter. Instead Racine's Hippolytus is in love with the young Princess Aricie, the daughter and sister of Theseus' sworn enemies. This accounts for his indifference, described below, to the advances of his step-mother Phèdre.

Seneca's influence, and Racine's own experience with court intrigue, led him to stress far more than had Euripides the problem of the dynastic succession. Phèdre, when she hears a false rumour of her husband Theseus' death, is anxious to protect the son she has by him from Theseus' stepbrother. (Racine takes this detail from Plutarch.) It is the mistaken report that allows Phèdre to confess to her attendant Oenone the cause of a mysterious malady she suffers – that an infatuation with her young stepson Hippolytus has overtaken her. If his father is dead, then her passion is not quite as odious as it might otherwise be.

Until this moment Phèdre has been wanting to die to erase the shame of her misdirected desire. She has been fasting to punish and destroy herself. Oenone, an inveterate dispenser of bad advice, persuades her mistress that her love is no longer criminal, that she should avoid thoughts of self-flagellation and even approach the fatally attractive Hippolytus.

The young Prince, believing that his father has perished, offers himself and the throne to Aricie. Meanwhile, Phèdre encounters him to plead that he treat her son kindly. Gradually she brings herself to avow her passion. Her stepson rejects her with anger and repulsion. Snatching his sword, she tries to kill herself, but Oenone intervenes.

Word comes that Theseus is alive and is about to return. Phèdre, fearing that her husband will hear of her proposal to Hippolytus, again talks of dying. Oenone suggests that her mistress forestall any revelation from the stepson by claiming that the young Prince had attempted to seduce her. At first appalled by the fabrication, Phèdre finally agrees. Theseus, disturbed by her story, sharply questions his son. The father's suspicions are further aroused when he learns that Hippolytus is planning to go away. The son does not dare confess that the reason for this journey is his wish to marry the alien Aricie.

Neptune owes Theseus the fulfilment of a wish in exchange for a past favour, so when Oenone, too, accuses Hippolytus, Theseus calls down the murderous wrath of the god on his now banished son. Hippolytus has been gallant and magnanimous enough not to expose

Phèdre's conduct, but has finally confessed his love for Aricie. Theseus, lamenting his son's defection, is inopportunely approached by Phèdre, who asks him to pardon Hippolytus. The King refuses to listen to her and tells Phèdre of Hippolytus' love for the foreign Aricie. This fills her with confusion and jealousy, but finally remorse overwhelms her emotions. She curses Oenone, who has persuaded her to lie and commit crimes against an innocent youth.

Again Hippolytus asks Aricie to marry him. Meanwhile, Theseus desperately seeks to discover the truth about his son and Phèdre. He is told that Oenone has drowned herself in the sea and that Phèdre, too, has been expressing a wish to die. Theseus wavers. Is Hippolytus guiltless after all? The father tremblingly begs Neptune not to carry out the fearful vow, but his plea is uttered too late. Hippolytus, driving his chariot along the shore, has been slain and dismembered by a sea-monster that rises from the waves at Neptune's prompting. This is related by another device borrowed from the Greeks, a *récit* or messenger's report. Phèdre appears before the grief-stricken King and reveals her passion for the dead youth whose behaviour towards her has been virtuous at all times. Then, having taken poison, she expires. Theseus, remorseful, adopts Aricie as his daughter.

There are further changes. In Euripides' version the spurned Phèdre hangs herself before Theseus returns and leaves a letter charging her stepson with attempted rape. Racine, though, keeps Phèdre in the play until almost the very end, which in many respects is a dramatic improvement. He borrows from Seneca the idea of enlarging Phèdre's role and making her rather than Hippolytus the principal figure.

But this also fits with his inclination to concentrate on the psychology of lovelorn women. As Francis Ferguson has put it, the consequence is a "reduction" of Euripides' far more universal study of frigidity in an intellectually arrogant young man. In the Greek's play, Aphrodite takes her horrible vengeance on the youth, through Phèdre who is under a spell.

For Euripides, who was writing about the consequences of the attempt to deny powerful natural human impulses, especially sexual desire, it is the priggish Hippolytus' singleminded dedication to the chaste goddess Artemis that offends Aphrodite. By contrast, Racine was more or less forced to scale the legend down so it would adhere to values the audiences of his own time held or appreciated.

Seneca anticipated Racine in having Phèdre confess her love openly to Hippolytus, while Euripides was hissed for attempting that in the first of his two versions of the tragedy. In Seneca, too, Phèdre is drawn to her stepson not by magical spells (a symbolic device employed by Euripides) but by a perception of the young man as a more attractive, more idealized replica of his father, to say nothing of his being much nearer her own age.

Theseus, also a principal figure, is portrayed as no less guilty, not only because of the *hamartia* of his quick temper but because of his past brutal treatment of Hippolytus' mother, the Queen of the Amazons.

Eric Bentley and others have commented on the "savagery" masked in this seemingly effete story. Phèdre is descended from the same tainted family that spawned the Minotaur, her mother having mated with a bull. In this play, as in the ancient Aeschylean dramas, the sins of the fathers are passed on to the children; the wild power of Phèdre's passion, which is beyond her control, is an inherited trait.

Madame de la Fayette relates that in a discussion Racine had stated that a good poet could inspire compassion for even the worst moral offenders. His hearers challenged him about this, and, easily irritated, he determined to write a play depicting the misfortunes of Phèdre in such a manner that the ill-fated heroine gains more pity from the spectator than does her virtuous stepson.

The playwright was eminently successful at this, and the role is perhaps the most cherished and sought after in all the French classical repertoire. Just as a young English or American actress dreams of some day playing Juliet or Ophelia, Lady Macbeth or Hedda Gabler, all French hopefuls aspire to be assigned to Racine's Andromaque, Bérénice and especially Phèdre. Among the notable modern portrayers have been Rachel, Sarah Bernhardt, Raucourt, Clairon and Duchesnois. Marcel Proust describes how the first time he went to see a Racine drama he tried to imagine himself at the première of the immortal work. Then he summoned to his mind's eye the procession of famed actresses who had essayed the character. The play was infinitely enriched for him, he wrote, by all these accretions from tradition and history.

The play represents Racine at his best – the language is most exquisite and the sensitivity of the portraits truly androgynous. Perhaps the most moving passage is that in which Phèdre, glimpsing Hippolytus with Aricie as they stand encircled, perceives their deep love for each other from which she is for ever excluded. Jealousy, grief and bitterness possess her, and she pours forth her torment in cadenced, beautiful lines that reach and stir the listener to share her sense of being deprived of life's most precious gift. She accuses herself most of all:

> Whose heart is this I claim as mine?
> . . . And from this time, my guilt has passed
> All bounds!
> Hypocrisy and incest breathe at once
> Through all I do.

She knows the enormity of her illicit lust and yet is unable to repress it in herself, and her self-abhorrence throughout makes her a sympathetic figure. In one moment, when Oenone urges her to occupy herself with affairs of state, Phèdre merely exclaims:

> I reign? To place the State
> Under my law, when reason reigns no longer

Over myself; when I have abdicated
From the empire of my senses.
[Translations by Kenneth Muir]

Racine achieves his poetic effect with the simplest vocabulary. His gift for lucidity would seem to an Anglo-Saxon writer to be inimical to verse, but, though his words and phrases are the plainest and though he must incessantly rhyme his Alexandrine couplets, there is never a prosaic line, never a hint of monotony in the rhythm. He had to obey a host of rules, established by tradition, many of them restrictive, and to work with a very limited vocabulary – in Lytton Strachey's phrase (from *Landmarks in French Literature*), he has to "soar in shackles" – but soar he does! He was able, with the plainest words, to attain an expressive and concentrated lyricism, a transcendent achievement. His language, by its very directness, has an added force. To quote from Strachey again: "Racine's poetry differs as much from Shakespeare's as some calm-flowing river of the plain from a turbulent river. To dwellers in the mountain the smooth river may seem at first unimpressive. But still waters run deep . . ."

The stir caused by *Phèdre*, including the hostility voiced by the cabal of Racine's enemies at court, brought about momentous changes in his life. In dudgeon at such display of malice, he withdrew from court life and largely from writing. For the next dozen years he composed only a few verses and essays, among them a sequence of confessional sonnets and a dutiful history of Port-Royal. He was now thirty-eight.

Some time after Mlle du Parc's untimely death he had taken a new mistress, also an actress, the Marie-Françoise de Champmeslé disparagingly referred to in Madame de Sévigné's letter. This liaison began about the time of *Bérénice* and lasted though the writing of *Phèdre*, whereupon the lady was won away from him – or, as a contemporary wit put it, *déraciné*, that is "torn from the root" – by the predatory nobleman Comte de Clermont-Tonnerre.

Racine, for many years something of an amorist, now decided to change his way of life. In 1677 he married – a wealthy lady who was very pious and never read any of his dramatic work – and began to raise a family, ultimately comprising two sons and five daughters. He enjoyed domesticity and was happily ensconced in it, away from the slanders and rapacious intrigue of the theatre and court.

He also returned to the aura of Port-Royal and, after his reconversion, grew very religious. *Phèdre* has often been called a Jansenist tragedy because the heroine passively wills little, acts little and submits to a predestined doom with no hope of grace and an innate sense of guilt and damnation. But even more Jansenist are the sentiments Racine expressed in his preface to the play's printed version, in which he insists upon the morality of this drama:

> I do not dare yet say that this . . . is the best of my tragedies . . . but this I do say: that I have written no play in which virtue has been more celebrated than in this one. The smallest faults

> are here severely punished; the mere idea of a crime is looked upon with as much horror as the crime itself; the weaknesses of those in love are treated as real weaknesses; passions are represented only to show all the disorder they occasion; and the vice is everywhere painted in colours that render its deformity recognizable and hateful. This indeed should be the end and aim of every man who works for a public audience.

He insists that Greek tragedy writers had held the same aim, and he argues that if all his contemporaries would embrace the same purpose . . .

> it might perhaps be a way of reconciling the art of the theatre with many persons celebrated for their piety and for their learning, who have during the past few years condemned it, and who would doubtless judge it more favourably if playwrights would study as much to instruct as to entertain their audiences.

The foremost Jansenist theologian and philosopher Antoine Arnauld, at whom this preface was primarily directed, duly responded with his approbation of *Phèdre*, and an erring son, long lost to a wanton life, was accepted once more into the austere fold of true believers from which he had wandered. Racine received a liberal pension from the King, as well as appointment to a sinecure in a financial bureau. In 1677 Racine and Boileau were named court historiographers, in which posts they travelled with the monarch on military campaigns in order to observe events first hand. Such duties, of course, were time-consuming.

But soon Racine's new tranquillity was disturbed by the charge that, some years before, he had poisoned his earlier mistress, Mlle du Parc. This accusation was made by a Catherine Monvoison, who was on trial for having disposed of several other persons by the same means. Though she professed to offer factual details as evidence, none could be substantiated, and her charge was further discredited by the fact that she had been in the hire of the Comtesse de Soissons, who was on the roster of Racine's most vicious antagonists. Even so, a warrant was readied for Racine's arrest.

Perhaps what spared him was that the investigation began to cast suspicion on Madame de Montespan, the royal mistress, and Louis XIV ordered the court findings kept secret; then the entire matter was discreetly dropped.

Despite the horrible accusations, Racine continued to enjoy royal favour. As Louis XIV grew older he also become religious. In a morganatic match he married the middle-aged matronly Madame de Maintenon, formerly the governess of his bastard children, and settled down to a more placid existence that rather paralleled Racine's routine. Madame de Maintenon, too, was very devout. One of her enterprises was to found a college at St Cyr for well-born girls in reduced circumstances, which under the patronage of the nun-like Queen soon took on many characteristics of a convent.

Her appeal to Racine, to write a religious play to be acted by the young ladies in her academy, was responsible for bringing him back to the drama. They had already put on *Andromaque*, but the girls had shown too much pleasure in the scenes of passion, so she now asked Racine to give her a drama without any love interest.

Accordingly, he chose a biblical theme and wrote *Esther* in 1689. As a former divinity student with a profound knowledge of scripture, he was exceptionally well prepared to attempt the subject. He further helped in the school production by giving personal instruction to the girls. The staging was elaborate, as the King (among the few males permitted to view the performance) contributed 100,000 francs for resplendent Oriental costumes and settings.

The return of Racine to the theatre in any form was widely recognized as an important event. So great was the demand to see *Esther* that a dozen more performances were given, first for the clergy, then for the courtiers. But the play was denied to the public until 1721, more than two decades after the author's death, when Louis XIV, too, was dead and piety was no longer the royal fashion. The revival had no marked success.

The play offers the familiar story of the wicked court minister Haman who plots to destroy the Jews and tells how they are saved by Esther, the Jewish Queen of King Ahasuerus, Persia's ruler. The verse is some of Racine's finest, and he introduces a chorus which recites passages that approach the sublime.

Topically, the script has allegorical references – to Louis XIV in Ahasuerus, to Madame de Maintenon in Esther and to Madame de Montespan, the discarded mistress of the Sun King, in Vashti. The troubles precipitated by the suppression of the Jews were instantly likened to the similar fate the Huguenots suffered in France after the Edict of Nantes which the somewhat narrow-minded Louis XIV had made into law – and Madame de Maintenon had once belonged to that sect.

All this helped account for the intense interest in the play in clerical and court circles, though the King apparently took no offence at what might have been interpreted as criticism of his intolerance. Worth repeating, too, is Madame de Sévigné's comment at the signal change in Racine's behaviour and thinking: "He now loves God as he used to love his mistresses."

For St Cyr, Racine was encouraged to compose a second play, *Athalie* (1691), by consensus a higher accomplishment than *Esther*. Indeed, some critics prefer it even to his youthful *Andromaque* and mature *Phèdre*. Voltaire, among others, considered *Athalie* the supreme French drama, though the play was not as highly esteemed in its own day as it was to be later, especially in the Romantic Age, when it was more in keeping with the general taste.

Racine, now fifty-two, had recently become "gentleman in ordinary" to the Sun King, whose effulgence was somewhat dimmed by age and domesticity. The post, however, brought the poet a much-enlarged income, adding 2,000 livres to his yearly stipend.

In *Athalie* the Old Testament was his source once more. The evil Queen is pitted against Joad (or Joash), the youthful heir to the throne who was raised by priests of the temple and is inspired with the true faith. Guilty of gory deeds, she has for six years led many of the Jews to participate in worship of the pagan deity Baal. When the Queen meets the young Joad, sole survivor of the royal family she has ruthlessly slain, she does not recognize him though she has dreamed that a rival to her power still exists; indeed she is attracted to the God-fearing youth.

But love is not a theme in this drama. A Levite rebellion, led by the High Priest, leads to the murder of Athaliah. Joad succeeds her as ruler, and the Chorus of Maidens lifts its voice in an ode to victory. The characters, surprisingly profound, are drawn with rare subtlety in sharp relief, with concise, simple strokes. The dialogue throughout is touched with "a bare lyric grandeur", in poetry that is often magnificent. The plot, though very simple, provides a vehicle for rhapsodic choric passages. The play is also filled with theatrical excitement.

At one point, for example, the High Priest warns his royal protégé to avoid thoughts of despotic rule and not to be deceived by sycophants, who will soon seek to beguile him: "Alas! They have misled the wisest of Kings." This remark, that might seem to have been directed at the absolutist Louis XIV, was daring and afterwards much cited in the eighteenth century; in context it is actually a plea for the elevation of priests over Kings. There was not much of the spirit of the rebel in Racine.

But he did finally contrive to anger the King and lose favour. In 1696 he bought the office of secretary to Louis XIV. Madame de Maintenon, wishing to perform good works, asked him to compile a list of sufferings inflicted on the French lower classes. The King discovered it, forced her to reveal who had drawn it up, and turned exceedingly wrathful. "Does he think, because he is a perfect master of verse, that he knows everything? And because he is a great poet does he want also to be a minister?" Banished from court, the playwright fell ill. Madame de Maintenon promised him that the King's anger would dissipate, as eventually it did. But though Racine returned on occasion and was allowed to approach His Majesty and the Queen, the warmth with which he had formerly been greeted was lessened; at least the poet thought it so.

Racine was tormented by a liver abscess. Not surprisingly, hearing his aunt's incessant, fanatic pleas to Heaven that for his salvation he should endure further humiliation did not relieve his pain. Surgery brought him ease for a short time, but he knew himself to be mortally ill and announced, "Death has sent in its bill." Boileau, also in bad health, came to visit him. In a touching scene, Racine said, "I rejoice to be allowed to die before you."

The poet, once a profligate, prepared his will, in which he begged for burial at Port-Royal:

> I know that I am unworthy of it, by the scandals of my past life and by the little use that I have made of the excellent education that I formerly received in that house, and the great examples of piety and penitence that I saw there . . . But the more I have offended God, the more I need the prayers of so holy a community.

His last day of life was 21 April 1699. He was fifty-nine. In recognition of the dramatist's contributions to the lustre of his reign, the Sun King granted a lifelong pension to the bereaved widow and children.

Subsequent generations in France have never ceased paying homage to Racine. He merits the top place in their literary hierarchy, as he combined genius as a poet with discerning psychological analysis and a superb mastery of form. What is more, his themes forever interest a people who have always dissected love and have been fascinated by its nuances and who sympathize readily with those seeking to live by the exercise of reason and self-discipline; that is, who *au fond* are temperamentally inclined to appreciate the innate beauty of order in every aspect of life.

But to drama lovers outside France, Racine's characters, like those of Corneille, are somewhat abstract. To a good many who do not speak French, and are therefore deaf to the beauty of his poetry, Racine's works often seem too static.

His other major contribution and influence, at home and abroad, has been as a theatrical technician. His works are the best examples of the *pièce bien faite*, the well-made play. The form that he perfected, in keeping with classic principles established by the ingenious Sophocles and summed up by Aristotle and Horace, has become the model for playwrights everywhere. Like Corneille, he links his scenes by having a character on stage at the beginning of each who is in view at the end of the one preceding.

The mood is consistent throughout. He eschews the slightest hint of comic relief and eliminates sub-plots and digressions. He shows how effective the three unities – time, place and theme – are in attaining compression. He is always concerned with a moment of crisis in the life of his principal protagonist, a hero or heroine possessing extraordinary qualities but beset by a fatal flaw – most likely hubris or insolent pride or an immoral trait.

The plays open *in medias res*, just before a crucial event. The exposition reveals information throughout the plays as their action unfolds; by withholding certain facts about the character's past, the author arouses the spectator's curiosity. The stories have numerous applications, so that spectators can readily identify with the plight of the hero or heroine.

Every line of dialogue is propulsive, hastening the action to a climax and resolution. The cunning arrangement of surprising but plausible – and logically yet subtly foreshadowed – reversals of fortune within a compact structure give a heightened sense of urgency. The casts are small; the atmosphere is claustrophobic as the tension forever mounts. The rapid pace leads the hero or heroine to make hurried misjudgements, the outcomes of which are very serious; the moral problems the troubled characters face are deep and lead to tragic conclusions.

The Baroque and neoclassical drama outran its inspiration in two generations or less, yet the format lingered on for almost two centuries. In lesser hands the compressed, direct and strictly limited design Racine used, alas, yielded overly artificial works in France, England and Germany. Serious plays of ensuing periods by writers lacking Racine's unique talent are declamatory, their language stilted and pretentious. Their plots are often confusing, packing too many incidents and emotions calling for fuller expansion into too small a framework of time and space.

But that did not happen when Racine wielded his artful pen. The firmer his control, the more rigid the decorous veneer of his play, the more uncomfortably aware the spectator is of the hurt and ominous pressure afflicting the characters. The writing of rhymed speeches in measured Alexandrines challenges a poet's ability to achieve full expressiveness – and Racine meets that challenge. His accomplishment is astonishing. If ultimately devices became a tired formula, cheapened by his successors turning out scripts for the commercial theatre, that unfortunate legacy cannot be imputed to him, nor can his chosen format be derogated. In the hands of a true craftsman, the structure Racine arrived at is the most effective a stage work can take.

— 3 —
MOLIÈRE

The Age of Baroque in France, particularly during the reign of Louis XIV, was a period of great comedy. The times and style of life offered a tempting field for satire. The elaborate and often hypocritical emphasis on decorum at court and at the higher levels of society, and the ridiculous gap between people's attempts to live a life of reason and their actual behaviour as self-indulgent, sensual human beings, presented the detached observer with all kinds of absurdities that could evoke laughter. It was easy to become cynical, to protect oneself with cruel wit, in the face of such a multiplicity of inconsistencies. Indeed, for a writer to stay compassionate or tolerant at the spectacle was difficult and unlikely. But one was to embody traits of objectivity and intellectual detachment and criticism, while seldom allowing himself to seem bitter. He thus became the ideal recorder of the manners and foibles of his epoch and indeed of humankind at all times.

Into what was to become the Sun King's artificial "grand world", but oddly placed at its periphery instead of at its centre, Jean-Baptiste Poquelin was born on 15 January 1622. He was the fourth of six children whose exhausted mother died after ten years of marriage. His father remarried then soon lost his second wife, so the task of raising his brood fell upon him. Fortunately, he had a steady and adequate income as an upholsterer and decorator. In 1631, when his namesake Jean-Baptiste was nine, the father bought from a brother the position of *valet tapissier de chambre du roi*, requiring his services only three months a year. He supervised the upholstery work at the palace and had the special honour of making the King's bed. For three months he lived in the King's residence. The father planned to pass this prestigious and lucrative post – one of eight like it in the vast royal household – on to his son; he even had King Louis XIII affirm his right to do so. A grandfather who enjoyed theatre-going upset the senior Poquelin's dream, however. He frequently took the child to performances at the Hôtel de Bourgogne, and this was the boy's undoing, since he was fascinated by what he saw.

The father, looking after his son's education, sent him to the Collège de Clermont, where sons of the nobility were students. It was the finest school in Paris, and he made friends who were to be very helpful. The college was a place where scepticism and even the search for rational proofs of faith – what looked like heresy – were nurtured. At the hands of the Jesuits, Jean-Baptiste had a thorough introduction to Latin and Greek and read the farces of Terence. Jesuit schools also staged plays, as tools for learning. Presumably, college dramatics interested the upholsterer's son, who was possessed of an unusually quick intelligence. Voltaire says that the youth had instruction from Pierre Gassendi, a friend of Pascal and Hobbes and an authority on Epicurus, a materialist, and Lucretius, an atheist. Gassendi was also renowned for his knowledge of science. The youth translated passages from Lucretius' *De rerum natura* and quoted them almost exactly in his most personal black comedy *The Misanthropist (Le Misanthrope)*.

From age fifteen on he also worked with his father at the palace to learn the upholsterer's trade. All that the bright-eyed lad saw there – the simpering courtiers, the flirtatious ladies, the wordly clergy, the intrigue, scandal, backbiting and pretension – he took in and remembered.

Most of the clergy in Paris deemed the theatres a threat to public morality. Magistrates were forbidden to attend performances. Priests could not conduct marriage ceremonies for actors, which meant that many were "living in sin", their unions all too brief. Too many plays dealt with illicit love affairs and other titillating subjects. The pretext given by Cardinal Richelieu for inviting actors to court and sponsoring plays was that their behaviour was "kept within bounds" under his scrutiny. He encouraged and supported the best companies while denying the less savoury ones his and Louis XIII's steady patronage.

To his father's growing disappointment, the youth showed no interest in becoming a royal bedmaker or decorator. Instead he studied law. His analytical mind suited him well for the profession, and after graduation it is believed that he practised for a short while.

From childhood, however, he had displayed a remarkable talent for mimicry. His family had often been embarrassed when he mocked the parish priest who came to visit at the Hôtel de Bourgogne. Now he could see the Italian comedians during their frequent visits. What probably led to his decision to quit law and enter the hazardous realm of theatre was an affair, beginning in his twentieth year, with the frivolous actress Madeleine Béjart, four years his elder. This good-humoured, warm-hearted young lady had been the mistress of the Comte de Modène for a half-decade and had borne him a son whom the count openly acknowledged.

Enamoured, Jean Poquelin left his father's home and went to live with Mlle Béjart, whose chief passion was the theatre. He obtained money by selling, for 650 livres, his hereditary right to succeed his father as royal upholsterer. Madeleine Béjart's young lover joined with her and her two brothers to comprise an acting troupe. They drew up a contract and named their company L'Illustre Théâtre. The date of this agreement, 30 June 1643, is now considered that of the founding of the present Comédie Française.

They leased a tennis court – a long rectangle, with a "shelf" at one end to serve as a stage – and offered a series of comedies and tragedies, without much success. Before long they were declared bankrupt. One of the chief creditors was a candle-maker. On three occasions in 1643 the young man – who now called himself Molière – was briefly imprisoned for debt. Each time his father rescued him, paying off the sums due, hoping that his son had learned a lesson and would renounce the theatre. This did not happen.

It was logical as well as customary for sons to assume a stage name and spare their families embarrassment, since the status of actors was so low. In turning from law towards the theatre, the young Poquelin was indeed assuming risks and losing social and legal standing. Actors were pariahs, an outcast class. Richelieu's tactic of introducing plays at court had somewhat helped to raise the profession in public esteem. By persuading Louis XIII to pension one company, who thereupon called themselves Le Troupe Royale, the Cardinal gave them more than a hint of regal sanction. Richelieu's successor, Mazarin, invited Italian comedians to France, a gesture that also lent the stage a bit more respectability.

Women now took feminine roles, except for character parts. One reason offered for this odd custom was that women refused to accept ugly or grotesque roles; they wished only to be beautiful in public. Less glamorous characters might be portrayed by a man who used a falsetto voice. A member of Molière's troupe, Beauval, was hired to do this, as had been Alizon earlier in Montdory's company.

As in Elizabethan England, the actors were expected to provide their own stage garb, usually in contemporary style, except where that would be too discordant, as in a fantasy, an allegory or a drama of ancient Greece or Rome. Those offerings would be adaptations, mixtures of the styles of the time and those of remote antiquity. Since many plays were given at court, costuming tended to be lavish, appealing to the public taste in this ostentatious epoch. For the most part, the players shopped for cast-off garments in markets selling second-hand clothes. But an enterprising merchant, suitably named M. Bourgeois, established the first known costume rental agency.

As with Shakespeare's company, the actors were shareholders who divided the take after each performance and were graded according to seniority and ability. The playwrights also shared, though they sometimes got a flat fee. Even the administrative staff – the treasurer, the stage manager, the usher, the ticket taker – were included. The company's life was arduous, and the actors worked unceasingly.

The scenery grew more and more elaborate. Candlelight still provided illumination. (The scene designer, who decorated not only the stage but also the playhouse, was entitled to collect and resell unconsumed taper-ends to enlarge his fee.) In the later works of Corneille and Molière stage machinery gradually gained in importance. It was modelled after that employed in the Italian theatre, and dazzling effects were obtained. This was particularly so when operas and ballets were put on, or music and dance were partially combined with the drama. Such effects appeared first at court and at Richelieu's private performances, then made their way into commercial theatres.

Acting styles were exceedingly broad at first. The Italian *commedia dell'arte* influenced the native French performers, who were awkward in comparison. Molière, an able comedian, successfully muted the comic style, subtly making his points and winning laughs. His attempts at tragic acting, however, were far less able. He had strong facial features, but his physical appearance handicapped him, and he had a speech defect, a sort of hiccup acceptable in farcical portrayals but not in the delivery of a poetic tirade. It was the chief reason Racine took his plays to a competing troupe. Another cause for his lack of success as a tragic actor may have been in his personality; he was intelligent and detached, balanced and "reasonable" – qualities that equipped him admirably to write and act in comedies.

Molière's efforts to subdue his cast's grandiloquent, emotional tragic style of acting largely failed, but some years after his death such performers as Baron did use the quieter approach that Molière, with his instinctive good taste, had sought. He was no more fortunate in composing tragedies than in acting in them. Eventually he recognized where his talents and intellectual bent lay and dedicated himself mostly to the smiling Muse.

Though the fledgling company L'Illustre Théâtre met only disaster in Paris, the small band of players refused to give up, and the 25-year-old Molière led them on a journey through the provinces. This tour – or detour – lasted twelve years, a time during which they overcame setbacks and hardships, slowly developing into reliable, resourceful professionals.

For competition they had the agile, tireless Italian comedians, whose journeys were also arduous and endless.

For a time Molière's troupe enjoyed the patronage of his former schoolmate the Prince de Conti, until that wealthy gentleman experienced a violent religious conversion, whereupon he severed his connection with the theatre in the belief that both the actors and their vehicles were sinful. He openly denounced Molière and his companions as foes of all good Christians, agents of the Devil who corrupted the young.

Another initial sponsor was the Duc d'Épernon, governor of Guienne. In Narbonne, Toulouse, Carcassonne, Nantes, Grenoble, Montpellier, Bordeaux, Dijon and especially Lyon, the company, headed by the ever more seasoned Molière, won praise and a delighted following.

By 1655 Molière had begun to write plays and to assume lead roles in them while directing his fellow players. His works were added to other tragic and farcical dramas in the repertoire. He launched his earliest success, *The Blunderer*, in Lyon, where love of the theatre was strong and the troupe was still favoured. In it appear characters borrowed from the *commedia dell'arte,* in particular the figure of the ingenious servant, in this instance called Mascarille, who schemes to further the amorous affair of his master Lélie, who is an incompetent in such matters and by his dim-wittedness is forever spoiling Mascarille's neatly laid plans. (In these earlier, imitative plays the actors still wore masks.) Molière had an undeniable charisma, and doubtless the success of this apprentice work was due to his deft staging and his skill in performing, not to good looks, which he did not possess. Though by no means unattractive, he was not conventionally handsome. His eyes were too widely set, his complexion was somewhat dark, his torso was short and his limbs were disproportionately long. But he had brilliantly mastered the tricks of his craft. He was charming and gestured well, and he spoke the prologues and epilogues most engagingly.

He was also steadily adding new players to his troupe. Many of these newcomers were very talented, including the astute Charles Lagrange, destined to be Molière's successor. Among them was also a Mlle Debrie, who eventually replaced Madeleine Béjart as Molière's beloved. Mlle Béjart had apparently long since wearied of him, though she remained the company's leading lady.

Another minor success, *The Love Tiff* (1656), enjoyed long popularity. Later playwrights, especially in England, were to pay it the flattery of imitation, among them John Dryden and Sir John Vanbrugh.

Emboldened by the esteem the troupe gained outside Paris, and encouraged by friends, Molière felt ready for a new assault on the capital.

An audition for the company before Louis XIV was arranged by the King's younger brother Philippe, Duc d'Orléans, and on 24 October 1656 L'Illustre Théâtre (or the "Troupe de Monsieur", as it came to be known) presented Corneille's *Nicomède* – but not very well. The fault was that Molière essayed the title role and was not deemed suited to it. Fortunately, a comedy – now unidentified – followed as an afterpiece. The King was immensely amused by it and ordered that the troupe should be granted permission to act at La Salle du Petit Bourbon, a theatre it shared with Scaramouche's Italian company. (Before his acting attempt at court, Molière had visited his father and had begged for and received his pardon for his unsavoury career as a player.)

Time and again the group put on tragedies and failed to capture the enthusiasm of Parisian audiences. Yet the actresses in the company wished to appear in heavy dramatic works that set off their physical and mimetic gifts. Molière's nature, like that of many comic geniuses, was basically melancholy, and he still aspired to the role of the tragic hero. After many humiliations and heartaches, his view of the world had become disenchanted. But, strive as he might, he could not persuade the public to take him as seriously as he deserved. Gradually he came to realize that comedy was his *métier*.

He proved this in *The Exquisite Ladies* (*Les Précieuses ridicules*) of 1659. He was already weary of the familiar characters and situations of the *commedia dell'arte*. Glancing around *l'haut monde*, as he had when he had been a younger visitor at court, he saw much – the ostentatious shallowness of the aristocracy, for instance – that was freshly yet also eternally risible. He declared, "No longer need I take Plautus or Terence for my masters, nor rob Menander. I have only to observe the world."

A cult of "exquisites" had established itself in Paris and especially at court. Headed by Madame Rambouillet, these ladies were insufferably affected in manner and speech, carrying their language to lengths that outmatched even that of the English author Lyly and his *Euphues*. Their excessive refinement, expressed in high-flown metaphors and fear of "inelegance", was a perfect target for satire. Molière wrote about two cousins, Cathos and Madelon, whose elderly parents command them to marry, if only because the family coffers are running low. The young ladies are loath to obey, as the game of flirtation whose pattern was set by the romantic ambience of the period appeals to them more. They wish to be courted with elaborate gallantry; their demands go to absurd extremes. Protests Cathos to her uncle, Gorgibus: "For myself . . . all I can say is that I think matrimony a mighty shocking thing. How can one endure the thought of lying by a man that's really naked?"

Two valets, Mascarille and Jodelet, deceive the young ladies by borrowing clothing from their masters and pretending to be a general and a marquis. They please the foolish *précieuses* by exaggerated wooing, following the prescribed ritual. They pay preposterous compliments, act out a meaningless but requisite lovers' quarrel, compose bad poetry and sing out of tune. Mascarille declares, "People of rank know everything without ever having learned anything." So grand and delicate is Mascarille, posing as a Marquis, that he will not even permit his feet to touch the ground and is carried into the salon where he intends to present himself to his hostesses. Madelon and Cathos are flustered at having a guest possessed of such hauteur and arrogance. Madelon calls for chairs. "Almanzor," she says to her servant, "convey me hither immediately the appliances of conversation." Then, in a famous phrase, typical of the language adopted by the cult, Cathos pleads with the "Marquis", "Dear sir, be not inexorable to that armchair which for the last quarter of an hour has stretched out its arms to you; satisfy the desire it has of embracing you." To oblige her, the Marquis seats himself.

At last the masters, the true suitors, arrive and unmask the low-born impostors. The young ladies, much embarrassed, are ready to capitulate.

This work had an immense success. The King ordered two more performances at court, personally attended both and gratefully awarded the troupe a bounty of 3,000 livres. After the première the demand for tickets at the public theatre was so great that Molière promptly doubled the price. During the first year the play enjoyed forty-four performances, enriching the author with royalties of 1,000 francs.

The effete cult was laughed out of existence at court by this one script. Madame de Rambouillet was clever enough to ward off any personal humiliation, however, by inviting Molière to stage the play under her aegis at a private performance for her friends. Graciously and discreetly, Molière responded to her gesture by composing a preface stating that he was not criticizing her circle but her bourgeois and provincial imitators.

None the less, the play earned him numerous enemies. Courtiers did not like being ridiculed. With *The Exquisite Ladies*, however, the polished French comedy of manners was established and began its long, bright career.

Prudently, Molière shifted his satire in another direction. *The Imaginary Cuckold* (1660) is a less effective piece. But Louis XIV was amused by it and sat through it nine times. The hero of this farce, convinced of his wife's infidelity, lacks the courage to attack her supposed lover. When he finally takes action, it is only verbally. "In the heat of my passion," he resolves, "I'm going to tell everyone everywhere that he is living with my wife." Molière himself portrayed Sganarelle, creating a new role in French theatre, the middle-class citizen who has a fund of native shrewdness yet is led into folly by self-delusions. The character was a forerunner of many who populate his plays, each the victim of a harmless yet obsessive quirk. These prosperous eccentrics testify to the author's realistic observation not only of the aristocracy but of the French bourgeoisie that was rising to unprecedented affluence and was anxious to copy the pretensions and graces of their social betters.

About this time, Molière lost his theatre at the Louvre, which was being renovated. Louis

XIV, as a new mark of favour, assigned him the private stage designed by Richelieu in the Palais-Royal. This became the troupe's permanent home for the rest of Molière's life. He had become a virtual appendage of the court, while his rivalry with the companies at the Théâtre Marais and especially at the Hôtel de Bourgogne continued. In *The Exquisite Ladies* he spoke slightingly of their acting styles, deeming them inept, ignorant and too intent on winning applause at the expense of their roles. They, in turn, declared that he was incapable of performing anything but low farces. To prove otherwise, Molière began the season in his new theatre with his tragedy, *Don Garcie de Navarre* (1661). The King went to see it three times, but even that kindness did not bring it success.

A new comedy, *The School for Husbands* (*L'École des maris*), of 1661, effected his recovery. His literary sources are Terence's *Adelphi* and Lope de Vega's *Discreta enamorada*, but some of it is autobiographical as well. Molière, nearing forty, was about to marry a girl of eighteen.

The play is concerned with how innocent girls should be prepared to enter marriage. Two brothers, Ariste – sixty – and Sganarelle – somewhat his junior – have as their wards a pair of attractive young ladies, Léonore and Isabelle. As in Terence's play, the elderly brothers have differing philosophies about how best to raise the young. Sganarelle believes in stern discipline, Ariste in a more lenient tutelage. He proposes that a young girl should have some freedom to indulge herself in youthful follies and pleasures.

The consequence is that at the end Isabelle outmanoeuvres Sganarelle and elopes with someone near her age, while Léonore marries her kindly if "mature" guardian. This apparently was Molière's hope, that if he was not too demanding he could please and hold a wife less than half his age.

The guardian brothers disagree in other respects. Ariste is a conformist, willing to adopt the conventions of society. He desires not to stand out, not to be singular, but always to be inconspicuous in dress and speech. Sganarelle is not only an individual but also an eccentric misanthrope, holding his own values and his often strange habits. He looks upon contemporary youth as inclined to insolence and libertinism and bewails the loss of a fixed morality. There is no reason to believe that the mature, judicious Molière wholly disagreed with the puritanical Sganarelle.

Suiting action to words, Molière, after considerable inner debate, startled his circle in February 1662 by his marriage to Armande Béjart, variously described as the younger sister or illegitimate daughter of Madeleine, his former mistress and long-time partner in the troupe. The consequences of the ill-fated match were not immediately apparent, perhaps because the ecstatic first days of the marriage did not indicate how unlucky it was soon to be.

Since the male parent of Armande was unknown, Molière's enemies promptly suggested that she was his daughter – he was old enough to be her father, and he had lived with Madeleine just two decades earlier. One of Molière's principal foes, the actor Montfleury, who headed the company at the Hôtel de Bourgogne, wrote to the King accusing Molière of incest. Louis XIV indicated his disbelief of the charge by standing as godfather to the new couple's first-born child.

But the scandal and mystery has never dissipated and is still hotly debated by Molière's biographers. Possibly he himself did not know the truth, for Madeleine had been quite promiscuous. The most reasonable assumption is that Molière, a decent man, did not regard Armande as his daughter.

Armande, who succeeded Mlle Debrie, had been constantly under his gaze from her childhood on. He had watched her flower into youth and womanhood. Interestingly, she had performed as one of the heroines in *The School for Husbands*. He was enchanted by her freshness and beauty. But she had been pampered by the other members of the troupe and was quite self-willed. With his help, too, she had grown into an adept actress, especially in light comedy. Unfortunately her temperament was as frivolous as Madeleine's had been: she was as flirtatious and perhaps as unfaithful – at least her husband, deeply enamoured, was convinced she was. She was also self-centred and had a streak of ruthlessness.

Molière's obsessive jealousy has become the subject of classic studies by psychologists. Mature and sharply intelligent, possessed of a detached and tolerant view of the world, he was still unable to control his disturbance over Armande's coquetry and real or imagined promiscuity. He suffered emotional torture over it, and the theme of infidelity entered his work and took on dominance there. His response to it was to invert it, to poke fun at cuckolds, indeed, to laugh publicly at himself, as if looking at himself and his plight ironically. He realized how unworthy she was but was still infatuated with her. What is more, his true feelings about her gave a darker hue to the humour of much of his remaining work. It reinforced the strain of melancholy in his nature. (Another cause of his despair was his incipient tuberculosis.)

The Bores (1661), a *comédie-ballet*, was commissioned by the financier Fouquet, who wanted to stage a pageant in the gardens of Vaux to entertain His Majesty. It presented various types of dull and irritating persons who habituated the court and angered those who recognized themselves or their friends. Louis XIV suggested to his dramatist other sorts who might be included – His Majesty did not mind teasing and offending the fawning, scheming opportunists, gamblers, untalented would-be poets and amateur musicians, overzealous duellists forever avenging imagined insults and boastful huntsmen who surrounded him. Molière introduced into this outdoor spectacle not only broad humour but also fairly sharp notes of social criticism, along with some lighter satiric overtones of unusual accomplishment. He would go on to perfect this unique form, the *comédie-ballet*.

The School for Wives (*L'Ecole des femmes*) of 1662 is longer than Molière's earlier works and is considered the first of his major comedies, perhaps the first great French script in that difficult genre. In it, his preoccupation with women and fidelity is raised again. The principal, Arnolphe de la Souche, is concerned with governing his young ward Agnès, whom he plans to marry. Like Sganarelle in *The School for Husbands*, the elderly Arnolphe is tyrannical. He has kept Agnès completely sheltered; indeed she is so innocent that she asks her guardian if it is true that babies are conceived through the ear – a question that was often repeated and begot merriment almost everywhere in France.

Inevitably, while Arnolphe is on a voyage, Agnès is besieged by a young man, the amorous Horace, a personable but not very bright character. When Arnolphe returns she tells him about this. Horace, not knowing who the old man is, also informs Arnolphe of the progress of his romance. Shocked and apprehensive, Arnolphe demands to know in detail from Agnès exactly how far the wooing has gone. The girl, in a stumbling narrative that torments her guardian by its halting and incomprehension, relates how Horace paid her compliments, described the delights of love and kissed her hands and arms. He also took away a ribbon that had been Arnolphe's gift.

> ARNOLPHE [*recovering himself*]: The ribbon's not the matter.
> But I want to know whether he did nothing but kiss your hands.
> AGNÈS: Why? Do people do other things?
> ARNOLPHE: No, no . . .

The guardian warns her that to permit such liberties is a mortal sin. But of course Agnès flees to the ardent Horace, who prevails. She is recovered by Arnolphe, however, who proposes to chastise her, but her charm – her melting voice and her figure – prevent him from carrying out his intention. He does read to her from a volume entitled *The Maxims of Marriage; or The Duties of a Wife: With Her Daily Exercises*. Inevitably, Agnès elopes with Horace, with the help of the young man's father, and the couple marry. Arnolphe can only console himself by reflecting that an unwed man does not have to worry about his wife's betraying him.

Commentators suggest that this is not merely Arnolphe but also Molière talking to himself and his tantalizing young spouse:

> That speech and that look disarm my fury, and produce a return of tenderness that effaces all her guilt. How strange it is to be in love! and that men should be subject to such weakness for these traitoresses! Everybody knows their imperfection . . . nothing is more frail, nothing more inconstant, nothing more false, and yet, for all that, one does everything in the world for the sake of these animals.

As in *The School for Husbands*, there is a character, Chrysalde, who advocates giving more freedom to the young. The conversations between good-natured, worldly Arnolphe and his friend afford the author an opportunity to discourse further on how to instruct a prospective wife. Arnolphe fails to heed Chrysalde's warnings that he is too strict. If anything, Molière at this point still seemed on the side of easy forbearance.

Though the King gave *The School for Wives* his blessing, and it was performed on thirty-one occasions during its initial two and a half months, it immediately caused the usual noisy controversy. Many of the more pious deemed it immoral, especially the scene in which Arnolphe and the naïve Agnès discuss the ardent Horace's physical advances to her. The dialogue in that passage was thought particularly degrading by the Prince de Conti. The powerful theologian and orator Jacques Bossuet also roundly condemned the piece. Molière's professional rivals were likewise quick to find fault, declaring the humour coarse, the characterizations inconsistent, the plot highly implausible. But the public went on liking it. Molière responded to all this outcry by writing first a one-act play, *The School for Wives Criticized* (*La Critique de l'école des femmes*), in 1663, portraying his foes as poltroons. To these ridiculous creatures he gave the words seriously uttered by his critics and then let them go on to preposterous exaggerations. To Dorante, a witty character, he entrusts his defence:

> I should like to ask whether the greatest of all rules is not to please, and whether a piece that attained that goal has not pursued the correct path. Do you think the whole public is misguided about this sort of thing and that each person can't judge his own pleasure?

For his still embittered rivals at the Hôtel de Bourgogne he produced *The Rehearsal at Versailles* (*L'Impromptu de Versailles*) in which he satirized them. Though a "play-within-a-play" was by now a familiar device, a rehearsal was a quite new idea (and was to serve Richard Sheridan much later to rich effect). Here it permits the author to continue his carping at shortcomings in the acting style of his competitors at the Hôtel de Bourgogne, while also offering his own credo: "The business of comedy is to present in a general way all the defects of humans and particularly the errors of our period."

King Louis XIV more or less settled the issue by showering approval on Molière, granting him a pension of 1,000 livres, having the company appear at court even more frequently and inviting him to dinner.

Molière now became an organizer of *fêtes* for the King and oversaw entertainment at St Germain and Versailles. This meant that his time was largely diverted to the staging of ostentatious spectacles in the royal gardens, but the assignment was lucrative.

More *comédies-ballet* followed, such as *The Forced Marriage* (1664) and *The Princess of Élide* (also 1664). Both are slight. In the first, Sganarelle wishes to wed but, aware of his betrothed's flirtatious nature, fears to assume the yoke. Significantly, in the *Impromptu* Molière inserted this exchange:

> – Hold your piece, wife; you are an ass.
> – Thank you, good husband. See how it is: matrimony alters people strangely; you would not have said this a year and a half ago.

Soon after, in the same year, Molière arranged a lavish festival lasting a week – it was called "Pleasures of an Enchanted Isle" and was replete with music, banquets and dancing, all lit by wind-fanned torches and 4,000 candles in swaying chandeliers. For this his fee was 6,000 livres. Strangely, the year was also marked by the inauspicious and inappropriate première of one of his bitterest works, *Tartuffe, or The Impostor* (1664).

This play had a long history before the public saw it. The King, taken aback by it, forbade its further presentation. It was an attack on the pious hypocrisy with which the court and French society of the period were infected. Louis XIV had good reason to applaud it, for his personal life, that is, his affair with Madame la Vallière, had brought open censure upon him from the devout. But he did not want to permit Molière recklessly to affront the Church, many of whose members immediately cried for the play's suppression.

Molière was allowed, however, to read the script a few weeks later at Fontainebleau to a chosen audience, including a papal legate. Another private reading occurred at the home of the Duc d'Orléans, with other members of the royal family – the Queen, the King's mother and the King – in attendance. Expressions of outrage grew louder. Pierre Roullé, vicar of St Barthélemy, issued a statement of praise for Louis XIV for having banned the play and demanded that Molière be burned at the stake, for being "a man, or rather a demon in flesh and habited as a man, the most notably impious creature who ever lived". The King replied that Roullé was over-stressing matters but prudently delayed permission for public performance of the much-disputed work. To compensate Molière for his loss, Louis XIV generously increased his annual pension to 6,000 livres; he also became official patron of the acting company, now to be known as the Troupe du Roi.

Over the next two years Molière revised the script; it is not known how much he changed it – no copy of the original version remains. He read the final revision to Louis XIV and asked for the right to present it openly, arguing that the play did not attack true religion but only those who merely pretended to practise it. The Queen urged her husband to consent, and Louis finally did.

The public offering took place while the King was away in Flanders in a military campaign. The next morning, the president of the parliament of Paris, a zealot, ordered that the theatre be shut; every poster announcing the play was torn down. A week later the Archbishop of Paris joined in the assault, threatening to excommunicate any who saw or read the comedy. Molière, infuriated, declared that he would withdraw altogether from the theatre. The King returned and told his favourite stage writer to bide his time.

A few months later the interdict was lifted. The play began a solid month's run, to crowds so large that spectators who had been able to obtain tickets entered hastily to escape suffocation.

Tartuffe still holds the stage, not only in France but all over the world. The Comédie Française, the descendant from the company founded by Molière, has by now produced *Tartuffe* about 3,000 times. Highly successful revivals in London and New York occur at short intervals.

The plot is extremely simple, as in all of Molière's plays. It was inspired, perhaps, by the author's personal acquaintance with the Abbé Charpy de Sainte-Croix, a member of the

Compagnie du Saint-Sacrament or Company of the Blessed Sacrament, and composer of a treatise on the mystical life, who was convicted of forgery, embezzlement and an immoral affair with the wife of a man in whose household he had been invited to stay. The Company of the Blessed Sacrament, to which the hostile president of the parliament of Paris belonged, was a secret society pledged to defend the faith. It sometimes put members in private dwellings to ensure that religious precepts were upheld there. In the play, Tartuffe is such an observer and, like many encountered in actual life, a dogmatist and a hypocrite. He has come to live with the family of the rich, fatuous Orgon, essayed on stage by Molière himself. The credulous Orgon has a young, second wife, Elmire, a pretty daughter, Marione, and a son, Damis. Another member of the household is the clever, voluble maidservant Dorine.

All these are soon unwillingly involved in Tartuffe's unscrupulous intrigues. Posing as saintly, he makes love to the wife while he pursues the daughter (whose love affair with Valère he tries to break up in order to marry her himself), lusts after the maid, poisons the father's mind against the son, extracts money from his host and sets himself up as a dictatorial ruler. All the while, he preaches morality. Complains Dorine:

> The other day, the big ox tore up right in front of us a handkerchief he found pressed into *The Lives of the Saints*. He said we'd committed the unpardonable crime of mixing the Devil's finery with holiness.

But the wealthy father, Orgon, dotes on Tartuffe.

> Tartuffe has bewitched him; he's become a complete fool. He calls Tartuffe "brother" and loves him a hundred times more than his brother, son, daughter or wife. Tartuffe's the only confidant of all his secrets and the advisor of all his actions. He embraces Tartuffe and pets him. He couldn't show any more fondness for a sweetheart. At dinner Tartuffe has to be seated at the top of the table. He eats more than six others, and the master makes us give him the best of everything. When he belches, the master says, "God bless you." He worships him. Tartuffe's his everything, his hero. [Translation by S.E. Mahir and Robert Hogan]

When charges are made against Tartuffe, Orgon refuses to believe them. Even Orgon's brother-in-law, Cléante, cannot persuade him that the intruder is an utter fraud. What is more, Tartuffe has a shrewd defence against all accusations: he admits to being human and imperfect, a sinner; he castigates himself and begs forgiveness of Heaven. Such a man is not easily trapped. "Why, just the other day he blamed himself for interrupting his prayers to kill a flea with too much anger."

As events reach a crisis – the son ordered from the house, the daughter about to be married to Tartuffe against her wishes – Elmire, an admirably self-confident and wordly lady, proposes that her husband conceal himself under a table and eavesdrop while she has an encounter with the importunate Tartuffe. Orgon finally consents to this. During the ensuing conversation Tartuffe assures her, "The only evil is in being found out . . . Sinning in secret isn't sinning at all." Orgon comes out from under the table, his eyes opened. He orders the psalm-singing humbug to leave at once.

But Tartuffe has obtained a deed of gift and certain compromising papers that put the gullible Orgon in his power. A troublesome new situation arises, in which Orgon verges on reduction to poverty, even eviction from his own house. Still, his mother, Madame Pernelle, refuses to credit Tartuffe with any wicked impulse. At this moment the hypocrite arrives with a police officer to arrest Orgon, who is about to escape Paris with the help of Valère. From this dilemma, Molière extricates the unlucky Orgon by a resort to a *deus ex machina*, nothing less than intervention by the King. The comedy ends with fulsome praise for the monarch, whose uncanny insight and pervasive sense of justice are paid almost embarrassing tribute by the arresting officer. Tartuffe is taken away to the prison that the unctuous rascal so well deserves.

Tartuffe is splendidly drawn. A thorough scoundrel, he is ever resourceful, turning every threat to his advantage. It is amazing how Molière keeps a slender story going for five acts. He does it by sharp dialogue, well-turned and interesting, frequent confrontations and new illustrations of the foibles and strength of his characters.

Goethe admired Molière's skill at exposition in the opening scenes.

The great weakness of the comedy is the extent of Orgon's credulity. James Rosenberg, in an introduction to his English translation, insists that the play is not about hypocrisy but gullibility. This makes Orgon, not Tartuffe, the focal figure. This has some logic, since Molière obviously wrote the role of Orgon for himself. His stupidity would gain him more laughter than if he were the sly, evil clergyman. In recent years, too, the play has been reinterpreted and given a quite different twist in which the relationship between the master of the house and his sly favourite is one of repressed eroticism: Orgon is a latent homosexual, infatuated with Tartuffe. This requires that Tartuffe be portrayed as younger and more attractive than in the traditional casting of the role. That does indeed make the play more plausible, even though it is contradicted by a few lines in which Tartuffe is derisively referred to as fat and red-faced – those lines, however, are spoken by Dorine, who thoroughly despises him. Many other passages in the dialogue would support a Freudian explanation of Orgon's subjection to the intruder. Explicit or even implied homosexuality or bisexuality could not have been articulated on stage in Molière's day, but the denizens of the court were worldly. Indeed, a younger brother of Louis XIV was a suspect; his being attracted by persons of his own gender was obvious and provoked mean gossip. Many would doubtless have been sympathetic if Tartuffe were portrayed by a handsome young actor; the bond with Orgon would have been highly believable. A mere stray gesture or two would have sufficed.

The moral of the play, however, is voiced by Cléante. When Orgon abuses Tartuffe and denounces all persons who profess to be devout, Cléante tells him: "Oh, come now! You're exaggerating again. Can't you ever steer down the middle of the road? You never keep within sensible limits. You're always hurtling from one extreme to another." Again, he counsels him, "Keep in the middle of the road . . . If you must lean to an extreme, better to be too lenient than too strict." It is mature, reasonable advice – Molière expressing his own balanced view.

In his preface he replies vigorously to the critics who for five years had kept this play from the stage. "Here is a comedy about which there has been a considerable noise." Hitherto he had satirized the nobility, pedants and doctors, yet all those classes of people were diverted by his picture of them; only the "hypocrites" sought to suppress his work. They did not, however, attack him openly, in their own behalf but proclaimed that he was offending God: "All the way through it [the play] is full of abominations. There is nothing in it that does not deserve to be burnt. Every syllable is impious . . . The least step to the right or left, all contain mysteries that they distort to my disadvantage."

He cites the King and Queen, and the great Princes and ministers of state, all of whom have expressed approbation of *Tartuffe*. He insists that his play has a worthy purpose, exposing and punishing evil, never presenting wickedness in a favourable light. It is not improper for comedy to deal with a religious subject; indeed, comedy in ancient times arose from mysteries and rituals in honour of deities. Even the theatre at the Hôtel de Bourgogne was in care of a religion brotherhood. Comedy is one way to correct the faults of the human race. It can be very effective at doing that. The fact is, he sums up, "We do not mind being wicked, but no one wants to be ridiculed."

He puts pious platitudes on the lips of a humbug. "But if I am to draw the character of a hypocrite accurately, how could I avoid it?" In conclusion, "One must either approve the comedy of *Tartuffe* or condemn all comedies in general." He lists the ancient philosophers who enjoyed going to comedies. If some of the offerings have had faults, that is true of nearly all human endeavours. But approval should be extended to "honest and instructive plays", and such a one is his *Tartuffe*. The preface is a strong brief for the soundness of his work and an interesting direct look at his mind.

The build-up for Tartuffe's entrance is remarkable. The play bears his name, but he does not appear until the third act. Incessant allusions to him, and sharp descriptions of him, pique the audience's curiosity. Once he appears he is characterized in a vivid, amusing exchange with Dorine. With one glimpse at her, he turns to his servant and exclaims,

> Tartuffe: Laurent, lock up my hair shirt and my scourge, and pray Heaven ever to enlighten you with grace. If anybody comes to see me, say that I am gone to the prisons to distribute my alms . . . [Turning to Dorine] What is it you want?
>
> Dorine: To tell you –
>
> Tartuffe [taking a handkerchief out of his pocket]: Ah! Heaven! Before you speak to me, take this handkerchief, pray.

DORINE: What's the matter?

TARTUFFE: Cover this bosom, of which I cannot bear the sight. Such objects hurt the soul, and are conducive to sinful thoughts.

DORINE: You must be awfully sensitive to temptation. I don't understand where all this heat comes from. I'm not that lustful. In fact, I could see you naked from head to toe and all that hide wouldn't excite me in the least.

Inserting the handkerchief, however, Tartuffe contrives to have his fingers explore the young lady's breasts.

For *Tartuffe*, with its moral earnestness, Molière is often likened to Jonson. But his anger is never as intense or slashing, and a larger share of his people are sympathetic.

His play did have the desired effect: the fanatical Company of the Blessed Sacrament was soon afterwards dissolved. It cannot be claimed, however, that hypocrisy for ever vanished from the world. (In the second half of our century, a revival of the play in Spain was obviously directed against another Catholic political movement, the Opus Dei. Its staging became a *cause célèbre*!)

During the five years that *Tartuffe* had to wait to reach the stage, Molière had been busy with other scripts. *Don Juan, or The Feast with the Stone Guest* (1665) was another challenge to the censorious. This is perhaps the most effective of all treatments of the Spanish legend of the cynical philanderer. No one can accuse Don Juan of religious hypocrisy: he is an out-and-out atheist and seducer, though on one occasion he does mask his lustful intent to complete a conquest. For Molière to write this audacious comedy while under siege for *Tartuffe* took courage. Especially shocking was Don Juan's paean to villainy and self-indulgence. Along with his atheism and satyriasis, the Don insists on his aristocratic obligations and privileges. He is arrogant and rude. The suspicion was strong that Molière's portrait of the prodigious lecher was an attack on the aristocracy.

He believes in neither Heaven nor Hell, only in the Devil. His catechism does not go beyond the fact that two and two are four. He scoffs when asked by his timorous servant to explain the wonders of Creation:

> I would like to ask you who made these trees, these rocks, this earth, and that sky up here; was all this built by itself? Look at yourself, for example; here you are; did you make yourself . . .? Whatever you say, there is something marvellous in humans, and that I have in my head something that thinks a hundred different things in a moment, and makes my body do what I wish.

But the servant, demonstrating his physical agility, stumbles while turning about. Gazing at the fallen believer, Don Juan says: "Your argument has a broken nose."

Most telling is a passage between the Don and a beggar who asserts his piety. "Surely," the sceptical Juan observes with irony, "a man who prays every day must be quite well off." The beggar confesses that very often he does not have even a crust of bread.

For Don Juan, sensual pleasure has a simple rule: "Constancy is only fit for fools." Again: "I have in this the ambition of conquerors, who go from victory to victory and cannot bring themselves to put limits to their longings." He claims to have possessed over 1,000 women; the exact figure, computed by his valet Sganarelle, is 1,003. (As a general practice, Molière gave his characters the same names as those of his actors, so that the same appellations appear in play after play but without consistency; it is the actor who is the same, not the character. Sganarelle may be an elderly master in one play, a youthful servant in another.)

Juan's chief fear is satiety:

> Once we have succeeded, there is nothing more to wish for; all the attraction of love is over, and we should fall asleep in the sameness of such a passion, unless some object came to awake our desires and present to us the attractive perspective of a new conquest.

During the course of his erotic adventures, Don Juan fights a duel with the angry father of a young lady whom he has seduced. Later, in a cemetery, he beholds a stone statue put up in honour of the dead commander, the girl's father, whom he mockingly bids to dine. The statue, accepting the invitation, arrives at the appointed hour. Juan, appalled at the threatening apparition, sinks to the floor, which opens beneath him. He sinks below it, enveloped in Hell's flames. None mourn him; only Sganarelle remarks his passing – by lamenting that now, with the Don gone, he will never collect his overdue wages.

The script is one from which Lorenzo da Ponte borrowed to piece together the libretto of Mozart's great opera *Don Giovanni.*

Molière's protest that the Don was presented as thoroughly evil and suffered dire punishment availed little. For, though the Don perishes in infernal flames, he is defiant and unrepentant. He is a Lucifer figure, sceptical of all conventional beliefs. It is a characteristic of Molière's heroes that they do not alter their nature or convictions. Tartuffe, though exposed, utters no promise of reformation, nor does the Don; nor, after them, shall Harpagon or Alceste.

The King protected Molière and the play; despite the outcries it was allowed to run, after some minor cuts. But when its comparatively brief career ended it was not revived in the author's lifetime. Following Molière's death, Thomas Corneille provided a verse adaptation, omitting the more scandalous dialogue. Molière's original version was lost; only in 1813 was a pirated Dutch edition found that is believed to be a close approximation to the original text; restored, it is acted today.

Lighter in tone, a *comédie-ballet, Love Is the Best Doctor* (1665), came next. Here Sganarelle is the father of Lucinde, who feigns illness because he will not let her marry Clitandre. The father summons a succession of four pompous medical practitioners, who dispute learnedly about their calling and prescriptions but cannot cure the girl's imaginary complaint. One orders an enema for her; this is countermanded by another, who fears it might be fatal. The girl appears to improve for a time without medication. "It is better to die according to the rules than to recover contrary to them," shouts a consultant, upset by a spontaneous recovery.

All this permits Molière to loose stinging shafts against the cant, charlatanry and self-interest of doctors, an age-old target of satirists. At last Clitandre, disguised as a physician, arrives. He persuades Sganarelle that what the daughter needs is to be humoured. Her problem is a troubled mind. "One must flatter the imagination of patients." He says the girl yearns to marry, and he – as her doctor – has generously promised to be her bridegroom. Sganarelle, thinking this to be only a pretended wedding, consents. The ceremony promptly occurs, after which Clitandre reveals his identity. The "false notary" who witnessed the ceremony proves to be a real one. Sganarelle, bowing to the inevitable, forgives his new son-in-law, and all ends cheerfully.

The little play took only five days to write. Molière claimed it had been suggested to him by no less a person than the King, who was doctoring and undergoing purges. But its darker origin may also have been the death of Molière's son, which he suspected was due to the misapplication of a remedy, antimony, and his own developing consumption, for which his physician offered nothing truly efficacious. Enjoying good relations with his own physician, a M. de Mauvillain, the detached, good-natured Molière once remarked, "We reason with one another; he prescribes remedies; I omit to take them, and I recover." That was a kindly gloss of the facts. His health was steadily deteriorating.

Molière's short interlude of seemingly pure gaiety with this *comédie-ballet* was followed by what is perhaps the best and darkest of his many works, *The Misanthrope* (1666), containing his best-drawn character, the ill-tempered Alceste.

As the title of the play implies, rich and high-born Alceste is at court, but all he sees there and in Parisian society displeases him; it is a panorama of corruption and pretence. Selfishness, sycophancy and intrigue prevail everywhere. No one ever speaks the truth if lies will serve better. Like Molière, the middle-aged Alceste is infatuated with a pretty but shallow and coquettish young widow, Célimène. (On stage, Molière played the role of Alceste, and Armande that of the fickle, heartless if witty Célimène, which in both instances was cruel typecasting.) Alceste's friend, Philinte, is more easy-going and tolerant; he seeks to reconcile the hotly indignant Alceste to the world.

The play is almost plotless; it consists of little more than incidents illustrating Alceste's candid contempt for the self-serving people he encounters, and his philosophical disputes with Philinte about how one should act and regard such persons. For instance, he meets Oronte, who fancies himself a poet and inflicts his verse on everyone by reading it aloud without being asked to do so. Oronte requests frank criticism; he gets it from Alceste, who tells him the poetry is quite worthless. Enraged by such candour, Oronte immediately vows revenge. Rebuked by Philinte for his tactlessness, Alceste explodes into a diatribe on the shortcomings of mankind.

Demanding integrity everywhere, he finds it nowhere. Consequently, he declares that "whoever is a friend of all mankind is no friend of mine".

Even the social amenities are laden with hypocrisy and should be abandoned. Trivialities, as well as important matters, send him into a rage. He is obsessive. Philinte exclaims:

> Philinte: What! Would you tell old Emilia that it ill becomes her to set up for a beauty at her age, and that the paint she uses disgusts everyone? . . . Or Dorilas that he's a bore, and that there's no one at court who isn't sick of hearing him boast of his courage, and the lustre of his house? [Translation by Henri Van Laun]

Alceste vows that he is prepared to do all that.

> Alceste: I would not spare anyone . . . It offends my eyes too much; and whether at court or in town, I behold nothing but what provokes my spleen. I become quite melancholy and deeply grieved to see men behave to each other as they do. Everywhere I find nothing but base flattery, injustice, self-interest, deceit, roguery. I cannot bear it any longer; I am furious; and my intention is to break with all mankind.
>
> Philinte: The world will not alter for all your meddling. And as plain speaking has such charms for you, I shall tell you frankly that this complaint of yours is as good as a play, wherever you go, and that all those invectives against the manners of the age make you a laughing stock to many people.
>
> Alceste: So much the better!

After the misanthrope has eloquently listed all the shortcomings of humanity, the pragmatic Philinte – doubtless speaking for Molière the detached, tolerant writer if not for Molière the agonized man – urges him to adopt a different attitude:

> Philinte: Great Heavens! Let us torment ourselves a little less about the vices of our age, and be a little more lenient to human nature. Let us not scrutinize it with utmost severity, but look with some indulgence at its failings. In society, we need virtue to be pliable. If we are too wise, we may be equally to blame. Good sense avoids all extremes, and requires us to be soberly rational. This unbending and virtuous stiffness . . . asks too great perfection for us mortals; we must yield to the times without being too stubborn; it is the height of folly to busy ourselves in correcting the world. I, as well as yourself, notice a hundred things every day which might be better managed, differently enacted; but whatever I may discover at any moment, people do not see me in a rage like you. I take men quietly just as they are . . .

But the intransigent Alceste does not heed this wordly advice. He is even more quickly sent into a rage by the light-hearted conduct of the flirtatious Célimène. She likes to be surrounded by admirers and to receive their compliments, and this Alceste cannot abide. In one of the most brilliantly written scenes in all theatre, he chides her. They have returned from a gathering, and he is finding fault with her behaviour. She protests.

CÉLIMÈNE: Am I to blame for having too many admirers? Can I prevent people from thinking me amiable? And am I to take a stick to drive them away, when they endeavour by tender means to visit me?

ALCESTE: No, Madame, there is no need for a stick, but only a heart less yielding and less melting at their love tales. I am aware that your good looks accompany you, go where you will; but your reception retains those whom your eyes attract.

He then demands to know what she sees in Clitandre, a rival, whose many failings he details. She explains that the gentleman will be helpful to her in a lawsuit she is pressing.

ALCESTE: Lose your lawsuit, Madame, with patience, and do not countenance a rival whom I detest.

CÉLIMÈNE: But you are getting jealous of the whole world.

ALCESTE: It is because the whole world is so kindly received by you.

CÉLIMÈNE: That is the very thing to calm your frightened mind, because my good-will is diffused over all: you would have more reason to be offended if you saw me entirely with one.

As their disagreement mounts, Alceste bewails the unwanted passion that binds him to her.

ALCESTE: Zounds! Why do I love you so? Ah! if ever I get heart-whole out of your hands, I shall bless Heaven for this rare good fortune. I make no secret of it; I do all that is possible to tear this unfortunate attachment from my heart; but hitherto my greatest efforts have been to no avail; and it is for my sins that I love you thus.

CÉLIMÈNE: It is true that your affection for me is unequalled. Your method, however, is entirely new, for you love people only to quarrel with them.

He has a choice, for a while, of another lady, Éliante, of surer virtue and more sober nature; but though he perceives that Éliante is more suited to him he is still irrationally bound to the whimsical Célimène, who lives only to play the callow social games and the game of hearts. Éliante accepts a proposal from Philinte instead.

Alceste also has a lawsuit pending but refuses to use any influence to win over the judges. He loses it. A mix-up in letters exposes Célimène's many instances of habitual duplicity. Eventually Alceste announces his decision to withdraw altogether from society, into solitude as a recluse. Philinte and Célimène join forces in hopes of dissuading him from taking such a step, but the spectator does not know whether they are successful.

In terms of dramatic action, scarcely anything has occurred. Alceste has barely altered. Yet the comedy has nary a dull moment, for two philosophical attitudes have been put forth with striking eloquence. *The Misanthrope* is universal and timeless. The problem it discusses – the need to wear a pleasant face in society, to adapt ourselves to the manners of the time – is as topical today as it ever was. Never before had a comedy had such depth, or more seriousness – indeed, it is often said that *The Misanthrope* verges on tragedy. What makes Alceste a comic figure is his excessive zeal for honesty, his self-congratulatory uprightness; any trait that is exaggerated is amusing when beheld and measured by a purely intellectual criterion, as well as by an onlooker with an ironic and practical turn of mind.

The reaction to *The Misanthrope* was mixed. The court circle, to whom it was addressed, did not much care for it. Today it is deemed not only Molière's best script but also the first true comedy of manners, not only because of its salon *mise-en-scène* but also because its humour arises from realistic characterizations. Alceste is not a caricature of the sort offered by Ben Jonson but is delineated if not with subtlety at least with psychological truth and other recognizable human qualities; for who has not known his like, the railer against society and its inconsistencies and mendacities? And who has not also met Célimène and the accommodating Philinte? What is more, the principal figures have a considerable degree of self-knowledge, which means that they are rounded, not flat.

With *The Misanthrope* begins a new comic genre, of a pattern not often followed by later writers, because few have been capable of emulating it. It requires plausible characters in credible situations, who are concerned with ethical problems and who can analyse them and discuss them fluently. Molière brought to comedy a new dignity. Only a Molière, a Wycherley, a Wilde, a Shaw, a Behrman is equal to the composition of such bubbly, light works with profoundly serious purposes.

It is interesting that Napoleon was to approve of Philinte's expediency, but the philosopher Jean-Jacques Rousseau deemed it detestable, compromising and time-serving and applauded the strictness and austerity of Alceste's code. But Rousseau did not see Alceste for what he is, an absolutist who wishes others to acknowledge his moral superiority. Besides, Alceste is a talker, not a doer, not a reformer. He enjoys denouncing others because it lifts his self-esteem. Whether he knows it or not, he often fulminates for the mere pleasure of it.

It is much to Molière's credit that he kept his balance in setting down *The Misanthrope*, satirizing Alceste as well as those whom he scorns. In Philinte's speeches, too, there is a measure of compassion for human frailty and folly. Molière was emotionally involved in what he wrote here, but he coolly kept his wits about him. *The Misanthrope* is Olympian as a result – a high point in the history of comedy.

As a curtain-raiser for this short dark comedy Molière wrote, also in 1666, a one-act farce, *The Doctor in Spite of Himself* (*Le Médecin malgré lui*). Sganarelle once more is the principal, now acting as the former servant of a physician. He has been earning his living as a woodcutter. He drinks too much and beats his wife. To get even, she passes him off as a doctor, and, cudgelled into accepting the role, against his will he begins to practise medicine.

His patient, a young girl, Géronte, trying to outwit her father, pretends to have lost her power of speech. The trick is inspired by her desire to marry against her father's wish. Sganarelle is pressed into furthering this scheme. When questioned by the parent as to the nature of the daughter's illness, Sganarelle cleverly launches on a farrago of irrelevant terms, mixing pig-Latin phrases, quotations from Aristotle and nonsense syllables. The father is duly impressed. Assuring himself that Géronte understands nothing, the impostor carries on his learned explanation in this fashion:

> SGANARELLE: Now, these vapours of which I have been speaking to you, in passing from the left side, where the liver is, to the right side, where the heart is, it happens that the lungs, which we call in Latin *armyan*, communicating with the brain, which we call in Greek *nasmus*, by means of the concave vein, which we call in Hebrew *cubile*, meets on its way the said vapours, which fill the ventricles of the omoplate; and as the said vapours have a certain malignancy which is caused – Be attentive; if you please . . . Which is caused by the acrimony of the humours engendered in the concavity of the diaphragm. It so happens that these vapours – *Ossabandus, nequeis, nequer potarium, quipsa milus*. This is precisely the cause that your daughter is dumb.

Nor is Sganarelle fazed when Géronte points out that he has mistakenly located the heart on the right side. "We've changed all that," he announces grandly. "Yes, formerly the heart was at the left, but today we practise medicine quite differently." Géronte, awed, offers an apology. "I wasn't aware of that, I beg you to forgive my ignorance," she replies.

Sganarelle works a miraculous "cure". The young lady recovers her voice, is united with her lover, and the impostor so enjoys his new profession that he decides to continue in it.

This merry if slight piece had a better reception than *The Misanthrope*, with which it shared a programme.

Molière, who was prolific as he always had to keep his company busy and the King and his circle entertained, sometimes fashioned new scripts at brief intervals. Some were *comédies-ballet* of only minor import. Inevitably he repeated his formula. *The Sicilian, or Love the Painter* followed *The Doctor in Spite of Himself* the next year.

In 1668 he adapted the story of Amphitryon earlier dramatized by the Roman farceur Plautus. Molière handled the legend with great adeptness, and the play has remained constantly in the repertory. Some read into the comedy about the amours of a divinity, Jupiter, and the mortal lady he loves, Alcmene, an allusion to a then-current affair between Louis XIV, the embodiment of divine right, and the compliant Madame de Montespan.

The theme of jealousy and a tormented and suspicious spouse arises once more in *George Dandin, or The Baffled Husband* (1668). A peasant who has grown wealthy marries the daughter of an impoverished noble family. He is a social climber. She arrantly deceives him. Both the betrayed husband and the conscienceless aristocrats are depicted satirically. But there is something self-punishing about the light way in which the author treats a subject that caused him so much anguish.

Shortly after the presentation of *The Misanthrope*, Molière left Armande to share quarters with the poet Jean Chapelain in another part of Paris. Chapelain, a founder of the Académie Française, was considered the leading poet of the day. Without his Armande, Molière was miserable. "If you knew what I suffer, you would pity me," Sainte-Beuve records his having told Chapelain.

> When I consider how impossible it is for me to conquer what I feel for her, I tell myself that she may have the same difficulty in conquering her inclination to be coquettish, and I find myself more disposed to pity her than to blame her . . . All things in the world are connected with her in my heart . . . When I see her, an emotion, transports that may be felt but not described, take from me all power of reflection; I have no longer any eyes for her defects; I can see only all that she has that is lovable. Is not that the last degree of madness?

After *George Dandin* came *The Miser* (*L'Avare*) of 1668. It, too, is derived from Plautus (*Aulularia*), who had taken the subject and character from Greek New Comedy. Molière's version is one of his best scripts; he enlarges upon the principal figure, giving him a family and a higher social status. Having rescued Harpagon's daughter Élise from the waves, Valère falls in love with her. He disguises himself as a servant in Harpagon's household to be near the charming young object of his affections, who returns his feeling. He hopes to win Harpagon's favour and attain a marriage with the daughter. Harpagon is wealthy but pathologically tight-fisted; his son Cléante lives with his widowed mother. The brother and sister are about to broach the subject of matrimony when their father takes them by surprise. He himself intends to marry the fair Mariane, and he is giving Élise's hand the very same day to a wealthy friend, the widower Anselme, who is willing to take her without a dowry. The girl argues to no avail against this plan. No matter what she says, her father responds almost as though hypnotized, "Without a portion." In other words, he strongly desires this marriage for his daughter because it will cost him nothing.

Cléante, Élise and Valère unite to circumvent these two proposed unwelcome matches. As part of his strategy, Cléante seeks to borrow a goodly sum and learns to his consternation that the secret lender, demanding interest at an extortionate rate of 25 per cent, is his avaricious father. This precipitates another quarrel between parent and son. In Harpagon's eyes, his son is wildly extravagant. He objects to the finery in which Cléante attires himself.

> HARPAGON: I should be glad to know . . . to what purpose serve all the ribbons, with which you are so finely larded from head to foot, and whether half a dozen hooks and eyes would not be enough to fasten your breeches' knees? What need is there to lay out money for perukes, when one may wear hair of one's own growth, that costs nothing? I'll hold a wager that what in peruke, and what in ribbons, there go at least twenty guineas, and twenty guineas bring in at least one pound thirteen shillings and eleven pence farthing per annum, at only eight percent interest. [Translation by H. Baker and J. Miller]

The old man starves his horses, lets them go unshod, permits only a single candle to burn on his table, waters the wine he serves his guests and never says, "I give you good morrow." Instead, his habitual greeting is "*Prête le bonjour*", equivalent to "I lend you good morrow." He orders his servants not to rub the furniture too hard lest it be worn out.

Frosina, arranging the match between Harpagon and Mariane, persuades him to take the girl without a dowry because, owing to her plain upbringing, she has a small, simple appetite, no liking for fine clothes and does not gamble. All this should result in a saving of 1,000 livres a year. Harpagon, though he would much rather get hard cash than profit from a negative expenditure, is won over upon hearing that the girl prefers bearded older men to feckless, clean-shaven young blades.

La Flèche, Cléante's servant, discovers and makes off with a hoard of gold that Harpagon has buried in his garden – much as in Plautus' *Pot of Gold*. The distraught curmudgeon calls the police and is asked, "Whom do you suspect?" "All the world; and I'd have you take into custody the whole city and suburbs!"

Misunderstandings ensue, ingeniously contrived. At last it turns out that Valère and Mariane are brother and sister, separated by the usual shipwreck, and both are the long-lost children of Anselme, the fiancé of Élise. Cléante offers to restore the lost money if Harpagon will permit his marriage to Mariane and Élise's to Valère. The old man grudgingly agrees, if there be no dowry and if Anselme defrays the cost of both ceremonies.

The taxing portrayal of Harpagon, who is in a constant state of agitation, marked as he is by his greed, was assumed by Molière himself. The play was not accorded a happy welcome; the first audience found the frenzied and stingy old man too unpleasant. Besides, the comedy is in prose, prejudicing its reception. But subsequently it became very popular, second only to *Tartuffe*, having been praised by Boileau. At the Comédie Française alone it has been performed over 2,000 times. A range of noted actors has essayed the role, including Guérin, Grandmesnil (whose own reputation for avarice contributed to the comic impact), Duparai, Coquelin, Baty, Dullin, Vilar, Sorano and Aumont.

Another of his numerous *comédies-ballet*, *Monsieur de Pourceaugnac* (1669), is an account of the misadventures of a provincial attorney in perilous Paris, where he falls afoul of intriguers who seek to exploit him. The piece is important chiefly because, by it, Molière considerably advanced the later-day "comic-opera" form to which his ventures in this genre logically led. *The Magnificent Lovers* (1670) is deemed to be of somewhat lesser calibre, but *The Bourgeois Gentleman* (*Le Bourgeois gentilhomme*; also 1670) is another of Molière's long-lasting triumphs.

It was a consequence of a visit to Versailles by a Turkish dignitary whose demeanour did not please Louis XIV. At the visit's end the King suggested that Molière and Lully, the composer, write a burlesque comment on the Turk's "haughty stolidity". However, Molière turned his little play, set to Lully's score, into a broader, more universal satire, concerned with newly rich middle-class Frenchmen who aped the aristocracy. His M. Jourdain, a modestly wealthy shopkeeper, falls in love with a disdainful marquise and is eager to improve himself in order to woo her. He seeks instruction from a music master, a dancing master, a fencing master and a tutor in philosophy.

They are to help him acquire polish but they spend a good deal of their time disputing among themselves which of the arts is superior to all others. Is it better to know how to carry a tune, to dance, to duel or to discuss matters metaphysical? (The figure of the music master is thought to be a caricature of none other than Jean-Baptiste Lully, who had his share of faults.)

When M. Jourdain wishes to compose a love letter, he is asked whether he desires it in verse or prose. He does not know the difference between them, and upon having it explained – "all that which is not prose is verse, and all that which is not verse is prose" – he is astounded. "To think that for over forty years I've been talking prose and didn't realize it!" At the curtain of this little farce, a group of pranksters in Turkish dress make the French "would-be gentleman" into a "*mamamouchi*", staging a lavish mock ceremony of investiture. The naïve M. Jourdain is never aware that anyone is taking advantage of him or making fun of him.

Some of the newly risen courtiers, who themselves were not long freed from the sordid ties of commerce, disliked the play, feeling that it struck a bit too close to the bone. But the King was delighted with these digs at *parvenus*.

In 1671 Molière and Lully worked together again, this time on a "tragedy-ballet". Much of the verse of this spectacular production was contributed by Pierre Corneille and Philippe Quinault, the latter an opera librettist and able dramatist. This was so sumptuously mounted that the stage of Molière's theatre had to be rebuilt at huge cost. It was an instance of a trend becoming ever more marked, of an emphasis on scenic investiture and the use of ingenious stage machinery as in Italy and of the ascendancy of dance and music – here, that of the gifted Lully – over the mere spoken word and limited gesture.

But Molière had not fully deserted his natural stage milieu: *The Rogueries of Scapin* (*Les Fourberies de Scapin*; also 1671) evokes the *commedia dell'arte*. The rascal Scapin, in this almost improvisatory farce, keeps everything in motion by his tricks. The script is the perfect vehicle for a virtuoso comic who wishes to display his energy and resourcefulness.

It should be kept in mind that Molière's company was sharing its theatre at the Palais-Royal with an Italian troupe and was on close and friendly terms with them. He studied their antics. He is said never to have missed a performance of their great pantomimist Scaramouche (Tiberio Fiorillo) and to have kept on learning from him. (One anecdote has it that the idea for *The Misanthrope* came from a conversation Molière had with another member of the Italian cast, who told him of a play of that same title put on in Naples some years before.)

Donald Lyons from the *Wall Street Journal* wrote this about a Broadway revival of the play:

> Molière's 1671 farce *Les Fourberies de Scapin* (*The Wiles of Scapin*) has always brought out the prude and the purist in critics. It's a formula comedy in which a maniacally inventive servant facilitates the bringing together of two pairs of young lovers despite the opposition of two grumpy rich old fathers. In it Molière grafted on to the plot of Terence's *Phormio* a good deal of rough-and-tumble action appropriate to the traditional *commedia dell'arte* character of Scapino, the runaway. The comedy was in prose, was frankly aimed at a popular audience, and had for its climactic scene the beating by a servant of a master hiding in a sack. None of this sat well with the oracle of French classicism, Boileau, who in 1674 knocked Molière for contaminating Terence with clowns and huffed: "I no longer recognize the author of *The Misanthrope* in that ridiculous sack Scapin gets wrapped up in." Boileau was wrong about Molière's brilliant mixing of comic genres: he should have saved his fire for a current adaptation, called simply *Scapin*, at the Laura Pels Theatre, an adaptation co-written (with Mark O'Donnell) and directed by and starring Bill Irwin. This is less *Scapin* than *Fun with Scapin*. The formulas of the plot are routinely mocked: signs reading "Exposition" and "Unbelievable Coincidence" are periodically deployed; charades are used to explain the narrative; characters' names are forgotten by their families (a girl called Hyacinth is referred to as Hydrangea or Heather). In addition to this perhaps forgivable cheek about the plot, the adapters kept emphasizing that we are at a play in 1997.
>
> Although Douglas Stein's set adopts the classical Roman *mise en scène* of two facing houses with upper windows, we are not for a second encouraged to imagine we are in Naples in 1671; references to 1997 abound. Characters comment on the Laura Pels Theatre, the Roundabout Company (the production's umbrella group), the niceness of the audience, the vanity of the star, etc.
>
> In Molière, Scapin has a famous and funny *tirade* against lawyers and law courts. Mr Irwin's version is full of references to dream teams and DNA experts – which both miss the point and are quite unfunny. Molière's mildly xenophobic mentions of Turks are here directed

> against French intellectuals; it's forgotten, I guess, that Molière was, among other things, a French intellectual.
>
> Still, it's hard to stay mad at Bill Irwin. The rubber-bodied, spaghetti-limbed performer is a nimble and acrobatic farceur, a nonstop mugger and, to all appearances, a nice guy. He's also a generous director who lets others shine. Christopher Evan Welch as a fellow servant is a standout. Marina Chapa brings a hyperkinetic zaniness to the second-banana ingénue. Mary Bond Davis brandishes a don't-sass-me ferocity as yet another servant. The cast as a whole is cheerfully multiracial, and Scapin provocatively wonders if "the community is ready" for the finale's mixed marriages.
>
> It's a likable, frisky puppy of a show, but something's missing. If you take away plot and character except as occasions for self-referential jokes, the humor has nothing to play against. It's not funny to watch one actor – as opposed to one character – beat another. Farce unstiffened by narrative is like a diet of chocolate; one begins to long for starch. This *Scapin* makes one appreciate how right the creators of *A Funny Thing Happened on the Way to the Forum* were: If you want to fiddle with old comedies, do it with music.

Yet another slight work by Molière is *The Countess d'Escarbagna* (1671), followed by one of his most deft comedies, *The Learned Ladies* (*Les Femmes savantes*; 1672). He was by now reconciled to and living again with his wayward Armande, whose own health had suffered almost as seriously as his and who was glad to take shelter with him. He was immensely pleased, none the less, to have her back.

All about him, the cult of the precious was once more prevalent: noble ladies were conspicuously dabbling in literature and science, gathering in pretentious salons, displaying their pedantry. They debated philosophy, linguistics and the classics. It seems he was not enthusiastic about education for women, or perhaps, a born satirist, he disapproved of its being carried to ridiculous lengths. *The Learned Ladies* presents Philaminte, the middle-aged wife of materialistic, respectable Chrysale, a worthy but henpecked bourgeois. The couple have two daughters. Armande emulates her mother; a prig, she aspires to be thought erudite. Henriette is more down-to-earth; her prime wish is to find a husband. She is besought by Clitandre, a straightforward young man who had formerly loved Armande but who has transferred his suit to her sister, after having been put off by Armande's affectations. Philaminte has a sister-in-law, Bélise, who shares her interest in matters intellectual while also fancying that hosts of men desire her, though she spurns them.

The conduct of these ladies is, of course, idiotic. Complains the badgered Chrysale (who was enacted by Molière): "Why do we need all these books around? All I want is one good Plutarch to press my neckbands in." Philaminte will not permit the honest Clitandre to marry one of her daughters; she prefers Trissotin, a fortune hunter with a glib tongue who pretends his only concerns are scholarly. He competes in writing poetry with Vaudius, a rival, a suitor. Armande professes to be shocked at the thought of marriage, because it involves a physical relationship. She advocates not the meeting of bodies but the matching of minds. Says Armande to Henriette:

> Armande: How small of you to hole yourself up at home and to see nothing beyond an adoring husband and little brats of children! It's pastime for the vulgar . . . Rather than be a slave to a man, my dear sister, marry Philosophy, who controls the animal side of our nature.

She urges her sister to emulate their cerebral mother. Henriette's rejoinder is pointed.

> Henriette: If my mother had only a noble side to her nature, you would hardly be today what you pride yourself on being. It is lucky for you that she didn't give all her attention to philosophy. Please now, Armande, grant me a few of the "low consequences" of marriage to which you owe your very life, and don't suppress some little scholar who wants to be born.

Yet secretly, though loath to admit it to herself, Armande is jealous of Henriette and anxious to regain Clitandre. Ariste, Chrysale's brother, finally solves the compounding problems of this family, declaring that they are bankrupt. Trissotin at once renounces his suit of Henriette, but Clitandre offers financial help.

A high point of the comedy occurs when the fanatical Philaminte dismisses a maid, Martine, for the improper use of a word. Henriette nobly refuses Clitandre's offer because his fortune is small and she has no dowry. Ariste explains that his news of bankruptcy is false, a mere device to rid the house of poseurs and parasites. At the end, Chrysale asserts himself and commands that Henriette's wedding contract be drawn up at once.

The comedy is best summed up in the line "Learning can make great fools." The characters are sharply delineated; the dialogue often sparkles. The tone is one of dry wit. The whole has verve and lean grace. It is well known that the portrayal of Trissotin, the fraudulent intellectual, was aimed by Molière against his voluble opponent the Abbé Cotin and the sketch of Vaudius against another foe, a poet and philologist.

Once more, Madame Rambouillet and her bluestocking coterie were outraged by this new attack. The Abbé Cotin could not withstand the ridicule to which he was now subjected, the laughter that suddenly surrounded him throughout Paris, and so he gave up the pulpit from which he had been inveighing against the marvellous playwright.

Tuberculosis was taking its toll, however. Though he was barely fifty, Molière's features were wasted. His large nose and thick lips stood out prominently. His brow was prematurely wrinkled, his eyes habitually sad. His life had been hard; he had worked indefatigably and had endured the torments of an unhappy match, pricked by barbs of well-founded jealousy. Of his three children, he had already suffered the loss of two, and his reunion with Armande was followed by the birth of another child who died a month later.

Constantly under attack by critics and competitors, he was forced to dance attendance and please a fickle King. His adult existence was a long round of travel, unceasing rehearsals, composition, business pressures and delicate and difficult personal relationships with his cast of temperamental artists. Small wonder that he was exhausted. He abandoned the strict regimen and diet prescribed by his doctors in order to resume the kind of social life demanded by his young wife.

With characteristic irony, and perhaps in a spirit of self-mockery and neurotic self-punishment, his final play was about a hypochondriac, *The Imaginary Invalid* (*Le Malade imaginaire*; 1673). He took the leading role of Argan, who fancies he suffers from any number of ills. Though frugal otherwise with money, he enjoys being swindled by quack doctors. His imaginary disorders do not interfere with his appetite, which is enormous.

He will not heed his brother, Beraldé, who advises him to trust to Nature and avoid physicians and drugs. "Almost all men die of their medicines, not their diseases." He revels in the attention paid to him as an invalid, but, the miserly side of his nature taking over, he plans to marry his daughter to a doctor, so that with a professional man in his family free medical service will be available to him. Everyone takes advantage of Argan's obsession: even his brassy maidservant, Toinette, teases him, posing as a diagnostician and prescription dispenser. His second wife flatters him, though actually she holds him in the lowest esteem. At last, he stages a dramatic death scene; slumped in his chair, he hears his wife expose her true feelings, cursing him. He returns to life, frightening the lady nearly out of her wits. He repeats the wicked trick to test his daughter's affection for him. She responds with genuine grief, deeply gratifying to him. His brother persuades him that he himself should become a physician, that it would be hard to know less than the members of the profession. He passes a fake examination, hilariously conducted in pig Latin, and earns a medical licence. He can now treat others as he himself has been treated, "burying his mistakes" as do the purported savants. The prospect makes him happy.

Wearing a robe and nightcap, Argan is constantly a figure of fun. He is play-acting all the time, exaggerating every twinge and ache, sometimes deceiving himself – though at moments he forgets his ailments, as when he is popping food into his mouth or walking without the cane he is fond of leaning on or thrashing about with.

The role was one that Molière filled to perfection. What lent his portrayal an extra authenticity was that he was gravely ill: it was foolhardy for him to undertake the part. So intense was his fatigue that Armande and other members of the cast urged him to cancel the fourth showing of the farce so he could rest. He was adamant about continuing, worrying lest his absence might cause the theatre workmen, who were paid after each performance, to miss a single day's wages. While he was still able to act, he felt compelled to do it for their sake, as well as for the sake of his long-established company.

That night he was again Argan, twice feigning death to evoke guffaws, then took the oath that confirmed him as a doctor – on the word "Juro" ("I swear"), according to legend, he began to cough convulsively. He concealed his seizure by pretending to be overcome by a fit of laughter and finished the scene. Backstage, he staggered and sank into an armchair, a prop that is still in the possession of the Comédie Française. He was assisted home by Armande and a young player, Michel Baron.

He recognized the seriousness of his attack and requested that a priest be summoned, but none answered the call. His coughing became more severe; a blood vessel in his throat was sundered, and the blood flowed out and choked him. He expired, gasping, attended by a sister of mercy. The date was 17 February 1673. Two parish priests refused him extreme unction, nor would they permit him interment in consecrated ground. Harlay de Champvallon, Archbishop of Paris, backed this decision, since the actor had neither made his final penitence nor been given absolution. For four days he lay unburied, denied a grave in the nearby parish cemetery.

Armande, in a belated show of loyalty, went to Louis XIV and pleaded for royal intervention, reminding the King that Molière's works had been given royal sanction. The all-powerful monarch negotiated a quiet compromise with the Archbishop; Molière's body was taken to an obscure corner of the Cemetery of St Joseph in the rue Montmartre at the twilight hour and lowered into the earth without Christian rites and only the barest of ceremonies. The site is unmarked and lost.

When his death became known, his enemies spoke derisively of Armande as "her father's orphan and her husband's widow", reawakening the ugly rumour spread earlier about the couple's true relationship. In spite of her promiscuity, however, and the disparity of their ages, it was believed that she was genuinely fond of him.

This sorry end marked the amazing career of France's most famous and influential dramatist. His accomplishment was vast, though comparisons of him to Shakespeare – which are too often made – are certainly far-fetched, as he lacked the great scope and depth of the English genius. Yet, more than any other stage writer, Molière fashioned the "comedy of manners", putting in it living people rather than stock caricatures and stereotypes, and he at times also shaped highly credible plots.

Because of his works, comedy took on new dimensions. (He also helped to advance the masque-like *comédie-ballet*, the prototype of latter-day comic opera or musical comedy.) If he did not entirely abandon the thinly outlined figures of the *commedia dell'arte*, he frequently went beyond that kind of exuberant farce; with no loss of vitality; the genre he invented had now a new depth and seriousness. His comedy offered a critical comment on society and human nature. This had been true in farce before, with writers such as Aristophanes, Machiavelli and Jonson, but Molière's style of presentation is lighter and often more identifiable and acceptable because it is so good-natured.

The disparity between the human and social ideal and the grotesque actuality is what sparks his deft satire. His characters fail to live up to the image of themselves they seek to project; they fail as parents, intellectuals, scholars, gallants, literary figures, philosophers, even as misers and humbugs. He is the most balanced of all comic authors. He preaches against every kind of excess. His characters are undone because they are obsessive. Many do lack self-knowledge. What is more, the follies he portrays and chucklingly deplores are universal ones; and, for the most part, he is as relevant today as he ever was.

Those who do not speak French are deprived of a true appreciation of his felicitous dialogue, variously described as "supple", "lean", "graceful" and "full of verve". He is not a great poet *per se*, nor much noted for his verbal wit; he has contributed only a handful of epigrams. But his lines have a lilt and his rhymes are effortless and are said to have a glint. He was an actor, first of all, and most of his humour lies in the skill with which he conceived amusing situations to be realized in action, some of them, of course, devices borrowed from his own long experience and his sharp and humble observation of Italian farce.

His roles offer superb opportunities for amusing pantomime; this is as true of a dark comedy like *The Misanthrope*, where Acaste boasts and displays the whiteness of his exquisite teeth and the elegance of his dress, as it is of *The Rogueries of Scapin*, where the anti-hero engages in tireless physical capers. If, as often happens in English and American productions, characters are not played richly and fully, each exploited for all its mimetic possibilities, then the plays, with their simple, often borrowed plots, can seem disappointingly thin.

As a craftsman, too, he was excellent: his scripts are lucid and well put together, and their development is neat and logical. His purposes were serious, as fundamentally was his temperament; he aspired to write and to act in tragedy. In another age, with a different and more considerate and receptive public, he might have sought less to inspire laughter.

He observed the classical unities very closely, yet he broke too many of the rules to be accepted by the Académie, which honoured him only a century later. Under less financial pressure, he might also have written more soberly, but, as it was, he had always to entertain the King and the frivolous court. Among his closest friends, besides the Grand Monarch (who did not fully appreciate his hireling's profounder gifts) were Boileau, La Fontaine and, for a time, Racine, three of the outstanding literary masters of Louis XIV's glorious epoch. They deemed him a worthy companion, as indeed he was, his reputation today having an even brighter lustre than theirs.

He was a sceptic and rationalist, like his own ill-fated Don Juan; as such he was a spokesman of his divided age, when religion – which he foreswore – and the new Enlightenment – at which he looked a bit tongue in cheek – were at odds. He despised and boldly baited, though with a veneer of deceptive gentleness, hypocrisy, bigotry, snobbery and sham of every sort. He was rigorously honest; and his compassion and objectivity led him to be remarkably tolerant, which betokened his emancipated spirit. It is all summed up in the quiet smile that is most frequently conjured by reading or seeing his plays, just such a smile as one imagines him wearing as he gazed at the fallible world about him. Sainte-Beuve, that eminent critic, wrote: "To love Molière – and I mean by that to love him sincerely and with all your heart – is really to have a protection within yourself against many faults, caprices and vices of the mind."

In 1680, several years after Molière's death, Louis XIV ordered the company, led by Armande and Lagrange, to be joined with that at the Hôtel de Bourgogne. Still subsidized by the royal coffer, the enlarged troupe grew into what eventually became the Comédie Française, also known as the House of Molière. Its members are also called the "children of Molière".

Every year, on 17 February, the anniversary of the playwright's death – which had almost occurred on stage – one of his many plays is revived. Then, in accordance with tradition, the curtain lifts again: set in the middle of the scene is the leather chair into which Molière collapsed while haemorrhaging on the fatal occasion that preceded his last curtain call. Ranged about the empty chair, to pay homage to him, is the entire company attired for the various Molière roles they habitually portray. They are acknowledging that tireless man's immortal contribution to French theatre.

His thoughtful comedies shaped a lasting form that was imitated all over Europe: in Italy by Goldoni; in Denmark by Holberg; in Germany by Lessing; in England by the Restoration playwrights and later Fielding, Sheridan and Goldsmith. Needless to say, he had his French followers as well. In many respects he is the inventor of modern comedy.

— 4 —

IF NOT MOLIÈRE . . .

Molière's immediate successor as "first playwright" was Jean-François Regnard (1655–1709). His was a minor talent, scarcely commensurate with the role now thrust upon him. He copied Molière's formula in some respects but broadened the range of characters portrayed, as well as deepening a little the realism of the backgrounds against which they move. What concerns them chiefly, though not exclusively, is money. (Eric Bentley has observed that tragedy is mostly taken up with murder and comedy with theft.) Regnard wrote both for the Italian players and in later years for the Comédie Française (to which, besides Molière's troupe and that of the Hôtel de Bourgogne, had been added by further royal urging the company from the Théâtre Marais). His works include *The Coquette* (1691), *The Fair at Saint-Germain* (1695) and *The Ball* (also known as *The Bourgeois from Falaise*; 1695–6). These are very light pieces, not without charm and raciness, yet on a level barely above farce. His *Démocrite* (1700) restates the theme of *The Misanthrope*. Best known is *The Gambler* (1696). The hero, Valère, a compulsive gamester, loses not only all his financial resources but also his beloved and a prospective legacy. *The Absent-Minded Lover* (1697) describes the misadventures of the *distrait* Léandre.

The Residuary Heir (1708) is a farce in a far more bitter vein. A young man, Éraste, eyeing a rich, dying uncle, Géronte, tries to win his favour and become his sole heir. Other relatives compete with him. Éraste learns that the old man intends to wed Isabelle, whom the young man himself loves. The girl's mother, Madame Argante, is also avaricious and furthers the inappropriate marriage. Éraste persuades the mother to defer the match. But the elderly Géronte has a mind of his own: he proposes to leave much of his fortune to another nephew and niece who are badly in need. At this point Éraste's rascally servant Crispin steps in. He pretends to be the chosen relative and convinces Géronte that the estate should go to Éraste after all. Before this happens, however, word comes of Géronte's death. Nothing daunted, Crispin now impersonates the demised uncle and dictates and signs before witnesses a document that satisfies the greedy Éraste. A new complication immediately arises: Géronte has only been in a coma and has revived from it. He is persuaded that the new will bearing his supposed signature was actually of his making – that his faint has merely obliterated his recollection of it. For the moment, at least, he consents to let the testament stand. This is a sour picture of the world, crowded with mercenary characters, and shows another facet of Regnard's mind and talent.

Alain-René Lesage (1688–1747) is more famed for his memorable picaresque novel *Gil Blas* than for his plays; none the less, he ranks higher than Regnard as a dramatist. His *Crispin, Rival of His Master* (1707) draws on the *commedia dell'arte* and relates the efforts of a clever servant who daringly seeks to steal and wed his master's beloved. This work is not without moral earnestness.

Even in Molière's later days the theatre in France was markedly changing owing to another Italian cultural invasion: opera was now the vogue. Along with it, as has been noted, was an emphasis on more grandiose stage effects and the use of improved machinery to provide them. Not only Molière but Corneille had to write for the dazzling costumed music plays and dance plays, all the rage at Versailles, that were presented in the city.

Cardinal Mazarin, importing the Italian players, brought in opera troupes as well. At first they performed only on state occasions at courtly festivals, as back in Florence and the other Italian duchies and principalities. But soon the King and his more aesthetic courtiers developed a taste for opera and ballet. In 1647 Mazarin commissioned a full-length opera by Luigi Rossi (1597–1653), *Orfeo*. It was coldly received, partly for political reasons – the French nobility resented the fact that Mazarin wished to surround himself with Italians – though the young King went to see it three times. Mazarin expended a huge sum to stage the foreign work, and this also stirred anger.

Rossi had chosen a subject favoured by composers from Monteverdi to Gluck, the legend of Orpheus and Eurydice. By this time an orchestra called Les Vingt-Quatre Violons du Roi had been established at court.

For his *Orfeo* Rossi and his group expanded the cast, adding sub-plots and new characters, some of them comic figures, probably to please the eight-year-old King who doubtless would grow restless listening to a six-hour mythological story sung in Italian, which was incomprehensible to most of the audience.

Orfeo is not without beauty. A late-twentieth-century shortened version – three and a half hours – was put on at the Boston Early Music Festival held in the Emerson Majestic Theatre. The stage designer was Robin Linklater. The poetry proved to be eloquent; Heidi Walbur, a *New York Times* reviewer, felt that it sounded Shakespearian. The score was restrained, with little effort at florid display. The best effects were subdued and depended on subtle vocal colour. Some dances were included. The period costumes were brought over from Sweden's Drottningholm Theatre, where early operas are frequently revived. From Boston, the offering moved to Tanglewood in the Berkshires for added performances.

A dozen years after Rossi's *Orfeo*, in 1660, Francesco Cavalli's *Serse* was staged at the Louvre to grace Louis XIV's wedding to Maria Theresa of Spain. (This work was subsequently adapted by Handel.) Once more the reception was hostile, perhaps because the text was sung in Italian and the role of Queen Amestris was taken by a castrato – a Servite father – which was anathema to the audience. Yet *Serse* did a little better than Rossi's *Orfeo*, and Cavalli was invited to return

Troisiéme Journée.
Le Malade imaginaire, Comedie representée dans le Jardin de Versailles deuant la Grotte.

Dies tertius.
DoKesinoson, seu Æger imaginarius, Comœdia acta in hortis Versaliarum ad fores Cryptæ.

Overleaf St Teresa of Avila, sculpted between 1644 and 1647 by Gian Lorenzo Bernini, Santa Maria della Vittoria, Rome
Above Performance of *Le Malade imaginaire* (Molière, 1673) at the garden of Versailles, 1676; engraving by Jean Lepautre
Right Set design for *Andromède* (Corneille, 1650); engraving by François Chauveau

Far left Pierre Corneille (1606–84); engraving by J.F. Bolt, 1824, after a seventeenth-century portrait by Charles Le Brun
Near left Jean Racine, 1639–99; engraving, *c.* 1690
Below left Molière (a.k.a. Jean-Baptiste Poquelin, 1622–73); engraving by Gerard van der Gucht after a painting by Pierre Mignard
Below Sarah Bernhardt as Phèdre (Racine, 1677), *c.* 1874

Above Elisa Rachel as Phèdre, *c.* 1850
Above right François JosephTalma as Nero in *Britannicus* (Racine, 1668), 1800
Below right Madeleine Béjart as Madelon in *Les Précieuses ridicules* (Molière, 1659); seventeenth-century painting
Far right *Tartuffe* (Molière, 1664); eighteenth-century illustration

Above left *Le Bourgeois gentilhomme* (Molière, 1670); illustration by Alexandre-Joseph Desenne, *c.* 1820

Above right *L'Avare* (Molière, 1668), Act V; illustration by Robert Smirke, *c.* 1785

Left Jean-Baptiste Lully (1632–87); engraving by Jean-Louis Roullet after a portrait by Pierre Mignard

Above *Les Indes galantes* (Rameau, 1735) at the Palais Garnier, Paris, 1999
Right *Roland* (Lully, 1685) performed by the Académie Royale de Musique, Paris, 1685; engraving

Left Pierre Carlet de Chamblain de Marivaux (1688–1763); copy of a painting by Louis-Michel van Loo, 1753

Below *The Triumph of Love* (Marivaux, 1732), McCarter Theatre, Princeton, 1991–2; directed by Stephen Wadsworth

Above Marie Sallé (1707–56); engraving after a portrait by Nicolas Lancret

Left Jean-Georges Noverre (1727–1810); engraving by Roger after painting by Jean-Baptiste Guérin, *c.* 1800

Above *Les Plaisirs du bal*, *c.* 1715–17, by Antoine Watteau

Left Marie-Anne de Cupis de Camargo (1710–70); engraving after a portrait by Nicolas Lancret

Above left Voltaire (a.k.a. François-Marie Arouet, 1694–1778); engraving after a portrait by Nicolas de Largillière
Above right Adrienne Lecouvreur (1692–1730) as Cornelia in Corneille's *Pompée*
Left Pierre Augustin Caron de Beaumarchais (1732–99); engraving after a portrait by Charles Nicolas Cochin

Above *The Marriage of Figaro* (Mozart, after Beaumarchais, 1786) as performed at Covent Garden, London, 1949
Right *The Marriage of Figaro*, Act I (Beaumarchais, 1781); engraving after an illustration by Jacques Philippe Joseph de Saint-Quentin

Above La Comédie Française, 1791; lithograph after an original watercolour, nineteenth-century French school

Left Sir William Davenant (1606–68); seventeenth-century engraving

Above John Dryden (1631–1700); engraving after a portrait by Thomas Hudson
Above right Sir Thomas Betterton (1635–1710); engraving after a portrait by Sir Godfrey Kneller, 1690s

Left William Wycherley (1641–1715); mezzotint by John Smith after a portrait by Sir Peter Lely, 1703
Below *The Country Wife* (Wycherley, 1675) performed at the Old Vic, London, 1936, with Michael Redgrave and Ruth Gordon; directed by Tyrone Guthrie

two years later, when he offered his unappreciated French masterpiece, *Ercole Amante,* dedicated to Mazarin who had just died. Enthusiasm was slight; the future of operas in France seemed uncertain.

The genius who finally created French opera was an aggressive young Florentine, Jean-Baptiste Lully (the Gallicized version of his name; 1632–87). Left an orphan at ten or twelve (some reports say at only seven) in his native city, the boy was brought to France by the Chevalier de Guise to serve as a page or kitchen worker in the employ of La Grande Mademoiselle, the King's niece. He was forever practising the violin, rasping the nerves of his fellow workers, but Mademoiselle noted his devotion and talent and found him a teacher. Before long he was a member of the King's private troupe of twenty-four violins. He caught Louis XIV's eye – or ear – and was given a small ensemble to lead.

Gaining experience as conductor of this string orchestra, he moved on to composition, eventually producing a host of works of every category: songs, dance tunes, violin solos, religious music, at least thirty ballet scores or suites, and nearly two dozen operas. His merit as a composer is much debated: some critics admire him; others deem his quality "dry".

Heidi Waleson, in the *New York Times,* wrote:

> Besides being gifted as a musician, Lully was an expert organizer who threaded his way through court cabals with astonishing success. Scruples seldom bothered him. In 1669, Louis XIV chartered an *Académie de l'Opéra* and chose the Abbé Pierre Perrin to mount musical dramas in Paris and several other French cities, to begin in two years' time. But Perrin spent too much money on spectacular scenery and machine effects and all too quickly bankrupted himself. Lully seized his opportunity and in 1672, with the connivance of the powerful Madame de Montespan, won the charter away from Perrin. He also disposed of Robert Cambert, an associate of Perrin. For the next fifteen years, Lully built up and dominated French opera, lastingly determining its character.

Lully had already collaborated with Molière on several *comédies-ballet,* as well as with Corneille on *Psyche*, which was almost if not quite a full-fledged opera. His principal librettist, however, was the distinguished poet Philippe Quinault, conveniently a friend of Molière. Together Lully and Quinault turned out musical dramas that first delighted the denizens of the palace and soon a broader public. Quinault's librettos added dignity to these endeavours.

A theatre was erected for them in the rue St-Honoré, into which a growing throng of the aristocracy crowded, so that on performance nights the street leading to it was blocked. The riders had to disembark from their horses and wade through mud.

Lully was elevated to the rank of nobility, with the title of Secretary to the King. In reply to a complaint that this was too lofty a rank for a mere musician, the King told his favourite composer: "I have honoured them, not you, by placing a man of genius among them."

Some said of Lully that he was a "diplomat" even more than a composer. With intuitive deftness he wended his way through the maze of intrigues, jealous feuds and political power-seeking that infused the life of the idle guests ordered to spend months at Versailles. He made enemies; some called him evil. He was short and ugly, had a swarthy complexion and was shortsighted. But he flattered members of the royal family shamelessly, and they doted on him, bestowing on him an endless succession of benefices. He earned fat salaries, dabbled in real estate and accumulated a fortune that his young wife and their four children inherited after his untimely death.

Lully has also been described as an "architect" because he had power and influence over the French musical world and used it to determine how a native French opera, as distinct from the imported Italian, should be constructed. He was dissatisfied with the Italian model, with its emphasis on melody, virtuosic display and vocal gymnastics in which the singer won applause as he or she climbed to high notes, at the expense of sense and sentiment. He was against too much violence in a libretto.

He was truly innovative. He kept the five-act structure but had fewer scene changes within each act. He saw to it that librettos were no longer in Italian but in French and that the singers' diction was clear and precise, as only the French language can be. Just as he had transformed himself by becoming a French citizen, he "naturalized" opera, creating a long-lasting new form that expressed the sensibilities of his adopted fellow countrymen and was more to the taste of the King.

He was able to impose this alteration on his rivals by the force of his strong-willed personality. He had yet another means of control; he had obtained a licence (1672) to manage the theatre in the Palais Royale on the condition that only operas be mounted there. Its stage had been mostly occupied by a group of comedians since Richelieu's death. Henceforth Lully alone decided what could be performed there. His dominance in Paris was monopolistic.

He was a perfectionist and extended himself to the utmost. For many of the productions he personally coached the singers, tirelessly rehearsed, designed the settings and helped build them, and engineered spectacular effects. Seated at a harpsichord, which he excelled at playing, he conducted the orchestra; he was also considered to be one of the best violinists on the continent.

The theatre was small but large enough. There was now a devoted if limited audience for this once foreign kind of entertainment, consisting of royalty, a segment of the nobility and a group in the public. The size of the playhouse created a feeling of intimacy and its ambience was elegant; that continues to be characteristic of French opera. The works were not written for the vast auditoriums in Venice, Rome and Naples that were packed with ardent, shouting tune-lovers.

Louis XIV had founded a Royal Academy of Music and Dance that Lully soon presided over. He decided who was chosen and who was kept out; that gave him even more influence over the music scene. He could justifiably paraphrase his monarch's purported claim and say, "*L'opéra, c'est moi.*"

Lully's monopolistic reign over French opera lasted until 1687, when he hurt himself while conducting – he struck his leg with a cane with which he was accustomed to beat time – and, mistreated by a purported doctor, died of gangrene.

Shrewdly, he provided each work with a prologue in which a divinity descended from the heavens to proclaim the virtues of Louis XIV, pleasing to the vain monarch. In his operas, Lully used a good deal of ballet. This, too, especially appealed to Louis XIV, who loved dancing and with his retinue took part in entertainments at Versailles. He is said to have been quite expert, appearing in a variety of guises, sometimes several in one ballet. Some of these *fêtes* were of extraordinary size and cost vast sums, exceeding even the amounts expended by the King's extravagant predecessors. He established the Académie Royale de Danse (1661), later to be merged with the Opéra in Paris, a not always happy association that continues today.

After Lully took over the Palais Royale the displaced troupe of actors took up quarters in a new house, the Guénégaud (1672), that had been built by an idiosyncratic nobleman of that name for opera – but not Lully – only a year or two before; it could seat more than 1,500 and was seldom more than half filled. Nor was there often a capacity audience for the subsequent theatre put up for the Comédie Française in a house accommodating 2,000.

The effect of opera's rise was making itself felt on all aspects of theatre, which became more opulent in setting, costumes – figured silks, high headdresses, plumes, helmets, velvet capes, brocaded trains – and broader gestures by the actor and by continued infusions of music and dance into comedies and tragedies alike. Hereafter, theatre interiors, too, became more ornate; the stage was also even more a place for gatherings of the élite. There they could promenade, flirt, gossip, as well as watch the actors. The ground floor of the auditorium was lowered, so that the first and second rows of boxes were more nearly level with the stage, affording the occupants the best view, at the expense of those beneath them in the orchestra. The new Comédie Française had the first horseshoe-shaped hall.

As early as 1660, Gaspari Vigarani prepared for Mazarin another special theatre in the palace that came to be known as the Salle des Machines because it was so fully equipped to put on awesome effects. It boasted 144 backdrops. (Eventually it became another possession of the King). Clouds and chariots could float above its stage, which was 59 feet high, 75 feet wide and 132 feet deep (the proscenium was 32 feet). Similar machinery was installed in the newer playhouses in the city, where perspective scenery was likewise introduced. Two other important scene designers of the period, both from Italy, were earlier Giacoma Torelli and later Jean Nicolas Servandoni, who followed the tradition of the famed Bibienas. Their productions, presented by sketches and small models, are striking. (Vigarani, jealous of Torelli's work for Louis XIV, destroyed as much of it as possible when he succeeded him at that court.) Before long, French designers were imitating them.

After Molière's death the Italian players, with less robust competition, regained their dominance. They also improved their situation by commissioning scenarios from French authors, something they had not bothered to do heretofore.

Among Lully's contemporaries at least two should be singled out and remembered, Robert Cambert (*c.* 1637–77) and Pierre Perrin (d. 1675). Lully's ambition to stop importing Italian productions was an aim that possessed Cambert, too. He wrote a short piece that was heard by Perrin, a poet, who was captivated by it. He offered to provide it with a libretto. The result was *La Pastorale* (1659). When published, its title page carried their assertion that it was "the first French play to music".

The short work pleased Louis XIV and Cardinal Mazarin when it was put on at the palace, and the Cardinal suggested that Cambert and Perrin write another like it, which the two promptly did: *Ariadne, or The Marriage of Bacchus* (1660). It was allowed to have the several semi-public hearings.

The pair were granted a licence to present more of their works. Perrin announced that he was seeking a style that would convey feeling without excessive embellishment, length and exaggeration; it should have "wit, lightness and intelligence". Subsequent ventures met that goal.

They now had a theatre, but unfortunately Perrin became the victim of unscrupulous associates and was soon in financial trouble that led to debtors' prison. To gain his release, he sold his royal licence. The purchaser was Lully, but within a fortnight the licence was revoked, though the King awarded the smooth-talking Lully a fresh one soon after (1672) and his singers and orchestra moved into the Palais Royale.

Perrin died three years later. Cambert went to London in a vain effort to have their operas staged there. Death overtook him in the foggy capital two years after he established residence there.

The next major composer in the still narrow precincts of French opera, Jean-Philippe Rameau (1683–1764), had a provincial background; he came from Dijon. His personality, described by all as sweet and modest, was very unlike that of the ruthless, wily Lully. His family, drawn to music, gave him an early start. His father taught him to play the organ. In school his thoughts and attention often drifted from what was under discussion to tunes and passages he jotted down as they occurred to him. He also sang so stridently that his fellow pupils were drowned out.

He learned to perform on the violin. After he finished his schooling he joined the violin section in a touring orchestra and next obtained a post as organist in the cathedral of Clermont-Ferrand.

But his duties there soon bored him. He intentionally and repetitively struck wrong notes during services. The discord was hurtful to the ears of the congregation and soon, to his delight, led to his dismissal, so that he was free to compose music full time. (Years later he was received by the cathedral and was much loved and honoured by its priests and communicants.) He wrote keyboard music, at first for the harpsichord (1706) and then in a variety of other genres. In his late thirties he published a technical treatise on harmony that for decades was a mandatory text for music students worldwide.

By his own account he had been drawn to writing for the theatre from age twelve on, and he pored over scores by Lully and others. His dream was to compose an opera, though he doubted his own competence. As the years went by, his unflattering self-appraisal continued to deter him; he was not ready. Only when he reached fifty did he feel up to the task. He had married at forty-two to a girl of nineteen. They seemed happy; he fathered four children.

Before he could attempt an opera he required a subject. He approached the blind playwright Houdan de la Matte, who was not amenable to a collaboration. Rameau continued his quest and finally had what seemed to be rare good fortune: no less a dramatist than the eminent Voltaire agreed to share his enterprise. They selected the scripture about Samson and Delilah as their theme and began to work on it; they stopped when warned that the subject was "unsuitable".

At this point Voltaire withdrew as a partner and Rameau renewed his search. At last he persuaded the Abbé Simon-Joseph Pellegrin (1661–1745) to take part. This time the source was the tragic myth of Phèdre, exploited by Euripides and Racine among others. Pellegrin made many changes, choosing a new title, *Hippolyte et Aricie*, feeling it was more appropriate to the altered story.

The young man in the story does not spurn his stepmother's advances because he is pledged to chastity and serves in the cult of the goddess Diane and is appalled by Phèdre's willingness to betray his father, here mistakenly believed dead, but instead because of his love for the virginal Aricie, arousing the infatuated Phèdre's anger and jealousy.

The father, Thesée, the King, has been in the underworld with his own father, Neptune. During ceremonial games staged to pay tribute to Diane, a dreaded monster rises from the turbulent sea. Hippolyte, challenging it, vanishes in flames and smoke. Phèdre, believing him dead, kills herself; but at Diane's command he returns borne by zephyrs and is reunited with Aricie while all rejoice. In this libretto the focus is on characters other than those in the great dramas on which it is based.

In rehearsal the singers had difficulty coping with the score. Rameau, discouraged, wanted to abandon the project, but Pellegrin and the wealthy music-lover Le Riche de la Pouplinière insisted on its continuance. Its first performance took place before an invited audience in the Parisian financier's mansion. Three months later it was moved to the Paris opera for greater exposure (1733).

As is usual with a new musical work it had a mixed reception. Some thought the story and score too "cerebral"; others welcomed its rare depth of thought. It caught on, however, and had thirty more stagings in its first year and many revivals, with some revisions, over the next two decades.

Rameau's confidence was bolstered and his genius unleashed by this success. After a late start he rapidly turned out many timely *comédies-ballet* and operas, only a few of which survive in revivals. Perhaps the most vital and admired are *Les Indes galantes* (1735), *Castor et Pollux* (1737), *Dardanus* (1739), *La Princesse de Navarre* (1745) and *Platée* (1745). An unusual feature of his composing was that his subjects became lighter as he aged. He had a number of different collaborators, partly because he outlived several of them.

Louis Fuzelier (1672–1752) provided the text for *Les Indes galantes*, a complicated, disjointed story that appealed to Rameau because of its exotic settings and multiple opportunities for spectacular stage effects, including a volcanic explosion. The "Indes" here are Peru, to which the principal characters have been forced to flee after four allied European nations enter into warfare. Osman, a Turkish pasha, has abducted Emilia, a provincial slave girl. The beloved Prince Taemus arrives to visit his erstwhile favourite, Ali. He is in love with Ali's slave girl Zairey. Meanwhile Fatima, his slave, is possessed by a desire for Ali. Taemus is disguised as a merchant and Fatima as a Polish male slave. Thinking she is an enemy, Taemus attacks her. But after identities are clarified, the slaves are exchanged and all concludes happily as the festival proceeds. In the next and final episode – the fourth – the action takes place in a North American forest near the Spanish and French colonies. Headed by Adaro, the native Indians seek to make peace with the European invaders. Damon and Don Alvar, French and Spanish officers, seek the favour of Zima, daughter of a native chief, but her affection is for Adaro whom she hopes to have as her husband. Don Alvar is enraged at being rejected. His anger is cooled by Damon. All ends quietly at a feast enhanced by a "pipe of peace" dance.

As before, the initial audience response was divided but the fanciful *Les Indes galantes* had music and ingredients that the public liked and the opera soon became widely popular, having productions all over Europe. It has continued to win new hearings now, especially a sumptuous staging for a gala at the Paris Opéra in the 1950s. The many parts are nicely matched to the characters; they are fully individualized and contrasted, and the action is lent emphasis by passages in the score.

Castor et Pollux almost defies synopses. Pierre-Joseph Bernard (1710–75) conceived its plot and characters. It is hard for moderns to appreciate the grip Roman and Greek mythology had on the imaginations of people in the eighteenth century, especially in matters dealing with the stage. Besides, opera always seems to fare better with settings remote in time and place; stories laid in the present usually have difficulty and seldom thrive.

Here the gods – Minerva, Venus, Mars – have leading roles and much of the action is allegorical or symbolic. Borne on a cloud, Venus appears, an enchanted Mars at her feet. Through the intervention of the goddess of love and wisdom, peace has been restored to a ruined world.

There is rejoicing. The hero Castor has been killed and preparations are under way for his funeral. His beloved, Telare, the daughter of the sun, weeps for his loss. She begs to share his fate. Pollux, his brother, has vowed to avenge Castor's death. Pollux is immortal. He, too, loves the grieving Telare. Having fulfilled his vow, he confesses to her his amorous feelings. She asks him to go down to Hades and bring back his brother alive. His dilemma: if he retrieves Castor it will cut off his chances of winning Telare. The decision he has to make is whether to appeal to his father Jupiter, ruler of Olympus; if he does, Jupiter will plead that he has no jurisdiction over Hades; he cannot help Pollux in his formidable endeavour. Also, Pollux must replace his brother in the underworld if Castor is to return alive from the kingdom of the shadows.

Pollux, searching, finds his brother; Castor refuses to accept the sacrifice, the gift of renewed life, but when apprised of Telare's prolonged mourning he agrees to go to her for just one day. The reunion of the lovers is an intense moment. Phoebe, who desires to belong to Pollux and is jealous of Telare, has called on the demons to prevent the meeting. But Jupiter is finally convinced that he must step in: Castor and Pollux are released from their promises and nearly all the characters are satisfied. To honour the estimable brothers, the deity gives them a place in heaven among the shining constellations.

This work is considered by many to be Rameau's masterpiece. It repeated the wide success of the two operas that came before; over the next forty-eight years it had 254 performances. In 1754 it underwent a complete revision that made it even more effective.

La Princesse de Navarre is a *comédie-ballet* for which Voltaire was the librettist. It was written to be part of the celebration on the occasion of the Dauphin Louis's marriage to Maria Theresa of Spain. The collaboration between these two superior artists was the Cardinal's idea; he hoped it would produce something truly remarkable. The music has withstood time better than the story. Mistaken identities, disguises, family feuds – all the familiar devices are pressed into service, but there are also some tragic overtones. The initial staging is said to have been exceedingly elaborate, as might be expected for a union between two rich neighbouring dynasties. One possible fault is that Voltaire's dialogue is often too literary.

The libretto for *Dardanus* by Charles-Antoine Leclerc de la Bruère (1711–54) is a fantasy dependent on magical tricks and transformations, like those being called for in many of the works by Handel in England. In a prologue, Venus summons the Pleasures to occupy the court of Amour. They do this so well that all who are there fall asleep. Venus has Jalousie (a role given to a dancer) arouse them, after which Jalousie is banished. The Pleasures enact the tragedy of Dardanus, which goes as follows:

Iphise, daughter of Teucer, King of Phygia, is in love with Dardanus, her father's sworn foe. Teucer wants her to marry Prince Anténor. In despair, Iphise seeks assistance from a necromancer, Isménor, who gives Dardanus a wand that alters his aspect to that of a magician. In that guise he hears Iphise confess her love for him; their passion is mutual. He reveals his true identity; startled and confused, the girl takes flight. He is captured by the Phrygians.

Jupiter bids a sea monster to rise, alarming the inhabitants of the nearby land. Anténor takes up arms against the menacing beast. He is defeated and about to perish but is saved by Dardanus. Grateful, he writes an oath of eternal friendship and gives him his sword as a token of his sincerity. He is not aware that the rescuer is also his rival for the hand of Iphise. An oracle, speaking for Neptune, foretells that Iphise will wed the man who kills the sea monster. Dardanus qualifies for that privilege; recognizing that, Anténor yields his claim and brings about the predictable happy finish by his renunciation.

The story and score were subjected to several revisions for subsequent stagings, mostly shortening and making the plot more compact; some of its melodies were lost in the process.

Even more fantastic is *Platée, ou Junon jalouse*, a comic opera with a libretto by Jacques Autreau (1650–1745) and Adrien-Joseph le Valois d'Orville. Its première took place at Versailles, to celebrate again the Dauphin's marriage. The prologue is enacted in a Grecian vineyard where Thespis presides over the birth of comedy. The action unfolds near a pool surrounded by expansive countryside. Jupiter wishes to vex his mate Junon (Juno). He enlists the help of King Citheron and Mercure (Mercury) and pretends to be enamoured of Platée, a vain, foolish nymph who lives in the pool. They stage a mock wedding while the jealous Junon spies on them from a hiding place in the greenery. The fake marriage is followed by a banquet attended by naiads, satyrs and peasants after a procession in which a coach is drawn by two large frogs; it is conveying Platée. Her face is veiled. As Jupiter is about to utter his vow, Junon rushes forth, assaults Platée and tears off the veil. All the witnesses to this altercation burst into laughter, to Junon's surprise. Jupiter and Junon are reconciled; Platée retreats to her refuge in the pool.

This strange frivolous work by Rameau is unique. It has been revived relatively often from the long list of his works. Recent productions have been mounted at the Spoleto Festival in Charleston, South Carolina, and at the New York City Opera in Lincoln Center. Costume designs and choreography for the naiads, satyrs and frogs present a challenge.

Before his death Rameau had earned a fixed place in the firmament of masters of music. His emotions had long life. He gave the chorus more to sing. To mollify the leads, who resented the choristers' intrusion into their time and space in the "spotlight", he allotted them additional arias. He had an abundant, prompt, rich store of melody at his command, and he was adept at word setting. His orchestra characterized the people in the drama and was able to reflect their heightened emotions. As no one had before, he evoked "pictures" from the orchestra to accompany the action and score onstage, by capturing the sounds of a sea monster, a whipping gate and thunder, the clamour of battle, a soft moment, birdsong, a tender exchange, an idyllic sunrise.

He usually avoided large ensembles behind the footlights or in the orchestra pit; the average number of his instrumentalists was forty. His overtures had snippets from lengthier passages that were conspicuous in the ensuing narrative and anticipated the mood that needed to be established.

*

Silenced for almost two centuries, two "lyrical tragedies" by Marc-Antoine Charpentier (*c.* 1634–1704) were reborn in 1984 when his *Medeé* (1693) was staged in Paris and New York and had heartwarming receptions. Soon after, his *David and Jonathan* (1688) had equal success. The librettos of both works are based on plays by Thomas Corneille, brother of the author of *Le Cid*. *Medeé* was later brought to the Brooklyn Academy of Music in 1993 by William Christie and his ensemble, Les Arts Florissants, specialists in Baroque. (See *Stage by Stage: The Birth of Theatre* for a fuller discussion of Charpentier.)

Doubtless other fine operas of the period await and would greatly reward discovery. Their titles are known and the names of their composers: André Destouches (1672–1749), André Campra (1650–1740), Henri Desmarets (1661–1741) and Marin Marais (1656–1728), to cite a few. Most were influenced by Lully, Charpentier's rival for favour at the Sun King's court.

In Italy fame came too late to Giovanni Battista Pergolesi (1710–36); after a lingering illness and stretches of obscurity and impoverishment he died at twenty-six and, like Molière, was buried in an unmarked grave. A cobbler's son, he limped and probably suffered from a lung infection.

Among his compositions are several tragic works now mostly overlooked, but shortly before his death he dashed off *La Serva Padrona* (*The Maid as Mistress*). Its success was explosive and carried his name throughout Europe and won over much of the Parisian public. (See *Stage By Stage: Dramatis Personae.*) With it was born comic opera, the insertion of songs and dances, as in light pieces by Molière or Marivaux and earlier forms of musical entertainment. In Pergolesi's farce the music was continuous; all the dialogue was sung or else rapidly enunciated in recitative to which Italian and French especially lent themselves: the more rapid, the more amusing. What is more, the characters were ordinary people, the setting contemporary and domestic. Soon composers everywhere were producing comic operas.

In France earlier forms of humorous music had been the ballads sung by strolling players. Light skits with music that were sometimes put on at the street fairs were also called "*vaudeville*"; even Henri III at times patronized them incognito. But comic opera was something quite new.

As might be expected in Paris, the cockpit of debates over aesthetic theories, controversy broke out. It was set off by Friedrich Grimm (1723–1807), a young German diplomat stationed in the capital. A self-appointed music critic who moved in Diderot's circle, he was delighted by Pergolesi's departure from the traditional model of French opera accepted by Rameau (though Grimm exempted Rameau from his attack). He wrote in an article that opera as staged in Paris was "the laughing-stock of Europe". The conductor, he wrote, was a "woodchopper", the instrumentalists seldom played together. The musical idol of the French, Lully, was a Florentine, not even a native.

Grimm also had praise for his friend, a budding young philosopher, Jean-Jacques Rousseau (1712–78), who, largely self-taught, had written a comic opera, *Le Devin du village*, in the mode perfected by Pergolesi. It had been put on in Paris and was approved for court and the public (1752). Rousseau himself then joined the fray, hurling pointed shafts at the traditionalists. He asserted that the scores were marred by "crude harmony", that the language did not lend itself to recitative and that French operas had no melody.

Rameau composed much music for ballet. As noted before, Parisian audiences insisted on having dance episodes inserted in every opera. He was very skilful in writing for dancers, adapting conventional forms such as the gavotte, the minuet, the tamborin and the chaconne to fit the mood and action to a particular moment in the story. The dancers were using more and more mime, enabling them to convey emotion and enhance the plot. They also moved away from the fixed patterns carried over from formal social dances of the past.

Ballet had gained a large, devoted audience in France, England, Italy, Russia and elsewhere. Much of this was owing to Rameau's having lifted the standard of music for theatrical dance. Two ballerinas were adored by the public; theirs was a fierce competition for popular acclaim and favour. Marie Sallé (1707–56), daughter of a musician and tumbler, was born in Brussels where her parents were visiting as members of a troupe of strolling players; it was headed by an uncle. The girl's beauty and strength singled her out at a very early age; she received lessons to prepare her for a career in theatre.

Her début took place at the St Laurent Fair (1718) – she was eleven or twelve. For several years she appeared in important venues while she studied with Françoise Prévost at the Académie Royale, becoming ever more the mistress of mime and ballet techniques. In 1721 – at fourteen – she performed at the opera in Paris. As she advanced in the art, fellow dancers with more seniority became jealous and saw to it that she was kept half out of sight, far from the footlights. She made such a vivid impression in Rameau's *Les Indes galantes*, however, that the status she was due could no longer be denied. Her rise to Prima Ballerina followed quickly. She was praised by Diderot and Voltaire.

The fashion of the day had women wearing very wide hoop-skirts. The stage at the Palais Royale was narrow. Actresses must have found it difficult to walk about and seat themselves gracefully. Even noble ladies in the side-boxes and the front of the pit were doubtless uncomfortable and awkward in such voluminous attire. More than any others, dancers were hampered by it.

In a bold stroke, Sallé dispersed with her mask, high headdress, hoop-skirt and panniers. She let her hair hang loose and wore only a diaphanous gown that revealed her slim, lovely figure. Her movements were free – and she occasioned a scandal. Soon many other dancers copied her. She was established as a bold reformer. She anticipated by two centuries the avant-garde American Isadora Duncan.

Sallé's reputation – and that of her frequent partner, her brother David – sped around

Europe. The English actor-producer David Garrick arranged to bring her to London, but his timing was unfortunate. England and France were on the verge of war with each other. Though the elderly George II was in attendance, the audience was hostile and unruly. At the next presentation a riot broke out and a spectator was injured. Garrick prudently cancelled the engagement.

In subsequent years, however, she spent much time in London, mingling there with the brightest of the intelligentsia; she could hold her own in any conversation; they considered that she was one of them. Her name was unsullied, and after her death her innovations, her emphasis on naturalness, expressions and mime, were championed by the still youthful Noverre who adopted many of them.

Marie Sallé's principal rival, Marie-Anne de Cupis de Camargo (1710–70), also claimed Brussels as her birthplace; she, too, was the daughter of a musician and early showed an aptitude for dancing. She was of Spanish descent. She was first a performer on stage in Brussels, then in Rouen and next at the Paris opera. The tall and romantic Sallé had the advantage in looks. Though some reports have it that Camargo was beautiful, her portrait by Vigée Le Brun does not bear that out, nor does Noverre's comment that she was "neither pretty, nor tall, nor framed". Yet one by Lancret suggests that she was attractive. And her technique was superior to Sallé's; she was remarkably agile and renowned for the dexterity of her footwork.

This led to reform as well: she discarded dancing in shoes with heels, replacing them with soft slippers that let her speed her movement. She shortened her skirts to show the rapidity of her steps or crossing of her ankles, allowing her to extend her acrobatic leaps and exude an air of fiery, impassioned emotion. The partisans of both dancers were vocally loud, often raising a din of applause to the ceiling of the Palais Royale.

To Camargo is attributed the introduction of the ninety-degree turn-out and the invention of the *entrechat quatre*, which makes the dancer seem to be feather-light in descent after having been airborne. (That has been questioned by scholars, but many other effects are due to her initiative.) She was so strong that she took lessons with the men and proved to be their equal. Yet she was feminine and inspired fashions in attire and coiffeur. At her retirement she was given a pension by the government (1751) and lived thereafter in care of the Comte de Clermont.

A better dancer than Sallé but less appealing, she was long remembered and celebrated in England. Charles Lecoq composed an opera about her, and the great choreographer Marius Petipa produced a ballet revolving around her. In London, after Sergei Diaghilev's death and the dissolution of his Ballet Russe, English dancers banded together to form a native troupe to perform works of English choreographers and revive classic works (1930). They called themselves the Camargo Society. It was the forerunner of societies of later British composers.

Other important performers of the day were Marie-Madeleine Guimard, who was very thin and who was described as "bird-like", and Marie Allard, who was stout but vivacious. Her life was a turbulent one. Among her several claims to historical notice was that she was the mother of Auguste Vestris, the superb male dancer. Anne Heinel was very temperamental, with an elegant figure, and was married for a time to another member of the gifted Vestris family. Her elevation and leaps evoked grand approval. Louise Madeleine was timid but excelled in ballets by Rameau; she appeared in nearly all those using his music.

The star male artists should not go unmentioned. The role of Danseur Noble called for a well-proportioned physique and natural grace. Assuredly, that requirement was met by Louis Dupré (1697–1774), who still performed with rare style at sixty. He was Noverre's teacher and had Gaetano Vestris as a student. Vestris belonged to a family whose men for three generations were hailed as "Gods of the dance". Dupré was exceptional in another aspect: he earned a fortune and retired very rich, an unusual outcome for a dancer. The Vestris family – male and female – played a very significant part in the growth of ballet.

Maximilien Gardel (1741–87) also removed the heavy mask that hitherto had been worn by performers. He did so to let the audience know that he was replacing Auguste Vestris in a role that evening. He was Noverre's successor as ballet-master at the Paris Opéra. He is believed to have created the *rond de jambe* as a choreographer there. He often partnered with Marie-Madeleine Guimard when he was in training with Noverre at the Académie Royale de Musique, where he became ballet-master. His technique was viewed as second only to that of the phenomenal Vestris Fils (1729–1808), who was deemed to have no peer in Europe.

Jean Lany (1718–86), though bow-legged, was praised by Noverre as "the most expert dancer I know". He had his turn as ballet-master at the Paris Opéra. One of the Vestris daughters, Thérèse, was his mistress. Gaetano Vestris challenged him to a duel but Lany elected not to fight. Gaetano was briefly imprisoned.

Jean Dauberval (stage name of Jean Bercher, 1742–1806) was yet another of those schooled by Noverre, who later complained that his former pupil, though at first "modelled by the graces, has grown heavy and muscular". None the less, his name endures as a clever, whimsical choreographer. At one time or another his *La Fille mal gardée* (1789) has been in the repertory of almost every ballet company. It uses music by various composers and, one of the oldest ballets still staged, has undergone endless alterations, always remaining very amusing. A long line of great ballerinas have enjoyed dancing the role of Lise: Mlle Théodore (married to Dauberval), Fanny Essler, Anna Pavlova, Irina Baronara and Alicia Alonso. Among the revisionists have been Marius Petipa, Mikhail Mordkin, Bronisla, Nijinsky and Frederick Ashton.

La Fille mal gardée had its première in Bordeaux a fortnight before the descent of the fear, din and anarchy spread by the French Revolution.

The Italian company's chief sketch writer proved to offer unique gifts and a very personal idiom. His lengthy name was Pierre Carlet de Chamblain de Marivaux (1688–1763). He was a novelist, and his fictional works are long and in many ways solid. But his stage writings, comprising thirty-five scripts, are brief, slight and delicate – perfectly suited to presentation by actors equipped with *commedia dell'arte* mannerisms. His plays have been called the "theatrical equivalent of the paintings of Watteau".

Certainly the fragile and fantastic spirit of Rococo is in them. As "bitter-sweet" treatments of the age-old subjects of love and deception, they represent a surprisingly fresh genre, a distinct break from the by then overused tradition of Molière that most other French authors were accepting without question. Indeed, Marivaux had a less than high regard for his eminent predecessor.

Soon many other writers were imitating Marivaux in turn. This established a different kind of theatre piece, the "sentimental comedy", or what the French aptly call "comedy with tears". Such plays fitted the new tone of society, the stage – as always – responding barometrically to the winds of change and overall climate of a new epoch.

Marivaux's little plays have exceeding subtlety. Some critics say that he adopts Racine's themes of passion but handles them with a refined, light, artificial touch that renders them droll. Frequently the *commedia dell'arte* characters reappear Gallicized: Perdolino, for instance, is Pierrot. The cast of Italian *zannis* is also softened, given a poetic quality. This author's verbal style is known as *marivaudage*. It is not precious, not *recherché* but nuanced and sensitive.

His most frequent (though not exclusive) subject is nascent love, the almost imperceptible start of attraction between young persons, taking place in a misty world of gardens and moonlight or elegant drawing-rooms to the accompaniment of guitars, mandolins or soft singing.

In general, only a half-dozen of his numerous scripts are considered true masterpieces. The early *Arlequin poli par l'amour* (1720) is among these. So is *La Surprise de l'amour* (1722), in which Lelio and a countess disavow love but then are reclaimed by it again. Both plays explore aspects of the emotion, the mysterious ways in which it unfolds in the human psyche, how people are drawn to and repelled by each other. What little dramatic action there is arises from their tentative approaches, doubts, withdrawals and returns. All this is delineated with amused sympathy and gentle charm.

Infinite variations of this recurrent theme are found in *La Double Inconstance* (1723), in which a pair of "lovers" – Arlequin and Silvia – mistake their infatuation for true love, only to discover that they are happier with quite other persons: at the end, Silvia weds a Prince, and Arlequin is head-over-heels about Flaminia.

Most typical is *Le Jeu de l'amour et du hasard* (*The Game of Love and Chance*; 1730), also one of Marivaux's best. Silvia is betrothed to Dorante, whom she has never met, since her father and his father are friends and have amiably made the match. Indeed, not even her father, Oronte, has ever glimpsed the young man, who reputedly is handsome and well behaved. Silvia protests, however, that many gentlemen present a pleasant face to the world but at home are horrid, even cruel and tyrannical, husbands.

Accordingly, she is frightened at the prospect, even though she has the option of refusing her suitor. She begs her father to let her change places with her maid, Lisette, so that she can have a better chance to observe Dorante when he arrives and also learn from his manservant the true nature of his young master. The indulgent Oronte agrees to this scheme. He is much amused to receive a letter from his friend, Dorante's father, telling him that the young man has proposed the same plan: he is changing roles with his valet, Arlequin. Oronte and his son Mario stand back to watch the playing out of this farcical situation. Predictably, the pretty Silvia, posing as Lisette, falls in love with the gallant Dorante, posing as his manservant; and the pert Lisette, impersonating her mistress, is fascinated by Arlequin, whom she thinks to be her intended husband; and Dorante is disappointed by Lisette, whom he believes is the girl he is to marry.

Silvia and Dorante are afraid of falling in love and wanting to wed beneath their station, while both Lisette and Arlequin are excited at the prospect of winning the hand of someone wealthy and far above them. Mario, Silvia's brother, interferes mischievously, creating new complications.

The dialogue is as frolicsome as the situation – the play's featherweight action is principally verbal. Mario rebukes Dorante for paying an initial compliment to Silvia, whose identity he mistakes. Silvia protests to her brother: "Why do you take that attitude? I want him to like me." Another exchange:

> Dorante: You are wrong to say you want, beautiful Lisette.
> Lisette: You don't need to give such a command, in order to be served.
> Mario: Monsieur, you pillaged that gallant trait from somewhere.
> Dorante: You are right, sir. I found it in her eyes.
> Mario: Be silent. That is still worse. I forbid you to be so witty.
> Silvia: He isn't witty at your expense. If he finds it in my eyes, he has only to take it.

Here is a similar exchange between the servants:

> Lisette: You must not doubt my affection.
> Arlequin: I want to kiss those little words and pick them from your mouth with mine.
> [Translation by Wallace Fowlie]

The Game of Love and Chance has now been offered more than 1,000 times at the Comédie Française. The basic plot premise – master and mistress passing themselves off as their own valet and maidservant – has since been used by many other dramatists, notably in England, among them Oliver Goldsmith for his *She Stoops to Conquer*.

Among Marivaux's later plays in this frothy new vein is *False Confidences* (1737), in which the penniless hero, again named Dorante, woos and conquers a wealthy young widow. Somewhat more tinged with social criticism are *The Triumph of Plutus* (1728), which deplores the misuses of wealth, and *The Isle of Slaves* (1728). In the premise of the latter, Sir James Barrie's *The Admirable Crichton* is anticipated. When an Athenian ship is lost, a few passengers take refuge on a deserted isle; a general and a lady are forced to reverse roles with the general's slave, Arlequin, and the lady's maid, of superior competence, who become the new master and mistress in these changed circumstances.

After 1747 Marivaux quit writing for the professional theatre. Having lost an inheritance, he had to earn a living by his pen.

Though he was well received in his own day, Marivaux's ascent to greater fame occurred in the more sentimental and romantic nineteenth century and later. His influence is marked not only on works by Goldsmith and Barrie but in France on the comedies of Alfred de Musset and on twentieth-century whimsical scripts by Jean Giraudoux and Jean Anouilh.

In the United States Marivaux and his works were known to only a few scholars of French literature. But that suddenly changed at the very end of the twentieth century. Enthusiastic reviews of his *The Triumph of Love* in France and England alerted American directors, and, as often happens, the play was sought out, scanned and put on by widely scattered groups: the Guthrie in Minnesota, the Court in Chicago, the Repertory in Berkeley, the McCarter in Princeton, Center Stage in Baltimore and Yale Repertory in New Haven.

Ironically, *Triumph* was deemed to be one of the playwright's lesser works and had not been well received when it made its début in the Théâtre des Italiens (1732), running for only six performances. In particular, the heroine's aggressive pursuit of the hero and the tricks she perpetrates on her elders were considered unseemly for a girl of noble birth.

New York was offered the comedy by the Jean Cocteau Repertory (1997), a bold, very active off-Broadway ensemble. The English translation was by Rod McLucas. Direction was by David Fuller, who added original incidental music by Charles Berrigan. Settings were by Roman Tatarowicz.

Many of the critics were charmed. The dialogue – Marivaux avoided rhymed verse – was well spoken by the leads, who carried off their roles with panache. And there was generous praise for the brightly fashioned period costumes.

In the play, the strong-spirited Princess Leonides is irresistibly attracted to Prince Agis, who is unaware of her existence. He is the true heir to the throne that has been usurped and awaits her. Meanwhile he has been closely guarded by an uncle and aunt, the one an ascetic philosopher, the other a dour old maid. The Princess dons male garb and presents herself to the Prince as a serious student of metaphysics and by this deception gains access to the innocent, isolated young man.

This situation yields many opportunities for discussions of the ethical and psychological facets of love, marriage and relationships between the sexes. Agis, long shut off from the outside world and an untroubled celibate, listens to the debates and is swayed by them. The unscrupulous and seductive Leonides wins over all by having both the guardian brother and sister-scientist enamoured of her (him). Eventually Agis claims the sceptre and tentatively embraces Leonides. There are complications involving the servants and touches of the *commedia dell'arte* – one of the characters is named Harlequin.

The comparative off-Broadway success of this work prompted another spate of productions around the country, some using the same English translation, some their own adaptations.

As late as 2003 the Cocteau Company's version was staged at the Walnut Street Theatre in Philadelphia. It evoked a protest by Nina da Vinci Nichols in *Theatre Scene*:

> No question the play is about romantic love, though it's not quite a romantic comedy. An adventurous young Princess, Leonides, adopts the guise of a student of rationalist philosophy, well sort of, in order to win the love of a true Prince, Agis. She first has to get past his brother and sister guardians, respectively, an ascetic philosopher and his spinster sister. She hits upon the clever scheme of courting both brother and sister gargoyles to win their trust and induce them to drop their guard duty. She acts as woman to the man and man to the woman, giving her male disguise more purpose than this theatrical standby usually holds. What's a romantic heroine without a little heroic posturing?
>
> This is a new company at work at the Jean Cocteau Repertory. The actors are lively, the production credible, and the direction fine enough to keep Pierre Marivaux's complex comedy moving at a fair clip. Several adaptations on stage and screen have brought the play firmly into the classical repertory and the Cocteau is to be commended for its dedication to keeping repertory alive. The stage looks lovely and the music is too, especially the tinkly piano. Yet *Triumph of Love* inevitably presents one or two difficulties rising out of its own period and style, respectively eighteenth-century and French, that may be insurmountable. A successful adaptation probably would need to overcome its origins entirely, which are distant from current audiences. This version, perversely enough, falls victim to its own fidelity to the original text.
>
> The minimal plot, after all, rests heavily on philosophical debate about the meanings of love and marriage, separately and together. Talk does not *lead to* action, it *is* action and calls for a level of coherence or intelligibility beyond the specific, witty lines.

Encouraged by the earlier favourable notices that the Cocteau offering had received elsewhere, a group led by James Magruder, who had staged his interpretation of the play at Princeton, decided to develop it as a Broadway musical and set about transforming it. Magruder provided the book – based on his own English translation – to which were added fresh lyrics by Susan Birkenhead, matching a new score. After out-of-town try-outs at Baltimore's Center Stage – where Magruder held the post of dramaturge – and at the Yale Repertory in New Haven, the production was brought to the appropriately named Royale Theatre on West 43rd Street, just off Times Square.

In Boston's *Theater Mirror* E. Kyle Minor reported on the Yale presentation and forecast a hit:

> Turning the eighteenth-century *Triumph of Love* into a musical works so well, you wonder why someone didn't pull it off years ago. *Triumph*, running at Yale Repertory Theatre, proves this chamber-farce was a musical waiting to happen.
>
> Composer Jeffrey Stock, lyricist Susan Birkenhead and book-writer James Magruder retain the light, romantic flavor of its source. In fact, they take it further, using music to briskly tell the tale of a princess who simply must get her man.
>
> Marivaux recently enjoyed renewed popularity in regional theatres. Hartford Stage successfully brought *False Admissions* out of mothballs two seasons ago. New Jersey's McCarter Theatre followed suit, as did several other New England venues. While this relative influx didn't quite bump Shakespeare or Molière from the "A-list" of most revived ancients, it introduced today's audience to a clever man previously rotting in the textbooks.
>
> Marivaux, as proven once again in Yale Rep's musical, remains fresh because he sticks to romantic comedy, or more specifically, love-driven farce. Since Marivaux was a French playwright writing the play for an Italian troupe, his flavour tastes very *Comédie Française cum commedia dell'arte*. The operative word here is comedy, no matter how you spell it.
>
> Borrowing from about 1,256 playwrights before him and more after his death, Marivaux drags Léonide in men's apparel, enabling her to woo her Big Moment in disguise. Unlike most other dramatists, however, Marivaux knows what avenues of comedy to click on to and when the gag has run its course. Magruder adds humorous anachronisms for his servants, but mostly leaves the story to Marivaux. Stock's music may be short on ballads and the repeating choruses we've grown accustomed to, but the piece is best served this way. Dreary exposition is economically and fetchingly doled out in song ("Men of Reason", "The Ballad of Cecile" and "Three Great Minds"). Stock's style ranges from musical scenes to soliloquy. Many of the melodies are of the highest order and would most assuredly be "hummable" if they were reprised at all. The cast is 99.4% lean. Michael Mayer's direction and Heidi Landesman's set design are models in tasteful economy.

The New York notices ranged from fervid approval to sharp disapproval, but there were not enough friendly ones to have newspaper readers wish to stand in line to buy tickets. The new arrival was certainly not Broadway's usual fare. The work remained at the Royale for two and a half months. There were reports of sell-out performances, but a run of that length would hardly earn the producers a full return of their investment.

The following year this musical version was seen in Philadelphia, again at the Walnut Street Theatre. It aroused the same praise and dissent from the local critic who cherished the non-musical version:

Someone simply must speak out on behalf of the eighteenth-century French playwright Pierre Carlet de Marivaux before it's too late, and I guess it has to be me.

Writing for a troupe of Italian comedians in Paris, Marivaux took the vulgar, rambunctious, athletic, improvisatory traditions of the Italian *commedia dell'arte* and transformed it all into something else entirely. For centuries the English-speaking world firmly believed that his plays were dainty, over-refined, effete and precious, with periwigged aristocrats prancing around manicured gardens in Louis Quinze satin breeches and waistcoats.

Then, less than a decade ago, Stephen Wadsworth directed Marivaux's 1732 comedy *The Triumph of Love* at the McCarter Theatre in Princeton and showed us that we were all wrong: Marivaux's plays are really heavy-duty dramas about human emotions at risk, about love and loss and suffering. Marivaux's plays (in translation by Wadsworth, James Magruder, and others) swept the country.

Then Magruder adapted his own widely produced translation into a musical that had a brief run on Broadway last year, and is now being produced in a carbon-copy production by the same director and set and costume designers. And if this production is right, then Wadsworth, too, was all wrong. Forget the human emotions, forget the suffering. And forget the daintiness and the preciosity. This stuff is just plain vulgar.

There's still a lot of potential for a real human drama here. Léonide (Jennifer Lee Andrews), meanwhile, has the Prince's presumptive friend, the disguised Princess, play at letting down their social guard and expressing their true feelings man to man. (This scene, long in the original, is wisely trimmed in the smooth, new translation by Rod McLucas.) Then they get to express themselves over again in their own identities. The point of the two parallel scenes was partly to contrast a formal and rather stylized courtly convention with a more naturalistic, sentimental confession of feelings. Instead, as these good and pleasant actors never quite conveyed the artificial constraints on behavior, including the manners of courtship, their first was nearly as naturalistic as their second.

Doubtless, a tightly structured, verbal play like this one demands more of an audience than, say, a physical comedy, or a typical boy-meets-girl plot, and the reverse, girl meets boy. Marivaux's play does not lead toward the altar, in spite of this heroine's aggressive strategies to get her man and in spite of the closing image of the couple's embrace. On its own, as I have implied, the script theatrically depends on the heroine's trouser role, and she wears them throughout. So, finally, the inspired clowning by a Harlequin and the servants supplied more than merely stage business to let in light and air.

It would seem that in Philadelphia, the "city of brotherly love", the subject of love is taken very seriously.

Interviewed by Elyse Sommer for *Curtain Up*, Magruder defends his very free treatment of Marivaux's script: "A truly stageworthy translation should only last twenty years. It would then be time for a new one." Asked why so many presentations of the play had sprung up around the nation, he had a plain, pragmatic explanation: "Marivaux wrote for the Théâtre Italien, a small playhouse, and his scripts do call for small casts, with few if any changes of scene, and simple unit sets. That appeals to regional companies whose financial resources are usually quite limited."

Besides the showing in Philadelphia, *Triumph* continued to reach the boards elsewhere in various translations and adaptations – Seattle, Palo Alto, San José. In the summer of 2003 it was revived again in Manhattan, this time in the open – and free – by the Classic Stage Company. Elias Stimac wrote in *Backstage*:

> Playwright Pierre Marivaux couldn't have imagined a more picturesque backdrop for his comedy than New York's Central Park. Neither could he have fathomed the overhead helicopters, sirens, bikers, and buses that accompany the outdoor setting. None of these distractions, thankfully, take away from his witty wordplay, marvelously translated into modern-day idiom by Stephen Wadsworth and Nadia Benarid, further adapted by Wadsworth, and playfully presented.
>
> The grassy grounds become the gardens in which Marivaux's characters play out their pent-up passions . . .
>
> Marivaux's plot blossoms with comic confrontations and flowery admissions of admiration. Director Stephen Burdmen neatly modulates the bluster and buffoonery, and draws audiences into the action by cleverly staging each scene in a different locale, requiring viewers to walk (and sometimes run) to keep up with the cross-dressed ladies and the objects of their affections. Shorts and jogging shoes are suitable attire for this moveable feast for the eyes and ears. Burdman's cast and crew are gregarious and game for their antic assignments.

Observing the many stagings of *Triumph*, the screenwriter Clare Peploe and her husband, Bernardo Bertolucci, a director of international repute, felt that it was promising cinema material. He prepared yet another English translation and devised a shooting scenario. They raised funds and initiated a production in Italy, with all the story's action occurring in a sun-laved garden. Well-known performers were chosen for the leads. The picture was released in the United States (2005). New York's film critics paid it little heed – perhaps because they were not attuned to *marivaudage*. Their opinions were widely diverse, as were notices in newspapers.

A lengthy, earnest summation is that by David Garrett, in *Identity Theory*, excerpted here:

> What is man, and what do men want? What is it that we love when we love, the spirit or the flesh? As love grows, are we guided most by reason or emotion? How do circumstance and history shape our openness to love and the importance we give it? These questions are addressed in *The Triumph of Love*, a film based on a play by Marivaux. It is about the daughter of a usurper king who decides to find the deposed king's son and then decides, out of infatuation

and justice, to marry him and have him become king. As he has been taught to hate all women in general and her in particular, she disguises herself as a man and visit the estate where he lives with his guardians and teachers, a philosopher and his scientist sister. To be allowed to stay at the estate, the princess dressed as a gentleman begins to befriend the prince and seduce the philosopher brother and scientist sister . . .

In *The Triumph of Love*, there are masters and servants, men and women, residents and visitors, with different perspectives and obligations, and the play and film are partly about how the characters seem to be conspirators, friends and lovers. When manners have the full force of society behind them, the force is so powerful it acts as a natural law and shapes personality so deeply one doesn't think to respond in an opposite manner. When one is aware of manners as an imposed or a chosen system of responses, one is inclined to be more flexible in their execution – or disregard them almost entirely. We think about our experiences as we have them, and we put our thoughts not only into action but also into words, sometimes very eloquent words: all human society is not gestures and grunts; and the most articulate works of art bear this out. Works made for sophisticated audiences often take into consideration not only experience but various interpretations of experience, and such a work is this.

The film is an amusement, and yet it asks provocative questions about love, deception, and justice – and it makes accessible a form of culture (the play by Marivaux) that might otherwise seem distant to us – and it provides us the opportunity to imagine other ways of being in the world, and, not least, the chance to laugh.

At the beginning of the film the princess and her friend and attendant are traveling toward the philosopher's estate by carriage and begin to change from women's clothes to men's, and once they arrive at the estate they think to roll up handkerchiefs to put into their trousers as substitute penises. This last act also indicates that the film will be not only about power and disguise but also about sex.

As soon as the gentleman-princess, played by Mira Sorvino, and the exiled prince meet, they befriend each other, making one think that possibly the prince, played by Jay Rodan, may be especially interested in male company – he later talks about this being the rare chance to make a friend. Later the gentleman-princess will say, "We liked each other as friends – do we like each other the same way now, or is it different?" and they'll agree they like each other more now than before.

The gentleman-princess begins a verbal seduction of the scientist sister, played by Fiona Shaw in a performance in which she goes from brainy and severe to floating on air. The gentleman-princess's gender seems a matter of signs – clothes, deep voice, and masculine bearing – but it is an impetuous passionate spirit that seduces the sister. Her brother, played by Ben Kingsley, realizes immediately when alone with the gentleman-princess that the man is a woman, and the princess explains she is attracted to him. We can find annoying and arrogant, or pathetic, the erotic desire of someone we do not find attractive, someone we do not want;

it's an act of imagination and affection to return someone's desire. The young woman's desire awakens that of the philosopher, and he feels conflicted, concerned about his reputation but eager for love. The solitude of the brother's and sister's lives had previously allowed them to remain committed to a set way of being – solitary, rational, and judgmental about the princess's family – and as they are seduced they begin to admit to each other that their way of life has had limitations. They can only admit these limitations when the opportunity to change has arrived – and possibly this explains why so often in life people refuse to engage in criticality (they do not see the opportunity for change). The princess herself begins to feel badly about exploiting the emotions of the brother and sister, her avowed enemies, in order to develop her bond with the exiled prince.

The sincerity in Mira Sorvino's eyes as she plays the princess throughout the film is a great part of what drew this viewer into the film and made the plot more engaging. She is a sensitive (and pretty) princess and a handsome, cordial gentleman, and does whatever she does in the film with sympathetic understanding and wit.

It is the height of farce when brother and sister both prepare to enter their carriages to leave the estate to meet their new lover(s), the same person; and they are humiliated by the revelation. The prince at first cannot forgive the princess – but the film ends in a triumph of love, love between a man and a woman, between siblings, and also for thought and science, as a scientific breakthrough occurs.

The film moves quickly, is well acted, and smartly edited. The color of *Triumph of Love* is often dark and dense, like the lush gardens of the estate. The estate itself, made up of stone walls and large rooms and attractive furnishings with a garden path adorned with the marble busts of great philosophers, seems to embody tradition, nation, and history, civilization in a word. The estate, like manners, like philosophy, may be an attempt to hold chaos, passion, and trouble at a distance, an inevitably unsuccessful attempt.

In 2005 New York play-goers were afforded a look at another Marivaux concoction. The Classic Stage Company, a long-standing off-Broadway institution, presented *The False Servant* at its theatre.

Once more the reviewers were of two minds, their responses remarkably at odds. For instance, here is the assessment of the *Village Voice*'s Michael Feingold:

> Pierre Carlet de Chamblain de Marivaux wrote plays that are the essence of Frenchness: totally easy to understand and utterly impossible to translate. The paradox is underscored by the new production of *The False Servant* at CSC, where Marivaux's rueful, subtle study of love's arbitrary rewards and disappointments comes through, pellucid as a spring of sparkling water despite the eccentric obstacle course of Kathleen Tolan's translation (made from a "literal translation" by Nelly Lewis and Pam Gould) that follows French usage doggedly, even

where it makes for antiquated diction or bad grammar in English. "Go Monsieur, return to the women who explain themselves more precisely than me." Tolan then compounds this fracture by salting the text with streetwise words (phony, crap, score, as a verb) that jar against the archaic phrases like cobblestones on a subway track.

Luckily, Brian Kulick's production, though it traces the delicate line of Marivaux's story with a heavy dark pencil, rarely gets in the way of his scampering, bittersweet narrative about a wealthy young girl who disguises herself as a roistering chevalier, in order to inspect the husband her guardian has selected for her, and finds herself the new love object of his current mistress. Call it *Twelfth Night* cubed. Against a sparse setting built from a wagonload of luggage, Mark Wendland's rich, somber costumes bask in Kevin Adam's flood of bright lighting. Martha Plimpton, in a Prince Valiant bob, makes a spirited hero-heroine, with Jesse Pennington suitably callous and dapper as the faithless lover whom she marries anyway. If Marivaux's grace has been left behind on this journey, he still has plenty of passion and brains left with which to fill the performance's speedy two hours . . .

Ironic awareness increases viewer pleasure . . . It is clear that there is no magical formula that can be used against human nature or against life.

In the *New York Times* Charles Isherwood was all frowns:

Decked out in a smart black tailcoat and shiny leather boots, her hair styled in a sleek blond cap, a sword dangling suggestively from her belt, Martha Plimpton cuts a debonair figure in the Classic Stage Company's revival of Marivaux's *False Servant*. Ms Plimpton, who spends the entire play in trousers, imbues Brian Kulick's production with a bright, puckish spirit, but there's little else to recommend this efficient but mechanical staging of one of the eighteenth-century French dramatist's lesser-known and less-lovable works.

The cross-dressing lass played by Ms Plimpton is on a mission to test the mettle of a young man's heart. Betrothed to Lelio (Jesse Pennington) before she has met him, she passes herself off as a dashing chevalier and is soon recruited by the scheming fellow to help him escape a romantic entanglement with a countess (Tina Benko).

Lelio has discovered, to his chagrin, that the countess's bankbook doesn't quite equal that of his as-yet-unmet mate. He encourages the chevalier to woo the countess, hoping to be freed from this misalliance without having to cough up the money he'd borrowed from her. Providing wooly comic counterpoint, as they try to manipulate their betters for their own aims, are the wily Trivelin (Bill Buell) and the bumbling Arlequin (Paul Lazar) . . .

As in his better-known comedies, like *The Triumph of Love*, Marivaux casts a cool eye on the vagaries of romantic love. A quintessentially Gallic worldliness rarely cedes its grip on his characters' minds, even as they seek to follow the impulses of their hearts. The temperature of *The False Servant* is particularly chilly: true feeling is not a significant factor in the complex calculations here. Lelio reveals his mercenary nature in the play's opening scene and remains unappealingly cynical to the last. The fun is in the faux-chevalier's playing a false fellow false.

But "fun" is probably overstating the case. Kathleen Tolan's new translation is credible but occasionally clotted in attempts to retain the intricacy of the original. Marivaux's characters engage in finely nuanced exchanges of badinage that can take on a wearisome rhetorical quality in translation. Ms Plimpton, with a roughish smile at the ready and mischievously darting eyes, is most skilled at warming up the analytical pulse of the dialogue. Mr Pennington's Lelio is affably raffish and Ms Benko's countess decorously self-possessed, despite her declarations of love for the ardent young chevalier.

Mr Kulick's production emphasizes the nip that never leaves the air, underscoring, with its stark simplicity, the sensation that we are watching a Shakespeare comedy unfolding in a cold-storage warehouse. The set, by Mark Wendland, is a large white square on which a cluster of battered trunks are arranged and rearranged, like pieces on a chessboard. It's an indication of the play's tepid dramatic temperature that the swapping of allegiances among the countess, the chevalier and the cad is hardly more involving than the trundling about of those trunks.

Somewhat less severe was William Stevenson in *Broadway*:

Unless one lives in Paris and goes to the Comédie Française regularly, it's not easy to see the works of eighteenth-century French playwright Marivaux. New Yorkers now have a chance to see one, thanks to the Classic Stage Company's production of this gender-bending comedy. With a lively new translation by Kathleen Tolan and an accomplished performance by Martha Plimpton, *The False Servant* is worth seeing. Just don't expect a riotous farce.

Marivaux's plays are more psychological than farcical, and Brian Kulick's direction emphasizes the writer's thoughtful side. That's fine. The only trouble is that Kulick often lets the pacing get too leisurely.

As in many of Marivaux's comedies, the plot involves disguise. Chevalier (Plimpton) dresses up as a man in order to spy on her fiancé, Lelio (Jesse Pennington). She suspects that he is carrying on an affair with the Countess (Tina Benko), so in disguise she befriends Lelio and spends time with him in the country. What she learns is even worse than she feared: Not only is Lelio having an affair, but he only wants to marry Chevalier because she has a larger fortune than the Countess.

To get even, Chevalier woos the Countess herself and attempts to extract money from Lelio. But her new servant, Trivelin (Bill Buell), is also a schemer and complicates her plans. He reveals Chevalier's secret to the Countess's servant, Arlequin (Paul Lazar), who becomes infatuated with the cross-dressing heiress and has a hard time keeping her secret.

All of the characters, nobility and servants, are preoccupied with money. Marivaux shows how finances frequently trumped affection in determining marriages in eighteenth-century

France. And, in timeless fashion, he shows that men like Lelio are pigs and that women like Chevalier can outfox them. Because she is smart and strong, Chevalier is a wonderful part for an actress. Plimpton is an excellent choice for the part. With her blond hair cut short, she looks like a pretty young man. More important, she is always fun to watch, whether Chevalier is verbally sparring with Lelio or delivering a sarcastic aside to the audience.

The rest of the cast provides excellent support. Lazar tries a bit too hard to get laughs. But he does have cute bits involving a mallet and a trunk.

From beginning to end, trunks figure prominently – too prominently, in fact. In the opening scene, there is a towering pile of trunks on a carriage. During the remainder of the two-hour play, trunks are moved around the stage, carried or pushed by the actors, opened to reveal puppets, and climbed into (by Arlequin). Director Kulick relies too much on the trunks, and all the business doesn't add up to much. He should have come up with other props.

Lesser contemporaries of Marivaux – their contributions now alive mostly on the page rather than the stage – include Florent Carton Dancourt (1661–1725) and Philippe Néricault Destouches (1680–1754). The former offers a succession of caricatures of the middle-class manners of his day in *Le Chevalier à la mode* (1687) and *Les Bourgeoises de qualité* (1700). These portray social climbers, making themselves absurd by emulating their social betters, and in the process being victimized by libertines and parasites. The women are stupid, their husbands gullible and greedy; the social picture is cynically drawn. By contrast to Dancourt, the works of Destouches are steeped in sentimentality and tend to moralize overtly. *The Married Philosopher* (1727) was his most popular. *The Conceited Count* (1732) depicts members of the *ancien régime* in conflict with the waxing middle class, a subject that had also appealed to Elizabethan and Jacobean comedy writers. Destouches had lived and worked in England and was acquainted with its literature.

Comedy like Marivaux's, with even more tears, was furthered by Pierre-Claude Nivelle de La Chaussée (1692–1754) with the *False Antipathy* (1733), *Fashionable Prejudice* (1735) and *The Man of Fortune* (1751).

After him, the sentiment and didacticism on stage became ever damper, threatening to engulf and drown any attempts at objective realism and social relevance. Yet this epoch advancing towards the cataclysm of the Revolution was to yield one writer, far more talented, whose spirit was more closely akin to that of Molière and who was therefore – in this changing political climate – a more solitary literary figure.

Pierre Augustin Caron de Beaumarchais (1732–99) needed no buttressing or spiritual encouragement from any of his fellow authors. He was one of the most exuberant and self-confident persons who has ever lived, in or out of literature. His career is as bizarre and adventurous as any in history; many biographers have vainly sought to do him justice, but the details go beyond credence.

He was born in Paris, on the rue St Denis, the son of a clockmaker whose last name was simply Caron. At nineteen the youth, too, became a watchmaker. (This was a period when the newly conceived timepieces fascinated men of a mechanically inventive turn of mind – even the French Kings tinkered with them.) Scarcely more than a year later the clever Pierre came up with an escapement that revolutionized the pocket watch.

Eventually this led him to Versailles and the notice of Louis XV, who bought a watch for Madame de Pompadour. Once able to approach the court, the glib and dandified Beaumarchais quickly ingratiated himself there. The King's four daughters grew exceedingly fond of him. For a span of four years, in his twenties, he tutored the royal young ladies in music, for he had remarkably diverse gifts. He invented a novel arrangement of harp pedals that is still used.

Young Beaumarchais was short-tempered and became involved in a duel in which he killed his antagonist, who was a far more experienced swordsman. "My children," commented the King. "See to it that nobody mentions it to me." It was not Beaumarchais's last engagement in physical combat: he defended himself ably in a no-holds-barred bout with a husky ruffian who happened to be a duke. The fearless future playwright risked his life many times; he was to serve four prison sentences; he was outspoken and never hesitated to make powerful enemies.

His protean abilities extended to the financial realm: he was an eager promoter, but like many of his kind he was carried away by over-optimism. Barely past thirty, he became a secret partner and agent of Pâris-Duverney, a leading banker, who placed him in an important post at court, but he lost this entry because of two sensational lawsuits. He attacked the judges in a series of pamphlets that made him known throughout Europe.

He kept his vituperative pen busy all his life, directing venom at his foes. He undertook commercial schemes of every sort: he joined lumber, shipping and publishing businesses; one of his most costly enterprises and failures was the complete works of Voltaire in ninety-two volumes. He became one of the controllers at the King's pantry and bought himself a judgeship of game cases. In the same way he twice attained rank in the bottom tier of nobility, buying the "de" that subsequently graced his name.

He never lost his interest in music; he composed songs and an opera, *Tarare* (1757).

He was also an orator and a political negotiator. His numerous political activities were oddly varied. He organized and headed a bogus company (secretly financed by the French and Spanish governments) to arm the soldiers of the Continental Army waging rebellion in the American colonies. He shipped vast supplies to the colonial forces, enough to equip 20,000 men during the most critical days of that war, but was never repaid. The provisions are given credit for the American victory at Saratoga.

He lost a huge sum; years after his death a belated Act of Congress awarded his heirs the money owed him by the new American nation. Yet his prime motive had not been profit. Though paradoxically he had purchased himself a grant of nobility, he was a liberal and genuinely wanted to help the American rebels. He now regretted having added the "de" to his name, as he had come to detest the aristocracy of his own country as much as they hated him.

He afterwards found muskets to aid the French Revolution. Later he was arrested; incarcerated by his fellow rebels, he narrowly escaped the guillotine but was banished instead.

He devoted a good part of his career to espionage, as a professional spy for both Louis XV and Louis XVI. Carrying out this furtive occupation, he concocted an imaginary criminal who supposedly possessed dangerous documents and pursued this phantom all about Europe, collecting substantial travel expenses. One episode in his role as a secret agent called upon him to flirt with a transvestite captain of dragoons.

His personal life was deemed scandalous. He was not above stooping to smuggling, impersonation, blackmail or slander. He was an ardent lover and married three times; each of his wives had formerly been his mistress. Amoral, he tried to arrange a liaison between one of his mistresses and the King of Spain.

He built himself a mansion that had two hundred windows and faced the Bastille, the royal prison in Paris – this seemed almost prophetic. When he himself was not bankrupt he was generous to his family and supported many indigent relatives. He knew poverty as well as success and affluence. He was fond of luxury.

Somehow this contradictory and impudent man also found time to be a major playwright. His first script, *Eugénie* (1767), failed. It was an inconsequential and rather sentimental comedy and was later revised and restaged. His second, *The Two Friends* (1770), had a somewhat kinder welcome. It sought to gain recognition for businessmen and suggested that they should be more respected. He also attempted a tragedy, *The Guilty Mother*, that is hardly notable.

His works of lasting acclaim are two robust and glittering high comedies, the first of which, *The Barber of Seville* (1775), he wrote while mourning the death of one of his wives in childbirth. Its scene is the beautiful, sunlit city in southern Spain, a country in which he often travelled. The plot of this immortal piece is all too familiar: Rosine is destined to marry her elderly guardian, Bartholo. She is sought by young cavalier Lindoro, really Count Almaviva in disguise. He wants to be cherished for himself alone. The young lovers are aided by the resourceful poet and barber Figaro who contrives by various tricks to gain Almaviva access to Rosine's dwelling, to further the courtship. "Lindoro" is able to enter by impersonating first a drunken soldier billeted in the house, and later a music master. Figaro drugs the servants.

The intrigue is adeptly handled, but it is the dialogue and unusual characterizations, and the complaints aimed at the aristocracy, that chiefly distinguish this script. Molière had used much the same plot in *The School for Wives*, but Beaumarchais's treatment has a fresh quality and the play is essentially radical, for it exalts the common sense and courage of Figaro, a man of lowly birth. It portrays him as kindly, generous, proudly independent and even insolent towards his "betters". In good measure this is a picture of Beaumarchais himself, who defied authority and outmanoeuvred his opponents; represented in the play in the person of Bartholo, he showed them to be rich and privileged and to have tradition and convention on their side.

Nor is old Bartholo easy to dupe; he is a worthy antagonist, suspicious and nearly as clever as Figaro. The barber is extraordinarily vital, in love with life and action, ready to reply at once to any challenge. The play has excellent timing, vivacious language, colourful Spanish atmosphere and never fails to hold the stage.

"I'm convinced that a grandee is good to us when he does us no harm," says Figaro. When rebuked by Almaviva, he adds, "My lord, people always expect a poor man to be faultless . . . From the virtues demanded of a servant, does Your Excellency know many masters worthy of being valets?" (translation by Wallace Fowlie). So run many sharp gibes at the nobility. Old Bartholo rues the "barbarous age" in which they are living. "You are always attacking our poor century," comments Rosine. "But what has it produced that we should praise it?" asks Bartholo, who further answers: "All kinds of silliness: freedom of thought, gravitation, electricity, religious tolerance, inoculation, quinine, the *Encyclopedia*, plays . . ." Obliquely, here again, is the voice of Beaumarchais himself, a bold, sceptical rationalist, emancipated, in favour of liberty of thought for all and fully aware of philosophical and scientific progress.

In another vein, Figaro sagely remarks: "If you want to teach cunning to the most innocent girl, just lock her up." Of his own attitude towards life, he confesses: "I hasten to laugh at everything for fear I may be obliged to weep." His cynicism is clear when he observes of the suddenly friendly Almaviva: "My usefulness has shortened this distance between us." To Bazile, the actual music master, is given a lengthy and eloquent tirade on how to get rid of one's enemies by slander: "Believe me, there is no vulgar form of evil, no horror, no absurd story that you can't instil in the leisure class of a big city if you go about it in the right way." He details exactly how to spread canards. Figaro, who has overheard him, is not impressed: "One needs station, a family, a name, a rank, solidity in a word, to create a sensation in the world by means of slander. But Bazile! If he slandered, he wouldn't be believed."

In 1784 Beaumarchais's redoubtable rogue-hero appeared in a sequel, *The Marriage of Figaro*. In this sparkling play his animus towards the aristocracy is even more outspoken. Almaviva and Rosine have been wedded a few years; the fickle count has already wearied of her and wants to stray from matrimonial bonds. His stare turns to Suzanne, his wife's vivacious maidservant. Figaro is about to make Suzanne his bride, but Almaviva intends to seduce her first, demanding an equivalent of the medieval *droit du seigneur*. He is foiled at this.

To head off Figaro, he seeks to have the barber marry the elderly Marceline. Meanwhile Rosine hears rumours of Almaviva's philanderings and acts to outwit him by having Suzanne assent to a rendezvous, to which the disguised Rosine goes in her maid's place. The complications mount rapidly, and in the highly amusing denouement Figaro turns out to be none other than Marceline's long-lost son.

Beaumarchais gives Figaro bitter lines flaying the arrogance of the ruling class. He reserves his praise for men of true ability whose rank does not depend on the lucky accident of their birth on silk cushions. That is to say, Figaro lauds and compliments himself, while commenting bitingly on those who have only blue blood to their credit.

As with Molière's *Tartuffe*, there was difficulty in getting *Marriage* produced; Louis XVI was set against it. The fiery author was determined and defiant. "The King does not want *The Marriage of Figaro* to be played. Therefore it shall be played," he vowed. It was, finally, nine years later (in 1784), and it caused a riot in the theatre.

To state, as it has been so often, that Beaumarchais hastened the advent of the French Revolution by the ideas couched in these two plays is perhaps hyperbolic. They were, rather, expressions of the growing social discontent, widespread malaise and moral degeneracy that led to the overthrow of the decadent Bourbon monarchy. Today the plays are still vigorous, not only as viable stage works frequently in the repertoire of the Comédie Française but also as librettos for three famous operas, a version of *The Barber of Seville* by Giovanni Paisiello, another even better known by Gioacchino Rossini and the scintillating and beloved *Marriage of Figaro* by Wolfgang Amadeus Mozart.

After the terror of the Revolution subsided, Beaumarchais came back to Paris. He sought to persuade Talleyrand to appoint him ambassador to the new United States of America, a post that might be useful in recouping the millions of francs owed to him. But nothing resulted from his efforts, and death overtook him at fifty-seven, well before the year 1799 was out and the tumultuous century ended.

The tragic theatre of France was never to see the achievements of Corneille and Racine equalled, but numerous writers busily undertook the composition of serious drama throughout the next few decades. As noted, sentimental drama, laden with moral instruction, took over. Most of these plays by minor or mediocre talents descended to the pathetic or bathetic. Here, as might be expected, the comedy of tears was outdone in works aspiring to tragedy. The fashion for such scripts came mostly from England, as with the comic author Destouches, or perhaps it developed simultaneously in both countries by a mutual exchange.

The foremost exponent of this sentimental drama in France was the philosopher and *encyclopédiste* Denis Diderot (1713–84), who with Voltaire and others assembled the huge compendium of knowledge to which the sputtering Bartholo alludes contemptuously in *The Barber of Seville*. The *Encyclopedia*, a grand accomplishment, years in the making, was meant to sum up the beliefs held by intellectuals in the Age of Reason. Beside his labours on this compilation of all philosophical and scientific theories, Diderot tried his hand at numerous plays and in doing so helped to set a long-lived pattern for stage works intended to inform and raise the moral sights of theatre-goers. They were to be spiritually uplifted and inspired by having their emotions disturbed, their sympathies aroused. *The Natural Son, or The Trials of Virtue* (printed 1757, produced 1771) is typical of this kind of drama, as is *The Father of the Family* (1758). In such plays middle-class life is depicted; the honest, decent man of commerce is offered as a model. At the same time there are emphatic lessons on the folly of vice and the wickedness of all sorts of oppression. Diderot was much influenced by the English plays of George Lillo.

Diderot is not as important for his heavy-footed *pièces à thèse* that are hardly likely to regain the stage, save possibly as outmoded curiosities, as he is for his other writings about theatre. His practical experiences as a playwright led him to publish several essays on the nature of drama and acting, the latter of which shall be referred to again shortly. In his *Essai sur la poésie dramatique* he calls for a bourgeois drama or tragedy concerned with middle-class characters, who should be portrayed in the social and economic settings that shaped them. This was a prophetic summons, as were his writings on acting, but he failed to embody its principles in his own creative endeavours, nor was anyone quick to accept his ideas.

A covey of other playwrights enjoyed contemporary success, some still following the strict classical tradition, others the new sentimental style.

Paul Scarron (1610–60) was another who had a life more dramatic than his plays, most of which were comedies. Outstanding were the burlesques he wrote for the actor Jodelet. His prose tragedy, *Zénobie*, is less memorable. Scarron was a prankish *abbé*, hideously deformed as a consequence of debauchery, syphilis and medical malpractice that had ruined his nervous system and left him so shrunken and misshapen that he had to sit propped up in a box with his head and arms protruding. None the less, he was courageous and charming; several of the most famous women of France adored him and brought him delicacies.

He conducted a salon; lacking money, he charged for the food his guests consumed. He married a poor young girl in a platonic match. When her first husband Scarron was paralysed she took his dictation and read and faithfully attended to him. The rewards of her virtue and devotion were great. When she was later widowed she became Madame de Maintenon and eventually the wife of Louis XIV.

Prosper Jolyot de Crébillon (1674–1762) offered gory melodramas with classical trappings. He thrived with this formula. A sample of it is to be found in *Rhadamiste and Zénobie*.

Antoine de Lamotte-Houdar (1672–1731) is barely recalled for his *Inès de Castro*, but deserves further mention for having advocated the liberation of drama from the constricting three unities as well as from having to write all dialogue in verse. "Why not in prose?" he demanded. But his protest was scarcely heeded.

Earlier there had also been Jean Galbert de Campistron (1656–1733) and Antoine de Lafosse (*c.* 1653–1704), now largely forgotten. Others of this period who might be listed are Joseph Saurin (1706–81) who wrote a *Spartacus*, Antoine-Marin Lemierre (1723–93) with a *William Tell* and Marie-Joseph Chénier (1764–1811), who penned a *Charles IX*. These were historical dramas that reflected the idealistic and patriotic spirit of the French Revolution and the Napoleonic era that followed.

Jean-François Ducis (1733–1816) attempted translations of Shakespeare and did not hesitate to "improve" the originals. Into his *Hamlet* (1769) and *Lear* (1783) he inserted overt moralizing, catering to the taste of his time, and took the liberty of making Ophelia the daughter of Claudius, hence Hamlet's first cousin.

The figure who dominated the age, however, was another philosopher. A waspy little man, his name was François-Marie Arouet (1694–1778). His *nom de plume* was Voltaire. He was of course the foremost intellectual and literary personality of his day, the very essence of the Enlightenment. His life and prodigious career are far too long and crowded even to outline: he was a wit, a businessman, a scholar, a historian, a metaphysician, a poet, an essayist, a critic, a fabulist, a satirist and a playwright. His feats as a lover (his sexual tastes are undetermined) are notorious. The multitudinous volumes of his published work omit his immense correspondence with eminent persons everywhere in Europe.

Though he was a great rationalist and an implacable foe of the Church and superstition, and radical in his approach to social conventions, he was nevertheless quite retrogressive in his theory and practice of drama. He was the most hidebound and dictatorial of classicists. The consequence is that the long roster of tragedies he turned out, mostly in the two and a half decades between 1718 and 1743, now seem lifeless, academic and cold. They are largely on standard themes already exploited by Corneille, Racine, Pradon and other predecessors: an *Oedipus* (1718), *Brutus* (1730), *Zaïre* (1740), *Death of Caesar* (1735), *Alzire* (1736), *Zulime* (1740), *Mahomet* (1741) and *Mérope* (1743). Among his scattered later scripts are *The Orphan of China* (1755) and *Tancrède* (1760). His greatest triumph was *Irène* in 1778, put on when he was eighty-four. "The marvel," said one unkind observer on that tumultuous occasion, "is not that he has written such a bad drama, but that at his age he has been able to compose anything at all."

By consensus, his best works are the much earlier *Zaïre* and *Mérope*. As the titles of his scripts suggest, his plots, melodramatic and complicated, are laid mostly in ancient times and remote places such as Greece, Rome, the Orient and the Middle East. His introduction of China and Peru as backgrounds (the latter in *Alzire*) is one novelty. He had some familiarity with Oriental literature and borrowed from it. His *Death of Caesar* is another attempt at a version more "correct" than Shakespeare's. The contrast is a lamentable one, hardly in Voltaire's favour. In *Nanine* (1749), a dramatization of Samuel Richardson's popular novel, he ventured into bourgeois drama and for once mixed moods by inserting comic passages.

His stage plays are not without eloquence, occasional sting or moments of onstage effectiveness. His chief resources were always his sharp intelligence and facile pen. His attack on bigotry and other forms of fanaticism in *Mahomet* is particularly strong and pointed, but today his dramatic writings sound stilted and superficial; his moralizing is too explicit, his characters externally motivated. Still, his was an inherently theatrical personality, and this often shows through and counts for him despite the handicapping constraints of the classical form he accepted. He stressed visual appeal – an example is the rich milieu of *Tancrède*. From the Elizabethan romantics he pragmatically took ghost scenes and an emphasis on love interest, because he perceived the audience's marked fondness for them.

His better works remain in the repertoire of the Comédie Française, as they were in his day, but elsewhere he is no longer important in the theatre, though in his own period he had an astounding influence abroad, especially in England and Germany (countries where he spent many years of political exile) and in Italy and even far-off Russia, where he was the guest of Catherine the Great. He was widely and slavishly imitated, with sterile results.

(Voltaire would have been surprised if he had known that a free adaptation of his satiric novella *Candide* in the guise of a musical comedy would finally reach Broadway in 1958, directed by Tyrone Guthrie, with a book by Lillian Hellman and a score by Leonard Bernstein. The cast had fine voices. Despite the collaborative efforts of these top talents – Guthrie's staging was described as "bountiful" – the run was a short one. A few years later, however, the work was brought back, restaged by Harold Prince who dispensed with most of the lavish scenery. The revised book was by another hand, but Bernstein's score was intact. Catching the public's fancy, it had a long engagement.)

As a critic, Voltaire commented in essays and prefaces – often harshly – on writers who had preceded him, judging them by whether they adhered to Aristotelian and Horatian precepts. He insisted on plausibility, compactness and clarity and was opposed to merely decorative verse; he insisted that poetic dialogue should have the "same purity as the most chastened prose", nor should rhyme hamper the thought or the delivery be too declamatory.

He was looked upon as infallible, and finally came to believe his judgements were always correct. His characterization of Shakespeare as "a splendid barbarian" is widely quoted. His analyses of some of Shakespeare's masterpieces are often unperceptive, but he also praises much in the English dramatist's works. He had kind words for Racine, especially that poet's *Iphigénie*, which he deemed unequalled. He assumed that French classicism was an advance even over that of Athens and Rome.

Voltaire had one salutary effect on theatre: he objected to seating noisy, restless gallants on stage and finally ended that distracting practice. He accomplished this reform by soliciting a grant of 60,000 francs from the Count de Lauraguais to recompense the actors who had sold tickets for the high-priced seats. The chairs had narrowed the acting space to a square not more than a dozen feet; now the cleared area was expanded.

Like Diderot, Voltaire took a decided interest in the styles of acting of his plays and sought to raise often deplorable standards.

*

Historically, during periods when new plays of quality are scarce, the theatre tends to revive past masterpieces and theatre-goers concern themselves more with performers, many of whom develop large popular followings by their outstanding skill or charisma. This came about in the late eighteenth century in France. The flamboyance in enacting tragedy against which Molière had inveighed in vain was gradually subdued by Michel Baron (1653–1729), who as a young man had been in Molière's troupe. He avoided the singsong declamation that stresses the rhymes in the Alexandrine couplets; instead, he introduced pauses to clarify what he was saying. He renounced the pompous mannerisms and bombast of his contemporaries. He modified gestures and softened his voice to a more natural pitch to suggest real emotion, believing gestures should be appropriate even at the sacrifice of a graceful pose.

Much acting was governed by strict conventions about how a line was to be spoken and how strong a passionate gesture was to be. Indeed some were codified and even symbolic, as in the Far East. With courage, Baron broke many of the inherited rules of the so-called "high style". His only guide was what conveyed the feeling of the character he was delineating. He stirred much controversy by raising his arms over his head, hitherto a movement frowned upon.

Like many actors, however, he was quite without modesty; he freely proclaimed his immense superiority. "The world has seen only two great actors: Roscius and myself. Every century has its Caesar; two thousand years are necessary to produce a Baron." Possibly because he felt lonely in his solitary eminence or was finally convinced there were no new dizzying heights for him to attain, he suddenly withdrew at the youthful age of thirty-eight. He stayed in retirement for three decades and then, near seventy, reappeared on the boards. He had immediate success and displayed growth in his interpretations and technique. A remarkable man, bold and innovative, his effect on his fellow actors was lasting.

Both Diderot and Voltaire urged actors to be more natural. In his *Paradoxe sur le comédien* and other essays Diderot called for realism in settings and costumes as well. He had also been annoyed by the foppish nobles who rimmed the acting space on stage and advocated getting rid of them. He declared that the new realistic plays should be in prose, which would of course obviate a good share of the musical declamation then in vogue.

Despite the progressive changes of Baron and the manifestos of Diderot and Voltaire, most acting held to the long-established manner. Two glamorous woman players of the epoch belonged to this school. Marie-Françoise de Champmeslé (1642–98) was more famed for the beauty and skilful use of her voice than her ability to simulate sincere emotion. Her pupil Marie-Anne Duclos (1668–1748) continued in this vein, to loud acclaim even after the declamatory style began to decline. Champmeslé's voice bewitched Racine, whose mistress she became, though she was married – he is said to have written many of his roles for her.

Legendary is Adrienne Lecouvreur (1692–1730), whose tragic story has been dramatized by Augustin Eugène Scribe and even provides the libretto (1902) for a minor but standard opera by Francesco Cilea. She tended towards "natural" acting; consequently when Baron returned to the stage it was to appear with her. Like Baron, she enchanted by her genuineness without losing a touch of "heroic grandeur". She deeply impressed Voltaire, who described her as "incomparable". As the star of the Comédie Française, and noted for the brilliance of her salon, she attracted the leaders of Parisian social and artistic circles.

Her lover, Maurice de Saxe, was the natural son of a German countess and the Elector of Saxony who later became King Augustus II of Poland. The affair between Lecouvreur and this illegitimate aristocrat was of long duration. Maurice, named Count of Saxony by his father, had to his credit an illustrious military career. His first marriage was annulled on the grounds of his infidelity. When asked to defend himself, he responded that he had "absolutely nothing" to say to the charge, that indeed his wife had not exaggerated.

To give him funds to advance himself, Adrienne sold her household and jewels. He rose to be Duke of Courland and promptly laid suit to a Polish duchess, but the marriage was prevented by the Russian and Polish governments. He returned to France. Obviously his fondness for his loyal Adrienne had waned. The Duchesse de Bouillon, fourth wife of the nobleman of that name, nurtured a passionate infatuation for Maurice. Supposedly she tried to dispose of her love rival, the famous actress, by a poisoning plot.

During a performance of *Phèdre* in 1729 Adrienne approached the theatre box from which the Duchess was watching and, gazing hard at her, recited Racine's lines about those who have practised to face the world without signs of hiding a crime. This caused a sensation, the audience recognizing the allusion and betraying its sympathies. Six months later Adrienne suddenly took ill and died – once again rumours of a poisoning spread throughout Paris. But the suspicion has never been proved.

Since she was an actress, albeit the most celebrated in France, she was denied a church burial. Her body was spirited from her dwelling at midnight and, like that of Molière, was interred in an unmarked grave. Her semi-royal lover did not mourn her long, if at all, but continued to show favour to her profession. Among many successors were Mlle Carton, a member of the chorus at the Opéra, and Mlle Chantilly, a stage name for Marie Justine Favart, the wife of a noted librettist and director of the Opéra Comique. Maurice, now a national hero and Marshal of France, used many harsh devices to rid himself of the unfortunate husband, including two *lettres de cachet* ordering his imprisonment on false charges. The young lady finally yielded her virtue to her determined suitor. But the reign of Madame Favart also ended. The Marshal's later love was a seventeen-year-old singer; she bore him a daughter who was destined to be the grandmother of novelist George Sand.

With the premature death of Lecouvreur, acting regressed to floridity. Voltaire struggled to have the ladies appearing in his tragedies exhibit a modicum of restraint, but he had little luck at persuading Marie Françoise Dumesnil (1713–1803) to modulate her portrayals. He had a bit more perhaps in the instance of Claire Josèphe Clairon (1723–1803), who erred by being too "natural" when she was his Electra.

He did enjoy hearing his poetic lines read sonorously. Mlle Dumesnil is said to have had little technique, but she could draw on emotional reserves for highly passionate moments. At other moments she dispensed with the "natural" and reached for the rhetorical "sublimity", and that also displeased Voltaire.

She was the favourite for many decades, performing long in a life that lasted ninety years. Mlle Clairon, possessed of physical beauty, was hailed by Garrick as "the perfect actress". Unlike Dumesnil, she prepared her roles meticulously and brought a wealth of imagination to them.

Among the men – apart from those becoming *commedia dell'arte* figures including Scaramouche and Dominique (the most notable being Giuseppe Domenico Biancolli) – admired performers were Quinault Dufresne, Henri Louis Lekain (1729–78) and François-Joseph Talma (1763–1826). Quinault Dufresne was a member of a famed theatrical family. Women found him very attractive. Voltaire, who frequently directed his own stage works, took a personal interest in the young Lekain and helped to train him. The youthful actor was far from good-looking but was talented and charming; he rose to leading parts at the Comédie Française where he was often paired and held his own with the tempestuous Mlle Clairon. He took on a series of Voltaire's heroes, as in *Zaïre* and *The Orphan of China*. He died young and was replaced by the handsome Talma, who survived the Revolution.

— 5 —

ENGLAND: THE RESTORATION

In 1649 Parliament tried His Majesty Charles I and sentenced him to death, and he was decapitated, to the shock of crowned heads everywhere in Europe. The execution was followed by conflict on the battlefield between the Cavaliers, loyal to the Stuart dynasty, and the Puritan dissidents.

Victory went to the opponents of the regime, who named Oliver Cromwell to serve as Lord Protector. Most of the Cavaliers fled abroad, chiefly to France to take shelter with its nobility.

The Puritans, finally empowered, issued an edict closing all playhouses and prohibiting theatre activity. As had happened centuries earlier in the eastern Roman Empire, the actors did not wholly abandon their calling. They sometimes performed surreptitiously, half hidden in out-of-the-way places. But any progress in the drama came to a full stop.

The players incessantly petitioned Parliament, asserting that they were honest citizens and begging that they be allowed to earn a living by their profession. Mostly Parliament chose not to hear them.

Two years after the death of Cromwell (1658), in the midst of a furious storm that alarmed the superstitious, the Stuarts were restored (1660) and life changed rapidly. The over-strict Puritans had exhausted popular support. Perhaps because the Cromwellian governors realized this, they had slightly relaxed the ban in 1656 and permitted one William Davenant to present an allegorical pageant that contained a fervent eulogy to the Protector. A few months later Davenant's operatic adaptation of Pierre Corneille's drama *The Siege of Rhodes* was staged. He presented the allegory, in emulation of the French, in a tennis court near Lincoln's Inn Fields, a site that at times was used for illegal performances that were raided by the police, who carted off the players as if they were criminals.

The producer of one such forbidden entertainment called *Claracilla* (1652) was Thomas Killigrew, a courtier who ultimately became Davenant's partner. The "opera" was put on in a hall, Rutland House. It was really a play with a minimal amount of music, but had it been described as merely a play it could not have obtained a licence. An "opera" was considered a more respectable offering.

The start of Restoration theatre was closely tied to William Davenant's courage and resourcefulness. His career as a playwright dated back to before the Civil War. Born in 1606, he was the son of a prosperous tavern-keeper (or vintner) at Oxford. The father was a lover of plays and playmakers, especially Shakespeare. Supposedly the poet frequently stayed at Davenant's inn on journeys to and from London, and legend has him godfather of the future dramatist. Further, goes the story, he may even have been the boy's true parent. Davenant never discouraged a rumour that he was Shakespeare's illegitimate offspring.

When the innkeeper died in 1622 he left instructions that his real or purported sixteen-year-old son William be sent to London and apprenticed there. But the independent youth obtained a post as page in the household of the Duke of Lennox, a cousin of James I; this began his long and sometimes close connection to the court. By 1627, when he was only twenty-one, his first play, *The Cruel Brother*, was produced at the Blackfriars. It failed. The actors would not accept his second work, *Albovine, King of the Lombards* (1629), which the resolute author then had published. Meanwhile the adventure-loving young Davenant joined two military expeditions led by the Duke of Buckingham against the French, both ending disastrously. Soon after he came back to London his tragicomedy *The Just Italian* (1629) was staged at the Blackfriars with success.

He put off writing for a long time, beset by illness of a venereal origin that was not treated. It left him with a disfigured nose and made him the victim of ridicule all his remaining days. Despite this handicap he married three times, improving his fortunes with each romantic foray. He was lucky in becoming a friend of Endymion Porter, a patron of the arts and a favourite of Charles I. When Davenant recovered enough to compose another play, *The Wits* (1634), he met objections from the Master of the Revels, but Porter bore the script to the King who read it with him, restored some of the deletions and granted permission for the performance at the Blackfriars. At last, Davenant had a success. The piece was subsequently acted at court. In it, two country gentlemen who are no longer very young come to London intending to advance their fortunes by taking advantage of rich women. Instead, a series of absurd mishaps befall them.

Charles I, though he disliked it, let it be enacted. It was revived twenty-five years later in a different societal and political climate and fared even better and thereafter was frequently restaged for many decades. It should be noted that in it city men, though knaves, triumph over dull-witted country folk.

Davenant followed *The Wits* with a tragicomedy, *Love and Honour* (1634), which earned the Queen's attention; she liked its "high-flown romanticism" which was the new vogue in England. Davenant was remarkably sensitive to rapid changes in taste, seizing on them quickly and furthering them. Though his talent was comparatively limited, his influence was to be very considerable.

The Queen commissioned him to compose a masque, *The Temple of Love* (1635), in collaboration with Inigo Jones. Her Majesty and the ladies of her entourage acted in it and then graced her royal presence with another, *The Triumph of the Prince D'Amour* (1636). Though reminiscent of John Fletcher at times, *Love and Honour* also anticipates the "heroic play" that is to follow in the next epoch. It concerns war and a dynastic struggle between families in Milan and Savoy. The characters are moved to heights of excessive virtue and evil and give voice to their exalted sentiments in inflated blank verse. An extravagantly mounted revival was a great success, too, during Restoration days. Members of the court, including Charles II and Prince James, lent their own finery to members of the company on that occasion. Samuel Pepys, the famous diarist, recounts in his journal that he liked the play so much he went to see it twice.

Two comedies, *News from Plymouth* (1635) and *The Platonic Lovers* (1636), followed in rapid succession, one realistic, the other romantic. The scene of the first is Sicily, for a script that pokes mild fun at the cult of "pure celestial love . . . abstracted from all corporal crass impressions" that was fashionable in the Queen's circle and flourished in France under the aegis of Madame de Rambouillet. The administration of an aphrodisiac by a learned doctor upsets the doctrines of the noble but over-spiritual ladies and gentlemen engaged in a court intrigue. At the end there is a double marriage and an admission: "There are Platonic lovers, though but few." On the whole the work is polished and graceful.

By now Davenant had won sufficient recognition as a literary figure so that, upon the death of Ben Jonson in 1637, he succeeded him as Poet Laureate, bringing him a pension of £100 annually. He continued with another play, *Unfortunate Lovers* (1638), and another masque, *Salmacidia Spolia* (1639). Both the King and Queen participated in this costly affair, the last of its kind before the outbreak of the Civil War. The same year Davenant was granted a permit to erect a new theatre, but now this was withdrawn. To requite him, he was anointed manager of the Cockpit's troupe.

With the start of hostilities Davenant joined the pro-royal forces and was knighted for his bravery in the siege of Gloucester. One of his duties was to smuggle arms and other supplies across the Channel. After the sentencing and execution of Charles I, the busy laureate became one of the cluster of exiles about the widowed Queen in Paris. When not engaged in political intrigues he worked on a poetic epic, *Gondibert*. In 1650, as a reward for his loyalty, he was named Governor of Maryland to replace Lord Baltimore, who adhered to the Puritan cause. Davenant set sail for the New World, but *en route* – he was still on the Channel – he was captured. He was taken to England and imprisoned.

A friend close to Cromwell got him released in 1652, and Davenant sought some means to return to the theatre. To start, he wed a wealthy French lady. Despite the hostile laws, he tried to form a company to erect a playhouse. He was blocked in this endeavour, and it was then that he boldly put on the pageant at Gibson's Tennis Court and, shortly afterwards, *The Siege of Rhodes.*

Since the authorities could find nothing offensive in them, he was able to proceed. Davenant had seen and learned much in Paris, and the music for *The Siege of Rhodes* – scanty but enough – was by the inspired composer Henry Lawes and was staged with machines and movable sets. Encouraged, he resumed his activity in the Cockpit, shrewdly selecting two patriotic plays, *The Cruelty of the Spaniards in Peru* and *The History of Sir Francis Drake*. Since Cromwell was at war with Spain, the government was inclined to look with favour on these rousing dramas. Growing still bolder, Davenant pushed onward with a sequel, *The Siege of Rhodes, Part II* (1659), once more but with less justification dubbed an opera. But the Puritans took exception and moved against him. Before any punitive action was decided on, however, Charles II returned to the throne. Davenant could now go on more openly.

With Killigrew, who organized the King's Company while he himself managed the Duke's Company, Davenant had sole control of London's two theatres. When the restoration of Charles II was clearly indicated, Davenant hastened to Paris to ingratiate himself with the new ruler.

Charles II had grown fond of play-going during his exile in France and Holland. Quite intelligent, he was also by nature pleasure-loving with a frivolous side, and he had the example of Louis XIV, observed at first hand, to guide him in seeking beguilement. The type of theatre now established by Davenant was particularly intended to please the royal taste as well as that of the courtiers surrounding the "Merry Monarch".

The royal return was hailed by hysterical mobs, but not everybody was happy to welcome the anointed heir. The Puritans gave up their leadership in public affairs, withdrew to their commercial enterprises and estates, and looked with stern disapproval on the new tone set by society. John Milton wrote *Paradise Lost* and John Bunyan his *Pilgrim's Progress* during this reign.

In securing his monopoly, Davenant had by means fair and foul driven other companies out of business: many had hurried to London, eager to re-establish themselves. The King, convinced that he should keep all theatrical activity in his own hands, issued "orders and patents" to that effect, vesting the direction of all stage affairs with Davenant and Killigrew. At first the Old Red Bull was available and after a short time was occupied by the King's Company. From there the actors transferred to Gibbon's Tennis Court on Vere Street, where there was only an impoverished platform stage now deemed inadequate.

The Duke's Company went into the Salisbury Court Theatre, while Lisle's Tennis Court was hurriedly remodelled and modern equipment was installed. What was needed was a new theatre, and the King's Company laid out money for a fine structure that was ready in May 1663; at the opening it was called the Theatre Royal. Later it was named the Drury Lane; after a fire it was replaced by a second playhouse of that name (1674) from designs by Christopher Wren.

For the next twenty-two years London had only two theatres; the Duke's Company finally put up a handsome building in 1671, somewhat larger than the Drury Lane. In Elizabethan days, when the city was much smaller, it had boasted six. In 1682 the two companies merged but continued to operate just the two playhouses for the ensuing thirteen years. What is more, the Restoration playhouses were small, the Drury Lane accommodating not over 500, the Duke's somewhat more, nor were the plays always well attended. Much of the time the plays lost money. Their appeal was too narrow. Now and then illegal minor companies sought to compete with the two established ones, but their efforts are of no consequence in theatre history.

The Drury Lane was of brick and timber, and roofed, topped by a windowed cupola through which daylight might pass, though that was of little help in winter or in London's grey spells. On cold, windy and rainy days the spectators might huddle in their wraps to keep dry. At first, performances began at 3.30 in the afternoon, hence the glass-sided cupola, but gradually the starting hour was delayed to 5.30. Ring-shaped chandeliers of fluttering wax candles lit the auditorium, and afterwards oil lamps served as footlights, lending a soft glow and enhancing the costumes.

There were no reserved seats, so servants might come well in advance to obtain good places for their employers. The pit had backless benches. On three sides of the oblong interior were boxes and above them two galleries, all decoratively gilded. The semicircular forestage and apron, matted and covered with green baize, protruded fifteen feet into the pit. A gold-painted and fancifully carved proscenium arch framed the stage. From the forestage to the furthest box was not quite thirty feet.

The orchestra, which played before the performance, during intermissions and at the end, was in a sunken space between the apron and the pit. This was an innovation, as heretofore music had floated down from a small balcony or a recessed room above the proscenium arch. The front curtain, once lifted, was not lowered until the end of the play; scene changes took place in full view of the audience. The floor of the stage had four rows of grooves allowing wing-flats to slide on and off, opening and closing each scene as the action unfolded. The painted wall of a room in a house could travel off, revealing a street or sylvan landscape behind it. By the same means, players could be "discovered" in a striking tableau in a new setting with an unbroken flow of the plot. To aid perspective, cut-out flats might give glimpses of distant vistas. The backdrop might also be painted with emphasis on sharp perspective for an added sense of depth.

The players entered chiefly through pairs of doors that opened on to the forestage, but the actors could also move directly from one scene area to another. It is believed that most of the action occurred on the forestage. Most works probably did not need new sets but could take advantage of those already on hand. The proscenium arch extended to the full width of the house.

The candles serving as footlights stood in cups that caught the dripping hot wax; there might also be a row of spikes to deter drunkards in the pit from attempting to climb on to the stage.

By the end of the century gallants were seated on the stage, as in France, though at first this was forbidden, as Charles II was annoyed by the practice. Puritans stayed away from the reopened playhouses. Thus Davenant's presentations were for a sophisticated élite. The Restoration stage was not, as it had been in Elizabeth's time, a democratic institution. Indeed, on occasion the general public was not even admitted. Contrary to previous custom, Charles II not only had special performances at Whitehall, his residence, but also attended the public theatres, in each of which a royal box was maintained. His frequent presence drew very welcome crowds.

The newer Duke's Theatre, being larger and having more stage machinery, was used more for operas and the more spectacularly mounted tragedies.

Even when His Majesty was present the onstage spectators were rude and inattentive; they offered audible caustic criticism, gossiped and even walked about paying visits. In the boxes, where the gentry sat, ladies wore vizards – half-masks – supposedly to conceal their identity. This encouraged flirtations and also made it easier for prostitutes to ply their trade. Sometimes performances were interrupted by loud quarrels and even fatal duels. The theatre was a social gathering place and had an intimate atmosphere that promoted risk-taking and scandal. Much as one went to the promenade in St James's Park, one attended the theatre to be seen and to observe what was happening in London's upper social strata. Between acts, fruit sellers called their wares. One of the best known of these was Orange Moll who for a while hired as one of her helpers a girl named Nell Gwynn, later a celebrated actress admired in light roles and even better remembered as mistress of Charles II.

Tickets to performances cost two shillings and sixpence in the pit, four shillings in the boxes, eighteen pence in the middle gallery and a shilling for the upper gallery to which servants accompanying their masters were admitted free for the last act. Such "tickets" were actually round metal tokens (that could be used repeatedly, hence saving money), though paper was occasionally printed for a benefit or other special event. A strange custom was that anyone was allowed in without a "ticket" to hear the music and see the first act. Presumably this was a way to drum up business; if interested, the spectators would stay on and watch the remainder. Consequently a suspenseful first act was essential. Double prices were charged for a first night.

There were no programmes to read. The plays were advertised by posters and handbills; some were tossed into passing carriages or sedan chairs or left at the doors of fashionable houses.

Davenant found that the supply of boys who could impersonate women had almost run out, so he introduced the casting of actresses in feminine roles. This move had the ready compliance of the King, who declared that such a change would heighten morality. Charles II, of course, had grown used during his Continental exile to seeing women on stage, and his motives were probably not as pure as he professed. Within a decade, by 1670, the capture of leading parts by actresses was wholly accomplished.

The level of morality was certainly not raised; the very opposite happened. At first the women drawn to acting were notoriously promiscuous, while most of the characters they were asked to portray were meant to be modest and very ladylike, representing the nobility and upper class. It took time for Davenant to gather enough players whose upbringing and family backgrounds equipped them to behave like duchesses and princesses.

Another consequence was that authors were called upon to enlarge the roles of women, to add more and increase their lines in classic works, even Shakespeare's. Miranda was given a sister and Ariel a distaff companion.

Annals of the period supply the names of several popular ladies who graced the stage, not only the pert, pretty Nell Gwynn who, though she was an illiterate cockney, has become legendary, but also Ann Bracegirdle, Anne Oldfield, Elizabeth Barry, an orphan brought up in Davenant's household with whom the playwright Thomas Otway was infatuated, and Moll Davis, also a favourite of the King. Among the most admired actors were Thomas Betterton, Jack Verbruggen, John Lacy, Edward Kynaston and Charles Hart.

The praise accorded Thomas Betterton by the public and his fellow actors makes extravagant reading. Colly Cibber, himself a very successful writer, producer and player of the time, wrote this tribute: "The most that a Vandyke can arrive at is to make his portraits of great persons seem to think; a Shakespeare goes farther yet and tells you what his pictures thought; a Betterton steps beyond 'em all, and calls them from the grave to breathe and be themselves again in feature, speech, and motion." He adds: "You must have been present at it! 'Tis not to be told you!"

Betterton also taught newcomers to the companies, shaping a new generation of actors. For this he got an extra fifty guineas a year.

Many others were also thought to be highly accomplished, some in tragedy, others in comedy. The older men, who were shareholders in the companies, tended to behave responsibly and respectably offstage, but some of the younger and lesser known were ill famed for wenching, drinking, rioting and debauchery. Actors were accorded many privileges; they could not be impressed for military service, arrested for a misdemeanour or sued for a debt – because they were under the protection of the Lord Chamberlain, who could punish them. To obtain a post with either company, a young aspirant would have to serve a three-month apprenticeship without pay.

Acting styles for both sexes were far from "neutral". As in France, a physical vocabulary was passed on from one generation of performers to apprentices in the next. So familiar and conventionalized were the gestures that it is said a spectator who could not hear well had a good chance of following the action by merely observing the actors' hands. A lover, in despair, assumed the stance of a hanged corpse, hands dangling, head tilted to the side or wandered about sighing, a hand on his heart, hat drawn low on his forehead. He suggested his obsession by an unswerving gaze at the object of his affection, while he folded his arms across his chest, again sighing heavily to indicate his pang. If he pointed to his brow or let a finger touch it, he was deep in thought. In other circumstances, his right hand pressed to his heart was meant to express an emotion of pity, grief or tenderness. Looking upward in a heroic tragedy he was addressing the gods and downward he was calling upon or defying infernal spirits. Shading his eyes, he gazed into the distance. He might fall to his knees to plead, extend his arms palms up to yield or, when standing, step back a pace or two to indicate astonishment. The ladies had to be adept at languishing, swooning gracefully, for they were often called upon to do so.

Comics, in particular, had to speak briskly, since their scripts abounded in bright repartee. The well-trained actor had to master a variety of vulgar, rustic dialects: much of the humour came from a patronizing contrast between elegant city and rude country ways. Folk beliefs and behaviours were not inserted for colour but for derisive laughs.

The male performer had to know how to fence, be acrobatically agile, curtsy, dance, sing and walk with a strut or a mincing gait.

For tragedy, firm voice control was necessary. A long speech, or "rant", mounted gradually to a full climax, with the actor, his face florid, shouting as he attained the finish. The tragedian's tone was required to be musical always, above all in long love passages and death scenes. Expiring he grimaced, stuttered and gasped to end on "a musical note".

To add to the artificiality of the acting, playwrights became ever fonder of asides and soliloquies; the intimacy of the Restoration theatre, with actor and audience near to each other, encouraged this. Supposedly, when the character betrayed his innermost thoughts to the spectators he was not overheard by the others sharing the scene with him.

Costuming was still mostly contemporary, as it had been in the Elizabethan and Jacobean theatre. Julius Caesar, for example, would be garbed like an eighteenth-century English gentleman. Now and then a period or exotic touch such as a tunic or scarf would be added to hint that the locale of the story was Turkey, Peru, Athens or Rome. The incongruity seemed to bother no one. The company supplied the outer attire. What counted most was that the dress should make a bold show. Male cast members had to provide their own periwigs, shoes and stockings, the ladies their own head-coverings, petticoats, gloves and personal garments.

Pepys, when he visited backstage, was disenchanted at the actual stuffs of which some of the "rich" dress was made and its tawdry condition. As was the long-standing custom, the men's resplendent clothing might consist of cast-off finery donated by the aristocracy. He remarks in his diary that much of its beauty onstage was due to the golden hue imparted by the candlelight.

In the tradition inherited from the masques, scenery might be elaborately decorative, though it was often simple, too, for reasons of economy, with certain stock-sets such as drawing-rooms, terraces overlooking a garden or smooth green lawns being used again and again.

Sound effects including cannon shots, fireworks, thunder and bells were added, as well as a full assortment of properties such as blunt swords, collapsible daggers and sheep's blood in a sponge or bladder that would spurt forth when pierced.

With the aid of stage-machines and trap-doors, ghosts and spirits could ascend or vanish, and witches flew, clouds lowered and suns and moons climbed or sunk. Operas, for which tickets were more expensive, usually called for the most spectacular effects.

With only two companies to write for, and only two producers to satisfy, dramatists had to create parts that could be aptly enacted by permanent members of the troupe, some of whom played only types; this accounts for much of the sameness of characterization in the scripts. For the same reason, great histrionic demands could not be made, since the actresses in particular were inexperienced – as already noted, the task of recruiting them was at first very difficult. Ladies of refinement would scarcely wish to appear on stage, and yet the comedies called for heroines well schooled in polite comportment.

Other reasons for the similarity of many roles were the delight audiences took in seeing women in male attire, the so-called "breeches parts", and the fact that the period promoted a style of dress betokening the wearer's rank and occupation. The plot-device of the disguise occurs in play after play. Of course no spectator was ever deceived into thinking a girl was really a boy, or was surprised at the final "unmasking". It was simply another convention that the audience took without cavilling because it liked to see young women in such unlikely dress. To behold a young lady's calf and ankle on stage was a highly stimulating novelty.

Clothing indicated the wearer's status and social role, and this also made the over-frequent plot-device of disguise acceptable and significant. A lady's maid, donning her mistress's gown, could deceive a gallant as to what she really was. The society was one in which "clothes made the man", and characters would be taken at face value depending on their garb at the moment. The audience was prepared to go along with this convention, too. Without it, the plots of many Restoration comedies would be too implausible.

For biographers, William Wycherley (1641–1715) presents many contradictions. Clive in Shropshire was his birthplace. His father sent the boy, only fifteen, to France to further his education at the salon of Madame de Rambouillet's daughter. This suggests that his family had wealth or influence or both. In England again, he entered Queen's College, Oxford, but did not matriculate. Instead he left the university and gained admission to the Inner Temple (1659) but then just as abruptly gave up the study of law and next aspired to be a courtier. Obviously he was trying to find his true vocation. He was to be a dramatist, a career probably inspired by his acquaintance with the works of Sir George Etherege (1636–92), though he tried to efface any traces of that source.

His first script, *Love in a Wood*, was produced in 1671; however, he claimed that it had been written a dozen years earlier (he would have been about eighteen), to have it seem that it predated Etherege's initial script. Wycherley was perhaps too conscious of his debt to his fellow writer. He also wished to pose as merely a cultivated amateur, a gentleman dabbling at pieces for the stage, which in fact Etherege had been. Many scholars, however, controvert Wycherley as to the date of the play's composition, placing it shortly before its presentation. Was he about thirty or a remarkably gifted prodigy in his late teens?

His subsequent career was wide-ranging, but his stint as a playwright lasted only three or four years, ending when he reached thirty-four – though he lived to reach seventy-six.

Wycherley was handsome and like Etherege he was a busy amorist, counting among his conquests the notoriously promiscuous Duchess of Cleveland, a mistress of Charles II. Therefore, when he dedicated himself to erotic comedy, he knew whereof he spoke. His name is usually joined with those of Etherege and William Congreve as the foremost comic dramatist of his time.

Love in a Wood was an immediate hit, though today's critics tend to think none too well of it. It borrows somewhat not only from Etherege but also from Sir Charles Sedley (1639?–1701), whose *The Mulberry-garden* (1668) is set in St James's Park where there was a fashionable promenade. (One recalls Sir Fopling Flutter saying, "All the world will be in the park tonight.")

Sedley, as rumour had it, was the original of Medley, Dorimant's friend in Etherege's *The Man of Mode*. He was a poet, a translator, a songwriter, a dramatist and an urbane jokester, combining in his person a disconcerting meld of qualities.

The plot of *Love in a Wood* is too complicated; it has been compared to the brambles and thickets of the park in which its overly intricate action occurs. There are passages that are witty and satiric. Like Etherege's *The Comical Revenge* it couples a serious theme and a comic one. Wycherley's satire is more earnest than that of most of his contemporaries.

His dialogue is not notably felicitous, nor is it memorable for epigrams. He is not lightly contemptuous but deeply critical, attacking the society he depicts. His anger, as he progresses, is even more marked. Yet he is still very amusing. He is at once the coarsest and, in his own estimation, the most "moral" of the Restoration school.

In *Love in a Wood* most of the fops, gallants and foolish or lovesick ladies are in search of marriages and property; their motives are overwhelmingly mercenary, though not wholly so. It is like *Vanity Fair*, thickly populated with one-dimensional characters with names like Sir Simon Addleplot, Lady Flippant, Gripe, Dapperwit and Ranger. At the last curtain, justice is meted out; a widowed fortune hunter is wed to a penniless knight, a rake accedes to a girl he sought to mislead, a gallant gets an alderman's pregnant daughter (the child's father is not her husband-to-be). A Puritan is exposed as a hypocrite, paid off by being matched to a lady of dubious virtue. The moral is that hardly anyone has been able to better themselves; their social climbing has been in vain.

Better is *The Gentleman Dancing-Master* (1671), with a plot taken from the Spanish master Calderón. The cast of five is also smaller. In this play, Hippolita is to be married against her will to a "cousin", the foolish M. de Paris, by command of her father, the fanatical Don Diegue. She resorts to a desperate scheme to save herself, obtaining by trickery from her fiancé the name of the man reputedly the most gallant in the city. She summons him, using her husband-to-be as her unwitting agent. As instructed, this gallant Gerrard breaks into her house. His curiosity has prompted him, and he beholds and is stunned by her beauty and charm; none the less, he is naturally wary, puzzled by the strange situation in which he finds himself.

She pretends to be naïve, though it is obvious that she is really shrewd and resourceful. He seeks to seduce her, and she agrees to an elopement without delay. But the arrival of her father and her ever-watchful, sour old aunt, Mrs Caution, thwarts this plan.

To explain his presence, Gerrard awkwardly passes himself off as a dancing-master. Once again the youthful pair are left alone and have a chance to escape, but this time Hippolita demurs, suddenly voicing doubts about Gerrard's true feelings – this is because she is falling in love with him. She suggests that they run off together at a later time, which they fix, and she tells him to leave and make preparations.

He returns. She confesses that she has been lying to him and tells him, among other things, that she has no dowry. He is willing to have her even so, and still she hesitates; he reveals his profound infatuations and awakened jealousy. Convinced of the sincerity of his passion, Hippolita consents to wed him and confesses that she does have a fortune.

In the early part of the play Gerrard speaks to her in an artificial and inflated style and she keeps up her appearance of unworldliness. But now their pattern of speech changes; they are two intellectual and rational persons striving to reach an understanding, in hopes that their relationship will be a lasting one. He has met and passed with honours a traditional "trial of love", not unlike the test administered by Harriet to Dorimant in *The Man of Mode*, except that in Etherege's play the resolution is not fully disclosed.

New York was recently treated to an off-Broadway revival of *The Gentleman Dancing-Master* at the Pearl Theatre (2005). A reviewer for the *Village Voice* commented: "Director Gus Kaikkonen encourages his actors to enjoy the plays, jokes and gibes, as well as the rustles and bustles of their costumes."

Of Wycherley's quartet of plays, *The Country Wife* (1674–5) is probably the most often revived and the most amusing by far. Along with Congreve's *The Way of the World* it is possibly today's favourite among all Restoration comedies. At the same time it is one of the most "lewd". Its plot, lifted from Terence's *The Eunuch*, is almost 2,000 years old and centres on Horner. With the aid of a Dr Quack, this unscrupulous rake spreads the whispered rumour of his sexual impotence. His friends cruelly snigger at his disability and have no qualms about leaving him alone with their wives, with whom he has illicit affairs. To apply his own phrase, he is a "Machiavel in love".

Actually Horner is disdainful of women, but he takes great satisfaction in laying plots involving them. Word of his sexual prowess flies about among the ladies, who are irresistibly drawn to him. Among his willing "victims" is Margery Pinchwife, the lusty amoral young "country wife" of an old man. She has just come to London, hears of the redoubtable Horner and is eager to meet this fabulous "capon". Hers is a barnyard realism. She so much enjoys her romp in bed with the redoubtable Horner that for a time she even refuses to go back to her doddering mate.

Meanwhile, Mr Pinchwife's friends defuse his suspicions about his wife, asserting that her association with Horner can only be harmless since he is supposedly "*hors de combat*" after a bout with the "French disease". The anxious Mr Pinchwife is also persuaded that his wife is an innocent, too simple and guileless to have committed flagrant adultery. The end finds the "country wife" reluctantly departing to rusticity again, and Horner continuing his merry way, unhampered in his lechery.

In a sub-plot, Harcourt seeks Mrs Pinchwife's more citified sister-in-law Althea. She reciprocates his feelings but insists that she must remain faithful to her fiancé, the dull Sparkish, because he deeply trusts her. Her dilemma is happily resolved when she discovers by a trick that miscarries that Sparkish has only a mercenary interest in her. His "trust" has only been a proof of his self-centredness; he has not cared for her at all.

The three decorous ladies who, unbeknown to one another, have been mistresses of Horner simultaneously while endlessly protesting their virtue, are exposed as shams.

Molière, as well as Terence, provided Wycherley with material for his robust farce; there are liberal helpings from *The School for Husbands* and *The School for Wives*. But Molière never handles a subject as indelicately as Wycherley has here. Innuendos and broad *double entendres* are frequent, as in the famed "china" scene, where Horner, using as an excuse that he is selling off his porcelains, is actually taking advantage of the ladies who visit him, while the deceived husband of one and the aged mother of another wait in the next room. *The Country Wife* has been castigated by generations of critics, including Lord Macaulay and Allardyce Nicoll, for its passages of gross indecency – or healthy vulgarity, depending on one's personal taste – but no one denies that it is uproariously funny; and play-goers in the twentieth century, their moral standards emancipated to the utmost, have gleefully rediscovered it.

Born a Protestant, though of a family opposed to the Puritans, Wycherley was converted to Catholicism during his youth in France, a defection that much provoked his family. Though he reverted to his former faith, it seems he became sceptical of all religious and ethical codes. He believed that man should give full vent to his natural instincts. This hedonistic philosophy, permitting libertinage, was doubtless reinforced when the success of his first two plays gained him admission to the Earl of Rochester's circle of decadent wits, where he exchanged quips with Etherege, Buckingham, Killigrew, Sedley and others of their brazen ilk.

With *The Country Wife* Wycherley had shaken off Etherege's pervasive artistic influence. Though the plot of the play is derivative, its style and the portrait drawing are rather much his own. The people exemplify "humours", as Ben Jonson defined comic characters; that is, they are dominated by a single obsessive trait, an inherited glandular imbalance such as avidity, jealousy or vanity, that leads them to behave foolishly and predictably.

His next and last play, *The Plain Dealer* (1671), owes a large debt to Molière's *Le Misanthrope*: "He that distrusts most of the world, trusts most to himself, and is but the more easily deceiv'd, because he thinks he can't be deceiv'd . . . Knew he loved his own singular moroseness so well, as to dote upon any copy of it; wherefore I feign'd an hatred of the World too, that he might love me in earnest."

Manly, a sea captain who prefers solitude on the bellowing main to life in festering cities, has been on a long voyage. Before his departure he entrusts several thousand pounds of gold and jewels to his false-hearted fiancée Olivia, and asks his close friend Vernish to watch over her.

The plan is that after their marriage Manly and Olivia will emigrate to the West Indies. Vernish, however, weds Olivia in secret. Meanwhile, though his sailors admire Manly's heroism at sea, he loses his ship and the other half of his treasure in an encounter with the Dutch. The play begins with Manly's reappearance in London. He has still to learn what has happened in his absence.

Two friends are true to him, one his good-natured lieutenant, Freeman, and the other his page, Fidelia, who is a girl disguised as a boy – a "breeches part". Implausibly, Manly is not aware of the sex of Fidelia, who loves him. He hearkens to Olivia and Vernish, who are gulling him. The "fops and fools" who crowd the London scene, seeking to ingratiate themselves with anyone of wealth or power, also surround him. Freeman, who is poor, hopes to better himself by marriage to a rich woman. He, like Philinte in Molière's comedy, believes that one must conform to society and be guided by its values.

Manly, discovering that Olivia has made off with his money and refuses to give it back, is appalled. He plans to wed someone else, unaware that Oliver has already married Vernish. Indeed, the beauteous if fickle Olivia has many suitors.

Wycherley's tone in *The Plain Dealer* is savage. Though he fully participated in the life of his times, particularly as a member of a degenerate coterie, he obviously despised his fellows and their society. He has little of Molière's gentle detachment or tolerance. He dedicated this last work to the theatre.

Manly is a violent sensualist. He is not suave or elegant like Dorimant, or cynical like Horner, but is fanatical in his railings against his world. As is the case with Alceste, his opinions are bitterly true, but they are absurd because they are carried too far.

Manly is in love with Olivia, who is merely leading him on. She pretends to concur with his condemnation of the vicious follies of conniving women, all the while embodying an evil representation of that very circle. Her alert, roaming gaze takes in the presumed youth, Fidelia, and she arranges a rendezvous with him.

Appraised of this, the hot-tempered Manly plots revenge. He still desires her and cannot erase her image from his passionate erotic thoughts, so he changes places with Fidelia and in darkness enters Olivia's bed and satisfies himself that he has fully possessed her. This violent cure for his increasing melancholy works exceedingly well for him, though it presents Fidelia – who herself deeply loves him – with very difficult moments, compounded when Vernish discovers "him", attacks "him" and, pulling off the wig and grasping the "boy's" bosom, realizes that Fidelia is a girl. Vernish immediately tries to rape her, but a mishap providentially stops him.

Manly still wishes to punish and expose the wicked Olivia. He returns a second time, again posing as Fidelia but is accompanied by witnesses. On this occasion he finds out that her husband is the equally false Vernish, who has been lying in wait, intending to murder him. In this fight Fidelia once more loses her wig. The villain fails in his attempt, and at last Manly perceives that the boy is a lovely young woman – learns that she is an heiress as well. After a series of events viewed sardonically, the play ends happily, yet even more than *The Misanthrope* it is often on the brink of tragedy.

Singled out for the bitterest satiric treatment in this dark comedy is the legal profession. Mrs Blackacre, "a petulant, litigious widow" surrounded by a covey of lawyers, enjoys filing costly lawsuits. Her targets include Blunder, Plodon, Quaint, Epilteause and Buttgawn. (Wycherley, who studied law for a while, doubtless had observed first hand the bribery and corrupt practices in Westminster Hall. His father, a perpetual litigant, could have provided his son with a model to copy.)

The widow Blackacre is pursued by the foolish, bold if ageing Major Oldfox and also by Freeman. The latter contrives to extort the annual sum of £300 from her. So, as can be seen, the play differs in details very much from *The Misanthrope*.

Surprisingly, London welcomed it. The eminent critic John Dryden exalted it. Wycherley was handled as a moralist and reformer. Indeed, *The Plain Dealer* might well have been the work of a Puritan, such was the fervency with which he described London's hollowness and viciousness. His audience, especially his most debauched friends, applauded his criticism of their way of life, though the play – a triumph at the Drury Lane – did not seem to affect them or change their ways in the least. The merry escapades at court and in the city went on undeterred.

The Plain Dealer marked the close of Wycherley's venture into theatre. He had gained the King's special liking. The monarch had even paid a visit to the playwright's bedside when Wycherley was ill and given him money for restorative travel to France and also considered appointing him tutor to the Duke of Richmond, the royal son.

But the King was angered by Wycherley's secret marriage to a widow, the Duchess of Drogheda. Legend says that she first attracted the playwright's attention when he was loitering in a bookstore and overheard her asking for a copy of *The Plain Dealer*, just issued. He lived extravagantly and had large debts, and a match with a lady of wealth seemed to promise salvation – but it was a mistake. Not only did it cost him the King's favour, but the lady, who was imperious and ill tempered, proved to have a jealous disposition and kept a close, irksome watch on him. Even worse, he contracted yet more debts, confident that he was able to pay them off, but in 1681, when his wife died suddenly, he found himself heir to little or nothing. Her estate was tied up in endless lawsuits, and he could touch none of it. He was cast into debtor's prison for seven years.

Charles II died. The incarcerated Wycherley was converted to Catholicism a second time – the date is not clear. James II succeeded his brother on the throne. The new King, perhaps inspired by a successful revival of *The Plain Dealer*, had him released by paying his debts and awarding him a pension. Wycherley returned to his ancestral home. By now he was nicknamed "Manly Wycherley". He was, however, said to be far more amiable than his saturnine hero. Men, and especially women, found him to be good company.

He spent much of his time rereading Seneca, the Jesuit Baltasar Gracián, Montaigne and Rochefoucauld, apparently still wrestling with his innate scepticism and the rational spirit of the age, which was in conflict with his inborn religiosity. He also turned out reams of bad verse and became a mentor of young Alexander Pope, who sought to improve if not correct the old man's rhymed output. Wycherley suffered, among other things, a strong impairment of his memory and became very repetitive. He also mourned the loss of his good looks.

Age did not stop Wycherley's wenching, though; he continued his pursuit of the ladies. At seventy-five, ten days before his death, he married once more, a young girl who inherited the few hundred pounds left in his diminished estate. His purpose was to provide for the girl, pay off most of his creditors' claims, and thwart a nephew who was his rightful heir. His last request to his young wife was that she would promise never again to marry an old man.

Quite the opposite in temperament and manner was Sir John Vanbrugh (1664–1726), a most improbable playwright. His Flemish grandfather, Gillis van Brugg, had fled from Spanish persecution in Ghent during the reign of the first Stuart King of England, James I.

John demonstrated so much talent with brush and pencil that his by now assimilated family sent him to Paris to study art. For a brief time he trained as an architect. At twenty-one he was back in England and a year or so later enlisted in the army where his first-hand knowledge of France was of value to the military. In 1690 he was caught in Calais and charged as a spy. He had a captain's rank. Finally freed, he took up dramatic writing, a fresh change of career.

He had chosen wisely, and in a short six weeks, by his own account, he conceived, wrote out and helped to stage a hilarious farce, *The Relapse* (1696). He quickly followed it with *The Provok'd Wife* (1697), which was even more fabulously successful.

Vanbrugh himself was not an affected man-about-town or a *flameur* like Etherege, though he wrote about such characters. Rather, he was a well-tailored gallant. He is described as having been the personification of John Bull, "rough, jolly, good-natured", "fond of food, and a heavy drinker". He is, of course, noted for being one of England's foremost architects, first as assistant to Wren and then as designer of Castle Howard and Blenheim, the magnificent and massive ancestral residence of the Marlboroughs and the birthplace of Winston Churchill.

He was also represented by the new opera house in Haymarket. A master of the Baroque style, his talent was for edifices on a vast scale. He possessed a most unusual combination of differing artistic gifts as expressions of a bluff, vigorous personality.

The idea for the *The Relapse, or Virtue in Danger* came to him after he saw *Love's Last Shift* or *The Fool in Fashion* (1696) by the actor-producer Colley Cibber. The hero of Cibber's script is Loveless, a reformed rake. (More shall be said about this play hereafter.) Vanbrugh scoffed at the ending of *Love's Last Shift* as too sentimental; he did not think a rake could repent and be changed into a faithful husband as quickly or as permanently as Cibber had him do. *The Relapse* concerns the further adventures of the same Loveless, who becomes helplessly obsessed with the charms of Berinthia, cousin of his formidably virtuous wife, Amanda. Especially amusing is a moment when Loveless sweeps Berinthia up into his arms and bears her off to a bedchamber, while she objects "[*Very Softly*]: Help! Help!"

As part of the plot, too, Young Worthy seeks to seduce the chaste Amanda but fails; his emotion after that is elevated to one of "sentimental adoration". But it is the other characters, the resurrected Lord Foppington, the country squire Sir Tunbelly Clumsey and the nymphomaniacal Miss Hoyden, who get the most laughs. Sir Tunbelly, keeping sharp watch over this exuberant young lady, believes her to be wholly innocent of the world and the nature of things masculine:

"Poor girl, she'll be scared out of her wits on her wedding night, for, honestly speaking, she does not know a man from a woman but by his beard and his breeches."

He is greatly mistaken about her, however. Miss Hoyden can scarcely await an introduction to the wedding bed. "It's well I have a husband a-coming, or egod, I'd marry the baker, I would so." She protests against the strict guard constantly placed over her: "Nobody can knock at the gate but presently I must be locked up; and here's the young greyhound bitch can run loose about the house all day long, she can." Her hand is sought by Tom Fashion, but Sir Tunbelly wishes to have the sanctifying ceremony postponed at least a week. This is much too long. "A week! – why, I shall be an old woman by that time."

A fresh aspect of *The Relapse* is that the scene is taken out of the city to the country, though the folk there are shown to be buffoons. In a good revival, this farce is still funny. When recently brought back in London, people left the theatre with tears in their eyes from laughing so much.

No one was more pleased than Colley Cibber by the success of *The Relapse*, and Vanbrugh chose him for the role of Lord Foppington once more.

The Provok'd Wife is even better. Sir John Brute, a coarse roisterer, loathes his married state. Here is the opening soliloquy:

> What cloying meat is love, when matrimony's the sauce to it! Two years' marriage has debauched my five senses. Everything I see, everything I hear, everything I feel, everything I smell, and everything I taste, methinks, has wife in't. No boy was ever so weary of his tutor, nor girl of her bib, no nun of doing penance, or old maid of being chaste, as I am of being married. Sure, there's a secret curse entailed upon the very name of wife. My lady is a young lady, a fine lady, a witty lady, a virtuous lady, and yet, I hate her.

His wife, poor woman, is indeed charming and long-suffering. Lady Brute has an attractive suitor, Constant, who dreams of leading her astray, but though drawn to him, she resists temptation.

Her niece, Belinda, is also fond of a sharp-tongued young blade, Heartfree. Like Sir Brute, who is a loud, self-professed misogynist, Heartfree is determined to elude matrimony.

> I always consider a woman, not as the tailor, the shoe-maker, the tire-woman, the seamstress, and (which is more than all that) the poet makes her; but I consider her as pure nature has contrived her, and that more strictly than I should have done out old grandmother Eve, had I seen her naked in the garden; for I consider her turned inside out. Her heart well examined, I find there pride, vanity, covetousness, indiscretion; but above all things, malice: plots eternally forging to destroy one another's reputations, and as honestly to charge the levity of men's tongues with the scandal; hourly debates how to make poor gentlemen in love with

> them, with no other intent but to use them like dogs when they have done; a constant desire of doing more mischief, and an everlasting war waged against truth and good-nature.

When Constant protests, "Very well, sir, an admirable composition truly!" Heartfree goes on:

> Then for her outside, I consider it merely as an outside; she has a thin, tiffany covering; just over such stuff as you and I are made of. As for her motion, her mien, her airs, and all those tricks, know they affect you mightily. If you should see your mistress at a coronation, dragging her peacock's train, with all her state and insolence about her, it would strike you with all the awful thoughts that heaven itself could pretend to form you: whereas, I turn the whole matter into a jest, and suppose her strutting, in the self-same strutting manner, with nothing on but her stays, and her scanty quilted under-petticoat.

In a cruel jest, Heartfree sends an unsigned letter to Lady Fanciful, a town belle, inviting her to meet him in the park. When she responds, attended by her French maid, Belinda, Heartfree insults her, saying that her affected airs and overuse of cosmetics have made her a laughing-stock. Lady Fanciful immediately falls in love with this rude fellow. The confidence that she has in her own beauty and style is immeasurable, and much of the humour of the play arises from her incessant self-flattery. "Is it possible," she demands, almost in awe, gazing into a hand glass, "my eyes can be so languishing, so very full of fire?" Again, she exclaims: "'Tis an utterable pleasure to be adored by all men, and envied by all the women. Yes, I'll swear, I'm concerned at the torture I give them. Lard! Why was I formed to make the whole creation uneasy?"

Her French maid Belinda, in self-interest, encourages her every folly. Says this mademoiselle, when Lady Fanciful asks if one should disobey one's intellect, "*Oui* . . . Because my nature make me worry, my reason make me mad."

Belinda and Lady Brute also venture in the park in a spirit of rebellion on a lark. Constant, who continues to woo the unhappy, ill-treated Lady Brute, draws her aside into an arbour. Lady Fanciful observes them.

Their paths are also crossed by Sir Brute himself, reeling drunkenly from a bout in a tavern and on his way to another. He becomes embroiled in an altercation with some watchmen, near Covent Garden, and to escape puts on the dress of a girl and is mistaken for one by constables who arrest him for breaching the peace. He is hauled before a justice but manages to disengage himself from the charge and staggers home.

Meanwhile, Lady Brute and Belinda have invited Constant and Heartfree to their house to play cards, not expecting the habitually inebriated Sir Brute to return before dawn at the earliest.

Fearing their presence will be misinterpreted, the two gallants scamper into a closet, where presently Sir Brute discovers them hiding, to the embarrassment of all. Sir Brute threatens everybody but is too drunk to do much more than verbally abuse his wife, then fall into a deep stupor.

Overnight Lady Brute concocts an explanation: the young blade and his friend had come to the house because Heartfree wishes to press his suit for Belinda's hand. He is ready to relinquish his single-blessedness and assume this new role, but Sir Brute's suspicions of his wife are not readily dispelled. When Constant challenges him to a duel, however, the timorous Sir Brute – more a bully than he is brave – suddenly practises the better part of valour, that is, discretion. As he puts it, it is better to be a "loving clog" than a "dead loon".

The domineering Sir Brute is a commanding figure, "stinking like a pig covered with dirt", and shouting, cursing and belching. In later decades it was a favourite role elected by the great actor David Garrick. To him are given such lines as "I never drunk my wife's health in my life, but I puked in my glass", as well as "If I were married to a hogshead of claret, matrimony would make me hate it." And "If women had been ready created the devil, instead of being kicked down into Hell, had been married." (Vanbrugh's contemporaries testified that he himself was rough-tongued and spoke in a manner resembling Brute's. Subtlety, they attested, was not one of this author's attributes.)

Seeking vengeance, Lady Fanciful writes a series of letters asserting that Belinda is pregnant and Heartfree is already married to someone else. However, Razor, Belinda's suitor, has a change of heart and Heartfree's marriage to her can be consummated. Sir Brute and the unfortunate Lady Brute are still in bond to each other, and the wife's seriously endangered virtue is still intact. Constant is left to yearn for her.

Though shallow and wicked, Lady Fanciful is still an engaging figure with her ridiculous pretensions and graces. Here Vanbrugh caricatured the feminine equivalent of the androgynous fops now a stock feature of the Restoration stage.

His plays depend on the physical action of hustle and bustle to elicit and sustain laughter, though the plot of *The Provok'd Wife* has a high degree of suspense as the spectator awaits the resolution of Lady Brute's dilemma.

Dryden said: "Vanbrugh . . . took the writings of others and made what he could of them; he took life as he found it and left it there."

Vanbrugh's subsequent scripts include *Aesop* (1696–7) and *The Mistake* (1705). With William Congreve and William Walsh he adapted Molière's *comédie-ballet Monsieur de Pourceaugnac*. The English title chosen by the collaborators for Molière's offering was *Squire Trelooby* (1704). A countryman visits the capital and attends a play; the world of theatre is strange to him, and his response is crude.

Left unfinished, *A Journey to London* was brought to completion by the actor-producer Colley Cibber, who renamed it *The Provok'd Husband* in 1728, two years after Vanbrugh's death. In it, a wife who is heedless and extravagant is frightened into mending her ways when her spouse threatens to divorce her. Cibber emasculated the work and introduced an element of sentimentality into it: while Vanbrugh intended that the erring lady should be guilty and that her wrathful mate should turn her away, Cibber had her prove to be innocent. Much of Vanbrugh's vigour remains and shines through, however, because the writing is rich in colloquialisms and folk epithet.

Vanbrugh's *The Confederacy* (1705), also adapted from a Dancourt farce, *Les Bourgeoises à la mode*, was probably his most "immoral" farce. A housewife, Clarissa, falls deeply into debt, and a valuable necklace she owns cannot save her. She is hounded by the wife of Moneytrap, an extortionate lender. The pawnbroker, Mrs Amlet, has a son Dick, a rascal with designs on Corinna, the daughter of a man called Gripe. Dick passes himself off as a colonel. He is assisted in this imposture by Brass, who pretends to be the "colonel's" footman, and by Corinna.

Moneytrap falls in love with Gripe's wife, while Gripe is smitten by Moneytrap's. The two women join forces to turn this to their advantage. The necklace meanwhile passes from hand to hand, causing much confusion and embarrassment to all involved. The servants extract funds from Gripe and Moneytrap, enough to pay the wives' debt.

The two married couples meet for tea. There is a general exposure; lies are retracted and identities are more truthfully established. Corinna accepts a remorseful Dick, and Mrs Amlet settles for £10,000, with which she helps the young lovers and so permits their marriage.

Some of Vanbrugh's late works, such as *The False Friend* (1705), reflect a new trend towards sentimentality paralleled in France by the "comedy with tears". A glance at the dates of these indicates how indefatigable he was. Probably his output fluctuated, however, as he alternated between turning out scripts and taking on commissions for architectural designs, many of them on a monumental scale.

In part his prolific period was made possible because he borrowed situations and characters freely, putting his stamp on figures like Sir Brute and Lady Fanciful while leaving others to remain all too familiar in comedies of this period. But originality was not a prime requisite of a writer as yet. As has been seen in this and earlier volumes of *Stage by Stage*, the ancient Greek dramatists exploited Homeric legends and religious myth for the subjects of plays; the Romans revived the Greek scripts. The Elizabethans and Jacobeans – Marlowe, Shakespeare, Jonson – plundered Italian literature and Roman history for their themes. The French – Hardi, the Corneille brothers, Molière – got melodramatic ideas from England and Spain; the Restoration playwrights, in turn, were indebted to Molière. Every major plot was more deeply probed and better travelled by the time it reached the eighteenth-century London stage. After 2,000 years no play could prove to be wholly fresh. Such is the nature of theatre practice.

On his accession to the throne, George I knighted Vanbrugh. He was the first person so honoured by the new King.

— 6 —

ENGLISH LAUGHTER

The Cavalier audiences had special ethical guidelines conditioned by their past impoverishment and humiliation in foreign exile. Restored to estates and wealth, they were giddily determined to enjoy themselves to the utmost. In court circles the spirit was overwhelmingly hedonistic; in the theatre fops mingled with courtesans and harlots. King Charles, who had a roving eye, set a bad example. In this anti-Puritan society, immorality was rampant. The plays both mirrored and competed with this decadence. Of course play-goers comprised only a small coterie, not large enough to fill both houses, not to keep a play running long; a few nights usually exhausted the contingent of paying spectators.

Generally this unthinking clique liked to see themselves portrayed on the stage as witty and elegant. In their social life, in their salons, clubs and coffeehouses they imitated the theatre; they sought to be *au courant*, mannered and cuttingly brilliant in speech. In boudoirs, too, they were as casual and flamboyant as the characters depicted in this narrow world. As the drama critic George Jean Nathan has said, for them sex was something transient and amusing, not to be taken seriously. They borrowed much of this behaviour from the idle French guests at Versailles.

Some of the people in the plays seem to be afflicted with satyriasis or nymphomania, depending on their gender. Many are avid for money and seek ready access to affluence by a marriage to a rich widow or a virginal, nubile heiress. The widows have sharp minds and the young heroines are not shy and demure but scheme and practise deception to captivate the man on whom they have set their rapt gaze.

Davenant gave his patrons a mixed fare of opera, heroic drama and comedy. But it was lightness that they preferred by far, and it is drawing-room comedy for which the period is esteemed. His ticket buyers were comparatively well educated, travelled and purportedly well bred. They could appreciate a witty sally, a well-turned phrase, a classical allusion, a honed insult, a lyrical touch or a nice distinction. To write for this clique was daunting. Nor was it easy to hold the attention of people whose minds so readily wandered to other, more physical pursuits.

To addressing those interests, the chief subjects of the plays were seduction and adultery. Pictured are not only upper-class life but also existence in debtors' prison and bawdy-houses, both of which were frequented by fast-spending, heedless young rakes of good families. Their conduct is candidly evoked on canvas by William Hogarth's unsparing, brisk and sharp pencil.

The aristocratic world was also infiltrated by swindlers busily cheating simple-minded ladies of quality and innocent rustic folk who visited the teeming capital city. Though its compass is narrow, the stage still offered a crowd of various types of citizens, to be encountered in the town's drawing-rooms, parks and malls.

One of the earliest Restoration authors reflecting the scene is Sir George Etherege (1635–91). His father is thought to have resided some years in the Bermudas, and later the son spent time in France. Young George was educated perhaps at Oxford or Cambridge, but that is not certain, as very little is known of his early life.

His first play, *The Comical Revenge, or Love in a Tub* (1664), was produced at the Duke's Theatre when he was not past thirty. By that time he was obviously a cosmopolitan man of the world. An aspect of Restoration comedy is the youthfulness of the playwrights. Either they died young or changed their careers when scarcely out of their twenties.

Etherege seems not to have written for money but only for the pleasure it brought him. *The Comical Revenge* is not pure comedy but is mixed with drama. It may have been inspired by his stay in France, but none can say for sure. The characters in the chief plot, which is not well handled, speak in rhymed couplets, while those in the sub-plot express themselves in prose.

Lord Beaufort and Colonel Bruce are rivals for the hand of Graciana. They fight a duel, and Beaufort, the loser, tries to kill himself. He is cured and consoled by Graciana's sister. That is the serious half.

The comic part arises from the antics of a French valet, Dufoy, whose fellow servants immobilize him in a tub. His master, Sir Frederich Frolich, a ruthless libertine, captures the fancy of an aggressive widow, from whom he gets hold of £200. He finally compensates by marrying her. Another victim of a confidence man is a foolish country knight, Sir Nicholas Cully, who loses £1,000. The rogues are exposed and punished by entering into wedlock against their will.

Too many characters! Four story-lines! The moods veer from satyrism to burlesque; this is the work of a talented novice. On opening night *The Comical Revenge* had a "barbarous" reception. To the first-nighters' surprise, however, the play appealed directly to London's new audience, and the word of mouth thereafter was decidedly favourable. The play became a huge success.

There are traces of Molière in the plotting and characterizations and amusing situations borrowed from the *commedia dell'arte*, but the work has little or none of Molière's detachment – and none of his moral earnestness. "Gentleman George" – Etherege's nickname – drew his people from those he knew at first hand and delineated the fast-living social scene he inhabited as he himself experienced it. Spectators recognized the characters as themselves, their friends and their acquaintances, whom they met and contended with everywhere. In this script – which qualifies as experimental – a new theatrical formula was born, a fresh, very welcome pattern set. With it, the English comedy of manners appeared on the stage.

Etherege had only begun, however. His next offering, *She Would If She Could* (1668), is nearer his mark. Here he advances towards drawing-room comedy at its best. The characters are more recognizable, the badinage even more lively, the mood more consistent. The action follows the flirtations and adventures of two young blades, Courtall and Freeman, idlers with nothing to do, as they try to fill their days. They pick up two masked young ladies, Ariana and Gatty, in the park and later discover quite informally, to their embarrassment, that these are the girls they are supposed to meet later in the day in more decorous circumstances.

But much of the plot has to do with Ned Courtall's affair with Lady Cockwood, who is so anxious to be bedded by a virile young man – it is she who "would" if she could – because her ageing husband, Sir Oliver, is verging on impotence but wishes to give the appearance of a still active rake. This hypocritical, ill-matched couple is always frustrating each other. The action is rapid: people not only hide in closets and under tables but even in wood-piles, not to be caught at delicate moments as the intrigue progresses. The scene shifts from drawing-room to tavern where both Lady Cockwood and Sir Oliver have guilty assignations that unhappily miscarry. Lewd ballads are supplied by Sir Oliver's crony, Sir Joslin Jolley, who abets the amorous hunts. If the older persons are near caricatures – they have a touch of the obsessive Jonsonian "humour" – the young lovers are beguilingly real. Such gallants as Courtall and Freeman are idealizations, of course; their wit is too ready, their wooing too persuasive. Etherege presented images that his audience took to its heart, the masculine onlookers very eager to resemble those glib, seductive young gentlemen, and most young ladies yearning to have such dazzling beauty.

The dialogue has some pith. Says the sceptical Courtall to Lady Cockwood, when she finally vows to mend her ways: "'Tis a very pious resolution, Madam, and the better to confirm you in it, pray entertain an able Chaplain." And facing his impending marriage, he laments: "That which troubles me most is we lose the hopes of variety, and a single intrigue in Love is as dull as a single Plot in a play."

Etherege often writes cleverly brittle dialogue, but this play is memorable not so much for its epigrams as for the comic momentum in the hilarious "business" or pantomime that he gives the actors. It is a work for the boards, far more than for reading. Pepys found its exact stage-instructions detailing the physical action "very merry, evoked only by gesture, not wit at all". There are numerous songs and dances, as well as two duels – one serious, one comic – and at the conclusion no less than six marriages, the high-born rakes to ladies, the fools to harlots.

Following the production of *The Comical Revenge* and *She Would if She Could* Etherege was admitted to a select group of gentlemen "pensioners" and celebrated wits who gathered under the aegis of the Duke of York. He was also appointed secretary of the delegation headed by the British ambassador to Turkey, the land of pashas, harems and multiple wives. He served for three years and is said to have been neglectful of his duties there. Returned to England from that hot, exotic land in 1671, he was made a member of the King's Privy Chamber.

His third and final comedy, *The Man of Mode* (1676), composed after a hiatus of seven years, is by far his best and is considered a classic of the English stage.

A notorious seducer, Dorimant, weary of an affair, seeks to rid himself of his mistress, Mrs Loveit, a lady of quick mind but passionate temper and obsessive jealousy. He is momentarily attracted to her pretty friend, Belinda, with whom he conspires to break off the old liaison; their intention is to form a secret new one. Almost at the same time his eye is caught by a vivacious, more respectable young lady newly arrived in London, Harriet, an heiress, daughter of the formidable Lady Woodvil. Though country-bred, she is resourceful, and her attention, too, has been taken and stimulated by this dashing gentleman, described as a "prince" among young blades.

In a sub-plot, Young Bellair is in love with Emilia, a girl with no fortune. Old Bellair, without his son's consent, has affianced him to Harriet. The father, a bluff country squire, meets Emilia and himself becomes infatuated with her; he toys with the idea of marrying her.

Much of the action occurs at the house of Lady Townley, Old Bellair's cynical, sophisticated sister, who tries to help the frustrated young lovers. Everybody is working at cross-purposes.

Yet another salient figure is Sir Fopling Flutter, the English dandy *ne plus ultra* (he has just returned from Paris and has an excessive fondness for misused Gallicisms), whom Dorimant cruelly employs as an unwitting tool in the break-up of his relationship with Mrs Loveit. It is the silly, lisping, affected Sir Fopling who is the "man of mode", as his name implies. An extravagant creation, he was soon copied by most of the other Restoration dramatists.

At the end, after innumerable setbacks and complications, Dorimant has rid himself of Mrs Loveit, has taken his pleasure of Belinda who deeply rues her loss of virtue and has become affianced to the cool, clever Harriet, though a marriage between two such calculating partners hardly promises lasting bliss. But they are well met and evenly matched. Young Bellair, a straightforward gentleman, weds Emilia. Old Bellair accepts the outcome, and Lady Woodvil, who knows Dorimant's heinous reputation and deplores it, is completely won over by his charm after he literally but pseudonymously dances attendance on her.

Lady Woodvil, who embraces the traditional morality of the conservative elder generation, is scandalized by the loose-living *beau monde* of London. The tolerant Lady Townley offers a contrasting picture of the city's fashionable hostesses and their opulent salons at which gallants and fops gather day and night to tell ribald jests, exchange quips and insults and above all to gossip maliciously. Here slander prevails and reputations are cut down.

Old Bellair, hearty, shrewd and coarse-grained, uses country dialect. His son is pleasant but viewed by Dorimant as somewhat simple and dull. But there are rewards in a close acquaintanceship with him. "He is handsome, well bred, and by much the most tolerable of all the young men that do not abound in wit," remarks Dorimant. He confides to his friend Medley that he, Dorimant, intends to lay suit to Young Bellair's wife Emilia after the intended marriage. She has chastely rejected Dorimant thus far, but after the ceremony her attitude might change. "I have known many women make a difficulty of losing a maidenhead, who have afterwards made none of a cuckold." Besides, he improves his own repute by associating with an honest, sober young man, while Young Bellair borrows an inflated air of intelligence by being seen in Dorimant's company. The acquaintance, therefore, is to the mutual interest of both. Dorimant is a remarkable portrait. Not even in Molière are the people drawn with more subtlety, complexity and perception as in this cold, clever, genuinely amusing script.

Presumably Dorimant is a portrait of Etherege's friend, the Earl of Rochester (1647–80), poet, satirist and libertine, who presided over the circle of wits to which Etherege belonged. It was the infamous Rochester who wrote this "epitaph" and mockingly pinned it on the royal bedroom door:

> Here lies our sovereign lord, the King,
> Whose word no man relies on;
> He never says a foolish thing,
> And never does a wise one.

A notorious scapegrace, he was adept at putting on disguises – as a German, an astrologer, a beggar, a porter – and deceiving even his closest companions. At thirty-three, his health ruined by alcohol and incontinence, impoverished and penitent, he was dead.

Dorimant also resembles Molière's Don Juan. A connoisseur of women, he pursues them and is widely pursued. In one scene, written with virtuosity, he is confronted by three angry ladies all at once, all emotionally involved with him; this almost overlaps Molière's Don, who on a not dissimilar occasion contrives to make love to two women simultaneously. Dorimant schemes elaborately to end his tie to Mrs Loveit, seemingly because to simply declare their affair over would be too easy. His pride demands that it appear that he has jilted her, not she grown tired of him. His tongue "would tempt the angels to a second fall". He is courting Belinda because for him any daily routine is unexciting. "I have not had the pleasure of making a woman so much break her fan, to be sullen, or to forswear herself this three days." He torments women and takes perverse delight in it. "Next to the coming to a good understanding with a new mistress, I love a quarrel with an old one." He is interested in Harriet for several reasons, but one is that she is rich. His manners are impeccable, but he can also be brutal. Mrs Loveit describes him best: "I know he is a devil, but he has something of the angel still undefaced in him, which makes him so charming and agreeable that I must love him be he ever so wicked." At the première Thomas Betterton enacted the role.

Dorimant's confidant is Medley, a jaded man-about-town, who is also given to commenting epigrammatically. Drawn along the same lines, but overly mincing, is Sir Fopling Flutter, who appears everywhere in public with his affected ways, androgynous lisping speech and six footmen and a dog. Medley depicts him as having "lately arrived piping hot from Paris", flamboyantly parading the latest French fashions in dress and manners. Reports an amused observer: "He was yesterday at the play, with a pair of gloves up to his elbows and a periwig more exactly curled than a lady's head newly dressed for a ball." And again: "His head stands for the most part on one side, and his looks are more languishing than a lady's when she lolls at stretch in her coach or leans her head carelessly against the side of a box i' the playhouse."

Sir Fopling's catalogue of the good qualities of a complete gentleman are in summary: he "ought to dress well, dance well, fence well, have a genius for love-letters, an agreeable voice for a chamber, be very amorous, something discreet, but not over-constant". He is stupid as well as pretentious and hence funny. An accomplished actor, undertaking the role of the preening Sir Fopling, steals every scene he appears in. Though Etherege's rivals sought to borrow from this acerbic caricature of a Restoration fop, no other ever quite equalled it.

Etherege's women are not only very real but also interesting. Mrs Loveit, her moods precipitously alternating, is passionate one moment, mature the next, caught in the throes of uncontrolled emotions the next. Along with her overwhelming bad temper, she has guile; she can think as quickly and slyly as the predatory Dorimant and thwarts him several times. Her suspicions are easily alerted and she reacts decisively. It is easy to sympathize with her, though she is a termagant. Her plight is that of all women, even the most worldly and intelligent, who love not wisely but all too well; she is in the toils of a man of satanic disposition. "Exquisite Fiend" is her name for him.

Belinda, naïve and bedazzled, abandons her principles, the obligations of friendship, her loyalty and her chastity, and all too soon regrets it, fearing exposure. "Love heeds no warning" is her plight.

Equally well delineated is the well-spoken, attractive Harriet, conscious of her beauty and always able to cope with each new situation as it arises. When she is not witty she is flippant. She is bored with country life and dreads having to leave the glitter and exciting tittle-tattle of London's salons. All the city's attractions are embodied in the confident, elegant bearing of Dorimant. Harriet has grown to dislike life in the country so much that she can hardly bring herself to look at a landscape painting. But though she has no illusions about the difficulty of being married to a man with Dorimant's history of infidelity, and though she has his measure she is ready to risk matrimony.

In *The Man of Mode* Etherege samples London – its society, its gambling clubs, its heedless displays of wealth and high fashion – incisively. Though polish and wit gleam throughout the script, the dialogue is not as refined as in the comedies of Congreve, Etherege's only peer among this period's playwrights. The speeches are, however, studded and strengthened by imagery from daily life, and the humour is critical and even caustic. When Dorimant is quarrelling with Mrs Loveit, who to his secret pleasure tears her fan, he chides her: "Spare your fan, madam; you are growing hot, and will want it to cool you." He explains why his eyes are always wandering, yet at the same time manages to compliment her:

> Constancy at my years! 'Tis not a virtue in season; you might as well expect the fruit the autumn ripens i' in the spring . . . Youth has a long journey to go, madam –

> should I have set up my rest at the first inn I lodged at, I should never have arrived at the happiness I now enjoy.

He confesses:

> Love gilds us over and makes us show things to one another for a time, but soon the gold wears off,

and he tells his angry mistress:

> When love grows diseased, the best thing to do is to put it to a violent death; I cannot endure the torture of lingering and consumptive passion.

Harriet challenges him:

> When your love's grown strong enough to make you bear being laughed at, I'll give you leave to trouble me with it: till then, pray forbear, sir.

She predicts, accurately:

> Beauty runs as great a risk exposed at Court as wit does on the stage, where the ugly and the foolish all are free to censure.

Especially good is the scene, too long to be excerpted here, in which Young Bellair gives Harriet a whispered lesson in how to convey the impression that they are in love with each other, to deceive their parents who are closely watching them. This is accomplished by a charming pantomime. Throughout the play, Harriet is created by Etherege in unnervingly effective gestures.

During another dispute, Dorimant upbraids her:

> There is an inbred falsehood in woman which inclines 'em still to whom they most easily deceive.

He adds:

> Women, when they would break off with a man, never want th' address to turn the fault on him.

Sir Fopling protests that Dorimant has no mirror in his anteroom:

Prithee, Dorimant, why hast not thou a glass hung up here? A room is the dullest thing without one.

Young Bellair points out the other theatre guests:

Here is company to entertain you.

Sir Fopling: But I mean in case of being alone. In a glass a man may entertain himself.

Dorimant: The shadow of himself indeed.

Sir Fopling: Correct the errors of his motions and his dress.

Medley: I find, Sir Fopling, in your solitude you remember the saying of the wise man, and study yourself.

Sir Fopling: 'Tis the best diversion in our retirements. Dorimant, thou art a pretty fellow, and wear'st thy clothes well, but I never saw thee have a handsome cravat. Were they made up like mine, they'd give another air to thy face. Prithee let me send my man to dress thee but one day. By heavens! an Englishman cannot tie a ribbon.

Dorimant: They are something clumsy-fisted.

Not all critics of the day approved of *The Man of Mode*. Sir Richard Steele, the essayist and playwright, wrote in the *Spectator*:

To speak plainly of this whole work, I think nothing but being lost to a sense of Innocence and Virtue can make anyone see this comedy without observing more frequent occasion to sorrow and indignation, than mirth and laughter. At the same time I allow it to be nature, but it is nature in its utmost corruption and degeneracy.

The Man of Mode was revived at London's National Theatre in 2007, meeting with mixed reviews. Michael Billington wrote in the *Guardian*:

Updating classics has become Nicholas Hytner's National forte. But what worked with *Henry V* and *The Alchemist* feels a touch strenuous in the case of George Etherege's 1676 comedy of bad manners. It's entertaining enough but it feels more like a gloss on the play than a genuine exploration of it.

Sex and wealth are, of course, common to Restoration and modern London. And there are contemporary equivalents to Etherege's cynical Dorimant who discards one woman (Mrs Loveit), beds a second (Belinda) and seems set to marry a third (Harriet). But, in making Dorimant a glossy-mag Don Juan, Hytner overlooks crucial differences between then and now: above all, the fact that the selfish hedonism epitomised by Etherege's hero found philosophical justification in the Hobbesian belief in the pursuit of pleasure.

I also detect a tristesse behind Etherege's rampant comedy. The fun certainly comes out here, most especially in Rory Kinnear's dazzling performance as Sir Fopling Flutter who arrives "piping hot from Paris". Kinnear brilliantly gives us a man who with his Gallic phrases and accompanying troupe of French mimes strives for an imported chic. But even in this absurd popinjay there is a narcissistic sadness which emerges when he says "in a glass a man may entertain himself": lines which go virtually unnoticed here.

In Etherege's world of masculine cruelty, woman are also seen as disposable objects. But, although Nancy Carroll turns the rejected Mrs Loveit into a shrewish corsetière, she never quite rams home her moment of revenge when she refuses to play Dorimant's game "to please your vanity". In fact, some of the most secure performances come from relative onlookers such as Bertie Carvel as Dorimant's camp fellow-traveller and Madhav Sharma as a rich businessman besotted by his son's secret innamorata.

The evening has a shiny modernity and Hytner assiduously follows the logic of his concept. In Vicki Mortimer's design we are in a world of trendy galleries and antiseptic bars filled with laptops, mobile phones and beau-monde fashions. Between scenes David Bolger's choreography also gives us a kaleidoscopic vision of modern London's hectic consumerist fever. I can't help wishing, however, that Hytner had chosen the harder task of transporting us back to Etherege's own distinct world of melancholic lust.

Had not Etherege not been so indolent he might have written more. But if diligence, prudence and sobriety had been his qualities, he might have written less well about the world he accurately captured and preserved for later generations. In that "artificial" realm, form and manners were promoted to desired ends in themselves, but the archness never succeeded in concealing the strong emotions that possessed the highly social creatures who struggled to present unfeeling masks to those similarly posturing in every encounter.

After *The Man of Mode* Etherege returned to the diplomatic service and wrote no more plays. He became the envoy to Ratisbon (1685–97) and then to Regensberg. He married a rich widow and purchased a title; he was now Sir George (1680). From what is known of his life he comes across as bibulous, nonchalant about practical affairs, and of an amiable disposition – he might have been a character in one of his own works.

Near the end of his life Etherege became an exile. Charles II died and was succeeded by James II, who sought to supplant Anglicanism with Roman Catholicism. This resulted in renewed armed conflict, and James lost his throne and was forced to go into exile. Etherege, a Jacobite – a supporter of the last Stuart – also left England. His last years were spent in France.

*

With almost no exceptions, critics deem William Congreve (1670–1729) to be the author of the best Restoration comedies. This is partly because of his exquisite style, but also because of his unnerving feeling for tone, his good taste, and his skill in conjuring intelligent, articulate characters that fascinate. Only Etherege approaches or equals him. Like Etherege, Congreve wrote little, producing only four comedies and a tragedy. Even so, his name is usually mentioned whenever the light stage of this period is discussed. At a play by Congreve the spectator is in good company and is grateful. His scripts are also kind to those actors who can meet their demands.

Born near Leeds in Yorkshire, Congreve was raised and educated in Ireland; this is an odd distinction he shares with several other writers of English in their formative years. (Perhaps the Celtic climate was salubrious for those who took pleasure in convivial banter.) His father was given a commission to join an army garrison at Youghal, in County Cork, and the son was enrolled at Kilkenny School and then Old Trinity College, University of Dublin, where Jonathan Swift was a fellow student.

Congreve was born an aristocrat and was perhaps unduly proud of his ancestors' long prominence. After he and his family moved back to England the elegant young man entered the Middle Temple to study law but soon found he had no calling for it. At twenty-one he had still not determined what his future course should be.

Within a year, however, he published a novel, *Incognita*, to which he had been applying himself for some time. It was light and sophisticated, though Samuel Johnson grumbled that he would rather praise it than read it. It earned the young Congreve some helpful funds, and showed his inborn flair for brittle, witty dialogue. As he himself pointed out, it is constructed according to prescribed dramaturgical guidelines. A few months later a volume of his youthful poetry came out.

He was twenty-three when his first script, *The Old Bachelor* (1693), brought him amazing, unexpected celebrity, and he abruptly became a playwright. A huge success, the play ran for fourteen nights. Among those greatly impressed was John Dryden, the Poet Laureate, who declared it the best "first play" he had ever seen. Congreve had already become Dryden's protégé, collaborating with that influential poet on translations of Greek and Latin classics, a means by which Dryden kept in funds.

The Old Bachelor is an innovative work; its borrowing is wide, including a plot device from an Italian Renaissance farce and Etherege's *The Man of Mode*, as was to be expected from a writer of his years with no practical stage experience. (It is suggested that Dryden and Thomas Southerne lent him hands at the last moment.) Some of the characters have predecessors in Wycherley's and Dryden's various comedies. The standard denizens of the Restoration drawing-room are here, some with the usual self-descriptive names: Vainlove; Captain Bluffe, the *miles gloriosus*; Bellmour, the unscrupulous seducer; Fondlewife, the old banker; Laetitia, his fickle spouse; Sir Joseph Wittol; the wealthy Araminta, who rejects Vainlove's proposal; Belinda, Silvia's maidservant who tricks Captain Bluffe into wedlock. They comprise an amusing ensemble, a covey of enchanting and distressed ladies and scheming suitors with mixed agendas and odd plans for accomplishing them. If anything, the play is overpopulated, the story overcomplicated, but the effect is rich.

Heartwell, the "old bachelor" of the title, hates women and dreads the prospect of matrimony. But he has finally fallen in love with Silvia; he might have been drawn by Wycherley. He is tricked into "marriage" to Silvia by Vainlove and Bellmour at a fraudulent ceremony presided over by Bellmour dressed as a cleric. Vainlove, Silvia's lover, is anxious to get rid of her; he is only really attracted to women who ward off his advances. The "marriage" is Bellmour's way of helping his friend. Wed to Heartwell, Silvia proves to be a very unpleasant mate, makes Heartwell miserable and deepens his antagonism towards the opposite sex. The hoax is finally exposed and he is emancipated.

Habitually Vainlove relinquishes to Bellmour the women who no longer interest him; this includes Silvia. It is Araminta who captures the jaded Vainlove, only by feigning indifference. When he finally proposes, she shrewdly evades giving him a definite reply, her reason being – as another character puts it – that "she dares not consent for fear he should recant". Vainlove is one of those who most want what they cannot have, which does present a dilemma to any lady who dreams of possessing him.

He is forever vexed by the women who encourage him, and employs ever-new strategies to escape them, thus missing the excitement of seeking a conquest. As Sharper, a friend, tells him, it is the stalking not the quarry that compels him: "Thou hast a sickly, peevish appetite; only chew love and cannot digest it." This is true, Vainlove admits:

> I hate to be cramm'd. By heav'n, there's not a woman will give a man the pleasure of a chase: my sport is always balked or cut short. I stumble over the game I would pursue. 'Tis dull and unnatural to have a hare run full in the hound's mouth, and would distaste the keenest hunter.

Meanwhile the others carry on their affairs.

The profession of writing was beneath Congreve's lofty social station. Before long, however, he was ready with *The Double-Dealer* (1694), which did not fare very well with its first audience. Dryden, the most authoritative voice in England's literary realm, continued to lend strong support, however. He paid a most extravagant compliment, declaring that this new play placed the young Congreve in the same category as Shakespeare, to say nothing of his being better than Jonson and Fletcher. Present-day readers might be amazed by that ranking, but standards and tastes change over the centuries. Dryden, considered a major poet and an acute critic, held fast to classical rules and derided the Bard for not observing them.

One reason for the initial failure of *The Double-Dealer* is probably that one of its themes – the incestuous passion of Lady Touchwood for her nephew Mellefont – is unpleasant. The young man is driven to all sorts of stratagems to ward off her unwanted attentions. There are serious scenes in the play, alternating with the comic passages: indeed it comes close to tragicomedy. The work is also shadowed by an arch-villain, Maskwell, Lady Touchwood's former lover, whose machinations lend the proceedings gravity.

When Touchwood learns of Mellefont's impending marriage to Cynthia Plyant, she enlists Maskwell to assist her in preventing the match by spreading lies about the designated bridegroom. Their scheme is about to succeed when Lady Touchwood discovers that Maskwell's intention is to win Cynthia for himself. Her jealousy stoked, she changes sides. An overheard incriminating conversation collapses their intrigue. All leads to a happy conclusion.

A sub-plot that parallels the main story-line adds further complications: Sir Paul Plyant, father of Cynthia, is Lady Plyant's oversexed but aged husband and is too often unable to take advantage of his marital rights, so Mellefont's friend Careless is able to seduce Lady Plyant. Her infidelity is partly the consequence of Mellefont's campaign against his aunt.

In another involvement, the pretentious bluestocking Lady Froth yields to the "pert coxcomb" Brisk. Her spouse, Lord Froth, foolishly overemphasizes a need to retain his dignity and never permits himself to laugh since he believes it unseemly. The true lovers, Mellefont and Cynthia, are the only attractive persons in the play.

All the action occurs within three hours, in one place (the Touchwood manor), a compression that would have pleased Aristotle. The plot is complex and better handled than is that of *The Old Bachelor*. Incidents dovetail neatly. The author was much criticized on the opening night for the overuse of soliloquies, particularly for one in which Maskwell reveals his thoughts about his desire for Cynthia and is overheard by Lord Touchwood. Congreve sought to defend himself for this and other structural faults but failed to do so effectively.

The Double-Dealer, though seldom revived, is still exciting and suspenseful; the characters are individualized; the dialogue is even more brilliant than that in its predecessor. The satire is keen and animated and there is more than a touch of moralizing in this somewhat dark script. The sensible Cynthia, gazing at the noble shams, eccentrics and dolts about her, says to herself:

> Why should I call 'em fools? The world thinks better of 'em; for these have quality and education, wit and fine conversation, are receiv'd and admir'd by the world. If not, they like and admire themselves. And why is not that true wisdom? for 'tis happiness: and for ought I know, we have misapplied the name all this while, and mistaken the thing: since
>
> If happiness in self-content is placed,
> The wise are wretched, and fools only bless'd.

This is the observation of an author twenty-four years old.

Congreve seems not to have been deterred by the cold reception of *The Double-Dealer*, though he did resent its failure. In 1695 he braved the town with *Love for Love*, which some feel stands as his best – that it is, therefore, the best of the best. It was London's greatest theatre hit in years, and was considered one of the most immoral plays staged during the Restoration. Its main character, Sir Sampson Legend, has two sons. Valentine, the elder and a scapegrace, has had innumerable affairs with women and has already fathered a bastard. He is portrayed, however, as having a literary bent and being inclined to philosophy; despite his "wildness" he is good-hearted.

Sir Sampson makes Valentine an offer, lest he be disinherited altogether: he agrees to pay Valentine's debts if the ne'er-do-well will relinquish his inheritance to his younger brother Ben, a hearty sailor now at sea, and accept instead a modest monthly allowance. Valentine reacts by feigning madness. In this role, which is often parodied and reminds one of a stalking Hamlet, he offers prophecies to Foresight, a foolish man who dabbles in astrology, saying, "Tomorrow, knaves will thrive through craft, and fools through Fortune, and honesty will go as it did, frost-nipped in a summer suit."

Valentine falls in love with the wealthy, lovely-eyed Angelica, who asks, "Who is this lunatic?" He describes himself in phrases that come from Shakespeare's melancholy Dane. Does he know who *she* is, she asks? He responds with the tirade that Hamlet addressed to Ophelia: "You're a woman – one to whom Heaven gave beauty, when it grafted roses on a briar. You are the reflection of Heaven in a pond, and he that leaps at you is sunk." Such remarks, of course, reveal a method in his madness.

The somewhat dim-witted Ben returns from a voyage to find that a marriage has already been arranged between him and Miss Prue, Foresight's unworldly daughter, a "country girl".

Valentine's love for Angelica ultimately leads to his reform, though at first she is cautious and cleverly enough puts him through several tests. This testing of a hitherto promiscuous suitor by his beloved is another device often employed in Restoration comedies.

The play is largely about the many false faces that people show in a society in which what is done is more important than is how it is done. Some pretences are to fool others, and some betray their own lack of self-knowledge.

Each of the main characters has a besetting folly. Mr Foresight is ridiculously superstitious; his wife is heedlessly unfaithful. The sexual peccadilloes of the characters are another chief subject; the mincing, unctuous Tattle is overwhelmingly vain; the heartless Miss Prue too simple; the merry Mrs Frail is, alas, what her name implies, and Sir Sampson is an impotent but lecherous petty tyrant. These are the inhabitants of a society where the principal motivators are sex and money. Valentine, Angelica, Ben and Miss Prue have plain ways and salty, sometimes uncouth, unaffected speech.

(Congreve's plays might be revived more often if the casts were not so large, and if elaborate costumes along with ornate sets did not make productions expensive.)

In a letter to a friend, Congreve wrote that humour was "a singular and unavoidable way of doing anything peculiar to one man only, by which his speech and actions are distinguished from all other men". This concept is particularly well embodied in *Love for Love*.

In all his comedies, love is a game that the women play as adroitly as the men, if not more so. Some of the attractive young ladies have fortunes but wish to be prized for themselves alone, a daunting demand in the materialistic and extravagant society of the time. Angelica, for example, tricks Sir Sampson into proposing marriage to her, obtains and destroys the document Valentine has generously signed removing his inheritance and of course weds him instead of his father.

Mention should also be made of Jeremy, the ingenious manservant who ably assists his master Tattle in marrying Mrs Frail after giving lessons in courtship to Miss Prue. Ben announces that he will select a wife for himself.

What carries the day are the brilliant verbal exchanges and the variety of idioms in which they are couched. "Oh, Lord, what have I said?" clucks Tattle, as he "accidentally" destroys another reputation. "My unlucky tongue." Whether his revelations are the product of ill chance or are deliberate and malicious, the London scene provides him with more than enough defamatory material, as most of this circle is made up of arrogant, cruelly cynical social climbers; the men are liars, the women wanton. This is the world in which such gossips as Tattle and his friends Trapland and Scandal flourished. Congreve's census is unsparing, and audiences recognized its truth and applauded.

Ben, whose father wishes him to marry the naïve, doltish Miss Prue, states, "I could never abide to be port-bound." Elaborating on this metaphor, he pulls a poor mouth at matrimony: a husband is likened to a galley slave, "chained to an oar all his life; and mayhap forced to tug a leaky vessel to the bargain".

The dialogue is lightly salted with incessant, imperishable wit. Valentine tells Angelica, in his "mad scene" with her: "You were all white, a sheet of lovely spotless paper, when you first are born; but are to be scrawl'd and blotted by every goose quill."

Though Congreve's touch is often delicate, at the same time the characters are obsessively practical and much concerned with money; his audience did not think ill of a man who chose a bride for the wealth she brought. The dowry was all-important. Congreve was a man of the world, a realist – no soft sentiment here.

The characters in *Love for Love* are treated harshly. The script is a rapid succession of dramatic scenes that make it lastingly stageworthy. Tattle is exposed. Mrs Foresight and Mrs Frail learn that they are "sisters" in more ways than one, and that they have both been incautious visitors to the notorious World's-End. Mrs Frail, who displays a gold bodkin lost by her sister-in-law, neatly traps Mrs Foresight, who in turn demands to know how and *where* Mrs Frail happened to find the bodkin. Foresight knows Frail cannot answer without betraying her indiscretion.

Throughout, Congreve's saving grace is the fact that a touch of poetry balances the obscene innuendo. Again, the affectation of poseurs in the salons is pointed out when Ben and Cynthia are heard, though they, too, are gently satirized. The robustness and fresh rhythms of Ben's jargon are generally recognized and admired as examples of Congreve's considerable virtuosity. The satire is wide in scope and is directed at many fields: no less than thirty images and metaphors are drawn from a sailor's life. The court, the legal profession, the clergy and the then-fashionable cult of "friendship" are also made fun of.

Congreve's prose can also be unexpectedly vigorous, as when Valentine seeks to know the excuse for his father's "barbarity and unnatural usage" of him. Sir Sampson explodes and shouts:

> Excuse! Impudence! Why, sirrah, mayn't I do what I please? Are you not my slave? Did I not beget you? And might not I have chosen whether I would have begot you or no? 'Oons, who are you? Whence came you? What brought you into the world? How came you here, sir? Here, to stand here, upon those two legs, and look erect with that audacious face, hah? Answer me that. Did you come a volunteer into the world? Or did I, with the lawful authority of a parent, press you to service?

Could not Congreve have written tragedies? He ventured to do so, calling his sole undertaking *The Mourning Bride* (1697). He has expressed himself interestingly regarding tragedy, commenting that the "passions are too powerful to let humour have its course". He observed that in "unspoiled youth" there is little character. "It grows with time like the ash of a burning stick, and strengthens toward middle life till there is little else at seventy years." If he himself had been more energetic, testing himself, experimenting, probing deeper, perhaps he might have been a writer of significant tragedy; perhaps his gift for poetry and his psychological insight might have been developed. Unfortunately, however, he made no further effort in that direction.

The Mourning Bride was staged, to an enthusiastic response. The production came about when a group of major players at the theatre called Lincoln's Inn Fields complained that Christopher Rich, a merchant who had purchased the acting company, was mean and unscrupulous. The group broke away, obtained a royal licence and founded a new troupe at the Dorset Gardens, another converted tennis court. They were led by Thomas Betterton, who was esteemed for his outstanding talent as a performer and his high character as a man. Lincoln's Inn Fields now had fresh competition. One of the ensemble's first productions was *Love for Love*, and after that it staged *The Mourning Bride*, a frenetic melodrama with an exotic atmosphere that falls into the category of "villain play" dear to Aphra Behn.

In it, a Princess of Granada, the lovely Almeria, daughter of King Manuel, secretly becomes the wife of Alphonso, son of her father's sworn enemy, the King of Valencia. The young man, taken captive, is held by force in Granada. Furious when he learns of the marriage, the fierce Manuel orders that Alphonso be put to death. The cruel King decides to hide in the Prince's cell and pass himself off as his son-in-law, so that when Almeria comes in an attempt to rescue him she will confront her vengeful father instead. He sees her disappointment and mocks her. By error, Manuel himself is then killed and beheaded.

A Moorish Queen, Zara, is in love with Alphonso, with whom she has been imprisoned, though he has rejected her advances. When she beholds the headless corpse and recognizes it for his, she is besieged by grief and swallows poison. The people of Granada revolt. Alphonso is freed and rejoins Almeria.

The play, a happy "tragedy" for Congreve, stayed on for thirteen nights and brought him more honour and financial reward. Many respected critics of the day liked it. Samuel Johnson, for one, professed himself awestruck by its power. It remained popular through the next century.

But tastes do indeed change, and *The Mourning Bride* is not viable today, filled as it is with noble characters of little complexity or depth, who express high-flown sentiments as the people did in eighteenth-century tragedies; now they sound inflated and bombastic. The plot is strong, however, and mystery overhangs the action, which turns on surprises. Whatever Congreve's shortcomings in tragedy, his innate gift as a dramatist is always discernible. Two lines in the script – the first words in the opening scene – are imperishable and are still quoted: "Music hath charms to soothe a savage breast" and in Act Three: "Heaven has no rage like love to hatred turned, nor Hell a fury like a woman scorned." This sums up the heroine, who is dark-humoured and dangerous.

The Restoration theatre stage was now shaped by a blast of indignation from an Anglican clergyman, Jeremy Collier, possessed of a zealous, dogmatic temper. In 1698 he published *A Short View of the Immorality, and Profaneness of the English Stage.* He launched his complaint chiefly against Vanbrugh but also specified Congreve's *Love for Love* as "giving aid and comfort to lechers". Other objects of his attack were Dryden's many farces, as well as Wycherley's sexual romp *The Country Wife.*

The playwrights tried to mount a defence against this assault, but Congreve, for one, was singularly inept in doing so. The theatre managers, sensitive to a shift in the wind, grew more cautious about what they staged; they operated by royal licence and the political situation was unstable. The merry monarch, hedonistic Charles II, was dead, and his less capable brother James II had been deposed in a coup after a short reign. The new sovereign, William III, a sober Dutchman, was offended and voiced his support for Collier's outrage. The Restoration farces had appealed largely to a coterie of courtiers, but now the tone at court was altered and with it London's moral and social climate.

It had been no secret that Charles II had mistresses, some – like Nell Gwynn – who were plucked from the lower classes and had risen by way of the theatre. That popular knowledge seemed to put a stamp of approval on the goings-on in that narrow precinct. But now the regal sinner had departed.

The Reverend Collier was a formidable antagonist. He was in ready command of classical learning, could quote scripture and was convinced that he was called to speak out. He believed that the purpose of drama was "moral instruction", and that was hardly the fare being offered. He soon won vocal reinforcement for this cause. Groups of displeased lady theatre-goers bonded together vowing to shun plays rumoured to be bawdy. The Lord Chamberlain and Master of the Revels were replaced.

There had also been a steady and expanding retrogression in the behaviour of the spectators. Drawn by word of mouth, hearing that the stage offered salacious entertainment, some of the newcomers were less than literate. They were coarser and even more impolite as the amorality of the plays themselves became more flagrant.

It was soon after Collier's intervention that Vanbrugh quit the theatre and turned again to architecture. Dryden also publicly recanted his having contributed to the lubricity of the stage, apologizing for his obscenities.

Apparently intimidated by Collier's jeremiad, Congreve, too, was silent for several years. When *Love for Love* had met a rousing reception, Betterton and Mrs Bracegirdle put him under contract to write a new play each year. Collier's protest, however, put an end to Restoration comedy with its free-and-easy lifestyle. A few playwrights turned out plays in the same sportive spirit, but not for long and without much success. The Restoration drawing-room play was swiftly replaced by the sentimental comedy of the sort provided by Colley Cibber and Sir Richard Steele.

Congreve was not finished, however. In 1700 he brought forth another script, *The Way of the World*, somewhat tempered to meet the new audience and the times. For all its accommodation to the social transition, it is the supreme achievement of suave, brittle Restoration comedy. It is not quite as cynical or as titillating as its predecessors, but essentially it belongs in the same category as the better works of Etherege and Wycherley and as Congreve's own earlier offerings.

Here the hero and heroine are fully realized, reaching their apotheosis in studied affectation and verbal scintillation. Here, too, the minor characters – they are so well drawn that they are scarcely minor – have a remarkable vitality. The plot is not as well designed as that of *Love for Love*; indeed, it is obscure and clumsy at some moments and slow at others. Characters are introduced a bit haphazardly and their relationships not clearly defined. Even so, says George Jean Nathan, it works well enough to display Congreve's people in action, "princes and princesses of farce . . . utterly gay and artificial . . . indulging in airy persiflage, contrasted with the broad humour of the more vulgar persons who surround them, bringing to life the street smells and stench of humanity. *The Way of the World* is indefatigable; its cast is delightful without exception. Along with *Love for Love*, this is one of his two comedies that are among the best written in English."

The title is an allusion, a lightly denigrating catchphrase used by the characters themselves to describe the loose conduct – the pursuit of money and erotic adventure – of people in society.

Mirabell, like other Congreve heroes, is a "legacy-hunter". He seeks to marry well, to Millamant, an heiress worth £12,000, half of which is already at her disposal. His difficulty is Lady Wishfort, Millamant's aunt, who detests him and schemes to have her niece marry a cousin, Sir Wilfull Witwould, of the country gentry.

Millamant deems Sir Wilfull a dreadful creature. Her hopes are fixed on Mirabell, though she is loath to acknowledge it. Mirabell had once wooed Lady Wishfort but only to gain access to her niece. When that stratagem was exposed, he had incurred the lady's lasting wrath. But now he conceives a new plan: he will present his manservant, Waitwell, as a rich uncle of his own and have him court Lady Wishfort. If she succumbs to "Sir Rowland's" charms, Mirabell will step in, reveal the suitor's identity and blackmail Lady Wishfort into consenting to Mirabell's engagement with Millamant.

Failing that, Mirabell will spread word of the deception, making Lady Wishfort the laughing-stock of London. The lady is most susceptible to a suit from any quarter, since she is "full of the vigour of fifty-five" and ready to "marry anything that resembles a man, though 'twere no more than what a butler could pinch out of a napkin".

Lady Wishfort is one of the funniest creations ever to cross a stage. Hers is the first appearance of the overweight, over-amorous widow on the prowl, equipped with the divine and at the moment the fierce temper of the "battleaxe" as she pursues men. Through the ensuing generations she is copied with superficial variations – by Sheridan's Mrs Malaprop in *The Rivals* and Wilde's Lady Bracknell in *The Importance of Being Earnest* and many others. She is as eternal henceforth as the *miles gloriosus* exemplified in Falstaff.

Congreve suggests effective stage business for her. She is seated before the mirror of her toilet table, calling for her maidservant, while lavishly applying cosmetics before presenting her face to a prospective husband.

> Lady Wishfort: I have no more patience. If I have not fretted myself till I am pale again, there's no veracity in me! Fetch me the red – the red, do you hear, sweetheart? An errant ash colour, as I'm a person! Look you how this wench stirs! Why dost thou not fetch me a little red? Didst thou not hear me, Mopus?
>
> Peg: The red ratafia, does your ladyship mean, or the cherry brandy?
>
> Lady Wishfort: Ratafia, fool? No, fool. Not the ratafia, fool – grant me patience! – I mean the Spanish paper, idiot; complexion, darling. Paint, paint, paint, dost thou understand that, changeling, dangling thy hands like bobbins before thee? Why dost thou not stir, puppet? Thou wooden thing upon wires!
>
> Peg: Lord, madam, your ladyship is so impatient. – I cannot come at the paint, madam; Mrs Foible has locked it up, and carried the key with her.
>
> Lady Wishfort: A pox take you both. – Fetch me the cherry brandy then.

Act III, Scene II

Lady Wishfort: I'm as pale and as faint, I look like Mrs Qualmsick, the curate's wife, that's always breeding. Wench, come, come, wench, what art thou doing? Sipping? Tasting? Save thee, dost thou not know the bottle?

Scene III

Lady Wishfort, Peg with a bottle and china cup.

Peg: Madam, I was looking for a cup.

Lady Wishfort: A cup, save thee, and what a cup hast thou brought! Dost thou take me for a fairy, to drink out of an acorn? Why didst thou not bring thy thimble? Hast thou ne'er a brass thimble clinking in thy pocket with a bit of nutmeg? I warrant thee. Come, fill, fill! So, again. She who that is. [*One knocks.*] Set down the bottle first. Here, here, under the table: – what, wouldst thou go with the bottle in thy hand like a tapster? As I'm a person, this wench has lived in an inn upon the road, before she came to me, like Maritornes the Asturian in Don Quixote. No Foible yet?

Peg: No, madam; Mrs Marwood.

Lady Wishfort: Oh, Marwood: let her come in. Come in, good Marwood.

Scene IV

[To them] Mrs Marwood

Mrs Marwood: I'm surprised to find your ladyship in *deshabille* at this time of day.

Lady Wishfort: Foible's a lost thing; has been abroad since morning, and never heard of since.

And here she is striking a pose and rehearsing how she shall let "Sir Rowland" gets his first glimpse of her:

Lady Wishfort: Is Sir Rowland coming, say'st thou, Foible? And are things in order?

Foible: Yes, madam. I have put wax-lights in the sconces, and placed the footmen in a row in the hall, in their best liveries, with the coachman and postillion to fill up the equipage.

Lady Wishfort: Have you pulvilled the coachman and postillion, that they may not stink of the stable when Sir Rowland comes by?

Foible: Yes, madam.

Lady Wishfort: And are the dancer and the music ready, that he may be entertained in all points with correspondence to his passion?

Foible: All is ready, madam.

Lady Wishfort: And – well – and how do I look, Foible?

Foible: Most killing well, madam.

Lady Wishfort: Well, and how shall I receive him? In what figure shall I give his heart the first impression? There is a great deal in the first impression. Shall I sit? No, I won't sit, I'll walk, – aye, I'll walk from the door upon his entrance, and then turn full upon him. No, that will be too sudden. I'll lie, – ay, I'll lie down. I'll receive him in my little dressing-room, there's a couch – yes, yes, I'll give the first impression on a couch. I won't lie neither, but loll and lean upon one elbow, with one foot a little dangling off, jogging in a thoughtful way. Yes; and then as soon as he appears, start, ay, start and be surprised, and rise to meet him in a pretty disorder. Yes; oh, nothing is more alluring than a levee from a couch in some confusion. It shows the foot to advantage, and furnishes with blushes, and recomposing airs beyond comparison. Hark! There's a coach.

Foible: 'Tis he, madam.

Lady Wishfort: Oh dear, has my nephew made his addresses to Millamant? I ordered him.

Foible: Sir Wilfull is set in to drinking, madam, in the parlour.

Lady Wishfort: Ods my life, I'll send him to her. Call her down, Foible; bring her hither. I'll send him as I go. When they are together, then come to me, Foible, that I may not be too long alone with Sir Rowland.

Congreve's genius for language shows in the variety of speech patterns and dialects from Lady Wishfort's "boudoir Billingsgate" to Sir Wilfull's rustic metaphors and glossary. He employs many accents, including the educated and classical nuances flowing from Mirabell and Fainall; their sentences are polished and balanced yet also sound "real" when uttered by that preening pair. Designed to be spoken on stage, the dialogue has pauses in which actors can catch their breath or hesitate to indicate uncertainty. This style, precise and fastidious, is often alight with happily chosen adjectives and images. Congreve's prose is also enjoyable to read on the printed page.

If one is inclined to condemn the busy, flamboyant adultery indulged in by this clique, let it be realized that divorce was hard to come by, and many marriages were not inspired by love or mutual physical attraction but were arranged by parents for reasons of social status or financial gain.

For a well-linked sub-plot, Fainall and Mrs Marwood are lovers but are a somewhat disagreeable couple. Fainall is the husband of Arabella Languish, Lady Wishfort's daughter. Mrs Marwood was a widow before her second marriage and now has an amatory interest in the suave Mirabell; for that reason she had exposed his motive in earlier wooing Lady Wishfort. The stares she directs towards Mirabell have aroused Fainall's jealousy.

Mirabell had once had an affair with Arabella; apprehensive that a child might be the result, he had arranged to have her wed his penniless "friend" Fainall. But there was no child. The good-natured Arabella despises her spouse. When she laments to Mirabell, "Why did you make me marry this man?" his response is characteristic: "To save that idol, reputation . . . A better man ought not to have been sacrificed to the occasion, a worse had not answered to the purpose."

Fainall has an equal dislike of his wife. He and Mrs Marwood, who carry on their liaison even in Lady Wishfort's house, are trying to get their hands on the Wishfort fortune. The remaining action is too complicated and at times too unclear to outline. At the final curtain, however, not only does Mirabell get his elusive Millamant, but he also thwarts Fainall's manoeuvres to obtain the rest of Mrs Fainall's estate, which Mirabell, with admirable foresight, has put in a trust for her.

All these capers and plots are to be expected: this is the "way of the world". Congreve illustrates it; he does not find fault with it. The comedy ends with a dance. If Congreve is a satirist, he is not a reformer; his plays are not designed to improve anyone's conduct. On the contrary, some critics think that the charming but calculating Mirabell is the author's amiable, self-serving self-portrait. He declared in his preface that his aim was not to ridicule innate follies for which no one is to blame but, rather, to comment on acquired ones.

Mirabell is genuinely enamoured of Millamant. Who wouldn't be? She is enchanting, pretty, wealthy and urbane. An intelligent, articulate conversationalist, she is arch, poised and self-possessed. She wisely seeks to hide her emotions from her suitor, with whose cavalier reputation she is well acquainted. But for her he is irresistible. Beneath her veneer of sophistication she is tender and sensitive, and possesses both self-knowledge and knowledge of the world. She is not portrayed romantically but as having a keen feminine intuition – she is believable and in many ways "modern". She is knowing about the ephemeral tricks of the heart and the flaws of society. She is no paragon and shares the weakness of other women of her day and milieu. She perceives in Mirabell a competence, an essential earnestness, braveness and sense of responsibility that she seeks in a husband-to-be. He exactly fits the bill for her. He is still physically young, yet in most ways quite mature. She has been discriminating and is still chaste.

Mirabell is philosophically inclined, given to sententious epigrams, and devilishly wily. At times he is more than a bit ruthless, yet is also capable of generosity. He is no saint, but he stops short at any deed that is malicious. Captured by Millamant, as well as attracted by her fortune, he offers her his name and hand.

The proposal scene is one of the most oft-cited passages in English literature. In writing it Congreve was following a formula used by other playwrights such as Dryden and Thomas d'Urfey, but none treats it as perfectly.

An actress proves her mettle if she speaks these lines for all they are worth, ending, as Millamant concedes a bit shyly, that she will "dwindle into a wife". Here are two overly civilized persons sparring, both witty, all the while aware that they are destined for each other and will have each other no matter what – but their code demands that they keep a façade of light-hearted doubt. It goes like this:

Millamant is singing; Mirabell enters, catching up the next line of the song: "Like Phœbus sung the no less amorous boy."

Mirabell: Like Daphne she, as lovely and as coy. Do you lock yourself up from me, to make my search more curious? Or is this pretty artifice contrived, to signify that here the chase must end, and my pursuits be crowned, for you can fly no further.

Mrs Millamant: Vanity! No – I'll fly, and be followed to the last moment; though I am upon the very verge of matrimony, I expect you should solicit me as much as if I were wavering at the grate of a monastery, with one foot over the threshold. I'll be solicited to the very last; nay, and afterwards.

Mirabell: What, after the last?

Mrs Millamant: Oh, I should think I was poor and had nothing to bestow if I were reduced to an inglorious ease, and freed from the agreeable fatigues of solicitation.

Mirabell: But do not you know that when favours are conferred upon instant and tedious solicitation, that they diminish in their value, and that both the giver loses the grace, and the receiver lessens his pleasure?

Mrs Millamant: It may be in things of common application, but never, sure, in love. Oh, I hate a lover that can dare to think he draws a moment's air independent of the bounty of his mistress. There is not so impudent a thing in nature as the saucy look of an assured man confident of success: the pedantic arrogance of a very husband has not so pragmatical an air. Ah, I'll never marry, unless I am first made sure of my will and pleasure.

Mirabell: Would you have 'em both before marriage? Or will you be contented with the first now, and stay for the other till after grace?

Mrs Millamant: Ah! don't be impertinent. My dear liberty, shall I leave thee? My faithful solitude, my darling contemplation, must I bid you then adieu? Ay-h, adieu. My morning thoughts, agreeable wakings, indolent slumbers, all ye *doceurs*, ye *sommeils du matin*, adieu. I can't do't, 'tis more than impossible – positively, Mirabell, I'll lie abed in a morning as long as I please.

Mirabell: Then I'll get up in a morning as early as I please.

Mrs Millamant: Ah! Idle creature, get up when you will. And d'ye hear, I won't be called names after I'm married; positively I won't be called names.

Mirabell: Names?

Mrs Millamant: Aye, as wife, spouse, my dear, joy, jewel, love, sweet-heart, and the rest of that nauseous cant, in which men and their wives are so fulsomely familiar – I shall never bear that. Good Mirabell, don't let us be familiar or fond, nor kiss before folks, like my Lady Fadler and Sir Francis; nor go to Hyde Park together the first Sunday in a new chariot, to provoke eyes and whispers, and then never be seen there together again, as if we were proud of one another the first week, and ashamed of one another ever after. Let us never visit together, nor go to a play together, but let us be very strange and well-bred. Let us be as strange as if we had been married a great while, and as well-bred as if we were not married at all.

Mirabell: Have you any more condition to offer? Hitherto your demands are pretty reasonable.

Mrs Millamant: Trifles; as liberty to pay and receive visits to and from whom I please; to write and receive letters, without interrogatories or wry faces on your part; to wear what I please, and choose conversation with regard only to my own taste; to have no obligation upon me to converse with wits that I don't like, because they are your acquaintance, or to be intimate with fools, because they may be your relations. Come to dinner when I please, dine in my dressing-room when I'm out of humour, without giving a reason. To have my closet inviolate; to be sole empress of my tea-table, which you must never presume to approach without first asking leave. And lastly, wherever I am, you shall always knock at the door before you come in. These articles subscribed, if I continue to endure you a little longer, I may by degrees dwindle into a wife.

Mirabell: Your bill of fare is something advanced in this latter account. Well, have liberty to offer conditions: – that when you are dwindled into a wife, I may not be beyond measure enlarged into a husband?

Mrs Millamant: You have free leave: propose your utmost, speak and spare not.

Mirabell: I thank you. *Imprimis* then, I covenant that your acquaintance be general; that you admit no sworn confidant or intimate of your own sex; no she friend to screen her affairs under your countenance, and tempt you to make trial of a mutual secrecy. No decoy-duck to wheedle you a *fop-scrambling* to the play in a mask, then bring you home in a pretend fright, when you think you shall be found out, and rail at me for missing the play, and disappointing the frolic which you had to pick me up and prove my constancy.

Mrs Millamant: Detestable *imprimis*! I go to a play in a mask!

Mirabell: *Item*, I article, that you continue to like your own face as long as I shall: and while it passes current with me, that you endeavour not to new coin it. To which end, together with all vizards for the day, I prohibit all masks for the night, made of oiled skins and I know not what – hogs' bones, hares' gall, pig water, and the marrow of a roasted cat. In short, I forbid all commerce with the gentlewomen in what-d'ye-call-it court. *Item*, I shut my doors against all bawds with baskets, and pennyworths of muslin, china, fans, atlases, etc. *Item*, when you shall be breeding –

Mrs Millamant: Ah, name it not!

Mirabell: Which may be presumed, with a blessing on our endeavours –

Mrs Millamant: Odious endeavours!

Mirabell: I denounce against all strait lacing, squeezing for a shape, till you mould my boy's head like a sugar-loaf, and instead of a man-child, make me father to a crooked billet. Lastly, to the dominion of the tea-table I submit; but with proviso, that you exceed not in your province, but restrain yourself to native and simple tea-table drinks, as tea, chocolate, and coffee. As likewise to genuine and authorised tea-table talk, such as mending of fashions, spoiling reputations, railing at absent friends, and so forth. But that on no account you encroach upon the men's prerogative, and presume to drink healths, or toast fellows; for prevention of which, I banish all foreign forces, all auxiliaries to the tea-table, as orange-brandy, all aniseed, cinnamon, citron, and Barbadoes waters, together with ratafia, and the most noble spirit of clary. But for cowslip-wine, poppy-water, and all dormitives, those I allow. These provisos admitted, in other things I may prove a tractable and complying husband.

Mrs Millamant: O horrid provisos! Filthy strong waters! I toast fellows, odious men! I hate your odious provisos.

Mirabell: Then we're agreed. Shall I kiss your hand upon the contract? And here comes one to be a witness to the sealing of the deed.

[Enter Mrs Fainall]

Mrs Millamant: Fainall, what shall I do? Shall I have him? I think I must have him.

Mrs Fainall: Aye, aye, take him, take him, what should you do?

Mrs Millamant: Well then – I'll take my death. I'm in a horrid fright – Fainall, I shall never say it. Well – I think – I'll endure you.

Mrs Fainall: Fie! Fie! have him, and tell him so in plain terms: for I am sure you have a mind to him.

Mrs Millamant: Are you? I think I have; and the horrid man looks as if he thought so too. Well, you ridiculous thing you, I'll have you. I won't be kissed, nor I won't be thanked. – Here, kiss my hand though, so hold your tongue now; don't say a word.

But Congreve is far more than a master of language. Lady Wishfort, half bourgeoise and half fishwife – she is blatantly *nouveau riche* – is a triumphant sketch behind the footlights; she reads the Puritan tracts of Collier and Bunyan yet is bursting with sensual appetites. Chary of her reputation, unsure of her social standing, she is by nature loud and brazen and must inevitably betray her carnal dreams – for good reason she is named Lady Wishfort. She is unconsciously vulgar, has too many drinks on the sly, is vain, foolish and virtually panting to be seduced or wed again.

Despite its bright, lively characters and quicksilver dialogue, however, *The Way of the World* had a cool reception and was soon withdrawn. Overnight the genre was outmoded; its day had passed. Usually theatre-goers want to be advanced, to be in the know, to be ahead of others. They ask, "What's new?" *The Way of the World*, though immortal, was already out of date. (Mostly revivals are not for spectators who have seen the play before but for a fresh generation who have heard of it and want to see what they have missed by having been born too late . . . or else the play returns in a film or in a musical form, the producer or composer choosing a story and characters that have been tested and proved to have broad public appeal.)

Congreve, embittered, left off writing for the theatre. He was thirty. He likened himself to Terence, foreign-born, whose fluent, aphoristic Latin was not appreciated by the illiterate Roman multitude. (To guard his felicitous style, Terence preferred to have his plays read rather than acted.) By now the campy Congreve was comparatively well-to-do, enjoying income from government sinecures – he had been careful to ingratiate himself with members of both political parties. While his pen lay idle he adopted the daily habits of an elegantly attired *flâneur*, strolling in the park in London's fashionable parade, carrying on flirtations with ladies of wealth and quality. He won the brief affections of a succession of women, among the most conspicuous being Sarah Churchill, following his intimate relationship with the talented Mrs Bracegirdle. (Sarah was an ancestress of the great Winston.) His affair with the devoted Duchess of Marlborough was next, and lasted longest – the pinnacle indeed. Valued for his smooth wit and patrician bearing and manners, he was invited to the very best and most exclusive houses.

When the exiled Voltaire was in London in 1726, paid Congreve the honour of a visit and began to speak of literature, Congreve tried to change the subject, dismissing his plays as trivial accomplishments. He wished his French guest to think of him as merely a "gentleman". Voltaire recalled that he was somewhat taken aback and exclaimed with some asperity, "If you were only that, I would not have come to see you."

In an earlier token of respect, Alexander Pope dedicated his translation of *The Iliad* to him in 1720. His role in English comedy could be equated to that of Marivaux in France.

He put his theatrical flair to the service of Handel, providing him with a myth-based libretto for *Semele*. The plot was used by Ovid, which gives a clue to Congreve's preference when reading classical literature. Jupiter, pretending to be a mortal, pursues the beautiful Semele. She, something of a social climber, demands that he appear in full array as the supreme god of Olympus. His mate Juno, her jealousy aroused, herself takes on the guise of a mortal to intervene and punish the adulterous couple. Handel said he had composed the work in the form of an oratorio, but his gleeful contemporaries spoke of it as "the bawdy opera". It contains several prized arias, among them "O Sleep, why dost thou leave me?" and "Where'er she walks".

The first professional staging of the work in the United States took place at the New York City Opera in 2006 as the eleventh entry in a series of Handel revivals there. Elizabeth Futral had the title role, and Anthony Walker conducted.

A serious accident befell Congreve in his thirty-eighth year. He was *en route* to the spa at Bath, long an established centre for high society. His carriage overturned, inflicting on him internal injuries that resulted in his death in January of the following year (1729). He was buried in Westminster Abbey, among the most celebrated.

His will puzzled those who knew him. He bequeathed £200 to Mrs Bracegirdle, who had taken the lead role in most of his plays and was now old and hobbled by penury. He also left her a claim to lasting celebrity, for her interpretation of his charming heroines as well as Portia and Shakespearean characters. She, too, is a permanent occupant in the Abbey, in the midst of England's great (she died in 1748). But most of Congreve's fortune – about £10,000 – went to the enormously rich Duchess of Marlborough. Her pious recollection of him is worth recording: she spent the entire legacy to purchase a pearl necklace. She had a wax-and-ivory likeness of her dead lover seated perpetually in his usual chair at her dinner table. She had its feet "regularly blistered and anointed for the gout", recalling an illness from which he had suffered in his critical later years.

He has his detractors, among them George Meredith, who grants that his style is bright – "a thrusting, flashing Toledo blade" – but thinks him superficial. It is possible that Meredith and other like-minded commentators have missed the point of Congreve's tolerant and amused picture of his times, drawn with discernment and an intuitive compassion. His figures are, after all, flesh and blood beneath their finery and despite their ultra-sophistication.

Finally, in the more open twentieth century, the exuberance and frankness of Restoration drama was rediscovered on both sides of the Atlantic. An offering of *The Way of the World* (1924) with a cast led by the popular actress Edith Evans did much to demonstrate again to Londoners the delights Congreve and his unfettered fellow playwrights afforded. Later Dame Evans was Lady Fidget in Wycherley's *The Country Wife* (1936). Cyril Richard played a series of fops in a staging of other farces of the period. A presentation of *The Way of the World* at the Tyrone Guthrie Theatre in Minneapolis drew Howard Taubman of the *New York Times* halfway across the continent for the pleasure of seeing Australian-born Zoe Caldwell as a charming Millamant, an independent spirit whose precise diction and guarded, dry humour had the audience leaning forward eagerly to hear what the exasperating, whimsical young lady vowed next.

In revival, *The Way of the World* in particular called for buoyant, skilled playing; some theatre companies are not up to presenting it. But done with flair it has a quality that is incomparable.

All too soon Congreve's plays almost vanished from London's busy stages. This also happened to his fellow writers of Restoration comedy. Even so, many of its elements made their way into new plays. The marriage proposal as a duel between members of the two sexes, for example, an "obligatory scene" in *The Way of the World*, was much imitated in subsequent comedies after Congreve, who himself had borrowed it from earlier works. Most of the later attempts at it by others, though, fell far short.

— 7 —

ENGLAND AFTER COLLIER

The galaxy of Restoration authors includes one more bright name, George Farquhar (1678–1707), whose works – though few, given the shortness of his life – indicate sharply the transition from pure comedy to the sentimental kind.

Like Congreve, Farquhar was Anglo-Irish. His father was a Londonderry clergyman. Young George failed both as an actor and as an army officer. He first tried his luck on the boards with the Smock Alley Theatre in Dublin, where he learned not only the stage-trickery but the stock plots and devices of English comic writers. Arrived in London, he had some success as a player – until in a fateful lunge and thrust in a simulated duel he pierced a fellow performer, cutting short his acting career.

He then turned to playwriting, knowing that audiences welcomed licentious fare of the sort Wycherley and the early Congreve provided. He complied with *Love and a Bottle* in 1698, the very year Collier issued his devastating critique.

The hero of *Love and a Bottle* is a scallywag called George Roebuck, who resembles his young creator in several ways: for one, he asks of life only sex and alcohol, and, for another, Roebuck has come to London from Dublin. The character's reason is that he has begotten a child while in Ireland, by a prostitute called Trudge, and his sternly ethical father insists on a marriage to the mother. Rather than assent, Roebuck has fled.

In London, by chance, he meets his friend Ned Lovewell, with whose sister Leanthe he had been in love. But he also encounters Trudge and their son, who have followed him. Once more Roebuck takes flight, while Lovewell undertakes to assist Trudge. Lovewell's inamorata, the beauteous and wealthy Lucinda, misinterprets his charity and breaks off with him, encouraging another suitor instead, Squire Mockmode, a rustic buffoon also just arrived in London.

By another of the legion coincidences, Squire Mockmode is lodging with Widow Bullfinch, where Trudge and her child, too, are staying. Complications multiply as Leanthe, Lovewell's sister, arrives in London disguised as a boy. When she presents herself to her brother with a letter of introduction, even he does not recognize her as his sister, let alone as a girl.

Seeking to be helpful, he obtains for her (or him) a position as a servant in the employ of Lucinda, whose amorous, drunken maid Pindress pursues the "page". A succession of mistaken identities, plots and counterplots, forged messages and misguided marriages follows, which are difficult to synopsize. Suffice it to say that Roebuck weds and sleeps with Leanthe thinking her to be Lucinda, Mockmode couples with Trudge the erstwhile prostitute, and Lucinda "marries" her maid Pindress, thinking her to be Roebuck in a woman's nightdress. Pindress "weds" the "page" – Leanthe in male attire.

But the ceremony linking Mockmode and Trudge is not valid because it is performed by the landlady, Widow Bullfinch, who is also in disguise. Trudge gets £500 from Mockmode, who is desperate to be free from the "bonds of matrimony". Finally all is set right and everyone is happy, except perhaps for the frustrated Pindress.

The play is completely absurd, but on its own terms as pure farce it is an entertainingly ribald exercise in wild, dream-like goings-on. A projection of the author's fantasy life, it also demonstrates Farquhar's philosophy that nothing should be taken seriously, that one should enjoy oneself at the expense of reason.

To balance the artificiality of the coincidences, there is a degree of realism seldom found in earlier plays of this era. Here, as elsewhere, Farquhar's treatment is ever more satirical and topical, his plotting neat, the tone good-natured and the pace fast. His dialogue, though not as witty as one might like, has force and local colour and is sprinkled with *bons mots*. Some examples: "Money is the sinews of love as of war"; "No widow dare be seen with a poet lest she should be thought to keep him."

The characters, though they populate a farce, are more than caricatures. Leanthe's behaviour conforms to the new moral standard for comedy on stage; despite being surrounded by men, she is chaste. Roebuck, though inclined to libertinage, embodies the ideal cherished by the free-thinking, upper-class young men of the Restoration.

There are also low-comedy figures – Lyric, Pamphlet, Rigadon and Nimble-wrist, for example – at whose expense the author and the audience have broad fun.

Having won public attention, Farquhar lost no time in submitting another work in the same year (1698), *The Constant Couple, or A Trip to the Jubilee*. He was intelligent if not wise, and saw the advantage of following up a hit. Though the play is similarly inconsequential, it earned him a good deal of much-needed money, of which he promptly rid himself in his typical spendthrift fashion.

A focal figure, the well-named Sir Henry Wildair – "an airy gentleman", "his wild Irish gaiety" resembling that of the author's, "entertaining to others and easy on himself" – greatly amused the spectators. Encouraged, Farquhar wrote a sequel, *Sir Harry Wildair* (1701) – but it failed. Time and familiarity deflated the boldness of Sir Harry's exploits, which comprised taking a fine lady to a brothel because of confusion brought on by mistaken identity.

Change occurred suddenly, and comedies became the favoured stage commodities. Farquhar bridged the change with two bawdy first plays and later sentimental ones, which still, however, retained some of the *risqué* wit that characterized works of the Restoration period. As early as 1702 he began writing some original comedies and some adaptations, the first two being *The Inconstant* and *The Twin Rivals*. *The Stage Coach* (1702), a collaboration with Peter Anthony Motteux, followed. Prompted by necessity, he was a fast worker, writing eight plays in all in a mere nine years.

The Beaux' Strategem (1707) is Farquhar's top achievement. His unchallenged claim to fame is due to this and *The Recruiting Officer* (1706), his two final scripts, which grace the boards wherever English is spoken and introduced new subject matter to his country's theatre. The setting and language are remarkably vivid; certainly his personal experience in the military enabled him to write about the army in accurate detail.

There is a good deal of human feeling beneath the jocularity in *The Recruiting Officer*, which is also notable for being placed in a rustic location, away from the streets, taverns, parks and drawing-rooms of London. As has been said, Farquhar let some fresh air blow around his characters and through his setting. Captain Plume, the hero of *The Recruiting Officer*, states, "I'm resolved never to bind myself to a woman for my whole life, till I know whether I shall like her company for half an hour." Silvia, the heiress in love with him, somewhat shares his view, maintaining that a man should not marry until he has had an assortment of sexual experiences.

Captain Plume knows all the standard tricks for collecting fresh troops. He flirts with the attractive local girls, to use them to lure gullible young men who are eager to don the plumage of fighting-men's uniforms to make a brave show. Kite, his sergeant, does the same.

Silvia, daughter of Justice Balance, falls deeply in love with Plume but has promised not to marry without parental consent. Rebellious, she puts on a masculine disguise and runs away from home. As a young man she is overtaken, charged with scandalous conduct, and brought to the court over which her father presides. He orders her drafted into Plume's contingent, to serve as a recruit.

At the same time Kite assumes a disguise as an astrologer. Another story-thread concerns Captain Brazen, a boastful rival of Plume. Though he seeks the hand of the wealthy Melinda, he has to be satisfied with marrying her maidservant. Plume, however, fares much better.

The plot is slender and far-fetched, but fills its purpose, to keep an audience laughing. Indeed, Farquhar handled this material with his usual skill.

The plays of the time were less salacious; even so there were elements aplenty remaining from a previous era. Silvia, for example, was given the traditional "breeches role".

In *The Beaux' Strategem* two young gentlemen, Aimwell and Archer, are close friends who have squandered their separate fortunes by reckless gambling and drinking. They embark on a tour of provincial towns to find themselves heiresses to refill their pockets.

Taking turns, because they can no longer afford actual menservants, each plays master to the other's servant, on alternate days. At Litchfield they reach an inn presided over by Boniface, assisted by his ripe daughter, Cherry. Boniface is secretly in league with Gibbet, leader of a local band of highwaymen.

Aimwell and Archer soon set their sights on a wealthy family that consists of Lady Bountiful, her pretty daughter Dorinda, and her brutish son Squire Sullen, recently and unhappily married to a young lady of good repute. Aimwell, much taken by Dorinda, sees her as the answer to his hopes of elegant plunder. Ingenious and histrionic, he attracts her gaze at a church service.

Shortly afterwards he feigns illness in front of the Bountiful mansion. Carried in, he promptly recovers and pays suit to the fluttering Dorinda, her youthful fancy caught. He passes himself off as his elder brother, Viscount Aimwell, rather than who he is, a penniless younger son.

Meanwhile Archer flirts with the smitten Cherry, the innkeeper's daughter, and with Mrs Sullen, the squire's repining wife. It is Mrs Sullen who becomes the next focus of interest. Against her wishes, her heartless father has wedded her to the stupid, rude squire. Now her eyes are drawn to Archer. Hers is a moral and psychological dilemma. Since he is posing as a footman his social status is far below hers, yet his manners seem superior to his position in life, so her emotional plight is intensified.

To increase the complication, she has another admirer, a French officer who is abetted by a priest. (The French, held in Lichfield, are prisoners-of-war.) Mrs Sullen exploits the officer's pursuit of her to make her husband jealous, in a vain attempt to reawaken his feelings for her.

The highwaymen, after weighing whether to rob Aimwell the traveller, elect instead to raid the dwelling of the rich Lady Bountiful. Aimwell and Archer rout the robbers. Cherry takes care to warn her father, Boniface, and he flees.

The sentimental bias of the author, and the effect of the new moral climate, are clear at the ending. Aimwell is so genuinely in love with Dorinda that he cannot maintain his imposture: he makes a clean breast of it. It hardly need be said that she forgives him his mercenary intent.

Mrs Sullen's long-absent brother, Sir Charles Freeman, suddenly reappears and forces the hateful, ugly squire to divorce Mrs Sullen, leaving her free to wed Archer. At Archer's request, Dorinda consents to take Cherry into her service. To mend matters further, word comes that Aimwell's brother has died, and so the young man has succeeded to a title and estate. (Aimwell greets this news jubilantly, uttering not a syllable of grief at the abrupt passing of his brother.)

All this provides a charming evening, and the play is frequently revived. An extract:

> Boniface: Sire, I have now in my cellar ten tons of the best ale in Staffordshire; 'tis smooth as oil, sweet as milk, clear as amber, and strong as brandy, and will be just fourteen-year-old the fifth day of next March, old style.
>
> Aimwell: You're very exact, I find, in the age of ale.
>
> Boniface: As punctual, Sir, as I am in the age of my children. I'll show you such ale! . . . I have lived in Lichfield, man and boy, above eight-and-fifty years, and, I believe, have not consumed eight-and-fifty ounces of meat.
>
> Aimwell: At a meal, you mean, if one may guess by your bulk.
>
> Boniface: Not in my life, Sir. I have fed purely on ale; I have eat my ale, drank my ale, and I always sleep upon ale.

Such lines are not witty but do have a virile timbre and give pleasure.

Farquhar is always in control of his Byzantine plot, developing it with remarkable lucidity.

Here, too, are all the durable stock dramatic devices – mistaken identity, disguises, danger, swordplay, would-be lovers hidden in closets, paternal objections to made-in-heaven matches – all cunningly varied so as to look fresh and up to date.

Though young, Farquhar, described as "a pretty fellow", had already gained much knowledge of life in many social strata and locales. Good-natured always, he laughed at what he saw. He declared that comedy should be "a well-framed tale handsomely told, as an agreeable vehicle for counsel and reproof". As one critic put it, Farquhar reproved hardly anyone, and offered no more advice than that a rake should give up his loose ways after he finds himself a pretty heiress.

He was voluble and softhearted, as sentimental as the characters he created. Preoccupied with marriages as luckless as his own, he favoured premarital experimentation. His humanization of his characters – with their moments of compelling seriousness so unlike the frolicsome inhabitants of plays by Etherege, Wycherley and Dryden – is a characteristic of the developing Augustan style.

In 1702, the same year he published *The Inconstant* and *The Twin Rivals*, he put out a collection of prose and poetry that contained his *Discourse upon Comedy*. He married soon after, to a woman who deceived him by pretending to have a large fortune she did not in fact possess. In spite of this he was kind to her, and concerned about her welfare. He worked as an army recruiter for three years. In 1706 the actor Robert Wilks gave him £30 in advance for the copyright, and *The Recruiting Officer* was performed successfully at Drury Lane. But Farquhar died deeply in debt at twenty-nine after a serious illness, just after the first presentation in 1707 of *The Beaux' Strategem*. He was buried alongside his father.

He left his two children to the care of Wilks. In a letter he wrote: "Dear Bob: I have nothing to leave thee to perpetuate my memory but two helpless girls. Look upon them sometimes and think of him that was to the last moment of his life thine, GEORGE FARQUHAR." Wilks obtained a benefit for the dramatist's widow, and the daughters each had a pension of £30 a year, which one of them received even up to 1764.

The British, having taken possession of Australia, used it as a far-off penal colony. The most violent criminals were sent there and soldiers were posted to control them. The convicts, finding life bleak, isolated and dull, decided to entertain themselves. They turned to amateur theatricalities and chose several plays to present, beginning with *The Recruiting Officer*, which became the first drama enacted on that remote, thinly populated continent.

The most prominent and influential figure of the Restoration was John Dryden. Milton, his undoubted superior as artist and man, had been forced into retirement by his encroaching blindness, by Cromwell's death, and also by the return of the Stuarts. In London, John Dryden was king of the coffeehouses where wits and writers gathered.

Born in 1631 in the village of Aldwinkle (also known as Aldavale), he was descended from minor gentry. A scholarship enabled him to gain a classical education at Westminster School and Cambridge. His family sided with the Puritans, which may have eased his obtaining a small government post after his graduation.

He began publishing poetry with political content that won him the notice of those in power. He continued doing this throughout his life, his sympathies fluctuating with the views of those able to be of most advantage to him. He could be described as a time-server, an opportunist. A kinder portrait is drawn by Howard Erskine Hill in *Dryden to Johnson* (edited by Roger Lonsdale): he was not an opportunist, Hill claims, but a "public poet", a spokesman for his fellow Englishmen. When Cromwell died, they mourned and he mourned with them. The return of Charles II was joyful because it was brought about without bloodletting, and Dryden felt relief and hope at that peaceful conclusion of a crisis.

Throughout his career as a poet he was very much a partisan, his time taken up with controversy. An incomparable satirist, his verbal thrusts cut deep. His anger was feared and the wounds were lasting. What distinguishes him, however, is the sharpness of his mind and eloquence of his quill pen. He was an antagonist on paper. The accession of Charles II evoked from Dryden a panegyric in fulsome verse to the new monarch. He likened Charles's risen star to the light that had shone over Bethlehem.

He changed his religion as the circumstances dictated, from Puritan to Anglican to Catholic. Settled in London, he tried to augment his limited income with poetry and found the going hard. Consequently he shrewdly turned to the theatre, where ventures could be more lucrative, especially since the King and court were fonder of plays than mere verses.

His first effort was a comedy, *The Wild Gallant* (1663), this a year before Etherege's *Love in a Tub*. He was, indeed, the very first of the Restoration comedy authors, though hardly the most inspired. He stated frankly that he wrote for the stage not to gain lustre but to earn money. He set Etherege and the others an example of sexual candour that they pragmatically followed. Pepys thought *The Wild Gallant* "so poor a thing as I ever saw in my life almost".

In the same year Dryden improved his prospects further by marrying Lady Elizabeth Howard, a daughter of the Earl of Berkshire. They had three sons.

He was not adept at comedy, as he himself confessed. But he did continue to have successes, and they added to his income. Some are not wholly without merit; he was thoroughly professional and could wield his pen most ably. *The Wild Gallant*, which owes much to Jonson's comedy of humours, was a failure initially, but four years later he revised it, and it was better received.

Dryden, like Shadwell, is somewhat of a link to the Elizabethan and Jacobean authors. He soon went beyond them, but he lacks the lightness of spirit and the airiness of phrase to match the better comic writers of his own period. He won a contract to turn out three plays a year but understandably seldom fulfilled it. With a share of the profits, he could earn £350 annually. The list of his comedies is lengthy.

In *The Wild Gallant* he created two characters, Lady Constant and Loveby, whose general traits he continued to delineate and refine over and over under different names, placing them in somewhat changed situations. Some of the plays are not pure comedies but tragicomedies, and some are heroic dramas with comic relief. Worthy of mention, perhaps, are *The Rival Ladies* (1664) and *Secret Love, or The Maiden Queen* (1667). In the latter, Celadon and Florimel are the principals and display Dryden at his best at depicting the men and women who inhabited the Cavalier world with its utter moral abandon. Also on the list should be *An Evening's Love, or The Mock Astrologer* (1668), along with *The Assignation, or Love in a Nunnery* (1672).

He was also responsible for a new version of *Amphytrion* (1690), a work on a mythological theme of such endless appeal to dramatists through the centuries that it would repay a thorough Freudian study. Dryden's adulterous Jupiter claims that his seduction of Amphytrion's lovely wife is justifiable because it will be of future benefit to humankind. The lustful god will beget her the young hero Hercules, who will right the world's wrongs by killing monsters and undertaking other superhuman tasks. Also, the god does not wish to have Alcemena truly mistake him for her dull husband: theirs has been a union that rises above such commonplace sanction:

> No, no: that very name of wife and marriage
> Is poison to the dearest sweets of love:
> To please my niceness, you must separate
> The lover from his mortal foe – the husband.
> Give to the yawning husband your cold virtue;
> But all your vigorous warmth, your melting sighs,
> Your amorous murmurs, be your lover's part.

This somewhat perverted standard of sexual morality is aptly designed to please Dryden's audience, which in theory – if not in practice – looked upon infidelity as amusing.

The anti-marriage theme is dominant in his more durable comic work, *Marriage à la Mode* (1673), which is still sometimes revived. The amorist Palamede learns that Doralice has a husband: "Art thou married? O thou damnable, virtuous woman." Rhodophil, her husband, describes himself to Palamede in a like vein: "The greatest misfortune imaginable has fallen upon me. In one word, I am married, wretchedly married, and have been above these two years." His wife is a jewel in every way, beautiful, amiable and clever. He confesses to having loved her for "a whole half year . . . but then the world began to laugh at me, and a certain shame of being out of fashion seized me".

Jealousy solves the problem of these "fashionable" lovers. Palamede is seeking to seduce the roving, flirtatious Doralice, while Rhodophil is pursuing the loquacious, immodest, coquettish Melantha, to whom Palamede is affianced. The prospect of being trapped in narrow marriage bonds to anyone as talkative as Melantha affrights Palamede. He muses:

> 'Tis true, in the daytime, it is tolerable, when a man has a field – room to run from it; but, to be shut up in a bed with her, like two cocks in a pit, humanity cannot support it. I must kiss all night, in my own defence, and hold her down, like a boy at cuffs, nay, and give her the rising blow every time she begins to speak.

When each man discovers the other's aim, he looks more kindly on the young lady to whom he is properly attached. Thus Dryden ends his erotic comedy on the side of the angels, and with a good deal of psychological validity: if others desire what one likes, one prizes it more highly.

The play is also satirical in its appraisal of the contrasted virtues of town and court manners and values. "Wit", as defined by this poet, is "none other than the faculty of imagination in the writer, which, like a nimble spaniel, beats over and ranges through the field of memory, till it springs the quarry it hunted after". He also carefully and helpfully distinguished between comedy and farce. The latter, as he saw it, deals with the "grotesque". In consequence, "the persons and action of a farce are all unnatural, and the manners false, inconsistent with the characters of mankind". He deplored the increasing fondness for farce in his time, "the world running mad after . . . the extremity of bad poetry". Yet some of his own works, a pertinent instance being *The Kind Keeper* (1678), very much fit into this category. An astute critic, he did not always practise what he eloquently preached.

Another of his comedies, *Sir Martin Mar-All* (1667), is also esteemed, some critics preferring it to *Marriage à la Mode*. In this work, too, there is a "breeches role", a love-lorn girl disguised as a boy and serving as a page. Some of its plot is derived from Molière.

Collier's attack hit Dryden hard. As has been mentioned, he openly admitted his fault. He declared that his "fat pollutions" had contributed to the "steaming ordures of the stage". He contritely added, "I am as sensible as I ought to be of the scandal I have given by my loose writings, and make what reparation I am able by this public acknowledgement."

Dryden's marriage had made him a brother-in-law of Sir Robert Howard, and a few years later Howard wished to share his new kinsman's literary fame and so persuaded Dryden to collaborate with him on a serious script. Together they concocted *The Indian Queen* (1664). The play concerns Montezuma, the triumphant ruler of Mexico, and a love affair, and its appearance created heroic tragedy, a fresh, popular sub-genre that was imitated by his contemporaries and dominated the English theatre for decades.

The Indian Queen undoubtedly owes much to Davenant's *The Siege of Rhodes*; like that work, it combines verse with music. A second source of inspiration was the great Italian poet Ariosto. *The Indian Queen* was staged with a spectacular *mis-en-scène* to much acclaim. To capitalize on this success Dryden on his own composed a sequel, *The Indian Emperor* (1665), depicting Cortez's invasion of Mexico, which was handily staged by using the same ornate sets and costumes.

Encouraged, he followed these lavish works with *Tyrannic Love* (1669) and then one even more grandiose, *The Conquest of Granada by the Spaniards* (1669–70), which is in two parts and at full length comprises ten acts. A fifth play, *Aureng-Zebe* (1675), completed the first cycle of his effort at poetic theatre.

In addition to Davenant and Ariosto, the models for English heroic tragedy were Tasso, another great Italian Renaissance poet, and of course Corneille, with whose virile and rousing work many of Charles II's courtiers had become familiar during their exile in France. Then, too, this was the neoclassical age, during which people profoundly respected the themes and styles of ancient Greece and Rome.

It is not certain that Dryden was the first to introduce this form of play to the London stage – he may have been preceded slightly by the Earl of Orrey – but he was to be the foremost practitioner of these serious dramas (which to today's spectators seem a strange stew), and numerous prefaces and essays expound his well-reasoned precepts and theories about it. He did not follow Corneille's example too closely: he wanted England to have its own kind of tragedy.

In his *Essay on Dramatic Poetry* (1668, revised in 1684) Dryden praised the French masters, singling out Corneille and Molière, yet cogently defended English forms of drama, including tragicomedy. He also states without apology that the English prefer the "variety and copiousness" of a main plot interwoven with sub-plots. (Racine had dispensed with the sub-plot in order to concentrate on one strong problem.)

To Dryden, plays complicated by many story-strands and mixed moods were not inferior. Certainly he felt the story should be coherent; the sub-plot and the people it introduces should not be wholly extraneous. They should be quite relevant, and then "our variety, if well ordered, will afford greater pleasure to the audience". Furthermore, he decried the overly strict French adherence to the three unities. "With their servile observations of the Unities of Time and Place, and integrity of scenes, they have brought on themselves that dearth of plot, and narrowness of imagination, which may be observed in all their plays." He proceeds to illustrate this by pointing out how much more the dramatic action could be developed in many instances, if only the author had a looser rein, and how absurd is the compression demanded by the Horatian precepts. He is not at all impressed by French dramatic poetry or the authors' fondness for regularity, declamation and the tirades. "I confess their verses are the coldest I have ever read." He continues:

> Their speeches being so many declamations, which tire us with the length; so that instead of persuading us to grieve for their imaginary heroes, we are concerned for our own trouble, as we are in tedious visits of bad company; we are in pain until they are gone. When the French stage came to be reformed by Cardinal Richelieu, those long harangues were introduced to comply with the gravity of a churchman.

He compares many long, moralizing speeches in Corneille's plays to sermons.

> Their actors speak by the hour-glass, like our parsons . . . I deny not but this may suit well enough with the French; for as we, who are a more sullen people, come to be diverted at our plays, so they, who are of an airy and gay temper, come thither to make themselves serious: and this I conceive to be one reason why comedies are more pleasing to us, and tragedies to them.

Brief exchanges are more natural to express emotions, he argues. "Grief and passion are like floods raised in little brooks by a sudden rain: they are quickly up; and if the concernment be poured unexpectedly in upon us, it overflows us."

In a further statement of independence, he declares that English writers of tragedy do not imitate the French. "We have borrowed nothing from them; our plots are weaved in English looms." The best patterns to be followed, he adds, are those set by Shakespeare, Fletcher and Jonson. Today Dryden is more esteemed for his criticism on the drama than for his plays.

It has been said that heroic tragedy of the kind advocated by Dryden and those who emulated him was a response to or compensation for a most unheroic age. In these plays, warriors of great courage, high idealism and patriotism meet challenges not only to their lives and the security of their countries, but also to their personal honour. They are capable of overwhelming fervour and love, and invariably their duty and honour are at odds with their passions, presenting them with dilemmas almost impossible to resolve. The hero has both an outer and an inner conflict: in the first, he faces and overcomes a dangerous foe; in the latter, he is torn by a crisis of love. The woman whom he seeks is always of spotless purity. The Restoration heroic tragedy is thus the complete obverse of the Restoration comedy, which is a vehicle for loose morality and cynicism.

Heroic tragedy played a secondary role to such comedy, for audiences in Charles II's time preferred to laugh. Dryden recognized that fact and lamented it, but there was no gainsaying it. The cultural and social climate was not right for exalted tragedy in England. Among the courtiers, too many things ordinarily held sacred were simply laughed at by the corrupt or amoral coterie that surrounded the pleasure-loving King.

Still, serious dramas did reach and hold the boards in considerable numbers. They were certainly not alien among the Cavaliers. Frequently a pompous passage evoked a ribald hoot or comment from a rake seated onstage. And of course the plays served to provide for flamboyant action that was of interest in itself. Women also liked them, flattered by the romantic image they reflected in the person of the adored, virginal heroine.

The age was monarchical; Kings still ruled by divine right, and in truth most of the Kings of England had been men of physical valour. A mystical aura still surrounded the King as a symbol. War, and participation in it, were still highly valued as proof of manhood by the aristocracy. By risking one's life, one evinced one's loyalty to the occupant of the all-powerful throne. Most nobles had been trained to fight with sword and pistol and had taken some role in the rapid succession of battles on home turf and at sea, in which England had steadily engaged during these decades, beginning with its own Civil War and the succession of military expeditions to the

Continent. The speeches of the beleaguered heroes did have meaning to the audience that heard them.

The question is whether these heroic dramas are adequate to the sometimes real problems they present. The answer is unhappily no: most of them are filled with what seems like miles of bombast; psychologically they are hollow; they strike one as offering mere literary attitudinizing. Not only were the times out of joint for heroic tragedy in this vein, but there was also a lack of poets with sufficient insight, intellect and genius to write them. What was missing in poetic splendour was often made up in dazzling music and stage spectacle, as in Italy and France.

John Dryden, with his ample command of language, was the best that England could offer at this moment. This run of couplets, in which an exclamatory Aureng-Zebe reveals the physical ecstasy he anticipates in the arms of Indamora, not only illustrates the sensual side of his poetry but shows how ably Dryden could handle this difficult and restrictive verse form:

> Oh, I could stifle you with eager haste!
> Devour your kisses with my hungry taste!
> Rush on you! eat you! wander o'er each part,
> Raving with pleasure, snatch you to my heart!
> Then hold you off, and gaze! then, with new rage
> Invade you, till my conscious limbs presage
> Torrents of joy, which all their banks o'erflow!
> So lost, so blest, as I but then could know!

In 1678, on the death of Davenant, Dryden had been made Poet Laureate. Whatever his moral shortcomings, he had a lucid intelligence: he was an excellent critic, one of England's best. But he was also a rationalist, above all a satirist – one of the most devastating in English history – and was without the qualities of heart that could imbue his work with the incandescent light and warmth that a Marlowe, Shakespeare or Webster had brought to a line of dialogue, a troubled character or a major scene.

Yet another handicap was Dryden's early determination to compose his tragedies in rhymed couplets. He was often masterly in fashioning them, but the artificiality of the style detracts from the high seriousness, the sustained eloquence and the full richness of feeling that one finds in *Hamlet*, *Othello* or *The Duchess of Malfi*. Nor is he the equal of a Corneille or Racine. He is further handicapped by the insistent preference of his audiences for happy endings. Not in all, but in most of the tragedies of this period, poetic justice is rendered: not only are the wicked punished but the virtuous invariably triumph. This is completely opposed to other basic concepts of tragedy. As a commentator has put it, tragedy is thus reduced to a "fairly tale". Even Shakespeare's plays were altered to fit this new concept. *King Lear* and *Othello* were given more pleasing outcomes.

In Dryden's earliest heroic tragedies, he complies with this demand of the spectators. Consequently, the plays lack truth to life; the hearer or reader senses their falsity. Even those who enjoyed the happy endings must have known that they were evading the harshness of reality.

The serious plays of those decades are filled with excessive emotion; expressions of feeling in them are hyperbolic. This may have been because the emotions are over-heated and the dramatists were aware of it and so strained and puffed to give size and substance to what they sought to express. They also dealt with absolutes only: the moral issues presented the plights of characters seeking to cope gloriously with them. There are no shadings. Essentially these are one-dimensional figures struggling with abstractions and much intricacy of plot – Love, Virtue, Duty, everything is over-simplified. Shadows are in conflict with shadows, while spouting a torrent of rant. The plays are also formless.

In part this was an inheritance from the Elizabethan and Jacobean drama, with its loose shape and plethora of incident. Dryden and his contemporaries did not learn from Racine the worth of unity or the wisdom of exploring limited situations in depth. Nor were they impressed with the aesthetic superiority of a plot handled with restraint.

To lend the plays a semblance of "life", a vast amount of blood is spilled; horrors are heaped high. Tortures were displayed in hideous detail to give the audience a frisson. An odd feature of the plays, too, is the habit of symmetry in plot construction. There is a marked parallelism; pairs of lovers, villains and dilemmas add to the over-supply of story turns and proliferating complications. This was perhaps in accord with a general inclination of the Baroque to over-decorate, manifested in all aspects of art and life.

The Indian Queen, *The Indian Emperor* and *Tyrannic Love* could be cited at length to illustrate all these characteristics. Every fault alluded to above is contained in them. In *The Conquest of Granada* the invincible Moorish hero Almanzor is large-souled and remarkably self-confident, deems war a "noble sport" and has been rewarded with endless victories. But after one glance he is hopelessly in love with Almahide, who is betrothed to Boabdelin, King of Granada, whom she dutifully weds, repressing her own passionate desire for Almanzor. To synopsize the story in even fragmentary detail would require pages, and the cast of characters is equally endless (and their names difficult to spell and pronounce).

Incident follows incident. There are ghost scenes and fights, dynastic intrigues, false accusations, tearful reconciliations and astonishing discoveries – voices from Heaven, for example, providentially warn Almanzor that the Duke of Arcos, with whom he is crossing swords, is his unknown father, as is attested by a birthmark and a token, a ruby-and-diamond bracelet encircling the hero's arm.

In the course of the play no fewer than seven characters are slain or kill themselves, to say nothing of a bull that is decapitated offstage. With King Boabdelin conveniently dead in battle, and Almanzor happily recognized as a nephew of King Ferdinand of Spain and hence of royal blood, the hero is enabled to marry his chaste, patient beloved. The action is epic and rousing throughout.

So popular was the leading role – enacted by Charles Hart in "long coat, breeches, periwig and plumed hat" – that "Almanzor" became a catch phrase for an irresistible, high-sounding warrior who is vulnerable only to the shafts of sudden and overwhelming love. At their best, such speeches, though they have the virtue of precision, are inescapably stilted and doubtless taxed the resources of the actor. The idea of employing rhymed couplets is said to have first been suggested by Charles II, who recommended it to the Earl of Orrey: the monarch was familiar with the ordered verse form of French tragedies and liked it. As Harley Granville-Barker has put it, that poetic arrangement suits the French language: it lends itself to clarity of thought and lucid exposition. It does not, however, serve to express "cryptic English emotions" or stir "intellectual excitement". Nor, when applied to ordinary, everyday affairs, does it sound anything but comic. The following, a request by Solyman, is typical:

> The Princess Melsinae, bathed in tears,
> And tossed alternately with hopes and fears,
> If your affairs such leisure can afford,
> Would learn from the fortunes of her lord.

To which Arimant replies: "Tell her that I some certainty may bring, / I go this minute to attend the King." Five hours of listening to such monotonous declamations, to say nothing of the rodomontade that was usually couched in it, must have been a trial for the audience, while speaking it at any length was surely an ordeal for the unlucky performers.

After *The Conquest of Granada* and *Aureng-Zebe*, Dryden ventured ever further and boldly adapted Milton's *Paradise Lost* to serve as an opera libretto, which he titled *The State of Innocence and the Fall of Man* (1677). (This was just three years after Milton's death.)

Other ambitious playwrights emulated Dryden's heroic dramas. The most prominent was Robert Boyle, Earl of Orrey (1629–79), already mentioned. He was a soldier and a statesman as well as a poet. He had apparently written similar scripts even before Dryden, but it is believed that they were not produced until a somewhat later date. His works include *The General* (1661), *Henry V* (1664) and *The Black Prince* (1667). Besides his exploitation of English history, very freshly interpreted, he chose such Oriental subjects as *The Tragedy of Herod the Great*, *Mustapha, Son of Solyman the Magnificent* (1665), *Tryphon* (1668) and *The Tragedy of Zoroaster* (1675). Here and there he turns a couplet felicitously, as when a lover in *Mustapha* imparts his bright vision: "As quietly as day does vanquish night, / I heard no noise, but saw resistless light."

On Boyle the influence of the French – Corneille and Racine – is stronger than on Dryden. He was not very popular in his own day but proved to be a precursor of the more restrained neoclassical dramas that followed.

Others are George Cartwright (*The Heroick Lover*, 1661) and Elkanah Settle (*Cambyses, King of Persia*, 1671; *The Empress of Morocco*, 1673), as well as John Crowne (*The Destruction of*

Jerusalem by Titus Vespasian, 1677). Settle's most unusual piece is *The Female Prelate* (1680). Actually the play is a biting attack on Roman Catholicism that relates the amazing adventures of Joan, a legendary lady who in masculine disguise becomes the Cardinal of Rheims and then Pope. Her chief opponent is the Duke of Saxony, whom she finally has burned at the stake and whose father she had murdered. Joan is far from chaste: her lover and co-conspirator is Lorenzo and ultimately she suffers a miscarriage in the street, which results in exposure and scandal.

Some of Settle's other scripts, such as *The Empress of Morocco* and *The Conquest of China* (1675), reveal his preoccupation with spirits, of whom he writes well. Crowne is much taken up with religious topics, with portents and miracles and with ghosts.

The exaggerated dialogue and attitudes and the sensational and implausible incidents and false psychology that made up these plays and lesser ones shortly provoked a parody, *The Rehearsal*, by the Duke of Buckingham with the help of some friends. Dryden, Crowne, Settle and others of their ilk were well taken off, sometimes most cruelly with direct quotations. The hero of *The Rehearsal*, a poet named Braye, is obviously meant to be Dryden. To make sure no one missed the point, Buckingham obtained a suit of clothes belonging to Dryden and lent it to the actor assigned the role, and then invited Dryden to accompany him to the première. From a public drubbing such as this, heroic tragedy could not hope to recover. (Dryden took his revenge on Buckingham a few years later in his blistering satire *Absalom and Achitophel*.) *The Rehearsal* was revived from time to time.

In any event, a change was soon to occur, led by the astute Dryden himself. By about 1677 he was ready to abandon the idea of writing tragedy in rhyme. He decided to go back to the blank verse of Marlowe and Shakespeare. The result is startling: he brought forth a tragedy of true stature and dimension: *All for Love, or The World Well Lost*. Almost at once the fashion for rhymed drama ended.

Despite his belittling comments on the unities, Dryden accepted them when composing *All for Love*; he also contradicted himself and excised Shakespeare's sub-plots; consistency was not a trait of his. The action is reduced to a short span of time, and the setting limited to Alexandria. The plot is simplified, with concentration on the fated lovers. If Dryden felt any qualms at attempting a new version of a tale handled by his great predecessors, he does not say so, though he often expressed veneration for the man from Stratford-on-Avon. Confidently he announced:

> Whenever I have liked any story in a romance, novel, or foreign play, I have made no difficulty, nor ever shall, to take the foundation of it, to build it up, and to make it proper for the English stage . . . The story is the least part . . . The forming it into acts and scenes, disposing of acts and passions in their proper places, and beautifying both with descriptions, similitudes, and proprieties of language, is the principle employment of the poet.

Above *The Way of the World* (Congreve, 1700) at the Lyric Theatre, Hammersmith, London, 1924, with Edith Evans as Millamant; directed by Nigel Playfair
Right William Congreve, 1637–1708; engraving after a painting by Sir Godfrey Kneller, 1709

LOVE FOR LOVE.
Buck. O Lord! let me be gone!
I'll not venture myself with a madman.

Left *Love for Love* (Congreve, 1695); eighteenth-century illustration
Above George Farquhar (1678–1707); seventeenth-century engraving
Above right *The Beaux' Stratagem* (Farquhar, 1707) at the Phoenix Theatre, London, 1949, with John Clements and Kay Hammond
Below right *The Recruiting Officer* (Farquhar, 1706), eighteenth-century illustration

Above left Aphra Behn (1640–89); engraving by James Fittler after a portrait by Thomas Unwins
Below left Anne Bracegirdle (1671–1748) as Belinda in *The Provok'd Wife* (Vanburgh, 1697); eighteenth-century illustration
Above Colley Cibber (1671–1757); engraving after a portrait by Giuseppe Grisoni
Right Nell Gwyn as Lady Knowell in *Sir Patient Fancy* (Behn, 1678); seventeenth-century engraving

Above John Gay (1685–1732); eighteenth-century engraving by William Aikman

Above *The Beggar's Opera*, Act III, (Gay, 1728); engraving after a print by William Hogarth

Left Oliver Goldsmith (1728–74); engraving after a portrait by Sir Joshua Reynolds, *c.* 1770

Below *Turandot* (Puccini, 1924), based on a play by Carlo Gozzi (1720–1806), Covent Garden, London, 1947

Below Richard Brinsley Sheridan (1751–1816); eighteenth-century engraving

Left *The Rivals* (Sheridan, 1775), with Isabel Jeans as Mrs Malaprop, Haymarket Theatre, London, 1967
Above *The Rivals*, with Anthony Quayle and Alec Guinness, Old Vic, London, 1938; directed by Esme Church

Left Henry Fielding (1707–54); engraving after a caricature by William Hogarth
Below *Venice Preserv'd* (Otway, 1682), with David Garrick and Susannah Maria Cibber, Drury Lane, London, 1762–3; painting by Johann Zoffany
Near right John Philip Kemble (1757–1823); eighteenth-century engraving
Far right George Frederick Handel (1685–1759); engraving after a painting by Thomas Hudson, 1749
Below right *Alcina* (Handel, 1735), Covent Garden, London, 1960

Left Farinelli (a.k.a. Carlo Broschi, 1705–82); painting by Jacopo Amigoni, 1735
Above left Carlo Goldoni (1707–93); painting by Alessandro Longhi
Above right Eleonora Duse as Mirandolina in *The Mistress of the Inn* (Goldoni, 1753), *c.* 1850

Above *Oreste* (Alfieri, 1783), directed by Luchino Visconti, Teatro Quirono, Rome, 1949
Left Gotthold Ephraim Lessing (1729–81); engraving by Albert Henry Payne after a drawing by Heinrich Wilhelm Storck

Now he and Davenant took the same approach to native material, as they had done earlier with Shakespeare's *The Tempest*. Some actors declare that some scenes actually play better.

Amazingly, Dryden has written a fine play in *All for Love*. It is hardly the equal of works of Shakespeare's, but it is a work of passion and beauty. Blank verse makes the difference. Belatedly, Dryden found the free, less regular line to be his true métier.

Within the play's scope, the conflict is between the divisive claims of love and honour, of sudden passion and calming reason. What is left is chiefly an illicit love affair; both participants are punished. This is not the vast, world-encompassing drama that Shakespeare evokes. Dryden makes few references to the passing of time, so one is not reminded how quickly the tragic tale is progressing, and how much action is compressed into it; the temple setting, on the stage as it was then constituted, would be somewhat simplified, so that it would be adaptable and suggest other places, not being too specific in detail or even outline. Though Dryden pares away many episodes that crowd Shakespeare's chronicle, in particular the earlier scenes, he adds a new contrivance – a confrontation between Cleopatra and Octavia, the deserted wife of Antony.

When critics objected to the tone of this encounter – the women somewhat lower their regal dignity – Dryden retorted that though one was a high-born Roman matron, the sister of Julius Caesar, and her antagonist was a Queen, "they were both women".

The plot is masterly, if not too neat – indeed, it has been described as almost "mathematical" in its precision and balance: again, the obsession with symmetry manifests itself. He cuts the size of the cast from thirty to a mere twelve. The characters have a lesser stature: Cleopatra is pathetic, rather than tragic, and Antony is shown at the last gasp of his glorious career, when he is weak, at times irrational. But his own speeches, and the remarks about him by his followers and the Egyptian Queen who worships him, are reminders of his former magnificence as man and warrior: "the lord of half mankind, vast soul", "the meteor of the world". His suffering and hers readily command our sympathy.

The poetry is at times periphrastic of the Bard's. In fact, Dryden wrote of *All for Love* that it was "Written in Imitation of Shakespeare's Style". It is interesting to compare a passage such as that which depicts Cleopatra as seen by Enobarbus:

> Age cannot wither her, nor custom stale
> Her infinite variety. Other women cloy
> The appetites they feed, but she makes me hungry
> Where most she satisfies.

Dryden's Antony murmurs to his inamorata:

> There's no satiety of love in thee:
> Enjoyed, thou still art new; perpetual spring

Is in thy arms; the ripened fruit but falls
And blossoms rise to fill its empty place,
And I grow rich by giving.

This is very good, but hardly an improvement over the original. In his Prefatory Note, Dryden explains that he has "disencumbered myself from rhyme . . . because this is more proper to my present purpose", and pays a splendid tribute to Shakespeare:

> I have not copied my author servilely – words and phrases must of necessity receive a change in succeeding ages – but 'tis a miracle that much of his language remains so pure; and that he who began dramatic poetry amongst us, untaught by any, and as Ben Jonson tells us, without learning, should by force of his own genius perform so much that in a manner has left no praise for any who come after him.

To this he adds, a bit immodestly, that "by imitating him, I have excelled myself throughout the play; and particularly, that I prefer the scene betwixt Antony and Ventidius in the first act, to anything which I have written in this kind". The scene is indeed an excellent one. It cannot be quoted in full, but here is a passage from a discussion between the two about their mutual foe, Octavius:

VENTIDIUS: I heard you challeng'd him.
ANTONY: I did, Ventidius.
  What think'st thou was his answer? 'Twas so tame!
  He said he had more ways than one to die;
  I had not.
VENTIDIUS: Poor!
ANTONY: He has more ways than one;
  But he would choose 'em all before that one.
VENTIDIUS: He first would choose an ague, not a fever.
ANTONY: No; it must be an ague, not a fever;
  He has not warmth enough to die by that.
VENTIDIUS: Or old age and a bed.
ANTONY: Age, there's his choice,
  He would live, like a lamp, to the last wink,
  And crawl upon the utmost verge of life.
  Oh Hercules! Why should a man like this,
  Who dares not trust his fate for one great action,
  Be all the care of Heav'n? Why should he lord it

O'er fourscore thousand men, of whom each one
Is braver than himself?
Ventidius: You conquer'd for him;
Philippi knows it; there you shar'd with him
That empire, which your sword made all your own.
Antony: Fool that I was, upon my eagle's wings
I bore this wren, till I was tir'd with a soaring,
And now he mounts above me.
Good heavens, is this – is this the man who braves me?

This is not only effective poetic dialogue but also sharp characterization of all three, the two speakers and the man about whom they are talking.

In the final scene the Egyptian Queen leans over her expiring lover and promises to join him in death:

Cleopatra: I will come: Doubt not, my life, I'll come, and quickly too: Caesar shall
triumph o'er no part of thee.
Antony: But grieve not, while thou stay'st,
My last disastrous times:
Think we have had a clear and glorious day,
And heav'n did kindly to delay the storm,
Just to our close of ev'ning. Ten years' love,
And not a moment lost, but all improv'd
To the utmost joys – what ages we have liv'd!
And now to die each other's; and, so dying,
While hand in hand we walk in groves below,
Whole troops of lovers' ghosts shall flock about us,
And all the train be ours.

A moment later Antony dies, and Iras tells her Queen: "He's gone too far to hear you . . ." The last two lines of the play, uttered by the priest Serapion, are a couplet: "And fame to late posterity shall tell, / No lovers liv'd so great, or died so well." Dryden continued to use blank verse in his later work – in all, he left twenty-seven tragedies, nearly all long since unacted and even unread, including a florid *Oedipus* he ventured in 1679. They are essentially operatic.

One of the best is *Don Sebastian* (1689). Its story is of Sebastian, of Portugal, held captive in Barbary, who falls in love with Almeyda, a Princess of that exotic land. They are secretly wed. After many vicissitudes, which once more include poisonings and the rout of villains, the pair seems destined for happiness. Then Sebastian learns to his consternation that Almeyda is his half-sister. Unwittingly, the lovers are guilty of incest. They part, Sebastian to become a hermit, Almeyda to closet herself in a nunnery. The sins of the parents have been visited upon the children: Sebastian's father and Almeyda's mother, the outcast Queen of Barbary, had enjoyed an adulterous relationship. In his Preface, Dryden explains that he visits no harsher punishment on Sebastian and Almeyda, because "an involuntary sin deserves no death". A strong religious feeling runs through it. The play contains some fine lines, among them: "Life is but air, / That yields a passage to the whistling sword, / And closes when 'tis gone."

Cleomenes (1692) has for its subject a contrast between the Spartan way of life and the Egyptian, the former austere, the latter decadent.

In 1679 Dryden essayed another correction of Shakespeare, this time of *Troilus and Cressida*; in this instance he added a fifth act in which Cressida kills herself, and thus is not left unpunished.

Dryden profited constantly from his theatre productions; his income often rose to £1,000 a year, some of his funds coming in pensions from the King. As a satirist, he provoked many enemies who quaked in anticipation of his barbs. On one occasion, perhaps through error, he was thought to be the author of an anonymous satiric attack actually not his; he was ambushed and beaten in Rose Alley, Covent Garden, by a hired band of ruffians, possibly paid by the Earl of Rochester. Dryden repaid his enemies with another scathing poem, *Absalom and Achitophel*, to which reference has been made. It was in this work that the belittling Buckingham, too, was flayed, along with others, including figures of political eminence.

He grew older, still enjoying royal favour in return for his loyal support to whomever was the monarch – and he himself reigned in London, in Will's Tavern, where his special chair stood near the embering blaze on the hearth during winter and on a wind-cooled balcony in the warm season. He stuffed his nostrils with snuff, discoursed on literature, and often generously praised and encouraged the young, as in the instance of Congreve. He was both courted and feared, his pen devilishly sharp when he deemed himself abused. As a critic, he was the arbiter of poetic skill in his day. He always had a ready word of self-congratulation.

Growing older, he became more respectable and even pious and, if anything, more conservative. When James II fled to France, Dryden for once held fast to his faith: he remained a Catholic, though the new regime was Protestant. All three of his sons had positions at the Vatican, which might well have influenced his decision. The cost to him was heavy. He lost his laureateship, his pensions and other sinecures; Shadwell, whom he had held up to ridicule and scorned, succeeded him in most of these. To support himself, he composed more plays, translated excerpts from Homer, Theocritus, Lucretius, Ovid and Virgil – the whole of the *Aeneid* – as well as Boccaccio. He adapted Chaucer.

He died at a ripe seventy and was given a tumultuous funeral, being entombed alongside Chaucer in Westminster Abbey, the resting place of so many of his talented contemporaries.

The standard comment is that Dryden was a better critic of the drama than a dramatist. He did not spare himself in his criticism. He was later to say, with respect to his earlier work, "I remember some verses of my own Maximin and Almanzor which cry vengeance on me for their extravagance . . . All I can say is . . . that I knew they were bad enough to please even when I writ them." By his own confession, he gave his audience what he perceived it crudely wanted. He enjoyed popularity in his own hour but at the cost of an unkind judgement by posterity. *All for Love* shows decisively that he is a dramatic poet of genius who might have done far better than he did.

Dryden's sole considerable rival is Thomas Otway (1652–85), author of the only other tragedies of the period that have survived. He was far less fortunate, unlucky in everything including in love, and he died young, at thirty-three. He entered Oxford but left without a degree. He sought to be an actor but failed. Pursued by poverty most of his life, he enlisted for military service, served in Holland, endured the horrors of a campaign and was commissioned. His death is attributed to starvation. He is described as having been temperamental, sensitive, bitter and brooding. His troubles were compounded by his unrequited infatuation for the actress Elizabeth Barry, notorious for the freedom with which she bestowed her favours.

Like Dryden, he began his playwriting career with works in rhymed couplets. His first two scripts, *Alcibiades* (1675) and *Don Carlos* (1676), are not works of salient merit, more or less conforming to the fashion of the times. Both contain moments of poignancy, however, and some redeeming poetry. In 1679, with *The History and Fall of Caius Marius*, he had turned in Dryden's new direction and wrote blank verse.

Alcibiades displays the author's lasting taste for violence: six members of ten are dead before the last curtain. With a nice sense of humour, however, Otway recalls one of them, the actress portraying Queen Deidamia, to appear before the audience and recite: "Now who says poets don't in blood delight . . . / Ours made such havoc that the silly rogue / Was forced to make me rise for the epilogue."

This curious play combines two themes: the quarrel between the Roman leaders Marius and Sulla, and the transposition of the Romeo and Juliet story to the Renaissance. The play is, like Shakespeare's, mixed in mood, with the Nurse providing comedy – in its initial presentation the role of this ribald gossip was played by a man.

Don Carlos brings to the stage the legendary figure based on the historical legend in the novel by the Abbé de Saint-Réal that later provided Friedrich Schiller a subject for a better play. This is not to say that Otway's work is meritless.

In 1676 Otway offered a farce, an adaptation of Molière's one-act play *The Rogueries of Scapin*, which often proved itself a handy afterpiece in an otherwise too short genre; there is more psychological realism in it than in others of its kind. There is harshness, cynicism and even nihilism in *The Friendship in Fashion* (1678), *The Soldier's Fortune* (1680) and, even later, *The Atheist* (1683). Very clear in these light efforts is the author's desire to shock.

He seems to have had a streak of both gallantry and courage. When John Churchill, the future Duke of Marlborough, struck a girl selling oranges in the Duke's Playhouse, she was defended by Otway who challenged the nobleman. In the ensuing duel both were wounded, but reportedly Churchill came out worse.

Blank verse continued to be followed in major works, first in *The Orphan* (1680). Otway attains his true stride as one of the masters of English tragedy. The scene is Bohemia. The twin brothers Castalio and Polydore love the same woman, their father's ward Monimia. Castalio weds her secretly. On the night of the marriage Polydore goes to Monimia's room, pretending to be Castalio, and ravishes her. Only then does Polydore learn of the marriage and, ashamed of his actions, challenges his brother to a duel he intends to lose. The part of the innocent Monimia was taken by Elizabeth Barry, of whom Otway himself was enamoured.

Stressed is the pathos of the situation and the characters, for the twin brothers have hitherto been strongly bonded. They had vowed never to quarrel with each other, regardless of which is successful with Monimia. The suspense is keen, the plot deftly manipulated. What is not clear, though, is why Castalio does not reveal his marriage. Both young men are good, though Polydore has less honest intentions in his affairs with women. But now unwittingly he is guilty of "incest" in having slept with his twin's bride. Learning the truth, he cries in horror, the verse reminiscent of Webster:

> Let's find some place where adders nest in winter,
> Loathsome and venomous; where poisons hang
> Like gums against the walls; where witches meet
> By night, and feed upon some pampered imp,
> Fat with the blood of babes. There we'll inhabit
> And live up to the height of desperation.
> Desire shall languish like a withering flower,
> And no distinction of the sex be thought of.

Polydore contrives his own end by provoking Castalio to a duel, suicidally impaling himself on his brother's blade. Monimia – who feels she can never let herself be touched by her husband, since she has in error enjoyed a night with his twin – takes poison and dies. Castalio, disconsolate, refusing all help from his father, stabs himself and expires, exclaiming, "Now all I beg is, lay me on one grave / Thus with my love. Farewell! I now am – nothing."

The play, a huge success, stayed in repertory for at least a century. Spectators were moved to tears, and even actors wept while portraying their roles at the sad climax. The virtues of the script are perhaps chiefly melodramatic.

Venice Preserv'd (1682) is the height of Otway's achievement; many critics argue that it surpasses Dryden's *All for Love* as tragedy, that it is indeed the finest serious play of its period. The subject of this, too, is taken from a book by Saint-Réal that had been translated into English a half-dozen years before. But it is believed that Otway was led to choose it by his perception of a parallel to a sensational incident of his own day, the so-called Popish Plot of 1678, which made his drama remarkably topical. Any work concerned with a conspiracy was certain to be talked about and to flourish.

Otway follows Saint-Réal's account closely, adding touches of characterization to round out the story. To provide the almost mandatory conflict between love, honour and duty he gives the hero a wife, Belvidera (the daughter of a wealthy Senator, Priuli), who is the focus of the drama; in doing so he also supplied another good role for his beloved Elizabeth Barry. A decent, sensitive young Venetian, Jaffier, enacted by Ballaton, has eloped with Belvidera. The father Priuli remains implacably opposed to the marriage and finally abets his son-in-law's financial ruin. Jaffier, Belvidera and their child are dispossessed from their home.

In this plight, torn between anger and despair, Jaffier is invited by his best friend Pierre, a soldier of fortune, to join a subversive plot to overthrow the Venetian Senate. He gladly enters into the conspiracy and takes an oath of loyalty to it. At his head is Bedamar, the Spanish ambassador, who wishes to see Venice removed as a competitor with Spain. All too soon Jaffier realizes that the malcontents, though they talk idealistically of liberty and reform, are actually nihilists, envious of those more prosperous than themselves and fascinated with the prospect of slaughter and destruction. They plan to pillage, slay indiscriminately and burn down Venice. Few of them are Venetians; they are mostly foreigners being paid through Spain.

Jaffier is further confused and disillusioned to learn that Renault, an aged leader of the revolt, had sought to molest Belvidera, whom Jaffier has entrusted to his companions as a hostage to ensure his own discretion. When Belvidera draws from him the details of the dangerous plot and its imminence, she is horrified by Jaffier's participation in it, especially since her father is marked as one of its victims. She persuades the constantly wavering Jaffier to betray the conspirators to the Elders of the Senate, to save the city from being reduced to ashes, in return for a promise that the guilty men shall be pardoned and allowed their freedom. The Senators readily give Jaffier their pledge, and the band of rebels is rounded up. But now the Senators revoke their promise: all the conspirators are tortured and put to death. The last of them, Pierre, is awaiting a similar fate: he will first be stretched upon the wheel and then executed. Jaffier is overcome with remorse; he is aware how much he has dishonoured himself. He blames Belvidera for having led him to inform on Pierre and the others, despite his oath to stand by them. As Pierre mounts the scaffold, Jaffier appears, begs his forgiveness, then at the condemned man's request spares him the ordeal of torture by plunging a dagger into his breast. A moment later Jaffier stabs himself, too, and perishes. Belvidera, who has pleaded eloquently with her father to save the plotters, beholds the bloody ghosts of the two dead men, goes mad and expires.

This entire story is compressed into not much more than twenty-four hours. There are a variety of day and night scenes – in a street, in the house of a Greek courtesan, Aquilina, where the conspirators gather, in the dwelling of Priuli, and at the palace where the Senate meets – but the action is limited to Venice; the unities are thereby observed. The style is virile, exceptionally vigorous, and one is again reminded of Webster, though the imagery is scarcely as rich or ever as vividly right.

There are some scenes of abnormal sexuality, which occur in the bedroom of Aquilina, who, in response to a plea from him kicks and whips a masochistic senator, the loose-tongued, aged Antonio. At the time the play was produced it was believed by some (possibly in error) that Antonio was meant to be Anthony Ashley Cooper, Earl of Shaftesbury, head of the Whig Party; in rumours, perhaps libellous and politically inspired, Shaftesbury was whispered to be a lecher of this kind. Needless to say, this scandalous portrait – and the frankness and bawdy humour with which the scene is written – added to the sensation the drama caused. The picture given of Venice, its senators and its people, is one of widespread corruption and depravity: the spectators can hardly hope for either side to succeed in the impending revolt, for neither is in the least sympathetic. The emphasis throughout is on Jaffier's personal problem; his fury against Priuli and the other vicious, self-serving men who rule Venice is in conflict with his relationship with his wife, the always unhappy Belvidera. Theirs is a strongly sensual conjugal bond, presenting Jaffier with a dilemma as to where his true loyalty lies once he has impulsively vowed to aid the conspiracy. The portrait of the fanatic and bloodthirsty dissidents, savouring in advance the carnage they will wreak, is most perceptive; even today it is most timely, and it anticipates in a measure a similar picture of terrorists pictured by Fyodor Dostoevsky in his nineteenth-century novel *The Possessed*. The strength of the friendship between Jaffier and Pierre, at least on Jaffier's part, is so exaggerated as to be explicable only in Freudian terms, though allowance must be made for the high value placed on comradeship in those days.

Highly melodramatic, filled with fiery and tearful encounters, clearly plotted, darkly atmospheric, *Venice Preserv'd* has undoubted power. Perhaps it is because of its concentration on the people – Jaffier, Belvidera, Pierre and Priuli – that it is artistically so successful. Some of its language is, of course, over-charged, yet it usually avoids rant, the chief fault of Restoration tragedy. In some details the characterizations are implausible – Jaffier and Belvidera scarcely mention their child, and it is hard to believe that Jaffier would offer his wife to the rebels as a hostage – but overall they are very real.

Otway, though hardly a major poet, has a gift for striking phrases:

> Jaffier: I'm thinking, Pierre, how that damn'd starving quality
> Call'd honest, got footing in the world.
> Pierre: Why, pow'rful villainy first set it up,
> For its own ease and safety: honest men
> Are the soft easy cushions on which knaves
> Repose and fatten. Were all mankind villains,

They'd starve each other; lawyers would want practice,
Cut-throats rewards; each man would kill his brother
Himself; none would be paid or hang'd for murder.
Honesty was a cheat invented first
To bind the hands of bold deserving rogues,
That fools and cowards might sit safe in power,
And lord it uncontroll'd above their betters.

An eloquent advocate of terrorism, Pierre exhorts and argues:

Burn! First burn, and level Venice to thy ruin!
What! starve like beggar's brats in frosty weather
Under a hedge, and whine ourselves to death!
... Rats die in holes and corners, dogs run mad;
Man knows a braver remedy for sorrow:
Revenge! The attribute of gods, they stamp'd it
With their great image on our natures. Die!
... Die – damn first! What! be decently interr'd
In a churchyard, and mingle thy brave dust
With stinking rogues that rot in dirty winding sheets,
Surfeit-stained fools, the common dung o' th' soil?

Obsessed with his passion for Belvidera, Jaffier exclaims:

O woman! Lovely woman! Nature made thee
To temper man; we had been brutes without you.
Angels are painted fair, to look like you;
There's in you all that we believe of heav'n –
Amazing brightness, purity and truth,
Eternal joy, and everlasting love.

When Jaffier protests, "Oh for a curse to kill with!" Pierre responds: "Daggers, daggers, are much better." Then he tempts Jaffier with his vision of a liberated empire:

All Venice free, and every growing merit
Succeed to its just right: fools shall be pull'd
From wisdom's seat – those baleful, unclean birds,
Those lazy owls, who (perch'd near fortune's top)

Sit only watchful with their heavy wings
To cuff down new fleg'd virtues, that would rise
To nobler heights and make the grove harmonious.

Thinking of Belvidera, he vents his feeling for her:

How could I pull thee down into my heart,
Gaze on thee till my eye-strings crack'd with love,
Till all my sinews with its fire extended,
Fix'd me upon the rack of ardent longing . . .

A vision of the destruction of Venice is quite as intoxicating:

How rich and beauteous will the face
Of ruin look, when these wide streets will run with blood;
I and the glorious partners of my fortune
Shouting, and striding o'er the prostrate dead,
Still to new waste; whilst thou, far off in safety
Smiling, shall see the wonders of our daring;
And when night comes, with praise and love receive me.

Jaffier tells Pierre of Renault's attempt to violate his wife, and his friend asks: "Was she in bed?" Jaffier confirms this:

Yes, faith, in virgin sheets
White as her bosom, Pierre, dish'd neatly up,
Might tempt a weaker appetite to taste.
Oh, how the old fox stunk, I warrant thee,
When rank fit was on him!

Awaiting death at the scaffold, Pierre rejects the offices of a priest, who remarks: "'Tis strange you should want faith." But Pierre is fiercely anti-Church:

You want to lead
My reason blindfold, like a hamper'd lion,
Check'd of its nobler vigour; then, when baited
Down to obedient tameness, make it couch
And show strange tricks which you call signs of faith.

So silly souls are gull'd and you get money.
Away, no more! – Captain, I'd have hereafter
This fellow write no lies of my conversion,
Because he has crept upon my troubled hours.

Dryden had strong praise for his young rival after Otway's too-early death:

> I will not defend everything in his *Venice Preserv'd*, but I must bear this testimony to his memory, that the passions are truly touched in it, though perhaps there is somewhat to be desired both in the grounds of them and in the height and elegance of expression; but Nature is there, which is the greatest beauty.

Some critics say that Otway and in particular this play shine forth only because the field is so bereft of outstanding drama; others contend that Otway, had he lived longer and developed his art, might have risen to Shakespeare's level. As with Marlowe, it is impossible to know. But never after Otway has England yielded a tragic dramatist of top stature.

There is, however, Nathaniel Lee (*c.* 1653–92), an important and interesting entrant. Mentally unstable, he is sometimes referred to as the "Bedlamite". Having become violently mad, he was confined in Bethlehem Hospital for four years. His plays, fitfully brilliant but at other times murky, contain elements of what might have been greatness. His writing frequently has a rhapsodic quality, and he is admired for his mastery of rhymed triplets, which sometimes alternate with more conventional couplets. Here are some lines from his *Nero* (1674), where Britannicus mourns the slaying of Cyara, a girl whom he supposes to be a boy (after the inveterate fashion of these stories, she is disguised in male dress):

My boy is dead.
To Heaven's bright throne his brighter soul is fled.
Yonder he mounts on silver burnish'd wings,
Each god immortal sweets around him flings.
Now, like a ship, he cuts the liquid sky;
His rigging's glorious and his mast is high,
Fann'd with cool winds his golden colours fly.

Such writing is truly Baroque; it makes one feel as though one were gazing at a tondo in a ceiling by Tiepolo, with flying angels and bright blue sky with sunsets flaming. Lee was a believer in the occult, as were Crowne and Settle, and like them he was fascinated by the twisted psychology of tyrants, perverse monsters of cruelty such as Nero and Caligula, who here appears as a ghost, Nero's spectral mentor, teaching his successor how to excel in deeds ever more vicious and pathological. The Roman scene attracted Lee: he evoked it in *The Tragedy of Sophonisba, or Hannibal's Overthrow* (1675) and in *The Court of Augustus Caesar* (1676). *Gloriana* and a play on the Hellenistic era, *The Rival Queens, or Alexander the Great* (1677), deal with much the same milieu. The conqueror is shown as impulsive, weak and effeminate, his affections divided between two Queens – Roxana and Statira – and his friend Hephaestion. In a drunken fury he hurls a javelin and kills Clytus, the most blunt and honest of those at his court. Later, poisoned, he dies babbling deliriously, his bowels filled with ice. The plot is based on a romantic novel, *Cassandre*, by Calprenède. Mourning the beautiful and innocent Statira, who has been stabbed by Roxana, Alexander declaims:

> Oh, she is gone, the talking soul is mute!
> She's hushed – no voice, no music now is heard.
> The bower of beauty is more still than death;
> The roses fade, and the melodious bird
> That waked their sweets has left them now forever.

Lee, one sees, has moved on from couplets and triplets to blank verse. All his plays are dynamic, filled with energy. His poetry is cosmic, as was his religious vision. His imagery is audacious, violent and large-scaled. The characters are intense, perhaps unnaturally so, possessed by the demons and ecstasies of their unwrought creator, who finally lost all self-control. His dramas tend to be shapeless; his quality, in more ways than one, is Elizabethan. His later work includes *Mithridates, King of Pontus* (1678), a study of the growth of conscience in a tyrant; *Theodosius, or The Force of Love* (1680) depicts the oncoming of Christianity, as does a subsequent play, *Constantine the Great* (1683). In both dramas Christianity is equated with meekness, by an insight or scale of values that is almost Nietzschean. The heroes of these plays love inordinately, which also unmans them. The author also seems to be obsessed with the agonies experienced by those who are tortured.

Lee's tendency to excess is noted even in his comedy *The Princess of Cleves*. The hero Nemours is a ruffian, a bisexual lecher who outdoes all other town rakes in his pursuit of sensual gratification. The play is disjointed, a strange mixture, about which there is difference of opinion: some think it is owed more attention; others deem his work too lurid and uneven, more fit for investigation by psychiatrists. Whichever position one agrees with, indisputably something most unusual is found there.

Lucius Junius Brutus, Father of His Country (1680) debates the merit of a republic as against rule by royalty. As might be expected, the argument for having a King is the more persuasive. But the play, at times rational and intellectual, also has a scene of gory sacrifice – blood is drunk – a death by fire and a crucifixion. The piling up of horrors is endless. A father orders his sons executed after having them scourged, to demonstrate that he is above personal bias as a democratic governor.

As is apparent, the serious dramatists of the day were disproportionately interested in historical figures, especially those of remote, ancient Greece and Rome. This reflects the pre-occupation by eighteenth-century intellectuals with all things "classical". Lee was educated at Westminster School and Trinity College, Cambridge. Like Otway, he undertook a career as an actor to scant avail. His plays, though, were decidedly popular, though *Lucius Junius Brutus*, with its anti-monarchical tirades, evoked official displeasure and was shut down by edict after three performances. His death ensued from a bout of excessive drinking.

One assuredly major figure stands outside the Restoration, though he lived and wrote through the height of it. John Milton (1608–74), the great, impassioned poet, was Puritan in spirit and also practice. He had served Cromwell's regime as Latin Secretary for the Council of State, as a thundering propagandist and pamphleteer. He had boldly opposed the Restoration, was imprisoned thereafter for three months and barely escaped hanging for his open resistance to the return of the King. His blindness, and the intervention of such friends as the poet Andrew Stage, as well as Marvell and Davenant, spared him.

Retired to a house in Holborn and then to the country with his wife and three daughters, he turned back from a dozen years of prose and political debate to verse again, beginning work on his great epic *Paradise Lost* and finally adding to his output a tragic play.

Milton assuredly never attended a theatre in the time of Charles II. Many histories of drama omit reference to him, yet he made two superb contributions to the dramatic form. The first is a masque, *Comus* (1634), written at the suggestion of, and in collaboration with, the composer Henry Lawes (1596–1652) for a fête at Ludlow Castle, a noble medieval edifice near Wales, the residence of the Earl of Bridgewater.

Milton's father, a prosperous property owner, was very musical: he played an organ and composed madrigals. The son, too, had a good voice and also played the organ. Music was in his soul, as well as in his sonorous prose and verse. Blind and retired, he spent much time singing and playing. *Comus*, fashioned while he still had sight, was a work of delicate poetry to which Milton added music to have it qualify as an "opera" and obtain a licence for production. It took advantage of the beautiful, well-wooded countryside in which the masque was presented, before the towering castle along the banks of the winding Severn.

It sings of "Such sights as youthful poets dream / On Summer eves by haunted stream". Since it was mandated that the Earl's offspring, two sons and a daughter, should have leading roles, the pastoral allegory recounts the perils overcome by innocent young travellers, the Earl's children, as they make their way through a forest to join their father on a festive occasion, his appointment as Lord President of Wales. The anti-masque is furnished by the antics of Comus, an enchanter, who vainly seeks to seduce a Lady. As might be expected of Milton, the stern young Puritan, this pageant-poem is a celebration of chastity.

In most opinions it is the finest masque written in English, by virtue of its rich and delightful language. To be appreciated fully it should be heard accompanied by the music of Lawes, the composer who first staged it. (A century later it was restaged with new music composed by Thomas Arne.) Few if any other masques boast a dramatic structure equal to Milton's *Comus*, as modern revivals have confirmed. He wrote just one other piece of this kind, *Arcades* (1633).

There is certainly evidence of a strong dramatic sense and flair in *Paradise Lost*, with its fiery and swirling conflicts between Heavenly Hosts and fallen Archangels. He had first considered putting it into the form of a play; it is hardly surprising, therefore, that when the poet later set himself to write a "Greek" tragedy, though on a biblical subject, he handled it with the same skill and assurance. *Samson Agonistes* (1671) was not written to be acted, though in recent years it has been staged with an effect described by some as "spell-binding". It was published the same year as *Paradise Regained* and represents Milton's last, high accomplishment as a poet.

He announces in a preface that his aim has been to observe all the strictures of Greek tragedy: his story fits within the three unities, and it avoids any intermixing of comic and serious incidents. A Chorus is employed. English literature indeed affords no purer example of drama in the Attic form than this tense work which – like the *Prometheus* of Aeschylus – is static yet pulses with emotional action that progresses towards a huge climax. The biblical story in the Book of Judges is followed in some details; it is considerably enlarged upon, and much of its barbarism is omitted or softened, so that the hero is shown much more sympathetically as chastened by suffering.

Samson, blinded and bound, is led forth from his cell to breathe fresh air:

> A little onward lend thy guiding hand
> To these dark steps, a little further on;
> For yonder bank hath choice of Sun or shade,
> There I am wont to sit, when any chance
> Relieves me of my task of servile toyl,
> Daily in the common Prison else enjoyn'd be,
> Where I am a Prisoner chain'd, scarce freely draw
> The air imprison'd also, close and damp,
> Unwholesom draught: but here I feel amends,
> The breath of Heav'n fresh-blowing, pure and sweet,
> With day-spring born; here leave me to respire.

To him, as to the bound Prometheus, comes a succession of visitors. Manoah, his father, is one, hopeful of winning his giant son's release by payment of ransom. But Samson is resigned to his lot and even feels that he deserves his punishment. He is taunted by Harapha. He bears this, too, with patience and fortitude. He feels himself reconciled once more with Divinity, whose ordained servant he had once been. What awaits him is a new destiny, which is not only his but that of his whole nation, which like him is yoked and enslaved.

His most important visitor, theatrically, is Dalila, hailed by the Chorus in a famous passage:

But who is this, what thing of Sea or Land?
Female of sex, it seems,
That so bedect, ornate and gay,
Comes this way sailing
Like a stately Ship
Of Tarsus, bound for th'Isles
Of Javan or Gadier
With all her bravery on, and tackle trim,
Sails fill'd, and streamers waving,
Courted by all the winds that hold them play,
An amber scent of odorous perfume
Her harbinger, a damsel train behind;
Some rich *Philistian* Matron she may seem.
And now at nearer view, no other certain
Than Dalila my wife.

The introduction almost adds a light note. Confronted by the woman who has betrayed him, in service to her Philistine masters, Samson's anger is aroused again. She has come, faltering and tearful, to beg forgiveness and offers several plausible excuses for her disloyal deed. As she spells out each pretext she is ever more clearly characterized, with traits not taken from the Old Testament but added by Milton. The stricken Samson denounces her, calling her a hyena, and, furious, she departs from his presence with an uncertain pardon and an insulting prophecy. Some commentators see this scene as one of temptation, as Samson is once more drawn by her physical attraction, which he must overcome to achieve moral regeneration. The Chorus says that in her last speech Dalila has bared herself as "a manifest Serpent".

Harapha, come to sneer at his prostrate foe, leaves crestfallen when his gibes evoke only a challenge to battle from Samson, newly resolute, blind but willing to fight with only an oaken staff.

A terrified Messenger, one of the few Philistine survivors, reports the final catastrophe, the destruction of the Temple. Samson has first offered a prayer to his God:

This utter'd, straining all his nerves, he bow'd;
As with the force of winds and waters pent,
When mountains tremble, those two massy pillars
With horrible convulsion to and fro
He tugg'd, he shook, till down they came, and drew
The whole roof after them with burst of thunder . . .

This catastrophe is the climax, but the true drama lies in Samson's penance and redemption, so that his death is a triumph. He has overcome the pride and a yielding to voluptuousness that led him to sin. God, who gave him a superhuman strength, has returned to him, and his final act is one of self-sacrifice.

The play is open to many interpretations. Some critics see in Samson, blind and impoverished, beset by enemies, a self-portrait of the author. The remarkable passage in which Samson speaks of his sightlessness would seem to bear this out:

O dark, dark, dark, amid the blaze of noon,
Irrecoverably dark, total Eclipse
Without all hope of day!
O first created Beach, and thou great Word,
Let there be light, and light was over all;
Why am I thus bereav'd thy prime decree?
The Sun to me is dark
And silent as the Moon,
When she deserts the night
Hid in her vacant interlunar cave.

It is possible to read the drama as an allegory in which the exultant, pagan Philistines are the Stuart Cavaliers, and the beset Hebrews the suppressed Puritans, the true believers. There is also a slight parallel between Samson's alliance with Dalila and Milton's own unhappy first marriage to Mary Powell. But others dispute this autobiographical interpretation. The second word of the title, "Agonistes", connotes the "competitor" or "struggler". Samson is chosen to be the champion of God. Has not Milton also set out to "justify the ways of God to man"?

To realize how far apart Milton's spiritual realm was from that of other Restoration playwrights, it should be noted that *Samson Agonistes* was published the same year as Wycherley's *Love in a Wood*.

He was a proud, obstinate man, self-righteous, difficult and often enraged. In controversy he was apt to be unfair to his antagonist and cruelly vituperative. Withdrawn from London and its theatre, he had a poor opinion of its practitioners. Dryden spoke highly of him, but the always self-confident, egoistic Milton in turn considered Dryden "a good rhymester but no poet", a certainly inadequate estimate.

All for Love, Venice Preserv'd and *Samson Agonistes* are rarely staged today, never in commercial theatres, only by subsidized troupes or else by academic sponsorship as curiosities and only at long intervals. They might almost be considered to be closet dramas.

Today none would deny Milton space for repose in Westminster Abbey, but he was long out of royal favour. He is buried alongside his father in St Giles, Cripplegate.

The new century in England and on the continent, as seen in France with such forerunners as Marivaux, Destouches and Diderot, brought an altered temper. The tone of life softened. Sentimentality prevailed in even more aspects of art. A reason for this was the rise and spread of a substantial middle class, with more compassionate values and less exacting taste. An economic process was under way, whereby the idle rich were growing poorer and refilling their purses by marrying their daughters to the *nouveaux riches*.

The composition of audiences changed, becoming broader, less patrician and cultured and more interested in domestic and everyday concerns. Playhouses were gradually opened in ever greater numbers in all parts of Europe as cities grew larger, and theatre-going was no longer solely a court entertainment or limited beyond that to an aristocratic coterie. The old forms of plays and in particular the comedies of intrigue continued, as presented by Corneille, Racine and Molière in France; in England, there were Shakespeare's comedies of manners.

But fresh, diverse types also began to appear. Tragicomedy was the new mode. From now on the theatre offered a more mixed programme, and it would not be as easy to categorize the style of any era or place. Seen in perspective, the century was hardly one that developed many outstanding playwrights or more than a handful of immortal works. All the same, it was an epoch when theatres were busier than ever before, appealing to more people and accommodating to their morality, which was stricter than that of the freewheeling nobility of the previous age. Plays, even comedies, became more didactic, expressive of the Enlightenment or the "Age of Reason" which was coming into being. The plays embodied the standards of people who had not inherited their privileges but who worked hard to improve their lot in life. This segment of the audience sought moral instruction and the reinforcement of solid pieties.

During this period, too, theatre was ever more cosmopolitan. Ideas were exchanged by dramatists in all European countries, as travel and other kinds of communication made rapid progress.

To continue with the scene in England: Colly Cibber (1671–1757), an actor-manager, became a leading if eccentric figure during the first decades of this new era. He shared control with two fellow actor-managers of a company that flourished at the Drury Lane. His plays, of no artistic importance, include *Love's Last Shift* (1696), in which he created the role of Sir Novelty Fashion, *The Careless Husband* (1704), *The Non-Juror* (1717), an adaptation from Molière's *Tartuffe*, and *Damon and Phillida* (1729), a ballad-opera.

Cibber, "an industrious poet and an honest man", wrote seven plays in all, which are chiefly memorable for the portraits he has left of theatrical personalities and practices of his time, and as a participant in – or at least the butt of – an amusing feud with Henry Fielding. Of plebeian origin, he was not an elegant Congreve. In the two plays mentioned above a remorseful rake is reformed and ecstatically reunited with his wife. Contemporary observers recorded that audiences were deeply moved, even to tears, by the happy ending.

Comedy was becoming genteel. The characters in the farces are much more decorous, and do not strive for verbal wit which is too often at the expense of propriety. Especially wives are shown as unfailingly faithful, if long-suffering. But invariably they are recompensed for their virtue. The philandering Sir Charles Easy in *The Careless Husband*, reprimanding himself for his faults, declares: "How mean a vice is lying! and how often have these empty pleasures lulled my honour and my conscience to a lethargy, while I grossly have abused her, poorly skulking behind a thousand falsehoods." Lady Easy, overcome by his efforts at a tender reconciliation, weeps and exclaims: "Oh my dear! distract me not with the excess of goodness."

An "excess of goodness" is exactly what Cibber introduced into his plays, and they were welcomed enthusiastically. When Sir Charles offers, "Take what no woman ever truly had, my conquered heart!" Lady Easy rhapsodizes: "Oh, the soft treasure! Oh, the dear reward of long deserving love! Now I am blessed indeed to see you kind without th'expense of pain in being so, to make you mine with easiness. Thus, thus, to have you mine is something more than happiness, 'tis double life, and madness of abounding joy."

Somewhat vague about his family and domestic matters, Cibber replied to a question that he had "about a dozen children". One of them, Theophilus, always in debt, became an actor and had a wife, Sussanah Arne (1713–60), who joined that profession.

A daughter, Charlotte Clarke, did, too. It was said of her that "oddity was her trademark" – she was a chip off the old block. She had a passion for firearms and horses that suited her for "breeches roles". She was in the cast of Fielding's *The Historical Register for the Year 1736* which was closed by the government when official censorship was legislated, a barrier that was retained until public protests finally removed it.

As a member of Henry Fielding's company, Clarke caricatured her father, whose signature role had been Sir Fopling Flutter. She excelled at parts that called for cross-dressing. Among her other roles was Captain Macheath in *The Beggar's Opera* by John Gay. Her loose living involved her in repeated scandals, and her career in the theatre rose, then tumbled abruptly.

Clarke's forays on the stage, like her father's, were affected by the changing expectations of audiences, as well as by new governmental strictures. Scripts now had to be submitted in advance for approval before a licence for production was issued. To get around this barrier, "theatre clubs" were organized. Purchasing the equivalent of a ticket bought membership, entitling the buyer access to a "private" viewing of a play for members.

More literary skill is displayed by Sir Richard Steele, best known as the founder of the *Tatler*, an innovative journalistic enterprise in which he was shortly joined by his long-time friend Joseph Addison and which was later succeeded by a similar and even more illustrious publication called the *Spectator*. Steele's *Tatler* came out weekly, the *Spectator* daily. In its widely read columns, along with social gossip, these two talented writers expressed their views on many aspects of life. Books and plays were reviewed. At its height, the circulation of the *Spectator* reached as many as 14,000 educated subscribers, who would read it at breakfast. In its pages, it might be claimed, were developed the forms of both the short story and the modern essay.

Steele, son of a notary, was born in Dublin in 1672. He studied at the Charterhouse School and Oxford but did not take a degree, going off to join the army instead. His nature was one of irrepressible high spirits. He roistered and drank heavily. He was excitable, open-handed and irresponsible. In many ways he fitted the picture of the Restoration gallant.

He fought a duel, almost killing his opponent. This shocked him, and he began to repent of his improvident, vagrant existence. Undertaking a campaign against duelling, he composed a tract, *The Christian Hero* (1701), and other religious essays in which he expressed dismay at the degeneration of the age and urged a return to Bible study and mutual decency and respect in relations between men and women. He lent support to Jeremy Collier's attack on stage obscenity.

When he was twenty-nine, finding that his own preachments were considered dull and were largely unheeded, he turned to the theatre as a better vehicle for his views. He wrote a trio of comedies in which the denouements are moral and evil-doers are drastically punished.

The Funeral, or Grief à la Mode (1701) was, in his own words, meant to show virtue and vice truthfully. Next came *The Lying Lover* (1703), in which the hero, believing he has slain a friend in a duel, undergoes pangs of remorse while in prison. Next came *The Tender Husband* (1705). None of these was very successful. His audience was not ready for him, and his craftsmanship was never too good. For seventeen years, occupied with other affairs, he abandoned the theatre but returned to it with *The Conscious Lovers* (1722), his most notable contribution.

In most of these moral comedies Steele's purpose is not so much to attack or satirize depravity as to show errant behaviour arising from error. The hero, being neither a fool nor a villain, is capable of finally recognizing his mistake and redeeming himself. The saving grace of Steele's plays is that, though sentimental, they are not mawkishly so. His message chiefly is that people should be benevolent and forgiving in their dealings with one another. In his preface he declares that some people have found fault with a comedy that elicits tears, but in his opinion "anything that has its foundation in happiness and success must be allowed to be the object of comedy, and sure it must be an improvement of it to introduce a joy too exquisite for laughter"; he argues further that "men ought not to be laughed at for weeping". In the rhymed prologue there is a plea for a more polite theatre:

No more let ribaldry, with licence writ,
Usurp the name of eloquence or wit . . .
'Tis yours with breeding to refine the age,
To chasten wit, and moralize the stage.

The play is based on Terence's *Woman of Andros*, though finally so changed that before the plot has gone far its source is barely perceptible. The hero, Bevil Jr, is a male paragon, an exemplary son. He, for one, is flawless. Though he is already of age and has come into a fortune left to him by his mother, he refuses to take any of it while his father still lives. Bevil Sr is anxious to see his son wed to a charming, pretty heiress, Lucinda Sealand. But she is in love with Bevil Jr's friend Mr Myrtle, and Bevil Jr himself has given his heart to a young lady, Indiana, who has experienced many vicissitudes since her childhood when her wealthy father disappeared at sea. Lucinda's mother, working at cross-purposes from her husband, is seeking a match between the girl and her cousin Cimberton, a noble coxcomb with intellectual pretensions and a high opinion of his social status, who wishes to enrich himself while begetting an heir.

These tangled strands of intrigue are separated and set straight, and all concludes happily when Indiana is discovered, by her ownership of a bracelet, to be Lucinda's half-sister; that is, Mr Sealand's long-lost daughter. As in Terence's comedy, this gentleman was rescued from his watery grave, and then – "for reasons now too tedious to mention" – changed his name and started a new family. Bevil Sr is gratified that his always obedient son is marrying well after all; Bevil Jr is delighted to claim his Indiana; Mr Myrtle is awarded Lucinda's hand. Mr Cimberton, losing interest when Lucinda's prospective inheritance is cut in two by the disclosure that she has a half-sister, huffily departs.

The exposition is clumsy and the main plot is often bland, centring as it does chiefly on the ambiguity of Indiana's position in being kept by a man who apparently has no designs of any sort on her; his solicitude and generosity baffle the poor girl. Since the audience knows what Bevil Jr has in mind, honourable matrimony at a propitious moment, no suspense is engendered. Indeed, a well-spoken servant, Tom, describes Bevil Jr as "the most unfashionable lover in Great Britain".

An old servant, Humphrey, one of the lesser characters, and a flirtatious maid, Phillis, have eyes for each other, and they are lively and clever. Their scenes together and neat speeches are invariably amusing and spark the frequently lagging script. In one welcome episode Mr Myrtle impersonates Cimberton's aged uncle; in another, Myrtle, unjustly suspicious of Bevil Jr's intentions towards Lucinda, challenges him to a duel. This permits the author another chance to derogate the, to him, pernicious custom of resorting to swordplay to save face and settle disagreements. In addition, Lucinda voices criticism of forced marriages made for material gain.

The dialogue is intermittently good. At times highly evocative, it offers vignettes of the life of the period. Tom scoffingly recalls the dignity and piety of customs of an earlier day when he says, "You could not fall to your dinner till a formal fellow in black gown said something over the meat, as if the cook had not made it ready enough." He depicts the saucy Phillis in this fashion:

> I met her this morning in a new manteau and petticoat not a bit worse for her lady's wearing, and she always has new thoughts and new airs with new clothes. Then, she never fails to steal some glance or gesture from every visitant at their house, and is, indeed, the whole town of coquettes at second hand – But here she comes; in one motion she speaks and describes herself better than all the words in the world can.

Indiana's wary, sour aunt Isabella initially holds a poor opinion of Bevil Jr: "[He] carries his hypocrisy the best of any man living, but still he is a man, and therefore a hypocrite."

Tom relates how he first met the piquant Phillis:

> I remember I was ordered to get out of the window, one pair of stairs, to rub the sashes clean; the person employed on the inner side was your charming self, whom I had never seen before . . . You could not guess what surprised me. You took no delight when you immediately grew wanton in your conquest, and put your lips close and breathed upon the glass, and when my lips approached, a dirty cloth you rubbed against my face, and hid your bounteous form; when I again drew near, you spit, and rubbed, and smiled at my undoing . . . We were Pyramus and Thisbe, but ten times harder was my fate.

Apparently he was so discomfited he had toppled off the stepladder. After that, he more than made up for his frustration in not having been able to kiss her.

It is also interesting, and indicative of social change, to hear Mr Sealand reply to Sir John Bevil:

> Give me leave to say that we merchants are a species of gentry that have grown into the world this last century, and are as honourable, and almost as useful, as you landed folks that have always thought yourself so much above us.

To which he adds,

> You are a pleasant people indeed because you are generally bred up to be lazy.

Steele was better at preaching than at practising moderation and good conduct. He was forever sinning and repenting. Of him it was said, "His tenderness for women rivalled his affection for alcohol." He married twice, and was a fond husband but hardly a faithful one. He borrowed and wasted money from friends whom he swerved into side streets to avoid meeting and was finally locked up in debtor's prison. Addison strove to help him, got him government jobs, lent him large amounts and once sued him to recover a loan. Steele was elected to Parliament in 1713 but was soon expelled for his use of "seditious language". His fortunes rose, with the aid of his political friends, but fell again when he spent too lavishly. He withdrew to his wife's estate in Wales, where he lived until his death in 1729.

Joseph Addison, whose name is invariably linked with that of Steele since they were co-editors of the *Tatler* and the *Spectator*, was actually possessed of very different talents and temperament. Born the same year as Steele, he was the son of an Anglican vicar and retained his piety life long. He, too, went to Charterhouse School, then on to Oxford where he displayed such brilliance, especially in Latin, that the Earl of Halifax marked him for government service, persuading the head of Magdalen College to divert the youth's interest from theology. The Earl also obtained for him a grant to travel on the Continent, to become acquainted with foreign languages.

The accession of Queen Anne put a stop to the grant, however, and the young man was forced to shorten his leisurely journey. He took employment as a tutor to extend his travel.

Returned to London, he was still short of funds. He began to earn notice and money as a poet, his outstanding attainment being a tribute to the victorious Marlborough after his triumph at Blenheim. Addison's *The Campaign* was later a favourite of George Washington.

Given a government post, he steadily rose to higher positions, becoming Undersecretary of State in 1706. Two years later he entered Parliament. With other posts bringing him a good income, he was soon prosperous enough to purchase a £10,000 estate. It was after the failure of the *Tatler* and its successor the *Spectator* that Addison took up writing for the theatre. His *Cato* was produced at the Drury Lane on 14 April 1713.

Taken from Plutarch's account, the play follows the fortunes of the republican hero and the remnant of the Roman senate after its members have fled to Utica, while Caesar and his legions seize Roman rule. The younger Cato, valorous and stoic, is resolved to oppose the conqueror. He has two sons and a daughter. The sons, Portius and passionate Marcus, are rivals for Lucia, whose father is a senator. Her choice is Portius, but she forswears him because she fears the effect on the excitable Marcus if he learns of her affection for his brother.

The daughter, Marcia, is beloved by the idealistic Numidian Prince Juba, who reveres Cato. Cato's secret enemies are Sempronius – a perfidious senator who is convinced that Caesar will prevail and wishes to court his favour – and an ageing Numidian general, Syphax, whose motives are much the same. The pair conspire to frustrate Cato's resistance to the new ruler of Rome. Sempronius, too, desires to possess Marcia.

Cato's eloquence puts down an incipient mutiny by Sempronius, who is still successful in hiding his participation in the plot. Sempronius orders the mutineers cruelly tortured and executed, lest they betray his own seditious role. Intending to desert Caesar's camp, he has Syphax's help in disguising himself as Juba. He means to kidnap Marcia and carry her off with him. But Juba, by sheer chance, intervenes and kills him. Marcia believes the dead man is Juba and laments him, and Juba, overhearing her, is now aware that his love for her is returned.

Marcus is slain. Cato pleads with the others to seek safety in flight. He then withdraws into solitude, where – after reading Plato's writings on the immortality of the soul – he bids his children farewell and slays himself by falling on his own sword. He is stintlessly praised and mourned by all who survive him, as they join their hands and prepare to ask for mercy from the approaching Caesar.

All this is compactly and lucidly told. The dialogue, though often stiff or high-flown, is at times vivid and effective. It is in blank verse, but lines at scene endings are in rhymed couplets or even triplets. (Steele also uses couplets as scene-closers in this way in *The Conscious Lovers*.) The best-known line is the exclamation of Portius: "'Tis not in mortals to command success, / But we'll do more, Sempronius; we'll deserve it."

The traitorous Numidian, Syphax, gives a cynical warning to Juba: "Honour's a fine imaginary notion, / That draws in raw and unexperienc'd men / To real mischiefs, while they hunt a shadow." He continues:

> The boasted ancestors of these great men,
> Whose virtues you admire, were all such ruffians.
> This dread of nations, this almighty Rome,
> That comprehends in her wide empire's bounds
> All under heav'n, was founded on rape.
> Your Scipios, Caesars, Pompeys, and your Catos
> (These gods on earth) are all the spurious brood
> Of violated maids, of ravished Sabines.

The general tone, however, is better represented in this adulatory exchange:

> Syphax: But how stands Cato?
> Sempronius: Thou hast seen Mount Atlas:
> While storms and tempests thunder on its brows,
> And oceans break their billows at its feet,
> It stands unmov'd, and glories in its height.

Such is that haughty man; his tow'ring soul,
'Midst all the shocks and injuries of fortune,
Rises superior and looks down on Caesar.

Yet Addison is capable of better poetry, as here, where Syphax predicts how destruction will pour in on Cato from every side, which he likens to a storm in his own South African homeland:

So, where our wide Numidian wastes extend,
Sudden, th' impetuous hurricanes descend,
Wheel through the air, in circling eddies play,
Tear up the sands; and sweep whole plains away.
The helpless traveller, with wild surprise,
Sees the dry desert all around him rise,
And smother'd in the dusty whirlwind dies.

Admittedly, a finer poet could improve on "dry desert".

To many today a speech such as Cato's on beholding the bleeding body of Marcus sounds false:

Welcome, my son! Here lay him down, my friends,
Full in my sight, that I may view at leisure
The bloody corpse, and count those glorious wounds.
How beautiful is death, when earn'd by virtue.

The strictness of the play's form is now called "pseudo-classical". Addison followed every Horatian prescription. Because of its enormous success, the play, too, set a pattern which most eighteenth-century English writers of tragedies followed as closely as they could. In lesser hands than Addison's, scripts were frigid and artificial.

Addison, however, enjoyed a triumph. Steele had tried to pack the house, on the first night, with friends drawn from their political party, the Whigs. The Tories who were present, though, joined in the perfervid applause. After that, the play ran for thirty nights, always sold out and was translated into Italian, French and German. It was read with interest and approval all over the Continent, as an example of English classicism. As such, it supplanted the "heroic tragedy" of Dryden and Otway. Today it would hardly do well on stage, though a reading of it is not without reward.

What most appealed was the portrait of Cato as a selfless, high-minded, dedicated Roman statesman–philosopher. He is a paradigm that fitted the dream of human perfectibility held by enlightened thinkers of the then dawning Age of Reason. Very little of Cato's greatness is demonstrated: he is mostly a stately, static if articulate figure, existing largely through the encomiums paid him by those who surround him, his sons, his loving daughter, the worshipful Juba. Dying, Cato himself doubts that his course has been the wisest: this is almost the only moment at which he comes to life and seems human.

Addison was so popular after the presentation of *Cato* that Jonathan Swift said he could have been elected King of England. Alexander Pope, who contributed a prologue to the play, declared: "Cato was not so much the wonder of Rome in his drama's days as he is of Britain in ours." Voltaire, who appreciated the close adherence to the unities that he himself so highly valued, wondered that Englishmen "could tolerate Shakespeare after seeing Addison's plays".

The author's place in theatrical history rests solely on this one script. His comedy *The Drummer* (1713) was a failure. With his insistence on propriety he was later called "the first Victorian".

Addison, whose public fault was a fondness for hard drinking, wed a countess, with whom he proved to be incompatible. He was awarded even higher government jobs, then retired with a large pension. A bit quarrelsome, he dismissed the Restoration writers as coarse and lost some of his friends, Steele and Pope among them. He died rich and full of honours in 1719 and was interred in Westminster Abbey.

Quite different from Addison's was the direction taken by Nicholas Rowe (1674–1718). He, too, is a transitional figure, a link to the tradition set by Otway, whom he much admired, and earlier by Shakespeare: he prefixes his *Tragedy of Jane Shore* with a statement that it is "Written in Imitation of Shakespeare's Style". Prepared for the law, like so many other English writers, Rowe found his way to playwriting. His style and form might be called "pathetic tragedy" and has often been described as a lachrymose complement to "sentimental comedy". His three best-known works are referred to as "she-tragedies" because they stress flamboyant leading feminine roles. For this reason he is also likened to Racine.

Still another influence on him is Marlowe. *The Ambitious Stepmother* (1701) is about a Queen whose nature is unusually turbulent. Cleone, dressed as a boy, affects a rescue at the expense of her own life. *Tamerlane* (1701) portrays the Eastern conqueror in a kindly light, as a peace lover. *The Fair Penitent* (1703) is a more notable example of Rowe's treatment. Lothario blithely seduces the proud Calista, in a portrait very different from Marlowe's. When he proves faithless, and she incurs her father's anger, she is led to repent of her wilfulness. What softens her self-assertiveness is the pardon extended to her by both her father and her husband. The plot is partly borrowed from Massinger's earlier *The Fatal Dowry*. *The Royal Convert* (1707) is laid in ancient Britain and is about the clash between paganism and early Christianity. Rowe is nearly always drawn to historical subjects, again like Shakespeare and Otway.

The Tragedy of Jane Shore (1714) parallels a theme originated by Shakespeare: the execution of the Lord Chamberlain Hastings by the order of the evil Plantagenet pretender, Richard III. In

Rowe's play Jane Shore, the former mistress of Edward IV, is left penniless at her royal lover's death. Hastings, speaking as her "friend", intervenes with Richard, now Regent, to have her confiscated estates restored to her.

Actually, Hastings is infatuated with the hapless Jane and wishes her to be his mistress. In Shakespeare's version she accepts that role; in Rowe's she indignantly refuses. Aware of the error of her past ways, she is seeking to live in piety and humility. Only the intervention of an old man, Dumont, saves her from being ravished by Hastings.

Richard, scheming to seize the throne, is hoping for Hastings's help. The Lord Chamberlain is adamantly loyal to the still uncrowned children of the late Edward IV. Richard then turns to Jane Shore for assistance, promising her renewed prosperity if she agrees. Still faithful to the memory of the dead King who was her generous lover, she also rejects the pretender's bargain.

Moving swiftly, Richard has Hastings and Jane charged with witchcraft and treason. The Lord Chamberlain, taken by surprise, is hastened to the Tower and beheaded. Alicia, Hastings's former mistress, is jealous and has helped Richard's plot since she wishes to avenge herself on him for his having shifted his desires from her to Jane, who is supposedly her best friend. Alicia falsifies an incriminating document that she has Jane unwittingly pass on to the Regent. Still in love with Hastings, whose execution she has abetted, Alicia goes mad.

Jane is left alone to work out her dire punishment: she must wander alone, no one speaking to her, no one sheltering her or offering food. Weak with hunger and despair, she collapses in a street. For the moment she is succoured by the mysterious Dumont, who strips off his disguise and reveals himself to be her husband, from whom Edward IV took her and whom she has long thought dead. She begs for and obtains his pardon for her past offences to him. Dumont and his friend Bellmour seek to revive her, but the distressed Jane dies where she had fainted in the street. Dumont and Bellmour are taken into custody by Richard's constables for having tried to rescue the outcast, and the dismal story ends.

The play is highly emotional and exceedingly romantic. It is often suspenseful, and in fact some scenes are powerfully envisioned. This is particularly true of the episodes between Hastings and the impassioned Alicia. The passages where he learns that his death is imminent, quarrels with her again, then forgives her and bids her farewell are very moving. Rowe also possesses considerable psychological insight.

Nor, as a poet, is he always deficient. The lines are often supple and mellifluous, but they frequently err because they are inappropriate. For instance, as Jane is expiring, Dumont offers her a drink and declaims:

> She faints! Support her!
> Sustain her head while I infuse this cordial
> Into her dying lips – from spicy drugs,

Rich herbs, and flow'rs the potent juice is drawn;
With wondrous force it strikes the lazy spirits,
Drives 'em around, and wakens life anew.

Whatever else this is, it is not dramatic poetry. In its context, such writing is absurd. A moment later Dumont urges Jane to eat a little. She protests that she cannot:

My feeble jaws forget their common office,
My tasteless tongue cleaves to the clammy roof,
And now a general loathing grows upon me.

But there is vigour and truth in the suddenly doomed Hastings's outcry when Alicia taxes him at a length he cannot brook:

Speak, and give ease to thy conflicting passions:
Be quick, not keep me any longer in suspense;
Time presses, and a thousand crowding thoughts
Break in at once; this way and that they snatch,
They tear my hurry'd soul. All claim attention,
And yet not one is heard. Oh, speak and leave me,
For I have business would employ an age,
And but a minute's time to get it done in.

An actor could do very well with a speech like that.

To Bellmour is given the final statement in which the play's moral is made most explicit:

Let those who view this sad example know
What fate attends the broken marriage vow;
And teach their children in succeeding times,
No common vengeance waits upon these crimes,
When such severe repentance could not save,
From want, from shame, and an untimely grave.

Rowe was a resolute and selfless patriot, as well as a student of classical philosophy, and his early death – at forty-four – ended his short stint as Laureate. If he was not a great poet or dramatist, he probably wrote the best tragic (or perhaps one should call them merely pathetic) works of the Augustan Age, or – as has been suggested – for as long a span as fifty or sixty years. Having long been preoccupied with editing Shakespeare's plays, it is not surprising that he announces in his preface to Jane Shore that his intention is to write dialogue like the Bard's. Alas, he did not. His inadequacy is often distressing; none the less, his works often thrived in his time. There was room for him in capacious Westminster Abbey, but his dramas are completely forgotten.

Addison and Rowe were but two of the men who wrote in contrasting veins. Ambrose Phillips (1675–1749) wrote historical dramas with rousing patriotic sentiments. He was one who, like Addison, was wedded to the pseudo-classical tradition. An example is his *The Distress'd Mother* (1712), largely an English version of Racine's *Andromaque*, with a more sentimental close. He also offered *The Briton* (1722), dealing with the Roman invasion of the British Isles, which compares the reputed "civilization" of the conquerors to the "savagery" of the "natives". His *Humfrey, Duke of Gloucester* (1723) concerns events in the reign of Henry VI and is anti-Catholic as was typical of much writing of the time.

James Thomson (1700–1748) also wrote historical dramas, among them *Sophonisba* (1729) about strife between Carthage and Rome. The theme stressed is patriotism, an emotion that the author thought should come before all others. *Edward and Eleanora* (1739) is about the Crusades. Once more the play is anti-Catholic, depicting the zealots of that faith as bigots who cruelly slaughter "infidels", while the Sultan is endowed with heroic traits. Thomson's masque, *Alfred* (1740), boasts the famous lyric "Rule, Britannia". His *Tancred and Sigismunda* (1745) has admirers.

Thomas Heywood's *A Woman Killed with Kindness* (1603) prefigured another type of work. The new middle-class audience wanted to see some aspect of its life reflected. The vogue for that sort of play had waned but now returned with fresh force. It was obvious that spectators would more easily have their emotions stirred if they were involved with the troubles of characters more like themselves.

Yet another trend of the pathetic drama was towards domestic tragedy. An early practitioner of such fare was Aaron Hill (1685–1750), whose *Fatal Extravagance* (1721) portrays only ordinary people. Earlier he had written classical tragedies in the manner of Voltaire, a *Zara* (1736) and *Alzira* (1736). More or less in the same category is John Dennis (1657–1734), a theatre critic who took part in controversies of his time. His *Liberty Assured* (1704) looks at the competition between the French and British in Canada. *Appius and Virginia* (1709) is yet another drama on a familiar Roman theme. The long-lived poet Edward Young (1684–1765) contributed *Busiris, King of Egypt* (1719) and *The Revenge* (1721), the latter bringing changes on *Othello*; here it is Zanga, a Moorish slave, who arouses a European's jealousy to trick into a criminal deed: "Let Africa and her hundred thrones rejoice . . . / Souls made of fire and children of the sun, / With whom revenge is virtue." Europeans are described as "pallid . . . cold white mortals". Young was apparently interested in the occult and the mystical, as was Dryden; yet overall his style and form are classical.

★

Hill's breakthrough towards domestic tragedy provided an opportunity for a more successful author, George Lillo (1639–1739). A jeweller's son who apparently followed his father in that trade, Lillo was born in London and clearly indicated his predilection for plays of this kind by an adaptation of *Arden of Feversham*, though he first produced *Sylvia* which was of no great consequence.

Lillo's two most important plays are *The London Merchant; or, The History of George Barnwell* (1731) and *The Fatal Curiosity* (1736). On the strength of these, Lillo became one of the most influential dramatists in all history, not merely in England but almost everywhere on the Continent. Though plays of this sort that dealt with lower-middle-class life had been written before – as has been indicated – they struck his first audiences as works of original genius.

In truth, however, his gifts are mediocre. What was startling was his subject matter. Except for the prologue, the scene endings retain the rhymed couplets. The hero of *The London Merchant* is not a Prince, a Roman statesman or an Oriental potentate but a humble apprentice. In a dedicatory preface Lillo argues that tragedies could do much good if they were concerned with such lesser persons. They could reach powerfully with example. He nimbly cites Shakespeare: "The play's the thing, / Wherein I'll catch the conscience of the King." In the play's prologue Lillo tells us that his plot is based on an old ballad. The background is Elizabethan London and its environs, just before the attack of the Spanish Armada.

George Barnwell is a decent, very handsome and incredibly innocent youth of eighteen, in service to a kindly, generous merchant, Mr Thorowgood, who has a pretty and virtuous unwed daughter, Maria. A fellow apprentice, Trueman, is George's close friend. One day Mrs Millwood, a beautiful kept woman with a mercenary obsession, observes George handling large amounts of money, which he and Trueman do for their employers. Having been ruined by men, a hatred of their whole sex dominates her.

She inveigles the pious, chaste young George into paying her a visit, and sets about seducing him. Her purpose is to rob Mr Thorowgood through him. She deceives the ingenuous boy by telling him romantic lies about herself and soon persuades him to embezzle money from his employer. When Trueman discovers the defalcation and informs Maria Thorowgood, the girl, herself smitten with George, covers up for him by replacing the missing sum. Barnwell's good-hearted master ruefully observes his erratic behaviour and pardons him for having committed, as he supposes, "the sins of youth".

The young man, repentant, is determined to break off his immoral, degrading relationship with Mrs Millwood, but her need for money is insatiable. She follows him and lures him back, claiming that she has lost her every worldly possession because of her indiscretion in having fallen irresistibly in love with him. Mesmerized by his unsophisticated passion for her, he yields to her again, and she prompts him to rob and murder his aged uncle, who has been his fond guardian.

The desperate Barnwell assents to undertake this deed, donning a mask and waylaying the old man at night on a country road and stabbing him to death. Overwhelmed by tearful remorse, he does not stop to steal his uncle's money or keys. Instead he reveals his identity to the dying man, kisses him and flees stained by blood.

Mrs Millwood's servants, Lucy and Blunt, learn of her scheme and are revolted by it. They warn Mr Thorowgood of what is afoot; too late he tries to prevent the crime, notifying the police. When she is accused, Mrs Millwood attempts to shift the blame entirely to Barnwell and her servants. She fails and together with George stands trial and is declared guilty.

Both are sentenced to the scaffold. George has freely confessed his misdeeds and, weeping, enters into a state in which he seeks reconciliation with Heaven. He recognizes the vicious results of his course of action and the harm he has brought, not only to his murdered uncle but also to his benevolent mentor, Mr Thorowgood, to the loving Maria and to his loyal friend Trueman.

Both criminals die on the scaffold, George praying, Mrs Millwood still hurling her defiance at a world she accuses of universal corruption.

Lillo is explicit about his intent in his prologue:

Forgive us then, if we attempt to show
In artless strains, a tale of private woe.
A London 'prentice ruin'd, is our theme,
Drawn from he a fam'd old song that bears his name . . .
If thoughtless youth to warn, and shame the age
From vice destructive, well becomes the stage;
If this example innocence insure,
Prevent our guilt, or by reflection cure;
If Millwood's dreadful crimes and sad despair
Comment the virtue of the good and fair:
Tho' art be wanting, and our numbers fail,
Indulge the attempt, in justice to the tale!

Certainly "art" is "wanting" in *The London Merchant*. It is execrably written, so badly that a modern reader is apt to find it comical. The prose is sententious and pompous; the sentences are long, intricate and clumsy. One marvels that actors were able to speak them. Every page contains a sermon: all the characters endlessly moralize and digress. In this epoch-making "realistic" play no one speaks naturally. There are frequent asides, all needless.

In the seduction scene of the play, for instance, George turns to the audience to exclaim: "Her disorder is so great, she don't perceive she has laid her hand on mine. Heavens! how she trembles. What can this mean?"

A few minutes later, the conversation goes on:

Mrs Millwood: What then are your thoughts of love?

Barnwell: If you mean the love of women, I have not thought of it at all. My youth and circumstances make such thoughts improper in me yet. But if you mean the general love we owe to mankind, I think no one has more of it in his temper than myself. I don't know that person in the world whose happiness I don't wish and wouldn't promote, were it in my power. In an especial manner I love my uncle and my master, but above all, my friend.

Mrs Millwood: You have a friend then whom you love?

Barnwell: As he does me, sincerely.

Mrs Millwood: He is, no doubt, often blessed with your company and conversation.

Barnwell: We live in one house, and both serve the same worthy merchant.

Mrs Millwood: Happy, happy youth! Who'er thou art, I envy thee, and so must all who see and know this youth. What have I lost, by being formed a woman! I hate my sex, myself. Had I been a man, I might, perhaps, have been as happy in your friendship, as he who now enjoys it. But, as it is – oh!

The friendship between Barnwell and Trueman, the two apprentices, is indeed remarkable. The farewell scene between them, in Barnwell's death cell, is more affecting than that between Barnwell and Maria, and the final embrace between the two young men is accompanied by much emotion and display of affection. Couple this intense relationship and the vicious image of Millwood, the female temptress who hates men and wishes to be avenged on all of them, and it is difficult not to look upon *The London Merchant* as a study of homosexual psychology. Indeed, the resourceful, dynamic and bold Millwood is by far the most interesting person in the play; the others are bland or implausible. It is hard to believe that George, a naïve but good-hearted, priggish youth, could so quickly and easily be led to acts of dishonesty and to the killing of the uncle to whom he felt so much gratitude.

The speeches quoted above are scarcely representative of the turgid discourse that weighs down Lillo's drama. Added to the natural dialogue – or what is offered as natural – are lengthy disquisitions by Mr Thorowgood on contributions by merchants to the salvation of England, and praise that members of the merchant class deserve, in contrast to those of the idle rich and privileged aristocracy. Doubtless such speeches were pleasing to the middle-class audience.

Nor is there ever an exchange of views from which some didactic point is not distilled, some pious lesson extracted. Lillo was a Dissenter; that is, he belonged to a Puritan segment of the population that had separated itself from and was at odds with the Cavaliers and both Catholicism and the Church of England. The merchant class was heavily present in the ranks of the often-persecuted Dissenters, whose lifestyle was austere and even ascetic, and whose concepts of good and evil were dualistic and rigid. Their goal was to live a "Christian life". Only three decades had elapsed between Wycherley's openly lascivious *The Country Wife* and the first performance of

The London Merchant, preaching that sexual indulgence leads to shame and damnation.

Whatever its artistic shortcomings, *The London Merchant* was a revolutionary work. It was the principal model and inspiration for Diderot and other French writers of the sentimental and didactic school; it brought a fresh fashion in plays to the English theatre and to the whole of Europe. Its appearance marked the beginning of the end for pseudo-classical tragedy. It also served as a forerunner and a preparation for the later Realistic theatre. Not only did people weep at it; they went again and again to see it.

A few months before *The London Merchant* was staged, Lillo's earlier play, *Sylvia*, had been presented without much notice. In 1735 his *The Christian Hero* was offered. This is in blank verse and relates how young Scandenberg, a Christian warrior, leads Albanians against infidel Turks. For Lillo, public duty had priority over love, in the well-grooved tradition of such dramas. But the play is also a paean to constitutional monarchy as opposed to absolutism, a topical subject then especially among Dissenters.

The next year's *The Fatal Curiosity* is considered superior to *The London Merchant*. Certainly its plot was to prove attractive to many later playwrights, as it is even today. Rupert Brooke and Albert Camus are just two authors who availed themselves of it: the former in his *Lithuania*, the latter in *The Misunderstanding*. (One cannot even be sure that the plot originated with Lillo.)

The scene in *The Fatal Curiosity* is the craggy Cornish coast. Two old people, husband and wife, have fallen on desperate times. When a prosperous-looking young stranger seeks shelter with them, the wife persuades the husband to murder and rob him. Too late, they discover that the slain guest is their own son, who has come back from the Indies and who has disguised himself hoping to give them a joyful surprise. After this horrible revelation, the husband kills his wife and himself.

Lillo handles this theme with more mature skill. The drama is sombrely atmospheric, the moral driven home with cruel impact. It is not only that crime is inexorably followed by punishment from on high, but also that those who are impoverished and helpless should trust more in the wisdom and mercy of Providence.

Lillo's *Elmerick, or Justice Triumphant* (1740) reached the stage next. Embarking on a crusade, the King of Hungary appoints Elmerick to dispense justice during his absence. He shall do so dispassionately, showing favour to none. The Queen commits serious offences, and the harassed Elmerick is forced to order the royal lady's execution. When the wrathful King returns, Elmerick submits to his fate, though he reminds the sovereign of the regal instructions. Recognizing that Elmerick has bravely performed his duty, the King takes no reprisal. Once more Lillo upholds the necessity of living by a stern ethic.

In the ensuing flood of works in the style of Addison, Rowe and Lillo, several names stand out. The lexicographer Samuel Johnson (1709–84), Dryden's successor as Literary Dictator or "Great Cham" of England, made one attempt to write for the stage: a pseudo-classical tragedy called *Irene* (1749). It failed, even though his friend and former pupil, the famed David Garrick, performed in it, largely as a favour.

Sweeping historical dramas in the manner of Rowe came from the novelist Tobias Smollett (1721–71), *The Regicide* (1749); from Aaron Hill, *Elfrid* (1710) and *King Henry the Fifth* (1723); from William Shirley, *Edward the Black Prince* (1750). John Hewitt (*fl.* 1730) continued so-called "naturalistic tragedy" like Lillo's in works such as *Fatal Falsehood* (1734), as did Thomas Cooke (1703–56) with his *The Mournful Nuptials* (printed in 1739, acted in 1743) and Edward Moore (*fl.* 1748–53) with *The Gamester* (1753). Of this group, Moore is probably the most adept; his drama, though steeped in misery, has strength, a unified structure and mood and an atmosphere of darkness that is well crafted and sustained. *The Gamester* traces the fall of Beverly, who descends to financial ruin through an addiction to gambling and commits suicide after being falsely charged with the murder of his sister's lover.

After Cibber and Steele, sentimental comedy – sometimes in combination with a more genteel form of comedy of manners and a moderated comedy of intrigue – filled the playhouses. The level of accomplishment is higher than that of serious drama, and several writers of at least modest genius appear. The most unique and interesting of these is John Gay (1685–1732). Gay should be seen as a leading critic of the excessive sentimentality of the stage, a movement to which Fielding and Sheridan also lent force. Perhaps these three writers are ranked higher than their contemporaries because more recent bias leans towards agreement with their critiques.

Gay's *The Beggar's Opera* (1728) was not, as is too frequently supposed, his earliest work. He preceded it with *The Mohocks* (1712) and *The What D'Ye Call It* (1715). Both these were burlesques of the underworld, making satirical fun of the penal system and showing thieves outwitting London's police.

Gay, who became a member of the Scribbler's Club, has been described as a "fat little dilettante who had great charm and a sweet, eager personality". He was welcome in the houses of all the titled ladies in the kingdom.

Among his friends were the "literary giants" Alexander Pope (who was to write his epitaph) and Jonathan Swift, who intervened with Bolingbroke to obtain a pension for him. Gay was greatly talented but seldom took up his pen, except to carry on a lively correspondence. Like Congreve he was indolent. Swift once said of him that a "coach and six horses" was the only exercise the bouncy little man could bear. Everyone who knew him coddled him; when he was ill, the Duchess of Queensbury's personal assistant attended him.

It was in an exchange of letters with Swift that Gay first got the notion for *The Beggar's Opera*. The two friends had been expressing their disapproval of the London stage and the unfortunate impact on it of Handel and his company of Italian opera singers, who had become the rage. "There's nobody allowed to say 'I sing' but an eunuch or an Italian singer," Gay complained, adding: "Everybody is grown now as great a judge of music as they were in your time of poetry, and folks that could not distinguish one tone from another now daily dispute about the different styles of Handel, Bononcini and Attilo."

In reply, Swift suggested that Gay attempt a lampoon on the Italian opera. In an uncharacteristic burst of energy, Gay undertook this. He turned it out neatly, apparently enjoying himself as he did so, and much of his infectious good humour is clearly apparent in it. For the music he collaborated with John Christopher Pepusch, a German composer, who had come to London around 1700. About half the tunes are original; the rest are arrangements of popular airs of the day and Elizabethan, Irish and Scottish folk songs, hence the term "ballad opera". In one or two instances Handel and Purcell were directly plagiarized – or, rather, plundered.

The ballad opera is said to be a form invented by Gay, though Durfey's *Wonders in the Sun* (1706) is somewhat similar. Its precursors are the farcical after-piece – a standard fixture of many programmes in theatres since Otway's introduction of Molière's *The Rogueries of Scapin* – and the pantomime – a dance-skit telling a brief story with expressive mimicry with elements of the *commedia dell'arte* – which were also favoured and given along with serious plays.

Opening in the little Lincoln's Inn Fields Theatre, *The Beggar's Opera* had a reception hitherto unsurpassed; it ran for sixty-two nights, a record not to be broken for nearly another hundred years. It was soon given in thirteen other English cities and towns, as well as Edinburgh and Dublin. Shortly afterwards, in 1733, it was performed in Jamaica, and finally in New York in 1750.

One reason it caused such a sensation is because of its added dimension of sharp-edged political satire. The chorus is comprised of cut-throats and bedraggled women-of-the-town, and it purportedly tells of the adventures of Macheath, a handsome highwayman whom the ladies much adore. He is captured and thrown into Newgate Prison, in the custody of Lockit, who is even more dishonest than his prisoner and has dealings with the notorious fence Peachum. When these two fall out, they make it up and resolve never to quarrel again, "because [they] have it in [their] power to hang each other".

In an effort to escape, Macheath pays court to Lucy, Lockit's gullible daughter. He secretly weds her, though he is already married to Polly, an offspring of Peachum, who would like to dispose of him. The best-known song in the piece results from the highwayman's dilemma: "How happy I could be with either, / Were 'tother dear charmer away." But he takes all such embarrassments lightly. His plot to break out is foiled. At the end Macheath stands on the gibbet, a rope around his neck.

At this point the author intervenes; asserting that the audience demands a happy ending in an opera, he provides one. For no good reason, Macheath is reprieved and returned whole-limbed to his wives.

To spectators it was obvious that the story of Macheath, Lockit and Peachum was a political allegory. The motley band portrayed was a reference to Sir Robert Walpole, the Prime Minister, and his corrupt government. Walpole was in the audience at opening night and was seen smiling; behind his public mask, however, he could hardly have been amused. If he suspected a drive against him, headed by Swift and other Tory satirists, he was correct.

Other songs in this delightful piece are "Pretty Polly", "If the heart of a man" and "Youth's the season made for joy . . ." They remain enchantingly fresh. It is said that music was put to the songs only at the last moment; the original plan had been for the words to be merely spoken.

(John Rich managed the theatre, and wags were soon saying that *The Beggar's Opera* had made Gay rich and Rich gay.)

Encouraged by his huge success, Gay quickly wrote a sequel, *Polly* (printed 1729), but Walpole's government was alert. The play was prohibited on the grounds that it was seditious – the Lord Chancellor had not dared move against *The Beggar's Opera* because it was too popular. Gay made money from the book sales; however, he himself acknowledged that *Polly* was inferior and was not too troubled that it was banned from the stage. It took almost fifty years until it was finally produced in 1777.

Meanwhile, in 1733, the bright little author ventured another burlesque, *Achilles*, which was apolitical. It failed. Gay died the following year, a mere four years after the unprecedented run of *The Beggar's Opera*.

In a letter to Swift, their mutual friend Dr Arbuthnot reports: "It was some alleviation of my grief to see him so universally lamented by nearly everybody . . . He was interred at Westminster Abbey, as if he had been a peer of the realm." A number of signal epitaphs ensued. The Duchess of Queensbury, the little man's favourite patroness and later his literary executor, wrote of him: "He knew the world too well to regret leaving it; and the world in general knew him too little to value him as they ought." A bit less kind was Alexander Pope's tribute: "Of manners gentle, of affections mild; / In wit a man, in simplicity a child." Gay's own words are often quoted and applied to him in final summary: "Life is a jest and all things show it; / I thought so once and now I know it."

The Beggar's Opera was widely imitated. One of the deftest practitioners in the form was Henry Fielding. From his legacy a linear descent is clear, leading to the development of English comic opera, reaching its apogee in Gilbert and Sullivan.

Gay's work, though, has had its own curious history, comparable only to that of Ben Jonson's *Volpone*. It has been endlessly revived. The Victorians found it necessary to expurgate it, then finally dropped it. In 1920 it was restaged in London by Frederic Austin and ran for 1,463 consecutive performances. That led to more revivals. In 1948 Benjamin Britten rearranged the music, and his version, too, became popular. A film was made with Sir Laurence Olivier as Macheath that was shown worldwide. In 1928 in Germany, Elizabeth Hauptmann translated Gay's libretto, Kurt Weill composed new music set to lyrics by Bertolt Brecht, some of them based on poems by François Villon and Rudyard Kipling. This revision, titled *Die Dreigroschenoper* (*The Threepenny Opera*), had another enormous success; it played an estimated

4,000 performances in 120 German theatres, and was produced in translation in eight other countries, including Russia, Hungary, Poland and Holland.

This was not the end. An "Americanized" adaptation, with Weill's music but newer words by Mark Blitzstein, with Weill's widow Lotte Lenya appearing in it, opened in New York in 1954; it played at a small off-Broadway theatre for 2,611 continuous performances, taking in $2.5 million. The cast was always changing, more than 700 performers taking part in it by turns. This was, up to that time, the longest run of any musical in the history of the American theatre. One of the songs, "Mac the Knife", made the gifted Weill known everywhere.

Gay's other works include *Fables*, and, most inconsistently, the libretto for Handel's English pastoral *Acis and Galatea*, as well as some comedies, a collaboration with Pope and Dr Arbuthnot called *Three Hours after Marriage*, and *The Distressed Wife* (1734).

As has been remarked, Gay became a model copied by Henry Fielding (1707–54). In his twenties this virile comic writer arrived in London, determined to have a literary career. Born in Somerset, the son of an army officer, he was of good family. He studied at Eton and elsewhere, mastering the classics, gaining a solid education that stood him in good stead. At nineteen he impulsively tried to elope with a beautiful heiress, but his romantic episode was foiled.

After further study he set off for London. There he first turned to the stage. Impatient, he formed his own troupe of actors, who performed at the Little Theatre in the Haymarket, and he produced his own works. His sharp style and bold choice of subject matter were a fresh breeze blowing through the city's stale, cluttered theatric scene.

Still too young and too hurried, he wrote no single work of salient merit – unless, as many critics have, one applauds his burlesque satire *The Tragedy of Tragedies, or The Life and Death of Tom Thumb the Great* (1731), which he expanded from an earlier two-act version produced a year before. Poking fun at heroic tragedy, he followed a fashion embarked on by Buckingham in *The Rehearsal*, a similar broad parody of bombastic, exaggerated scripts that in fact scarcely needed parodying.

Fielding interwove into this travesty lines and situations from at least forty-two identifiable scripts from the quill pens of his serious contemporaries. His "mighty" cast includes King Arthur, Tom Thumb the Great, the whimsical ghost of Gaffer Thumb, Lord Grizzle, Merlin, three courtiers named Noodle, Doodle and Foodle, Queen Dollallalla and Princess Huncamunca, this last lady "equally in love with Lord Grizzle and Tom Thumb, and desirous to be married to them both". To Doodle is given the much-quoted opening invocation in the mock-heroic manner that delighted spectators then and now:

> Such such a day as this was never seen!
> The sun himself, on this auspicious day,
> Shines like a beau in a new birthday suit:

This down the seams embroider'd, that the beams.
All nature wears one universal grin.

To some readers a little parody of this sort goes a long way, but *Tom Thumb* has long had its admirers and from time to time is revived by university acting groups. To appreciate it fully, of course, one needs to be familiar with the type of drama it satirizes.

In its printed version Fielding appended footnotes that add remarkably to the humour. They very neatly and astutely take off the academic zeal for annotating trivial points for disputation.

Fielding's other plays were numerous and include *The Grub Street Opera*, which had its title changed from *The Welsh Opera* to appease sensitive Welshmen. Along with *A Virgin Unmasked, or An Old Man Taught Wisdom* and *Miss Lucy in Town*, he turned out other burlesques and playlets such as *Love in Several Masques* (1728), *The Author's Farce* (1730), *The Covent Garden Tragedy* (1732), *Pasquin* (1736) and *Tumble-down Dick; or, Phaeton in the Suds* (1736).

Some of his other titles attract interest: *Rape upon Rape or The Justice Caught in His Own Trap* (afterwards more politely called *The Coffee-house Politician*), *The Lottery*, *The Intriguing Chambermaid*, *Don Quixote in England* and *The Wedding Day*. As Fielding approached his thirties his satiric sense matured and sharpened, until it had an uncomfortable bite. This is best exampled in *The Historical Register for the Year 1736*, which purports to be a report and commentary on notable political events of that year under Walpole's dishonest administration.

The government, nettled by the stinging attacks by Gay and Fielding, retaliated at last. Walpole pushed through Parliament the Licensing Act of 1737, ostensibly to restrict immorality but really to silence his critics and thereafter promptly closed Fielding's playhouse. In his own words, the young author was driven from the stage when he was just beginning to learn how to write plays.

Thus it is Fielding who is particularly responsible for bringing to England a censorship that persisted beyond the mid twentieth century. The young man himself was forced to shift to the study of law, and so entered politics and became a magistrate. That position allowed him to behold the less seemly aspects of human nature first hand.

This experience, together with his early grasp of dramatic structure, enabled him to become one of the world's most eminent novelists, the author of two of the finest books of fiction in English, *Joseph Andrews* and *Tom Jones*. What the novel gained, the stage was deprived of: Fielding might well have been the source of England's best and most thoughtful comedies. He was born with a true flair, but the theatre knew him only while his talent was still unripe.

Yet another playwright who seems to have laughed off gentility and sentimentality is Oliver Goldsmith (1728–74). He came of a Saxon and Protestant family which had settled in Ireland; he was the fifth child of an impecunious clergyman whose parish was in the county of Longford.

At three he was examined and termed impenetrably stupid; all the same, the boy was taught to read and write by a maidservant and then, at the age of seven, entered a village school presided over by a retired quartermaster who added to his lessons a store of local lore about "ghosts, banshees and fairies". Goldsmith later memorialized his schoolmaster in *The Deserted Village*.

Afterwards he was sent to several grammar schools where he gained some acquaintance with classical languages. He was badly scarred by smallpox, his gait was ungainly, his head was too big for his body, his chin weak and his upper lip protruding, and he was much persecuted by school-mates.

Despite this he obtained a scholarship to Trinity College in Dublin, though in return for it he had to sweep the court, bear up trays to the fellows' table, carry off soiled plates and pour ale. Feeling humiliated, he studied little, barely passing his examinations and graduated at the bottom of his class. He was also given to playing pranks that won him no favour with his tutors, one of whom caned him for an infraction.

When Goldsmith's father died he left a pittance. The youth lived for a while with his widowed mother in their humble dwelling, attempting to make a living and failing in a half-dozen professions. He seemed happiest when dressing in gaudy attire, playing his flute or singing Irish airs, fishing, or repeating ghost stories at night before the hearth. In desperation, he emigrated to the New World but returned after a mere six weeks. Deciding to study law, he ended instead in a gambling house where he lost all his money.

He decided to take up medicine, went to Edinburgh and dabbled for a year and a half in the study of chemistry and natural history. He moved on to Leyden but left there still without a degree. By now he was twenty-seven and owned nothing but his flute and the clothes he wore.

He set out on foot on a tour of the Continent, through Flanders, France and Switzerland. Possibly in Italy, though no one is certain how, he finally got himself a medical degree. His friends claimed that he was so "ignorant of biology that he could not tell the difference between any two sorts of barnyard fowl until he saw them cooked and on the table".

In 1756 he returned to England penniless, friendless and jobless. Attempting to practise medicine, he obtained no patients. He endured a spell of intense poverty during which he ventured to become a vagabond actor; he was an apothecary's assistant and was even reduced to begging at times. He served as an usher in a school, hated the work, tried his luck as a bookseller's hack, loathed it and went back to being an usher.

He found and lost other positions. At thirty, in lieu of some better means of earning a living, he embraced literature. By luck he met Ralph Griffiths, publisher of the *Monthly Review*, an important journal. He began to sell articles, reviews, children's books, a biography, a *History of England* and a series of letters supposedly by a Chinese traveller. All this time, however, he remained anonymous, signing his name to nothing. But he was gaining recognition in booksellers' circles and among editors and other writers.

Goldsmith was really quite ignorant and filled his books with howlers, in one instance writing of the tiger as a beast native to Canada. On another occasion he was nearly persuaded by a jokester that Alexander the Great had done battle with Montezuma, a "fact" that he was about to include in a history of Greece, one of a long series of textbooks he had prepared. ("If he can tell a horse from a cow, that is the extent of his knowledge of zoology" was Dr Johnson's comment.)

The pontifical Samuel Johnson, the painter Sir Joshua Reynolds and the eloquent statesman Edmund Burke gradually accepted him as a friend. Still without funds, he was about to be dispossessed by his exasperated landlady. He rushed off an alarmed message to Johnson, who dispatched him a guinea. Arriving on the scene shortly after, the Great Cham found that Goldsmith had already spent part of the guinea on a bottle of wine and was imbibing from it, while berating his landlady for having sent for the sheriff's deputy to evict him.

But he showed Johnson the manuscript of a novel, *The Vicar of Wakefield*, which he had just finished, and Johnson took it to a publisher who bought it for £60. Even before the novel appeared, Goldsmith became famous for a philosophical poem, *The Traveller*, the first work to bear his name. The novel, though it took four years to see print, was also a huge success. If Johnson had not generously intervened, it might never have been published. Even before the century's end it went through a hundred editions.

Emboldened by this turn in his fortune, Goldsmith considered writing for the stage. The result, *The Good Natur'd Man* (1768), was not well received; none the less, it is one of the better comedies of the eighteenth century. Goldsmith, who has a surprising command of irony, satirizes the "man of sentiment", the conventional hero of the comedy-with-tears. His hero, Mr Honeywood, is indefatigably benevolent; he is as kindly and generous as Mr Thorowgood in Lillo's *The London Merchant*.

The play was an attack on the manners of two popular contemporary dramatists, Kelly and Cumberland. Though Goldsmith himself was emotional, he disliked false excesses of feeling and made a point of exposing mawkishness and treating it ironically. Since he was opposing the taste of the new audience, he suffered because no spectator wished to see his or her emotional indulgences held up to scorn. People came to the theatre to weep and would not be denied the privilege. They dismissed *The Good Natur'd Man* as "low".

Goldsmith had criticized "genteel comedy" as early as 1759, in his essay *The Present State of Polite Learning*, and he returned to the critical fray in 1772 with his *Essay on the Theatre, or A Comparison Between Laughing and Sentimental Comedy*, in which he deplores the fondness of his contemporaries in the theatre for their tearful laughter and over-fastidiousness and pleads for the restoration of something franker and more vigorous, praising Vanbrugh in particular.

Despite this iconoclastic attitude, however, he had not – in *The Good Natur'd Man* – written a comedy that was too different from others of his period. He was more a creature of the age than he realized. The play, which contains platitudinous moralizing and has an ending meant to please everyone, is not without its share of sentiment. Only in certain episodes, resented by his audience, does he break from it. He does his best in holding up to scorn the corrupt police, whom he himself had encountered.

The play also shows that the author was still an apprentice at his craft, of which he was never to become a full-fledged master; his plots are filled with too many implausibilities. His dialogue is not distinguished by wit but conveys a pervasive geniality. It has been described as "natural, fresh and tender".

Even if *The Good Natur'd Man* failed on the stage, being a little too advanced for its day, it brought him much profit. He cleared a good sum from his benefit nights and from the sale of the copyright. The two in combination brought him £500, many times as much as *The Traveller* and *The Vicar of Wakefield* in tandem had earned. Indeed, his famous novel was to sell only after his death.

In 1733, after the astonishing success of his narrative poem *The Deserted Village*, Goldsmith tried the stage again with *She Stoops to Conquer*. In it, Mr Hardcastle, a country gentleman who has a marriageable daughter, is expecting the son of his best friend Marlowe to pay a visit as a prospective husband. The young man is unknown to the father.

Though the young Marlowe has a reputation for being handsome and intelligent, he is strangely bashful. It is said of him: "He's a very singular character, I assure you. Among women of reputation and virtue, he is the modestest man alive; but his acquaintances give him a very different character among creatures of another stamp; you understand me."

Travelling to the Hardcastle manor, Marlowe and his companion Charles Hastings arrive at an inn, where they meet Hardcastle's crude stepson, Tony Lumpkin. In a prankish mood, without identifying himself, the hard-drinking Lumpkin directs them to his house, telling him it is an inn that can accommodate them for the night. Arriving there, the newcomers, who believe they are lost, act in what seems an impudent manner to their host, whose talkativeness they, in turn, think is presumptuous for an innkeeper.

Miss Hardcastle, meanwhile, has changed roles with her maidservant, to get a closer glimpse of her suitor-to-be, who believes her to be a barmaid. From these disguises arise the usual quota of mistaken identities and misunderstandings.

Finally all is set straight, and Marlowe gladly claims the lively Miss Hardcastle to be his wife. A sub-plot concerns a match proposed by Tony Lumpkin's mother between her son and the wealthy Miss Neville, who is in love with Hastings, Marlowe's friend. This, too, ends happily, with Miss Neville getting her wish, though she calls off a planned elopement. There is also a to-do about some jewels, supposedly stolen, that is cleverly handled.

In all appraisals of the play, the role that gets the most attention is that of Tony Lumpkin, a very original creation. A drinker, a wencher and a seeming booby, he is actually cunning. Many famed actors have essayed this noisy part of the brazen fool. Lumpkin has been compared to

Puck and Falstaff, Shakespeare's clowns, though perhaps too kindly. But he does have remarkable vitality. The other characters are drawn with clarity, and Miss Hardcastle especially is vivacious.

The play, though its plot is a bit simple and unlikely, has a warmth that makes it endearing. On the opening night its reception was uproarious, and it has remained a constant favourite in English repertories and theatres ever since.

Earning huge sums of money, Goldsmith spent them faster than they came in. He shared the best society in the kingdom, and to his circle added the actor-producer David Garrick. In the presence of brilliant men, all noted conversationalists, his contribution was often inappropriate. Horace Walpole described him as "an inspired idiot". Garrick penned an acid couplet about him: "Here lies Nolly Goldsmith, for shortness called 'Noll', / Who wrote like an angel, and talked like poor Poll."

He gave away money to everyone who asked him for it and finally owed over £2,000. Worried and ill, he made the mistake of dosing himself. "I do not practise. I make it a rule to prescribe only for my friends," he is reported to have said. To this a friend replied: "Pray, dear Doctor, alter your rule, and prescribe only for your enemies." This advice was well meant and sound.

The medication only worsened his sickness. By the time he called in a more qualified physician it was much too late. He was forty-six when he died. Many honoured Goldsmith at an elaborate funeral at Westminster Abbey (1774). His pallbearers included Lord Shelburne, Lord Lowth, Sir Joshua Reynolds, the Hon. Mr Beauclerc, Mr Burke and David Garrick. When it was discovered that he had died in poverty, however, and had not left enough money to pay for the ceremony, he ended up interred privately in the graveyard of Temple Church, without his eminent friends in attendance.

When a cenotaph was erected to him in Westminster Abbey, Dr Johnson wrote a tribute, recalling that this oddly ineffectual man had excelled in so many branches of literature: "There was hardly any kind of writing that he did not attempt, and all that he touched he adorned."

During Goldsmith's lifetime changes in manners added a new burden on the authors of comedies. It became unacceptable to laugh when in a social setting, even in a playhouse. To do so came to be seen as a mark of ill breeding. Laughter in a theatre is contagious and inspires widespread hilarity that prompts the actors to become more antic, and this came to be frowned upon. A smile or a titter was enough; a loud response to a jocular line or amusing twist in the plot was improper. Samuel Johnson, a hearty man, was given to guffaws but lectured his disciples on greeting clever words and situations with quiet dignity. In much the same spirit wrote Lord Chesterfield, Jonathan Swift, Alexander Pope and Addison, who had similar views on this subject.

Sobriety also descended on the players. Costumes gradually became less glittering. The material of ladies' dresses was no longer as rich and costly. The men no longer wore white knee breeches exposing their silken-clad legs and perhaps well-turned calves; instead they wore trousers. It was the advent of a more democratic age.

The scenery changed, too, becoming less ornate than before. It is a precept in the theatre world that comedy should not be staged in front of a dark or subdued backdrop. Brightness must prevail on every side. But more and more this was not happening as the Puritan influence steadily gained.

Today the answer seems of little importance and not worth all the shouting, but at that time there was a great deal of public dispute on how to define "comedy" and "tragedy". Nowadays aesthetic categorizations are not of much concern. What is Beauty? What is Truth? These are questions that are no longer asked.

Goldsmith wrote during this period of changing expectations in England. Richard Brinsley Sheridan (1751–1816), with a very different personality, pursued a very different kind of career. Anglo-Irish, born in Dublin, son of a respected actor, his mother was a novelist. He was sent to study at Harrow, where his teachers and classmates treated him with contempt because his father was a mere "player". From this he developed an early aversion to the stage. He had reason for pride, however, in his lineage. Over a span of 250 years his family was to produce twenty-seven authors of more than two hundred books.

While he was still at Harrow, his father sent for him to come to the resort city of Bath, where the company was performing. He was introduced to the dazzling idle society of that fashionable spa. The young man held his own with éclat, displaying a significant verbal wit. There began a romantic melodrama that involved him and a high-born young lady, Elizabeth Linley, already noted for her beauty. She had an unpleasant suitor, a Captain Matthews, and to "protect" her Sheridan eloped with her to Calais. This provoked a great scandal revolving around the "Maid of Bath" – Miss Linley – and her husband; at first, it seems, their relationship was platonic, though they had gone through a marriage ceremony of a kind. Their families were furious, and Sheridan found himself compelled to fight two duels in defence of his honour. In the second he was seriously hurt. The parents finally reconciled, and by 1774 that phase of the celebrated affair had a happy ending.

By now Sheridan had fallen genuinely in love with his bride. He settled with her in London. His intention was to study law, but he was destined never to follow that profession.

He found himself pressed for funds. Though he had tried to avoid any connection with the stage, in desperation he wrote no less than three plays in a single year, *The Rivals*, a brief farce called *St Patrick's Day, or The Scheming Second Lieutenant* and a comic opera, *The Duenna*. It is amazing that Sheridan was only twenty-three when he composed *The Rivals*, one of his two major works. He proves that the theatre was in his blood.

The play's title is most appropriate, for the over-romantic heroine, Miss Lydia Languish, has no less than four suitors for her hand. The principal one is young Captain Absolute, whose chief competitor is himself, under another name, Ensign Beverly. Aware that Miss Languish, after the sentimental fashion of the day, wishes to be loved for herself alone, not for her very considerable fortune, he has presented himself to her as an impecunious naval officer. Enraptured by the prospect of sacrificing all for love, she is determined to elope with him, forfeiting her legacy, which comes to her only if she marries with the consent of her guardian, her aunt Mrs Malaprop. She has been reading too many novels from the lending library. Says Mrs Malaprop, with a touch of shrewdness, "A lending library in a town is an evergreen tree of diabolical knowledge."

Bob Acres, a bumptious, rustic gentleman, also seeks the lovely if fanciful Lydia, as does Sir Lucius O'Trigger, a mad Irishman, who believes he has been carrying on an amorous correspondence with her. In reality, the person to whom he has been sending his letters, and from whom he has been receiving billets-doux, is the elderly Mrs Malaprop, still intent on a flirtation.

Ordered by his father, Sir Anthony, to wed a girl selected for him, Captain Absolute refuses, but quickly changes his mind and countenance on learning that the lady in question is none other than the delectable Miss Languish. But first he must with delicacy and tact reveal to her his true identity, while also changing his image in the jaundiced eyes of Mrs Malaprop, who has developed a strong aversion to the upstart "Ensign Beverly". He accomplishes her conversion with much difficulty, and when Lydia discovers that she need not run away from home or relinquish her fortune after all she is not pleased at the unromantic prospect:

> There had I projected one of the most sentimental of ropes! so becoming a disguise! so amiable a ladder of ropes! Conscious moon – four horses – Scotch parson – with such surprise to Mrs Malaprop, and such paragraphs in the newspapers! Oh, I shall die of disappointment! . . . Now – sad reverse! – what have I to expect, but, after a deal of flimsy preparation, with a bishop's licence, and my aunt's blessing, to go simpering up to the altar; or perhaps be cried three times in a country-church, and have an unmannerly fat clerk ask the consent of every butcher in the parish to join John Absolute and Lydia Languish, Spinster! O, that I should live to hear myself called Spinster!

Lydia describes the raptures of her illicit love affair:

> How mortifying to remember the dear delicious shifts I used to be put to, to gain half a minute's conversation with this fellow! How often have I stole forth in the coldest night in January, and found him in the garden, stuck like a dripping statue! There would he kneel to me in the snow, and sneeze and cough so pathetically! he

> shivered with cold, and I with apprehension! And while the freezing blast numbed our joints, how warmly would he press me to pity his flame, and glow with mutual ardour! Ah, Julia, that was something like being in love!

Meanwhile Bob Acres and Sir Lucius O'Trigger are separately pushing their claims, and Captain Absolute finds himself challenged to fight not one but two duels in the same day. Indeed, such is the mix-up, he is even asked to be his opponent's second. The duelling scenes are broadly amusing and provide a melodramatic conclusion to this brisk, rollicking comedy. Bob Acres, forced into fighting against his will, turns volubly craven.

One suspects more than a hint of autobiography here, recalling the author's own much-publicized elopement. But there is also delightful irony, at the expense of sentimental comedy.

Sir Lucius is advising Acres on how to comport himself at the coming encounter:

> ACRES: There, Sir Lucius – there [*puts himself in an attitude*] – a side-front, hey? Odd! I'll make myself small enough: I'll stand edge-ways.
>
> SIR LUCIUS: Now – you're quite out, for if you stand so when I take my aim – [*levelling at him*]
>
> ACRES: Z—ds! Sir Lucius – are you sure it is not cocked?
>
> SIR LUCIUS: Never fear.
>
> ACRES: But – but – you don't know – it may go off of its own head –
>
> SIR LUCIUS: Phoo! be easy. Well, now if I hit you in the body, my bullet has a double chance, for if it misses a vital part on your right side, 'twill be very hard if it don't succeed on the left!
>
> ACRES: A vital part!
>
> SIR LUCIUS: But, there – fix yourself so [*placing him*]. Let him see the broad side of your full front – there – now a ball or two may pass clean through your body, and never do any harm at all.
>
> ACRES: Clean through me! a ball or two clean through me!
>
> SIR LUCIUS: Aye, may they; and it is much the genteelist attitude in the bargain.
>
> ACRES: Look'ee! Sir Lucius – I'd just as lieve be shot in an awkward posture as a genteel one – so, by my valour! I will stand edge-ways.

After this Mr Acres' "valour" drains away from him completely when he welcomes the first pretext to avoid the exchange of pistol-shots.

The subsidiary theme is an engagement contracted between Faulkland and Julia, friends of the principals. The affianced pair is always at odds. Faulkland has once saved Julia's life at sea, and she feels perpetually grateful to him. The forthright Lydia Languish scoffs at this:

> Believe me, the rude blast that overset your boat was a prosperous gale of love to him . . . Obligation! Why, a water-spaniel would have done as much! Well, I should never think of giving my heart to a man because he could swim.

The swain, Faulkland, is beset by neurotic uncertainty. He is forever in doubt as to Julia's affection for him, and every proof of her sincere love provides a new cause for doubt. He is a very original character, and though he conveniently reforms before the final curtain one suspects that the change will not last and that he will go on lacking assurance and seeking it, always a poor prospect for the faithful and unlucky Julia.

The solemnity of their wooing, too, and the stilted speeches, are also satirical of the sentimental poetic dramas of the day. The chief attractions of the play are not the principals but Bob Acres and Mrs Malaprop. The noisy, hustling, garrulous Acres is reminiscent of Tony Lumpkin in Goldsmith's *She Stoops to Conquer*. He is almost as stupid but somewhat more warm-hearted and not as boorish. His speech-pattern is wondrous to hear, a rapid musket-fire of expletives. Here he is talking to himself, as he clumsily practises a dance step:

> Sink, slide – coupee! Confound the first inventors of cotillions! say I – they are as bad as algebra for us country gentlemen. I can walk a minuet easy enough when I'm forced! and I have been accounted a good stick in a country-dance. Odds jog and tabours! I never valued your cross-over to couple – figure in – right and left – and I'd foot it with e'er a captain in the county! But these outlandish heathen allemands and cotillions are quite beyond me! I shall never prosper at 'em, that's sure. Mine are true-born English legs – they don't understand their curst French lingo! Their *pas* this, and *pas* that, and *pas* t'other! No, 'tis certain I have most anti-Gallican toes!

The role has tempted a succession of adept comic actors, offering endless chances for hilarious "business".

Even more amusing is the character of Mrs Malaprop, described by Absolute in a letter to his Lydia as "the old weather-beaten she-dragon who guards you". She is, to a degree, modelled on Congreve's vulgar Lady Wishfort, corpulent but still amorous. Absolute's letter continues: "It shall go hard but I will elude her vigilance, as I am told that the same ridiculous vanity which makes her dress up her coarse features, and deck her dull chat with hard words which she don't understand –" Whereupon Mrs Malaprop cries out:

> An attack upon my language! What do you think of that? – an aspersion upon my parts of speech! Was ever such a brute! Sure if I reprehend anything in this world, it is the use of my oracular tongue, and a nice derangement of epitaphs!

A "nice derangement" of language is a precise depiction of Mrs Malaprop's mistreatment of English or her "oracular tongue" – she either mispronounces words or misuses them, as when she calls upon her niece to "illiterate" the English from her memory or declares to Sir Anthony that she would by no means wish "a daughter of mine to be a progeny of learning". She would be satisfied if the girl had merely "a supercilious knowledge in accounts . . . and know something of contagious countries". And "he is the very pineapple of politeness".

From this tirelessly loquacious, coarse and addled lady comes the term "malapropism", designating words pronounced wrongly or incorrectly applied. She is truly an archetypal figure. Mrs Malaprop is also anti-romantic:

> 'Tis safest in matrimony to begin with a little *aversion*. I am sure I hated your poor dear uncle before marriage . . . and yet, Miss, you are sensible what a wife I made! – and when it pleased heaven to release me from him, 'tis unknown what tears I shed!

Her name is, of course, derived from "*mal apropos*". Sheridan's mother, besides writing novels, had turned out some plays, and some say that Mrs Malaprop is an elaboration of a character found in one of them.

The Duenna also has charm, and it has had a revival in the twentieth century as a libretto for a light opera by the Russian composer Sergei Prokoviev. (In some countries, including England, it is called *Betrothal in a Convent*.) Its setting is Spain; it has many effective scenes. It is claimed by some to be the work that bridges the transition from the ballad opera to the comic opera. It was hugely successful.

Sheridan adapted Vanbrugh's *The Relapse* under a new title, *A Trip to Scarborough* (1777); it did not go over and left him in need of funds again. He hurriedly pieced together two shorter pieces that lay about unfinished; *The School for Scandal* (also 1777), his masterpiece, is the very happy result. It is a play richer in human and comic values than its predecessors.

Sheridan himself purported to disesteem *The School for Scandal*. He asserted that it was "one of the worst plays in the language" and he would "have given anything not to have written it". In print, certainly, it is not anywhere near as hilariously effective as it frequently proves to be on stage. In any event, the author's aim was not literature but royalties.

Charles Surface, an improvident rake, and Joseph Surface, an unctuously suave hypocrite, are brothers. They vie for the favour of their wealthy uncle and, as always in these comedies, the hand of a well-endowed heiress, Maria. Perceiving that Charles is beloved by Maria, the envious Joseph conspires with Lady Sneerwell, who also harbours a passion for the extravagant Charles.

It is announced that the profligate Charles is bankrupt. Unbeknown to the Surface brothers, their rich uncle Sir Oliver has returned from the East Indies, where he has long resided. He conceals his identity from them, to discern their true natures. His close friend, Sir Peter Teazle, is the guardian of Maria. Sir Peter, an elderly bachelor, has recently married a young woman, but it has turned out badly. The new Lady Teazle, from an impecunious country family, has too eagerly entered into a circle of malicious idlers and gossips, presided over by Lady Sneerwell. When her husband rebukes her for spending too much, she replies to him impertinently:

> Sir Peter: 'Slife, madam, I say, had you any of these little elegant expenses when you married me?
>
> Lady Teazle: Lud, Sir Peter, would you have me be out of the fashion?
>
> Sir Peter: The fashion, indeed! what had you to do with fashion before you married me?
>
> Lady Teazle: For my part, I should think you would like to have your wife thought a woman of taste.
>
> Sir Peter: Aye – there again – taste! Zounds! Madam, you had no taste when you married me!
>
> Lady Teazle: That's very true, indeed, Sir Peter; and, after having married you, I should never pretend to taste again.

Their relationship is a strange one, yet implicit with psychological truth. Muses Sir Peter, when alone:

> With what a charming air she contradicts everything I say, and how pleasantly she shows her contempt for my authority! Well, though I can't make her love me, there is great satisfaction in quarrelling with her, and I think she never appears to such advantage as when she is doing everything in her power to plague me.

Sir Oliver, to test his nephews, dons two different disguises. First he impersonates a money-lender, answers a summons to the house of the financially distressed Charles and is taken aback when Charles sells him all the Surface family portraits – all except one, that is: his scapegrace nephew adamantly refuses to part with the picture of his Uncle Noll, because of the gratitude and affection he feels for him. The rather vain old man is touched and is even more impressed to learn that Charles has lent some of the money to help Mr Stanley, a poor relation of the Surface family.

Sir Oliver and his brother, the father of Joseph, had been equally irresponsible in their youth, and to Sir Oliver his nephew's energetic sowing of wild oats is not too heinous. Snorts the tolerant Oliver: "I hate to see prudence clinging to the green suckers of youth; 'tis like ivy round a sapling, and spoils the growth of the tree."

Meanwhile Sir Peter has begun to suspect that the flighty, tart-tongued Lady Teazle is having an affair with young Charles. In reality she has been carrying on a dangerous flirtation with the hypocritical Joseph. He is about to seduce her, when her husband arrives unexpectedly.

What follows is the world-famous "screen scene". The worried Lady Teazle hides herself behind a panel and overhears her husband discuss his fears about her with the equivocating Joseph. She also discovers for the first time that Joseph is seeking to marry Maria. At a delicate moment, Charles bursts in. Sir Peter conceals himself in a closet, to eavesdrop on what Charles has to say about Lady Teazle. Joseph's liaison with her is unhappily revealed. Charles, mistaking who is behind the screen, knocks it over. The glib Joseph immediately concocts a plausible excuse for Lady Teazle's presence in his room, but Lady Teazle refuses to let the lie pass. Overcome by having heard Sir Peter's generous plans for her, she confesses to her husband, berates Joseph as a double-dealer and, vowing to be a good wife to her elderly mate, departs with him.

Act IV, comprising the sale of the portraits and the awkward business with the screen, is one of the most original and brilliantly constructed in all comic literature. Sir Peter's shocked and hurt realization that the "person" behind the screen is not a little French milliner, as Joseph has declared, but his own errant wife is truly poignant. This is comedy, not farce; the people in it are real.

The spectator is moved by the old man's emotional plight. It is said that on the first night the audience's applause greeting this episode was so stormy that it startled passers-by outside the theatre.

Sir Oliver, disguised as the indigent Mr Stanley, goes to his nephew Joseph to beg assistance. Joseph, that elegant "man of sentiment", turns "Mr Stanley" away with smooth talk but not before he hears a few aspersions cast on himself as miserly, though in fact he has already given £12,000 to each of the Surface young men. There is no longer any doubt that the foolish but good-hearted Charles will be the chosen heir.

Lady Sneerwell makes a last attempt to ensnare Charles but fails. He is given his Maria; Sir Peter and Lady Teazle are reconciled. The conclusion is sentimental, a concession on Sheridan's side to the known predilection of his audience. He could not afford to flout entirely their wishes. Still, Charles is too honest to promise to reform.

As the title indicates, the comedy is meant chiefly as an indictment of the malicious gossip-mongers who surround the Surfaces and Teazles: in this babbling circle are Lady Sneerwell, Mrs Candour, the poisonous Mr Snake, old Crabtree and his absurd nephew, Sir Benjamin Backbite. Sheridan himself had suffered from the falsehoods and exaggerations of tattlers and scandal-mongers and here he pays them back, directing a good many whiplashing lines against them and their ceaseless libels.

Very nicely conceived is Mr Snake, who at a propitious moment tells the truth because he is paid twice as much for doing so as for telling a lie. He begs that no one reveal what he has done:

> Consider – I live by the badness of my character; I have nothing but my infamy to depend on, and if it were once known that I had been betrayed into an honest action, I should lose every friend I have in the world.

The dialogue is sharp, volatile and witty. Sheridan's timing is perfect. Joseph assures Lady Teazle, "When a scandalous story is believed against one, there certainly is no comfort like the consciousness of having deserved it." Indeed, he argues that she will be more careful of her reputation if she has a guilty secret to hide. Her knowledge that she is wholly innocent makes her too unwary: it is an oddly persuasive pretext for her to commit adultery, as she very nearly does. Maria exclaims, "The male slanderer must have the cowardice of a woman before he can traduce one." After selling the portraits of his ancestors, Charles says, "I suppose you are surprised that I am not more sorrowful at parting with so many near relations. To be sure, 'tis very affecting; but you see they never move a muscle; so why should I?" The script also contains a splendid drinking song that begins:

Here's to the maiden of bashful fifteen;
Here's to the widow of fifty;
Here's to the flaunting extravagant Queen,
And here's to the housewife that's thrifty –
Let the toast pass, –
Drink to the lass,
I'll warrant she'll prove an excuse for the glass.

With *The Rivals* and *The School for Scandal* Sheridan is credited with having revived the dry and brittle vivacity of Restoration comedy, but without its salacity, and with a good deal more humanity. Sentimental comedy was seeking to compensate for the lack of heart in the Restoration farce; its own fault was that of unwarranted emotion. Sheridan attains almost the right balance between the two extremes. When his characters do become "soft" they take the edge off it by laughing at themselves.

The major phase of Sheridan's playwriting career, which lasted but four years, ended with *The Critic* (1779). This is very much in the manner of Buckingham's *The Rehearsal* and akin in spirit to what Fielding had accomplished in his burlesque *The Tragedy of Tragedies*. But *The Critic* is hardly as broad as Fielding's slapstick work; its humour is more deft, and the faults it satirizes are so timeless – one is almost tempted to say universal – that this brief piece has not dated; it is often brought back with marked success. It is testimony to Sheridan's sagacity that he kept his play short, for the joke at its core is not sustained for long. Once again his keen comic intelligence is evident.

With shrewd perspective and amused detachment Sheridan views his special world – the theatre – and correlates it to the larger world. Here is the author Sir Fretful Plagiary asking his friends for their "frank opinion", then being hurt and resentful and instantly rejecting it when he gets it. Here, too, is a playwright railing against the blindness and obtuseness of newspaper reviewers while he claims to be indifferent to them.

It is not different now than then, and Sheridan puts them down exactly. Here, in the person of the voluble Mr Puff, is press agentry, writing letters to editors and planting anecdotes and stories in the journals to get a play noticed. This gentleman offers a disquisition on "the puff direct, the puff preliminary, the puff collateral, the puff collusive, and the puff oblique, or puff by implication".

Sheridan, tongue in cheek, was baring secrets of the entertainment business as he – a writer and manager – well knew it. We attend with two critics, Sneer and Dangle, a dress rehearsal of Mr Puff's new tragedy *The Spanish Armada*. What follows is a mock blank-verse play-within-a-play, with comments from the three guests.

Puff explains how he has put his drama together; to start, he has to have a "love-interest", so he immediately has "the governor of Tilbury Fort's daughter fall in love with the son of a Spanish admiral". Improbable – "But what the plague! a play is not to show occurrences that happen every day, but things just so strange, that though they never did, they might happen."

The son of the Spanish admiral is Don Ferolo Whiskerando; he is a prisoner in the fort, and in no time at all the young lady, Tilburina, is torn "between her passion and her duty". Before long the author is protesting at mangling cuts made by the actors. In the play-within-the-play there is soon a discovery scene, a mad scene, a battle scene and a climax of action in which five characters simultaneously point daggers at one another and finally nothing less – with cannon shots and thunder – than the sinking of the Spanish Armada.

But the wittiest passage is an utterly silent one. Lord Burleigh, Queen Elizabeth's Lord High Treasurer, enters, goes slowly to a chair, meditates, rises and comes forward, shakes his head, and departs. Asks the astonished Sneer: "Now, pray what did he mean by that?" The enthusiastic Puff responds:

> Puff: Why, by that shake of the head, he gave you to understand that even though they had more justice in their cause, and wisdom in their measures – yet, if there as not a greater spirit shown on the part of the people, the country would at last fall a sacrifice to the hostile ambition of the Spanish monarchy.
>
> Sneer: The devil! did he mean all that by shaking his head?
>
> Puff: Every word of it – if he shook his head as I taught him.

Earlier Mr Sneer has referred to another play, "a genteel comedy . . . written in a style which they have lately tried to run down; the true sentimental, and nothing ridiculous in it from the beginning to the end".

> Mrs Dangle: Well, if they had kept to that, I should not have been such an enemy to the stage; there was some edification to be got from those pieces, Mr Sneer!
>
> Sneer: I am quite of your opinion, Mrs Dangle: the theatre, in proper hands, might certainly be made the school of morality; but now, I am sorry to say it, people seem to go there principally for their entertainment.

Slyly, Sheridan is hitting at the lachrymose sentimental comedy that he disdained.

The following year, 1780, he entered the realm of politics and was elected to Parliament, where he served the rest of his life, rising to be one of the leaders of his party and a renowned orator, in the distinguished company of Burke, Fox and Pitt the Younger. During this time he continued to manage the Drury Lane with the help of his father-in-law and others.

He was also a member of the Literary Club in London, which made him an intimate there of Dr Johnson, James Boswell, Sir Joshua Reynolds, David Garrick and the historian Edward Gibbon.

In Parliament he defended the abused American colonies. His most acclaimed oratorical performance was his charge against Warren Hastings, accused of having been a dishonest administrator of India; on this occasion the impassioned Sheridan held forth for nearly six hours, then, exhausted, collapsed and was caught by Burke.

Sheridan's company at the Drury Lane contained such notable players as John Philip Kemble (1757–1823) and Mrs Sarah Siddons (1755–1831). For his troupe he adapted A.F. von Kotzebue's spectacular verse drama, *Pizarro* (1799), which was immensely popular.

But he was most unlucky concerning his playhouse. In 1791 the Drury Lane was declared structurally unsound and had to be completely renovated. Then in 1809 the rebuilt theatre burned to a heap of ashes, ruining Sheridan financially. Besides that, he had always lived much beyond his means.

He became a widower and married a second time but not compatibly. His debts overtook him; he was arrested. He never recovered from his setbacks. His appearance changed: the once dandified gallant of Bath became shabby, gross and bloated from excessive drinking. His friend and patron, George IV, now shunned him, as did the Whigs whom he had led.

Even as he lay dying, at sixty, the bailiffs waited to carry him off to prison; he expired before ignominy befell him again.

Incongruously, his funeral was a grand event. Two royal dukes strode beside his coffin as it was borne into Westminster Abbey, while a parade of London's élite followed them. Byron, in Italy, wrote an apt epigrammatic tribute:

> Sighing that Nature formed
> But one such man
> And broke the die
> In moulding Sheridan.

(The reader of this history will have noticed how many playwrights drank too much, were imprisoned for debt and died poor, after which they were unceremoniously buried, more honoured in death than in life.)

*

Oddly enough, neither Goldsmith nor Sheridan had much influence on their contemporaries; they did not turn back or stem the foaming tide of "laughter and tears" with which the eighteenth-century stage was awash. Emulating Cibber and Steele with "comedies of intrigue" and "sentimental comedies" were such writers as Mrs Centlivre, Hugh Kelly, Richard Cumberland, Edward Moore, Thomas Holcroft and the Colmans, father and son. By mid-century, "sentimental comedy" was the dominant genre, a very anaemic form that grew more and more genteel.

The life of Mrs Susanna Centlivre (1667–1723) was as picturesque as her name. A literary descendant of Mrs Aphra Behn, she lost her first husband when he was slain in a duel. She took to the stage for a livelihood and later married M. Centlivre, a cook to Queen Anne and George I.

Indefatigable at composition, she poured out a number of scripts, one of which – *The Gamester* (1705) – was substantially successful. (This is a much-used title; at least a half-dozen well-known dramatists chose it.) In it, the evils of gambling are deplored. When the spouse of the heroine breaks his promise to quit the tables, his ingenious wife dons male attire, outwits him at betting and convinces him to stop before he is utterly ruined.

The short-lived Hugh Kelly (1739–77), son of a Dublin publican, first met players in his father's tavern and later won plaudits when he went to London with his *False Delicacy* (1768), which Garrick then staged at Drury Lane. The comedy was as popular there as it later became in Paris and Lisbon, and when the printed version appeared it sold 3,000 copies in a single day.

The play traces the troubles of the three pairs of somewhat ill-suited lovers and contains much moral platitudinizing. It is more didactic than amusing, but it was what spectators wished to see. Kelly repeated his success with *A Word to the Wise* (1770), which was a better play. He also had luck with his *School for Wives* (1773), which was similarly replete with preachments against the folly and perils of duelling.

Richard Cumberland (1732–1811), grandson of a Master of Trinity College, Cambridge, and son of an Irish bishop, began his very different career as secretary to the Lord Lieutenant of Ireland, before selecting the drama as a field of endeavour. He was fortunate with *The Brothers* (1769). His *The West Indian* (1771) lifted him to celebrity. This is a very ambitious work in which Cumberland introduces what he calls "a new type of man". The hero, Belcour, was born under the "vertical sun" of Jamaica. He comes to London to meet his guardian (who is really his father), a merchant. As Cumberland sees him, Belcour is mostly "natural" and has difficulty adapting himself to London's sanctimonious, mercenary society, embodied in Lady Rusport, who professes high morality but attempts to defraud her nephew Charles of an inheritance. Belcour seeks to seduce a young lady, Louisa Dudley, but is finally brought to marry her and mend his wild ways. Then he learns that she is an heiress.

In a sense, the impulsive, rather primitive and even extravagant but generous character is a prototype of Sheridan's Charles Surface, whose shortcomings are to be overlooked because, whatever his derelictions, he is a good fellow. Besides, he is a free spirit; he acts from innocent instinct and is full of amusing confrontations and surprising discoveries. His chief trait is sincerity.

After this work was successfully performed all over the Continent, Cumberland kept busy with other scripts: *The Fashionable Lover* (1772), *The Natural Son* (1784), *The Jew* (1794) and *The Wheel of Fortune* (1795). In passing it might be noted that the performer who played the leading role in this last-mentioned play was a handsome, club-footed young man, none other than Lord Byron.

Cumberland's influence was felt in the theatre throughout the Western world, as he became for a time the pre-eminent English playwright of the sentimental school. *The Jew* reveals Cumberland's own human impulses. He portrays a Jew in a kindly light. Old Shiva, believed to be avaricious and miserly, is secretly helping others, in particular two young lovers. *The Wheel of Fortune* treats another of Cumberland's favourite themes: Penruddock, who has been a recluse, comes into a fortune. He returns to the world, finds it abhorrent, has a chance to avenge himself on his enemies. But, after a severe inner struggle, his natural goodness prevails. He forgives those who have injured him and spends his money on worthy causes. He yearns to return to the beauty and quiet of nature.

Cumberland wrote serious dramas, too, among them *The Battle of Hastings* (1778), which throbs with patriotism. It is in the tradition of Rowe, Ambrose, Phillips and Thomson and still has some fervent admirers. He also wrote an adaptation of *Timon of Athens*.

It was specifically against the strained, old-fashioned and artificial dialogue and far-fetched situations found in the comedies of Kelly and Cumberland that Oliver Goldsmith was protesting in *The Good Natur'd Man* and the critical essay that accompanied it. But is was a tribe of dramatists including Kelly and Cumberland, rather than the likes of Goldsmith and Sheridan, who drew people to the theatre and prevailed. We are indebted to Cumberland, however, for an interesting *Memoirs* that tells us much about the playhouses and players of his day, especially David Garrick.

Edward Moore (1712–57), one of several writers of plays called *The Gamester*, did well at comedy. *The Foundling* (1784) is well plotted and resembles *The West Indian* because it deals with the long-popular theme of the changeling and the discovery of lost parents.

Thomas Holcroft (1754–1809) was a friend of two very progressive thinkers of his time, William Godwin and Thomas Paine. His own sympathies were revolutionary or at least liberal. His plays, especially the later ones, are forerunners of the pure melodramas of the Gothic Age to follow. *The Road to Ruin* (1792) tells of kind-hearted Harry Dornton, impoverished from gambling, who goes to a friend whom he helped to make rich. His wealthy friend refuses to succour him. Dornton learns that his father, too, is about to be involved in the catastrophe he has brought on. He decides to marry an elderly wealthy widow to repair his fortunes and make amends. Eventually all is straightened out for the reformed, repentant wastrel. This play earned and kept for a long time a place as a standard work in the English repertory. Other Holcroft contributions are *Man of Ten Thousand* (1796) and – more important – an adaptation of the French melodrama *Coelina, or The Child of Mystery* (1800) by Guilbert de Pixérécourt. This is the play that began the vogue, soon to swell to large proportions in England, for scripts with sensational plots and few or no literary pretensions. They were meant merely to seize, titillate and thrill an audience.

The Colmans, father and son, provide another example of inherited talent. George Colman the Elder (1732–94), a theatre manager, is noted for *Polly Honeycombe* (1760), *The Jealous Wife* (1760) and the very lively *The Clandestine Marriage* (1766), the latter written in collaboration with David Garrick, a play still revived with good effect. Another of his pieces is *The Man of Business* (1774).

In general, he opposed the overdosing of plays with sentimentality and, in his critique of social follies, had some kinship with Sheridan, whose detached attitude he anticipated. He, too, brought back the Restoration fops, as with the elderly Beau Lord Ogleby in the chucklesome *The Clandestine Marriage.*

His gifts are not very literary, but his dialogue is adequate, his craft professional. In *The Jealous Wife* a hen-pecked husband, Mr Oakley, seeks in vain to free himself from his wife's dominance. These are two people who love each other, yet torment each other ceaselessly. The play is populated with other interesting characters: Squire Russet, whose daughter runs away to avoid marriage to an unappealing suitor, the horse-and-hound lover Sir Harry Beagle, the young heedless hero Charles, another gallant with weak discipline but a sensible, full heart – it is said that Fielding's *Tom Jones* inspired the image of many of these virile, irresponsible young rakes. By contrast, two city patricians, Lord Trinket and Lady Freelove, illustrate the wickedness of town life. He wrote, altogether, some thirty plays.

George Colman, the son (1762–1836), was more attached to the cult of melodrama. His works are wide-ranging, embracing almost every genre. Critics and the public somewhat mistakenly hailed him as Sheridan's successor.

His lighter pieces include *The Heir-in-Law* (1797) and *John Bull* (1803). In both, snobbery and false friendship are satirized, and the superiority of plain and humble folk who have kind and generous hearts is demonstrated.

In the latter play the hero – appropriately called Job Thornberry – falls on hard times. A wealthy stranger, who turns out to be an orphan Thornberry had once befriended, rescues him. Virtue is rewarded. In both plays false friendship is condemned, as well as the pursuit of money, social affectation, marriages for status and sexual promiscuity.

Colman's comic opera, *Blue Beard, or Female Curiosity* (1798), takes place in Turkey. In this offering, with a display of skilful light verse, Colman establishes himself as a precursor of W.S. Gilbert, another master of zany thought. Like Gilbert's Lord High Executioner in *The Mikado*, the Turkish ruler does not look upon the beheading of a wife as a serious affair. His solution to domestic squabbles is arbitrary:

How many there are, when a wife plays the fool,
Will argue the point with her, calmly and cool;
The bashaw, who don't relish debates of this sort,
Cuts the woman, as well as the argument, short.

An admirable bit of chop-logic! A similar flow of nonsense in rhyme is found in *The Review, or The Wags of Windsor* (1800).

Versatile and prolific, the younger Colman scored a hit with a serious work in blank verse, *The Iron Chest* (1796), taken from *Caleb Williams*, a novel by William Godwin. This is an exciting play; its elements are those of melodrama. Sir Edward Mortimer has been tried for murder and acquitted. He keeps this incident hidden, and is now head-keeper of the New Forest. When he learns that the hero Wilford possesses the secret, Sir Edward recklessly accuses him of a robbery. The young man is cleared, however, by the discovery of a document in a locked chest.

Other serious plays are *Inkle and Yarico* (1787), celebrating as does Cumberland humankind's innocent and primitive instincts – a Rousseauan concept – and *The Law of Java* (1822), offering criticism of imperialism and international trade – not English, but Dutch. The work has many splashes of Oriental colour and attempts a nicely balanced exploration of its theme: if the Dutch traders have shortcomings, so have the natives, whose Sultan is cruel and tyrannical. Of interest is a priestly recluse, Orzinga, betrayed by a friend in the past and now withdrawn to meditate in a spot close to nature. Through him the author expresses many ideas that he presumably shared.

In plays such as these the formula was developed of stock characters and stock situations that can be manipulated by the melodramatist to arouse and grip the imagination and feelings of less sophisticated spectators, who gazed with bated breath and mouths agape.

This new type of play had incidental musical accompaniment – hence the term "melodrama" – that further affected the audience's emotional response. The scripts show notations by the author or stage-manager specifying what sort of music is required: "solemn", "mournful", "menacing". They very much resemble the soundtrack of a modern film or television programme, where music is employed to insinuate a mood, enforce an emotion or create an atmosphere.

Plays like this were at first offered only in the smaller theatres, those that had no patent or licence to present spoken works but were free to give those that incorporated music. The audiences drawn to these houses were not intellectually demanding, asked no literary qualifications of the dramatists and sought only sensation and novelty. They loved violent action, surprise – no matter how illogical – and florid sentiment. This is the beginning of the purely commercial theatre that would eventually comprise most of the Western world's stage. It grew and flourished most rapidly on the Continent, and the English playwrights followed the German and French lead, adapting and translating more works from those countries.

As yet, however, this degrading change was only incipient; nor was the theatre ever to cease being, for other writers and theatre-goers, a place for searching psychology, earnest social concern and ethical debate.

Elizabeth Inchbald (1753–1821) attacked the dreadful conditions in prisons in one of the earliest plays dedicated to social reform, *Such Things Are* (1787). Craftsmen of some note were Samuel Foote, who wrote *The Orators* (1762) and many other farces, John O'Keefe with *Wild Oats* (1791), Arthur Murphy with *Three Weeks after Marriage* (1764) and Thomas Morton with *Speed the Plough* (1800). John Home (1722–1808), a Scot, offered a good many patriotic dramas including *The Siege of Aquileia* (1760), *The Fatal Discovery* (1769) and *Douglas* (1756), which were filled with wild poetry and gloom. Here, too, are seen the first sproutings of Gothicism.

When playwrights falter, actors are likely to get more attention. This happened in the latter half of the eighteenth century in London. One stage figure in particular rose to an almost dizzying prominence and popularity. David Garrick (1717–79) was seen as one of the most inspired ever to stride the boards and declaim verse or speak prose. An intellectual, he was an intimate – as has already been observed – of the most eminent men of his day, Samuel Johnson, whose pupil he was, James Boswell, Oliver Goldsmith the whimsical physician, John Arbuthnot, the statesman Edmund Burke, Richard Sheridan and Sir Joshua Reynolds.

Born in Hereford and raised in Lichfield, he was a member of a good Huguenot family. His father was a French recruiting officer; his mother was English. In Lichfield he was enrolled at a private school initiated by Dr Johnson, his teacher. When the school failed, David accompanied Johnson to London where they briefly shared quarters.

Going out on his own, he joined a brother in the wine trade but soon responded to his desire to seek a career in the theatre. He was taken on for several minor roles and then suddenly caused a sensation by his fierce portrayal of Shakespeare's Richard III in 1741. Thereafter he became famous for his enactments of Macbeth, Othello, Hamlet and Lear in a small theatre. Garrick's Hamlet was apparelled like an affluent English gentleman visiting an eighteenth-century drawing-room. He also excelled at comedy.

In his acting he emphasized reliance on appropriate gestures and movement. (Diderot in his essay on acting praised Garrick's practical theories and instruction to his players. His ideas were not communicated in print but subsequently were verbally transmitted from generation to generation.)

As his reputation grew and he prospered, he was able with John Lacey to purchase the Drury Lane in 1747, the seating capacity of which he expanded, and establish a company of sterling actors whom he managed and who appeared in a repertory of works by Shakespeare and others, some imported from the Continent and some that Garrick himself wrote or collaborated on. Of the twenty-one scripts he wrote, most of them farces, *The Clandestine Marriage*, composed with the elder Colman, is the most enduring; its revivals still earn incessant laughter. He also contributed numerous prologues and epilogues to works produced at Drury Lane. He was very much the pragmatic showman, and for once an actor and director triumphed over an author.

The company Garrick assembled and ruled sternly was comprised of many whose names, like his, are legendary. One was Peg Woffington (1714–68), the shrill-voiced daughter of a Dublin bricklayer. She was a charming comedienne who shone especially in "breeches roles" and off-stage doubled for a time as the infatuated young Garrick's mistress. She never disdained any role, however minor and unattractive.

Garrick was innovative in other ways. Like Voltaire, he ended the sale of tickets to seats on the stage, silencing the distracting chatter and rude flippant comment from the buyers. To compensate the players for this loss of revenue, he raised their wages. He dispensed with footlights, setting lights overhead, at the sides and below, where the audience could no longer see them. This alteration reduced the heat and smoky smell they gave off.

With the help of a scene designer, P.J. Loutherbourg, he brought the first "realistic" settings to the theatre, as well as many spectacular effects to which spectators had by now become accustomed. They were insatiable in their demand for them; he answered their desire.

He continued to operate the Drury Lane for nineteen years, until 1776, when Sheridan bought it with two partners who had far less luck with it. In 1769, somewhat belatedly, he organized a national jubilee in Stratford to mark the Bard's 200th birthday.

He idolized Shakespeare, but he was another who tampered with the texts, giving some of the tragedies happy endings to appease his audiences. In his defence, mounting plays is an expensive undertaking. The producer must buy a script at the start and promise to pay royalties afterwards. (Though not to Shakespeare!) A theatre is purchased or rented and a director engaged along with a scene designer and scenery constructed and painted. A cast is gathered; some ensembles, especially for Shakespeare, may be quite large. Musicians and dancers may be required.

Rehearsals are costly. A costume designer is given an assignment; dressing the players may add considerably to the budget, especially for richly garbed historical dramas. Stagehands are needed to pull the curtains, to oversee the lighting and to shift the properties and sets. There must be a ticket-seller, a ticket-taker at the door and ushers. Posters have to be printed and distributed citywide and put up. Money for such an enterprise is not easily raised; theatrical ventures are highly speculative – the odds are long. Some offerings vanish after a mere one or two viewings. The box office dominates. If theatre-goers insisted on happy endings, their voices could not be ignored.

After his retirement from the Drury Lane, Garrick decided to dwell in France, perhaps influenced by his ancestral ties. He had many friends there. On occasion he performed in French cities and was greatly extolled, his experiments debated. This phase of his life lasted three years.

For most of his adult life he was happily married to Eva-Maria Violetti, a dancer whose family origins were mysterious, rumour having it that she was the illegitimate daughter of a duke.

His death, at sixty-two, was sudden. His wife long survived him, dying at ninety-eight.

Though an actor, he was accorded a magnificent funeral at Westminster Abbey. Another long-standing tribute: centuries later, theatres throughout the English-speaking world bear his name.

Garrick is important in the history of theatre because his personal qualities – his decorum, wit, amiability and analytical intelligence – gained him entrance into the most élite circles in London. His unique accomplishments on stage added to his lustre; well read, he approached plays in a new way. He did much to raise the social acceptability of acting as a profession.

Charles Macklin (*c.* 1700–1797), Garrick's elder, alternated in some of the major roles with the younger man. Macklin was Irish and was a link to the tradition of Betterton and Barton Booth. He shared and even anticipated Garrick's view that acting needed restraint. His physique was a disadvantage, as he was shorter than most of his celebrated leading ladies – a Romeo less tall than Juliet, a small Macbeth, a short Othello . . . His temper was tempestuous, his diction rolling with a brogue. He was not handsome but graceful. He had fiery eyes and a voice that was infinitely flexible, quickly modulating from soft and harmonious to suddenly chilling.

He broke from the flamboyant style that had long prevailed, performing instead with quiet restraint, assuming most often an easy, natural manner. There was to be no more tearing of passions to tatters. His characterizations were so intense and real, so insinuating, that they disturbed and haunted the spectators. Nor did he approve of the stilted, oratorical, declamatory stance used in France for *tirades*. The story is that the pathos he evoked in *The Merchant of Venice* made King George II go home to spend a sleepless night. He boldly reinterpreted the image of Shylock, making him sympathetic rather than comic, which caused a controversy.

He threw himself into a part with such fervour that he caused the death of a fellow actor by thrusting a cane through his eye. He had to stand trial for murder but won acquittal. One of his favourite stage tricks was the carefully timed pause: he discriminated among three kinds, that he called his short, long and grand pauses.

Macklin also began a move towards more historically authentic costuming, in which he was even far in advance of Garrick. He dressed in ancient Scottish attire as Macbeth and in a gabardine as Shylock.

In mid-career he turned to writing plays that had profitable runs.

He lived to be ninety-seven and possibly older, and his stage career lasted more than half a century. He appeared in plays for at least sixty years. He was still strong enough to perform when he was past ninety. He did not always act with Garrick, and they finally separated. After extreme age forced him to quit the stage, he returned to watch his former colleagues and took perverse delight in heckling them from the pit.

When Sheridan controlled the Drury Lane, Mrs Sarah Siddons (1755–1831) joined the company. The daughter of Roger Kemble, an actor-manager, she toured for many years in the provinces, though she made one sally to London when Garrick invited her to play Portia. In 1782, however, she captured the town and her 37-year reign as England's most esteemed tragedienne was never challenged. She was especially admired for her Belvidera in *Venice Preserv'd* and Lady Macbeth. Reynolds painted her as the Tragic Muse.

In personal life having a cold dignity, she was admired for her virtuous reputation and intelligent discourse. On stage, however, she immersed herself so deeply into her tragic roles that she was often reduced to tears after the curtain's fall. Her emotional distress lingered even after she went home.

She used little makeup and refused to powder her hair. Her manner on stage was stately and noble – hers was what was called the "classic" manner. But matched to her dignity were fire and passion that elevated her impersonations and thrilled all spectators.

James Quin (1693–1766) was an actor of the older ranting and bellowing school, another hulking Irishman whose physical proportions suited him perfectly to enact Falstaff, which from all accounts he did wonderfully. He was fine in comedy and essayed tragic roles to less applause. He is long remembered for having said, when he first beheld Garrick's reserved style, "If this young fellow is right, we are all wrong."

John Philip Kemble (1757–1823) was the brother of Mrs Siddons and later managed both Drury Lane (for Sheridan) and Covent Garden. He had for a time prepared for the priesthood, evidence of his inherent seriousness. As an actor he was famed for his Hamlet and Macbeth, playing the latter part opposite his sister as Lady Macbeth. He staged revivals of Shakespeare and devoted much care to preparing them. Not recalled as a truly great actor, he was none the less important and influential over a 25-year span.

Davenant's *Siege of Rhodes*, to which he added music, was the impetus for yet another form of theatre in Restoration England. As in France during the reigns of Louis XIV and XV, opera became quite popular in London. The aristocracy embraced it. The Puritans had not objected to musical entertainment, and the Lord Protector was known to be very fond of it; that was what had emboldened Davenant to propose reopening a theatre to present a play with songs and orchestral accompaniment. The music for this was by Matthew Locke (1630–77), and the scenery by a pupil of Inigo Jones. As noted, the playhouses of Charles II's era were available for operatic productions, and Dryden, Shadwell, Tate, Settle and Lee wrote or edited librettos of some of the works offered there. Furthermore, England brought forth at this time a composer of the first rank, Henry Purcell (1659–95), whose *Dido and Aeneas* (1698) and *King Arthur* (the first with words by Nahum Tate and the latter with text by Dryden) contain some of the finest music of any in British history.

One source of librettos was Shakespeare's plays, and operatized versions were the consequence: *The Tempest*, *A Midsummer Night's Dream* and *Measure for Measure* underwent this metamorphosis. Many liberties were perforce taken with the original texts. *A Midsummer Night's Dream* as reshaped by Shadwell became *The Fairy Queen*. Other of Shakespeare's scripts were inset with masques, or given entr'actes that involved dancing as well as songs. This was emphatically done in Shadwell's revision of *Timon*, where the first-act feast is enhanced by elaborate ballet. It was Charles Gildon who prepared the new version of *Measure for Measure* (1692). The Restoration writers had not the slightest doubt that they were improving on Shakespeare, and – as has been remarked – they often changed the plays' endings as well, to make them more acceptable to a supposedly more cultured and sophisticated audience.

In these operas, as has also been said, the most elaborate scenic investiture was to be seen. Davenant had followed *The Siege of Rhodes* with two more spectacular productions: *The Cruelty of the Spaniards in Peru* and *The History of Sir Francis Drake*. At first no women took part in these works; young men assumed feminine roles. But after Charles II's return this was abruptly changed. Stage instructions for presenting these musical works are extant; they often call for eye-dazzling effects.

In addition to native operas, some works were imported from France or adapted – as was *Psyche* (1674) by Locke and Shadwell, from a script by Molière for which the original music had been by Lully. For the most part all these "operas" used music only at intervals; they were not entirely sung but were interspersed with songs and for the rest tended to consist of recitatives, that is, speeches accompanied by music.

Certainly mention should be made of Niccolò Piccinni (1728–1800), a busy Italian chiefly remembered for his feud with Glück, a German, for dominance at the Paris opera. Among his works is *La Cecchina, ossia La buona figliuola* (*La Cecchina, or The Good Girl*; 1760).

A performance of *The Tempest* in 1674 was the first at which the orchestra, an ensemble of twenty-six instruments including a harpsichord, was arranged in front of and below the stage, its present position, rather than on a balcony or niche above the stage as formerly. This allowed more room, and the orchestra was enlarged; but it also became visible. Hitherto, as in Italy, the musicians had been more or less out of sight, unless one looked upwards.

Dryden theorized about opera; he thought it should treat mostly with gods, goddesses and mythological heroes. But shepherds and shepherdesses might also appear in them. He wrote a libretto for an experimental work, *Albion and Albanius* (*c.* 1684), with a score by a French composer, Louis Grabu, that was a disaster, possibly because Grabu was hardly acquainted with English and mangled Dryden's poetry. In it are classical divinities and other allegorical figures, though the subject is English history – a strange juxtaposition.

Henry Purcell came from a family of devout Catholics who were adherents of Charles II. After the Restoration, in which they had participated, several of them were rewarded for their loyalty to the exiled Stuart monarch with minor posts at court. Henry senior, the composer's father, was a well-trained musician; as a boy he was a chorister and later he became master of a boy's choir at the Abbey.

When *The Siege* was revived in 1661 Henry senior was in the cast; he needed extra money to sustain his large brood – six children, of whom Henry junior was the fourth.

At the Abbey, Henry junior became friends with a Venetian musician; through him he got to know the works of Monteverdi and was greatly impressed and influenced by them. At twenty he was appointed organist at Westminster Abbey. He succeeded Blow there and poured forth a flood of compositions, mostly anthems and other liturgical pieces but also two hundred songs using biblical texts and *The Book of Common Prayer* or lyrics by contemporary poets. (Some biographers believe that Henry senior and Henry junior were Protestants, unlike other members of the Purcell family, but prudently kept it secret.) He contributed songs to plays by Dryden, Shadwell, D'Urfrey and Southerne. He was widely admired. His gift reached its fullest expression in *Dido and Aeneas*, his sole opera, with a libretto by Nahum Tate (1652–1715).

Besides Locke and Purcell, mention might be made of John Blow (1648–1708), whose *Venus and Adonis*, commissioned for the King's amusement, is a little jewel; it probably served as a model for Purcell's much greater *Dido and Aeneas*. One reason for thinking so is that Purcell was a pupil of Blow. Both works were intended for performance at a girl's school, by its young students. From there *Dido and Aeneas* moved on to become an ever-living classic, outlasting Purcell, its grand composer, who died a mere half-dozen years after its première, at thirty-six. The choice of subject – a classical myth given by Virgil – accords with the then dominant preference for references to Greek history and literature. He left incomplete scores for several semi-operas, including some meant for music-dramas based on Shakespeare's plays.

The story goes that he was in the habit of staying out late drinking with friends in taverns. One freezing night his wife locked him out; he caught a cold that grew serious and proved fatal.

Charles II was not especially fond of opera and did little to encourage the form. He preferred to import them from Paris. When Purcell died, the chance to establish a strong native opera tradition perished with him.

William III was more partial to musical stage works, but in his time foreign composers – Italians, the French, Germans – fared best in London. Chief among them was Georg Friedrich Handel. A fuller account of Handel's activities and those of Italian companies in London is given in *Stage by Stage: Dramatis Personae*, a previous book in this series.

Opera companies were Italian for the most part, and held forth at Vanbrugh's Haymarket, largely depriving English actors of a licensed stage.

Besides, audiences preferred this musical drama and spent their money there. Apparently there were not enough well-trained English voices after Purcell's day, so operas were presented by adding famous Italian artists who had no knowledge of English. Since this compromise was not generally very acceptable, famed Italian castrati with "nightingale tones" finally superseded English singers; the operas were wholly performed in a foreign tongue. Some received large sums, since they were much in demand on the Continent.

The profusion of castrati was the result of a decree by the Vatican that women could not be members of church choirs. Confronted by this quandary, musical directors turned to male sopranos for the liturgy. Congregations liked the compelling sounds of boys' shrill voices; more and more such passages were inserted. Poor families with many sons could send one for the surgery to augment their income and perhaps give him a chance to gain fame and fortune, as many did. The Vatican, appalled by this practice, forbade castration, but too late. The second rule was unheeded. Castrati continued to appear as late as the next century, when they were finally replaced by counter-tenors and mezzi.

Attracted by this favourable situation, the German composer Georg Friedrich Handel (1685–1759), who had been working in Italy, ventured to London. He had already made a name for himself in his native Germany. A Saxon, his birthplace was Halle. At eighteen he went to Hamburg where he played the violin and the harpsichord in the opera orchestra. Absorbing the forms, he began writing for the stage and had two youthful works enacted, one *Almira*, to surprising applause, the other *Nero*, which failed.

For further study, he left for Florence, where he met Arcangelo Corelli and the Scarlattis, father and son. To support himself he travelled about Italy as a performer on the organ and harpsichord. Before he reached England he had already made a name for himself with a more ambitious offering, *Rinaldo*, which he had written in a fortnight. The work triumphed in Venice and was produced throughout Europe. The Elector Georg Ludwig invited him to Hanover and gave him a well-paying post, but Handel found that city provincial and stodgy and in 1717 grew restless, broke his contract and returned to England to stay for the next thirty years.

He established his own company, which brought him unending troubles with temperamental singers and caused him a succession of financial embarrassments. He also had a formidable rival in Giovanni Battista Buononcini. Handel was spiritually an Englishman and acquired legal citizenship. A gluttonous eater and heavy drinker, he made and lost fortunes, grew grossly fat, and more and more resembled "John Bull". This German, who worked in London and wrote operas to Italian texts, was buried at the end in Westminster Abbey, a rare tribute to a foreigner.

His feud with the much older and more experienced Buononcini, whose light tunes are now almost completely forgotten, was not the only source of Handel's difficulties. The Elector of Hanover, whose service he had quit rather abruptly, was now on the British throne as George I. Fortunately he was so appreciative of music that he forgave Handel's defection and graced a revival of *Rinaldo* with his presence.

The King sided with Handel in the quarrel that divided the public and the Royal Academy of Music's shareholders as to who was the better composer, the sober German or the sensuously tuneful Italian. The noisy struggle between these two lasted for seven years, until Handel was finally victorious.

To obtain the best singers possible he promised huge fees, bankrupting himself and his backers. His artistic superiority had the effect of driving less gifted English composers from the operatic stage. The chance for any opera in English also vanished, since Handel was wedded to the idea of Italian librettos rendered by Italian singers, especially those with whom he had worked while in that country. Before his arrival in London, and after Purcell's earlier reign, there had been Thomas Clayton's *Arsinoe* (1705) and *Rosamund* (1706), the latter with a libretto by Addison; the former, though possibly the music was not original, was a success, the latter an utter failure. Thereupon the chastened Clayton withdrew to Ireland.

In addition to the factionalism between the two prominent composers and their vociferous admirers, jealousy overtook the highly strung prima donnas. London was shocked and entertained on 6 June 1727 by a hair-pulling match between Cuzzoni and Faustina on stage, accompanied by a battle between their partisans in the pit, before the startled eyes of Caroline, Princess of Wales.

During his long tenure Handel was also involved in court politics – a royal family struggle between the new King and his heir George II. The Royal Academy, producer of the operas, closed its doors a year later, in June 1728. One of the reasons was the vast success of *The Beggar's Opera*, a novelty drawing crowds that by now were tiring of works in the style of Buononcini and Handel. The mythological, historical and biblical tales, and tales of magic and witchcraft they unfolded, were beginning to pall. *The Beggar's Opera* was meant to parody the *opera seria*, and Pepusch, who arranged the ballad tunes, had a personal grudge against Handel, who had replaced him as private musician to the free-spending Duke of Chandos.

Handel, mistakenly assuming that the craze for *The Beggar's Opera* and light pieces was temporary, returned to the fray, offering new works. For another decade he persisted, composing eighteen more operas – in all he created in his career forty-six scores and productions. In this later phase he had some momentary successes, but the tide was now increasingly against him. Besides, he had a new competitor, the Neapolitan Niccolò Porpora, who was sponsored by enemies of George II and the Whigs, that is, the adherents of the Prince of Wales and the Tories, who spread vicious libels against Handel. Porpora headed a rival company at Lincoln's Inn Fields and split what audience for opera there was left.

Handel's consistent use of texts in a foreign language made that a permanent feature of musical drama in England's capital. The Handelian operas are static, resembling oratorios performed in costume. Emotionally they are inherently progressive and stirring, but they call for too little action, relying upon the sublimity of the music and the Baroque elaborateness of the staging to enthrall audiences. Here, too, the lavish, costly spectacle of operatic stages set a standard that tragic drama, and melodrama as well, had to equal in order to attract audiences.

Though the librettos are often stilted and dull, imaginatively staged twentieth-century revivals prove that there is moving drama and suspense in Handel's operas. With no native development of *opera seria* after Handel's invasion, the future of England's musical genius was to lie in the direction of *opera buffa* or comic opera, as exampled by *The Beggar's Opera* and the mocking caprices of Gilbert and Sullivan.

Handel suffered a stroke in 1737 and began to go blind. He worked for another twenty-two years with a paralysed arm, fashioning only three more operas in the last part of 1741. He mostly shifted his efforts to writing oratorios of surpassing beauty. From year to year he narrowly escaped being thrown into debtors' prison.

— 8 —

THEATRE IN ITALY AND SPAIN

The beginning of the eighteenth century saw a craze for opera in Italy. When the young Handel was studying there, Alessandro Scarlatti (1659–1726) was very busy. In all, the elder Scarlatti composed 114 operas, half of which have disappeared; of those remaining, none are deemed viable now. In Italy in 1700 there were already grand theatres built to house the performances. Venice was a notable centre of activity in this realm; it had sixteen stages. A public devoted to the music dramas packed the nightly offerings. Singers, whether castrati or prima donnas, were widely adored. Each had zealous partisans who prized them above all others, punctuating the excitement of the performances with cheers and catcalls.

An important early figure was Apostolo Zeno (1668–1750), court poet to Emperor Charles IV in Vienna; he furnished over sixty librettos, in which he reduced the number of acts from five to three, shaping a form for them that became standard.

After Zeno, another royal laureate in Vienna, the fine poet Pietro Metastasio (1698–1782), provided subjects for numerous librettos. Plebeian by birth, the son of a soldier who became a Roman grocer, the eleven-year-old Pietro was fond of reciting on street corners. A wealthy jurist, Giovanni Gravina, witnessed him performing and adopted and educated him. Recognizing his amazing poetic gifts, he became Metastasio's patron. Pietro inherited a sizeable fortune from Gravina and quickly spent it. Still youthful, he became familiar with many of the prominent composers of his time and studied music, including singing, with Porpora.

His poetic style was influenced, he asserted, by Ovid and Tasso. For many years an older woman, a famed singer, aided him. Growing tired of her favours and driven by financial necessity, he took a lucrative position in Vienna. His exquisite verses were precisely suited to *bel canto*, the exacting technique of the virtuosic castrati who were then the spoiled monarchs of the musical stage.

Italian composers in Austria and elsewhere liked Metastasio's lyrical scripts so well that they used them over and over; the same subjects and words were appropriated by a succession of melodists. Though distinguished, the dramas of Zeno and Metastasio are unvarying in theme, so that no little monotony and rigidity sets in. As with the plots Handel favoured, the subject of each is drawn from myths or legends of antiquity, the scriptures or medieval history, and the story always has a happy ending, with the leading characters – always noble lovers – reconciled or paired off at last. Invariably there is a villain, often a usurper. The pattern was for solo songs to be linked by recitative. Italian operas of this sort flourished during the first half of the century.

Following the elder Scarlatti's death, Naples was where many operas were composed and produced more or less to this formula, which was not to change until the appearance of C.W. Gluck in the 1760s. From Italy, public enthusiasm for music dramas spread to France, England, Austria and more slowly to Germany.

An offshoot was *opera buffa* – in France *opéra comique*, in England ballad or comic opera – which also first developed and grew popular in Italy. Probably originating in Naples, it tended to celebrate peasant life and have a contemporary setting, as opposed to the violent and sombre themes of *opera seria*. These little farces with vigorous music, often in the spirit of *commedia dell'arte*, rose to be a distinctive art-form when Giovanni Battista Pergolesi (1710–36) offered his *La Serva Padrona* (*The Maid as Mistress*; 1733) and *Il Flaminio* (1735). Pergolesi, doomed to an early death at age twenty-six, from consumption exacerbated by dissipation, wrote *opera seria*, too, but those works were less appreciated. Some critics say that he was not more talented than other composers of his day but luckier in that by some chance his *La Serva Padrona* has survived while other similar works have vanished.

More ordinary folk came to *opera buffa*, which greatly broadened the audience, making plays with music even more appealing. Conniving young lovers, servants, doddering and miserly old guardians, dim-witted notaries, eccentric music-masters and a host of other such characters were derived from ancient pantomime.

In Italy, as in England with Dryden and Addison, French influence was pervasive, and the neoclassical drama continued. The most illustrious name associated with the genre during this century was unquestionably that of Count Vittorio Alfieri (1749–1803). A group who worked towards the same ideal preceded him: Giovanni Delfino (*Medoro*, 1630) and Pier Jacopo Martello (*Marco Tullio Cicerone*, 1715) are examples, though not wholly happy ones. Francesco Scipione di Maffei (1675–1765) comes much nearer with *Merope* (1713), with its sharper characterizations and emotion strong enough to break through a formal reserve. It strengthened the tie to French neoclassicism. Impressed by Maffei's accomplishment, Voltaire wrote his own version of its subject.

Three decades later Antonio Conti offered *Marco Bruto* (1743) and *Duso* (1747); Alfonso Varano wrote a drama titled *Giovanni di Giscala* (1754). Artistically, neither is a major success.

Count Vittorio Alfieri, a native of Turin, was brought up with French as his first language and turned to Italian when he was in his twenties. Yet he became celebrated for his pure, sensitive, precise handling of that language. In a period of Romantic political ferment, Alfieri paradoxically reflected his time's passionate concern for reform by force. Though his classically disciplined dramas are almost invariably laid in ancient days, they have contemporary references. His characters talk of liberty and yearn for individualism. They have the high-flown idealism typical of Romantics. Perhaps this is why, though Alfieri's subjects and dramatic form are traditional and austere in shape, his plays have fire, enthusiasm and relevance derived from the author's own heroically emotional temperament.

Alfieri's canon consists of twenty-one dramas, from *Cleopatra* (1775) to *L'Alceste Seconda* (1798), in a literary career lasting twenty-three years. Like Schiller, he wrote a play, *Filippo*, about the ill-fated Don Carlos, portrayed as a Spanish liberal opposed to his oppressive father, Philip II. Mary Stuart is another subject that he shares with the German playwright. He also produced some very remarkable comedies. His best works are based on Schiller and biblical stories. He wrote eloquent essays on political topics.

He proved the sincerity of his liberalism by giving away his inherited estate. He is remembered and honoured as an ardent patriot and lover of freedom.

A taut tale of incestuous feeling touched with Oriental colour and interwoven with the Psalms, his gory *Agamemnone* implies an incestuous relationship between father and daughter. *Saul* (1782) and *Mirra* (1780) are among a series of tragedies that freshly treat plots already explored by the Attic dramatists.

In *Oreste* (1776), as in his other verse-drama, he followed Voltaire's example, observing the unities in tightly organized scenes. But he gave the situation new values. In slaying the usurper Egisto, Oreste in a blind rage has unwittingly killed his mother, too, and is not yet aware of it. His companion Pilade seeks some way to inform him of what has happened. When the bloodstained Prince learns of his deed, he is shocked into madness. Alfieri creates the climactic scene with great yet sparse power.

Antigone (1783) is also freely reconceived. The widow of one of Oedipus' sons, Polinice, comes in darkness to bury the ashes of her husband, a slain and disowned claimant to the throne. She comes upon his sister, the Princess Antigone. The two strong-willed women vow to carry out the ritual in defiance of Creon's strict edict. Surprised by the guards and held, the pair are sentenced to perish, after Antigone boldly proclaims her guilt and rebelliously argues against the edict. But Emone, son of Creon, loves her. The young man pleads with his father to spare her. Creon finally relents. The tyrant permits Antigone to choose between death and marriage to the enamoured Emone. The Princess, determined not to accede to the tyrant's might, proudly elects to die. Enraged, Creon orders her buried alive. Emone and his armed supporters arrive. He denounces his father, resolves to kill himself, and leaves bearing the corpse of his beloved.

These tragedies, with their always lofty and sometimes exalted sentiments, have gained little recognition in Italy. His plays call for passionate declamation and vigorous acting. A revival of *Oreste* directed by Vittorio Gassman was a sensation in 1962, suggesting that other Alfieri scripts, if staged with the requisite fire and skill, might fare as well.

Alfieri held that the theatre's duty is to teach people to be "free, strong, generous, transported by true virtue, truly aware of their individual rights and in all their passions keen, noble and magnanimous". An idealist, surely! Working with a highly conventional form that today seems too restrictive, he demonstrates, as did Racine, that neoclassicism can engender exciting theatre.

For this reason Byron highly esteemed Alfieri, and it was why the Italian exerted influence on other dramas in his country. His closest imitators were Vincenzo Monti (1754–1828), who wrote *Aristodemo* (1786), *Galeotto Manfredi* (1788) and *Caio Gracco* (1802). But neither Monti nor his fellows reached the world stage. One reason was that the Age of Romanticism was at hand.

With comedy, Italians did better in the eighteenth century. Two Venetian leaders of the theatre of laughter left scripts that are still alive and honoured. Each was temperamentally very different from – and held views antagonistic towards – the other, and they wrote in opposite ways. Before they rose to dominate the scene, Italian farce had continued in the by then overly familiar and exhausted tradition of the "improvisational" *commedia dell'arte.*

It was also divided as before into two rather distinct categories, the literary comedy in classical form and the farce in regional dialect. But the literary comedy, after flourishing in the sixteenth century, had declined in quality during the seventeenth and first half of the eighteenth. Scarcely any script of merit had come forth for decades. The field was all too open for at least one new author of genius, and fortunately two appeared: Carlo Goldoni (1707–93) and Count Carlo Gozzi (1720–1806). Perhaps it was all to the good that they were at odds with each other. The competition called upon their resources and debate sharpened the artistic faculties of both.

Remarkably fertile, Goldoni wrote between 250 and 300 plays, the majority of them in Italian, but some in French – these during the last phase of his career when he moved to Paris. It is manifestly impossible to survey an output of such magnitude adequately here. Indeed, many of his plays are not readily available even to scholars.

Carlo Goldoni was the son of a Venetian doctor. His first playthings were puppets for which he devised stories. Later he ran away to join a troupe of players and stayed with them for a time. His father wished him to take up medicine, but the young man, having an independent disposition, chose law. Earning a degree, he served in several chanceries, but his thoughts were always drawn to the theatre.

His first scripts were tragedies; the earliest failed, but soon he had better luck. Shifting to comedy, he found his true *métier*. He disdained the *commedia dell'arte* and was anxious to change the form, believing it was too casual and more than a little worn out. He was inspired by the Greek and Latin farces but wanted to improve on them.

While in Pavia he produced an early script, *Il Colosso*, that satirized several prominent local families; for this the youthful author was driven out of town. But his goal, he declared, was realism. To further this aim he sometimes wrote in Venetian dialect. He read Molière and consciously set out to emulate that French master whose careful craftsmanship and balanced wisdom about life he fully appreciated. Some of Goldoni's earlier works are based on personal experiences.

Fortunately, he associated himself with a company of actors headed by Girolamo who staged his works quite as fast as he penned them. They asked him to provide them with sixteen plays in a single year, and the prolific Goldoni recklessly promised to deliver them. Not only did he keep his rash pledge, but the scripts he hastily turned out in this short span are still deemed among his very best. Widely known was his prolonged affair with a duchess; one wonders how he found time in his incredibly crowded life for amorous dalliances.

Along with Pietro Chiari (1711–88), a dramatist who shared some of his views, Goldoni flourished in Venice until the advent of Carlo Gozzi. Then at last, finding Gozzi's criticism and competition too keen, having already been to Rome, he accepted an offer from Paris, where he was to write scripts for the Italian Comedians active in the capital. On the occasion of the last performance of a play before his departure from Venice he was given a public ovation and wept like a child; he was fifty-five.

In Paris, besides carrying out his duties for the Comedians, he taught Italian to the royal children. He was commissioned to write a play for the marriage of Marie Antoinette to Louis XVI. Endearing himself to the royal family, he was granted a pension. Growing old, he retired to live on it. The French Revolution, however, cut it off, so that in his extreme age he was penniless and miserable. The French poet André Chenier proposed to the turbulent Assembly that Goldoni's pension be restored, and at his urging the measure was passed – but too late. Goldoni had died the day before. A lesser sum was voted to his widow, however.

To winnow through Goldoni's prodigious output and choose examples of his best work is a daunting task. As might be expected, the plays are uneven in quality. Perhaps a few could be cited, mostly because they are still on the boards. When he was starting, he had to work with the *commedia dell'arte* whose undisciplined methods he deplored. He gave them fresh outlines for sketches and masked plays for which they improvised dialogue. Gradually he began to supply written speeches, at first only monologues for one character but then for several of the characters and finally complete scripts. He slowly effected the reforms he had in mind.

Among his early works for the masked comedians is *Arlecchino, Servant of Two Masters* (1745), a rollicking account of a personal retainer, Arlecchino, who, to augment his purse, takes two jobs simultaneously. Each master is unaware that he is not solely in that one's service; Arlecchino nimbly keeps his double employment a secret from both. When a gentleman stops him on the street and gives him a written message to "take to your master", the startled recipient is uncertain which of his two masters is meant. He delivers the message to the wrong one, of course, and all manner of funny troubles and misunderstandings ensue, until his deception is finally revealed. Goldoni handles this remarkably deftly; the fun is spontaneous and unremitting. This farce is frequently revived.

Another favourite, *The Liar* (1750–51) (adapted from Corneille), is among the sixteen scripts Goldoni rushed out in that twelve-month period. The hero, Florindo, is excessively timid. He refuses to admit that he writes love sonnets or sings amorous serenades to the girl he adores. He suffers at the hands of a mendacious rival, Lelio, who is so skilful at falsehoods that he almost wins the heroine's heart and hand. At the end, Lelio's cunning lies are exposed one by one. He is rejected by the Venetians whose decorous social order he has sought to penetrate. As punishment, he must return to the Roman girl to whom he is engaged, though he no longer loves her. *The Liar* was brought to twentieth-century Broadway, one of the few Goldoni scripts to be professionally staged in New York City.

Another has been *The Mistress of the Inn* (1753), which was a frequent vehicle of the acclaimed actress Eleonora Duse. The woman who keeps the inn is Mirandolina, the most successful of all feminine roles Goldoni created. She was meant to show off the gifts and personality of Corallina, a popular soubrette of the Venetian stage. Two aristocrats patronize the inn, one of good lineage but reduced circumstances, the other *nouveau riche*. Jealous of each other, they court her, debating before her whether social rank or wealth is more important. She cares for neither one of them – though she readily accepts the generous presents they bring.

To be rid of the pair, she introduces them to two actresses who pretend to be ladies of high social position. The *nouveau riche*, the first to see through the impostors, is made to appear less fatuous than his rival. Goldoni seems to be making the point that "rank without money . . . is more ridiculous than money without rank". Indeed, he always betrays a bias against the nobility that was doubtless pleasing to the middle-class audience for whom he chiefly wrote.

Meanwhile, Mirandolina flirts with the Cavaliere de Ripafratta, a misogynist. That he is a self-proclaimed woman-hater is a challenge to her, and by tricks fair and unfair she succeeds in teaching him a lesson, bringing him to propose to her, only so that she can reject him. At the end she chooses to marry a servant at the inn, as her late father had urged her to do. This had been her intention all along, but first she has wished to assert herself and learn what men are really like. In this, as in so many of his other plays, Goldoni shows how shrewd is his observation of human behaviour, yet for the most part he lacks a deep insight.

In *The Boors* (1760) four figures, Simon, Lunardo, Canciano and Maurizio, represent the lower middle class in northern Italy. The people of this fortunate region enjoy comparative prosperity and look with scorn on those less practical than themselves. Self-important, viewing themselves as the leaders of their community, Lunardo and Simon are burdened with unpleasant wives, one shrewish, the other stupid. Lunardo has married a second time, and his attractive daughter is forever quarrelling with her stepmother. Stepmother and stepdaughter join together, however, to thwart the obstinate Lunardo. Thus discord prevails at home.

Simon is tiresomely opinionated; Maurizio, also elderly, is a cantankerous widower with a son courting Lunardo's daughter. Their fathers, who have other plans for them, oppose the match. The women busily intrigue to assist the young pair. The fourth boor is Canciano, who is also ill-tempered but lucky enough to have a clever wife, Felice, who influences him more than he is ready to admit.

The four grumblers like to gather and complain about the decline in the manners of the younger generation and compare them unfavourably to young people in times past. They declare that social and parental disciplines have broken down and that the young are granted too much freedom. Morals, they say, have grown slack, and women have become too bold. Felice takes issue with this, telling the old men that they are tyrannical, selfish and narrow-minded. If they wish to be loved, she scolds, they must give love and be more generous. In the end she rather easily creates a reconciliation among all those who have been at cross-purposes.

In his *Memoirs* Goldoni states that he sought to show how men who have social stature and are congenial in society are often too stern at home. But there can be no doubt that he sides somewhat with the criticisms voiced by the old men he portrays. At this point in his life, apparently, he was looking both ways, forward to an emancipated new age and backwards to a happier time.

The Boors was made into an opera by Ermanno Wolf-Ferrari in 1906, as were three other of Goldoni's farces. In it, as in most of his work and particularly the pieces in dialect, Goldoni acts as a social historian. He offers a broad and detailed picture of the daily life and habits of people in Venice and other regions of Italy in his era that is as evocative of that animated, colourful scene as paintings of Guardi and Canaletto. This dimension of his plays is fascinating.

His play *The Accomplished Maid* débuted in London in 1768, with a libretto by Goldoni, music by Piccinni and an English translation by Edward Toms. Actually it is a musical version of Samuel Richardson's novel *Pamela*; here the beset heroine's name is changed to Fanny. Occasional stagings in England and America reveal it to be light, filled with pleasurable melodies.

He is a child of his period, but he softened the traditional lineaments of many of the harsher and crueller *commedia dell'arte* characters, especially Pantalone. He does not have the cool, clear detachment of a Molière, though Goldoni's comedy in verse overtly attests to his admiration for his French predecessor, and he paid similar tributes in other poetic plays about Terence and Tasso. These are not among his better works, however, as he does better in prose than in verse.

One of his most revealing pieces is his *The Comic Theatre* (1750). In it, a company of actors headed by Orazio is rehearsing a Goldoni script, *The Father a Rival to His Son*. Making use of the familiar device of a play-within-a-play (which was used before by the Elizabethans and Jacobeans and by Buckingham and Sheridan, and after by Shaw and Pirandello), Goldoni was able to express through his performers the many faults of the stage as he saw them. He condemned actors for their vanity, their disregard for dialogue as written and their intruding of indecent jests, and most playwrights for having shallow purposes, in sum, for the evils he opposed and sought to overcome in the theatre.

He believed in inculcating morality by showing examples of goodness rather than by presenting evil and then denouncing it. Other ideas of his are contained prodigally in *The Comic Theatre*, a rewarding treatise to read. His spirit is optimistic; he has a contagious good nature and a sense of fun. At moments he is a bit too mild, and he borrows plots from the classics and elsewhere, yet his fancy is enormously fecund and vivacious. His portraits of women are affectionate yet sharp, and he has a keen eye for masculine foibles. He creates on his always busy stage a whole delightful world of his own. His gift for bringing to life the palpable influence of inanimate objects – a house, an inn, a street, a coffee-shop, a fan – is so strong as to be almost mysterious. Many of his plots revolve around just such tangible and inert "things" that he contrives to endow with vitality. He transformed caricatures of people delineated by masks into recognizable human beings and stock scenery into real settings. He is at his very best, indeed, in depicting interactions among small groups with a variety of persons, some amusingly eccentric, some typical, in places like a tiny village, an inn or coffee-shop. Humanity as he depicts it is a social species.

Voltaire wrote of him:

> Any day now I am looking forward to seeing one of Goldoni's plays performed at my country house. I once described him, and I still think of him, as the great painter of nature. This worthy reformer banished pointless farce and vulgar buffoonery from the Italian stage, at a time when we had adopted them in some of our Paris theatres. One thing always struck me about the plays of this prolific genius – how they all finish with a moral lesson that sums up the play's subject and plot, demonstrating that such subject and plot are designed to make men wiser and better members of society.

Italian composers and others found Goldoni's farces a rich source of ideas for librettos; some adapted works that had been staged or else fashioned librettos to order for them. A list of those who made use of his fertile fancy includes many illustrious names.

As has been said, Goldoni was plagued by the attacks and competition of his fellow Venetian Carlo Gozzi. Though the Gozzis were titled and of an esteemed family, they were poor. Consequently Carlo entered military service at sixteen and remained in it for three years. Once out, he made a place for himself in high circles by the dazzling wit he displayed on many occasions. Though he had a brother who wrote tragedies, he attached himself to a scholarly group that was very interested in preserving Venetian traditions, one of which was the lively *commedia dell'arte.* They were aroused by Goldoni's attacks on the institution that Gozzi nostalgically cherished.

As a critic, Gozzi frequently took sides against Goldoni; though he was aware of the shortcomings of *commedia dell'arte,* he felt it should be reformed but not replaced. One account states that Goldoni encountered Gozzi in a bookshop and remarked, "It's easier to find fault with a play than to turn out a worthy one." Accepting the gage, in a few days Gozzi came forth with his script, *The Love of Three Oranges* (1761), incorporating his ideas and ridiculing Goldoni and Chiari.

Its success was instantaneous, and before long Gozzi was at the very top in the theatre world of Venice. *The Love of Three Oranges,* like its several successors, is a philosophical fairy tale, an Italian equivalent to Marivaux. Since it is an odd mix of verse and prose, sometimes in Venetian or Neapolitan dialect and sometimes in clear Tuscan, and contains satire, necromancy and ironic grotesquery, it is almost impossible to synopsize well. Gozzi writes out some of the "business" and dialogue, but leaves space for improvisation by his cast of *commedia dell'arte* players, to whom he pays very generous deference.

In all these plays there are magical transformations, scenes of hilarity and absurdity and also moments that are very real. The plot revolves around the melancholy Prince Tartaglia, who is put under a spell by the evil Fata Morgana and is certain to die unless he can be induced to smile. All sorts of fantastic adventures follow when a second magician, Celio, lends assistance to the doomed Prince and sends him out to search for the three oranges that turn out to be young girls, two of whom quickly perish. It was clearly apparent to the Venetian spectators that the two sorcerers, Fata Morgana and Celio, were intended as caricatures of Goldoni and Chiari. Indeed, the phenomenal impact of the play was a factor in persuading Goldoni to leave Venice for Paris, because his day in his beloved native city was done.

Gozzi's emphasis is on pure theatricality and illusion that stimulates fantasy; at the same time, through allegory and symbolism deeper meanings are inferred. The language is sometimes poetic and adumbrant, the serious passages rich with the dialects of Venice and Naples, the humorous episodes reverting to the lyrical.

Gozzi continued in this strange vein in more runic fairy tales, perfectly suited for enactment by the resourceful ironic pantomimists of the *commedia dell'arte* who had been despised by his erstwhile rival. Indeed, the company that first presented *The Love of Three Oranges* had done so with special zest, owing to the hostility they felt towards Goldoni.

Critics liken Gozzi to Marivaux, but he has little of the psychological penetration of that French writer. He does have something of the same delicacy, a similar bent towards the whimsical, the artificial, the precious. He envisioned enchanted castles, reached after dangerous journeys and created astonishing metamorphoses: an orange is cut open and a girl appears; a girl is enspelled and becomes a dove. The surface appeal is always to the child's sense of wonder in people. But running throughout is a subtle parody apparent to the sophisticated spectator. The serious notes are sounded again and again, often at unexpected places.

In his subsequent plays the dialogue is fuller, the freedom to improvise somewhat diminished. After *Three Oranges* came *The Crow* (1761) and then *The King Stag* (1762), in which King Deramo possesses a statue that signals to him when people lie to him. He is anxious to select a bride, but the statue proves a hindrance since no maiden of noble birth passes the test; the statue invariably betrays the wiles of each aspirant.

Accordingly, the King extends his search beyond court circles. A poor girl, Angela, is acceptable. But this angers Tartaglia, who himself is enamoured of Angela and also wishes his daughter Clarice to marry the King. By evil magic the King is changed into a stag; as such, he is hunted and barely escapes being slain. It is a parrot – who is actually another sorcerer, Durandarte – who saves him.

In *Turandot* (also 1762), an even better-known script, a Chinese Princess whose temperament is cold refuses to heed her father's pleas that she choose a husband. She propounds a three-part riddle that every prospective suitor must answer if he is to be successful; whoever fails to solve it must die. Many do perish in attempts to possess the frigidly chaste and heartless Mandarin Princess, until there appears at the Emperor's court an unidentified Prince who accepts the challenge, solves the riddle and, after further vicissitudes, does gain the love of Turandot and triumphantly weds her. A fairy tale like this, one that poses a test to a suitor, of course has anthropological roots, and echoes earlier plays about Oedipus and the Sphinx.

The Woman Serpent (also 1762) followed. *La Zobeide* (1763) is another much-admired work, though its tone is darker. Others are *The Fortunate Beggars* (1764), *The Turkish Wonder* (also 1764) and *The Magic Bird* (1765). In this last, Renzo and Barbarina, who are poor but full of pious sentiments, are altered completely when they become rich – they display pride, they are ungrateful and their actions are wicked.

Gozzi's last offerings have a more serious hue; they commingle tragic and comic scenes, not always to interesting effect. In the ensuing Romantic era, when he had a considerable influence on Ludwig Tieck and Ferdinand Raimund, as well as on J.R. Planché, enthusiasm for Gozzi was unbounded; some German critics even rated him as superior to Shakespeare, a judgement that is hard to sustain today. His work continued to inspire in the twentieth century – this can be seen in plays by Chiarelli and Antonelli – and in countries as far-flung as Russia, where Evreinov and Blok owe him a solid debt.

The Love of Three Oranges serves as a libretto for a comic opera with music by Sergei Prokoviev (1921). Giacomo Puccini captivatingly adorned *Turandot* with lush melodies to translate it into an opera as his final and not quite completed work.

An unprecedented event occurred in the twentieth century, when a Gozzi play reached the precinct of Broadway. In 1996 *The Green Bird*, a translation of Gozzi's *The Beautiful Little Green Bird*, opened at the New Victory Theatre for a two-week engagement. Julie Taymor, renowned for her uniquely colourful, imaginative treatment of fantasies, was the director. Her production was revived a few years later for a fortnight at Lincoln Center (1996) and again at the Cort Theatre (2000). In the interim it was on view at the Playhouse in La Jolla, California. These various performances brought Taymor and members of the cast a slew of nominations for Obies (off-Broadway awards) and Taymor an Emmy, grants from the Macarthur Genius Foundation, a Guggenheim, a Brandeis Creative Arts Award, an International Classical Music Award and a Chandler Performing Arts Award.

The casts were not all "live" – unexpectedly large puppets interpreted some of the roles, and some of the flesh-and-blood players wore half-masks. Some listeners described the show as "haunting, unnerving, and hard to get out of your head". Taymor designed the masks and puppets, assisted by Christine Jones.

In the play, Renzo and his twin sister Barbarina have been separated from their father and mother the King and Queen by a wicked grandmother; believing themselves to be orphans, they are living with unkind foster parents. The children run away, encounter wild adventures and meet a collection of extraordinary characters and objects: a sorcerer's garden, dancing waters, singing apples, clowns, giants, ogres, a statue that comes to life and is beloved by the boy and a magical green bird that the girl cherishes. The names of these beings indicate that they have an affinity with *commedia dell'arte*.

After visiting the Cort, the exacting critic John Simon wrote in *New York Magazine*:

> The enchanting surprise of the month, if not the season, is *The Green Bird*, the 1765 fairy-tale comedy by Carlo Gozzi. As translated by Albert Bermel and Ted Emery (with added prose by Eric Overmyer and lyrics by David Suehsdorf), choreographed by Daniel Ezralow, and graced with funky pastiche music by Elliot Goldenthal, this is sheer delight, made sheerer by Christine Jones's sets, Constance Hoffman's costumes, Donald Holder's lights, and especially Julie Taymor's masks, puppets, and staging.

Another of his many fables, *The Serpent Woman* (1763), was performed at a gala benefit at the National Arts Club, in its New York début. The enactment was attended by the Italian Consul General and a select audience who paid very generously for tickets.

Enchanted by this script, Richard Wagner availed himself of it for his first opera, *The Fairies* (1833). Cheristani, a fairy queen, marries Farrascad, a mortal prince. Their journey from youth to maturity is "half-horrifying and half-humorous". Puppets and Venetian masks were used, and the costumes were spectacular. As in *The Green Bird*, there are bawdy passages and some of the characters are borrowed from *commedia dell'arte*. At the climax, love conquers all.

Also in 2000 *The Love of Three Oranges* was staged at the New York City Opera and Puccini's enhancement of *Turandot* was in the season's repertory at the Metropolitan Opera. Gozzi would have considered 2000 a good year.

The Italian theatre during the Baroque era was not solely dependent on Goldoni and Gozzi. A list of others might include Pietro Chiari (1712–58), Girolamo Gigli (1660–1772), Jacopo Angelo Nelli (1673–1767) and Giovan Battista Fagiuoli (1660–1742). These writers were preceded by Carlo Maria Maggi (1630–99), whose *The False Philosopher* (1698) offers ideas that comedians were not likely to express through improvised dialogue, which helped prepare the way for Goldoni's compact scripts. Fagiuoli was a shrewd observer of manners. Such plays of his as *Trying to Control Girls Is Folly* (1715), *Appearance Ain't Truth* (1728) and *The Fashionable Husband* (1735) move at a fast pace and are entertaining. *The Power of Reason* (1736) and *Love Unseen* (1737) have slightly more sober themes.

Venice's contributors to Italy's stage disappeared in time, but to its credit the city of canals alone had seven playhouses. Their companies travelled to other towns during the off-season. All the large cities had public theatres where comedies, dramas and operas were given; in addition, Italian noblemen employed private troupes in the palaces to amuse themselves and their guests. To keep all these actors furnished with scripts required inspired poets to keep busy with the scratching of their quill-pens.

As has been remarked, the multiplication of playhouses all over Europe was a feature of the latter half of the eighteenth century. In Paris a royal decree caused the number to shoot from ten in 1784 to fifty-one by 1791.

Spanish playwrights made a meagre artistic advance during the eighteenth century. The public had become infatuated with *comedias*, slapdash melodramas largely about the country's struggles with the Moors of North Africa. Spain, having withdrawn from its ventures to the north, now turned its gaze again across the straits to the south. The physical action in the plays was largely concerned with the plight of imprisoned Spanish virgins facing impending rape by sultans or handsome Moorish princes lured into illicit romances ending in conversions or heroic rescues. (*Comedias* are more fully described in *Oriental Theatre*, the second volume of the *Stage by Stage* series. Such plays grabbed the fancy of theatre-goers in the Philippines while Spain ruled that far-off archipelago.)

There were attempts to revive respect for Aristotle's dicta and infuse the three unities in scripts, without much success. Ignacio de Luzán led the campaign with difficulty. He was abetted by a journal, *Diario de los Literatos* (1736–46), that promoted French models. Luzán spent several years in France (1740–50); he wrote a *Poetics*. Slowly the neoclassic polemics took hold and the wild popular stage was somewhat tamed. Luzán translated *Hamlet* into Spanish and published a history of his nation's theatre; it reached print after his death.

The *Antisacramentales*, the religious allegories that the masterly Calderón had raised to a superb art form a century before and that were so lavishly staged, were finally ended by royal edict in 1715; Church and civil authorities felt that they had become vulgarized and out of control. The neoclassicists were also opposed to them.

Madrid had only two permanent theatres for public performances; they preserved the shape of the sixteenth-century *corral*. They were finally demolished in the mid-1740s and replaced with a "modern" building. A private theatre was erected in Philip IV's palace, El Bien Retiro (1632). Here royalty and their guests saw operas splendidly presented, sometimes in a sylvan setting.

Sentimentality infused comic works, as evidenced by the box-office success of Nivelle de la Chaussée's *The Fashionable Prejudice* (1735), a French script that Luzán translated. Tears were also elicited by the new neoclassical tragedies, which were much given to moralizing. Writers embracing this trend included Nicolas Fernández de Moratín and Vicente García de la Huerta. Of the two, Moratín was the better poet but de la Huerta's *Raquel* (1772) was a triumph.

Flouting neoclassical precepts, Ramón de la Cruz brought back the *sainete*, the brief, light musical comic afterpieces affixed to *comedia*, often risqué and meant to send spectators home in good spirits. He also devoted himself to perpetuating the *zarzuela*, expanding it so that it more closely resembled the operetta – the genre into which it ultimately evolved. His plots were based on incidents in daily working-class life.

Moratín's son, Leandro Fernández, also a dramatist, contributed more neoclassical scripts, fashioning them in the manner of Molière and Goldoni, including *The New Comedy or The Café* (1792) and *When a Girl Says Yes* (1800), filled with *esprit*.

— 9 —

THEATRE IN NORTHERN EUROPE

Holland had long had a tradition of vigorous theatre, dating back to medieval and Renaissance times, when religious drama had flourished there. The Jesuits had developed there a style of production that consisted largely of *tableaux vivants* and was used to present what was known as "school-drama", dedicated to teaching morality and glorifying the Church. These were mostly Latin and were done on framed, curtained platforms.

Some were secular in origin, daringly adapted from Plautus or Terence. Another and somewhat later form of theatrical activity was the Chambers of Rhetoric – Rederijker Kamers – put on by amateurs who collected into societies with distinctive emblems to hold annual contests. They mounted pageants, recited poetry, sang and offered plays similar to the moralities – discourses on abstract theological or ethical themes.

These visually colourful affairs continued into the seventeenth century. In 1638, in Amsterdam, theatrical events were at last housed in the renowned Schouwburg, an arch-roofed, two-galleried building that closely resembled Shakespeare's playhouse. Much was done from then on in the Netherlands that kept up with developments in the design of the platform and the auditorium, and which at the same time reflected structural innovations in Italy and England – the proscenium arch, the vista stage, the wing flats, the installation of machinery. The Jesuit playwrights were of all nationalities, since the order was thoroughly cosmopolitan. Just as the architectural style of every country and period – medieval, Renaissance and Baroque – was represented in the theatres of Ghent, Antwerp and Amsterdam, so in the Jesuitical drama classical, medieval and later influences entered.

A secular theatre also came into being. In the eighteenth century Pieter Arentz Langendijk, for example, offered comedies such as *The Mutual Marital Deceit* (*c.* 1712), in which a young man and a young lady, both impoverished, pose to each other as having wealth; indeed, he claims to belong to the Polish nobility. The work contains much valid observation of manners and the impact of social values on personal behaviour.

Northern Europe's most important playwright by far is Baron Ludvig von Holberg, who has been called Molière's most distinguished disciple and one of the leading figures of the eighteenth-century theatre. Whether he merits this designation is often debated. Some deem him little more than mediocre. To strike a judicious balance between these two points of view, one would have to go through all his plays and read them in their original versions. Anyhow, he has zealous admirers.

In early childhood von Holberg was left an orphan and was raised by an uncle who planned to have him go into military service. Instead a cousin adopted him and he went to live in the mountains. Later he studied in Bergen, and then at the University of Copenhagen. To support himself he became a tutor in French. In 1704, with only 60 thalers in his pocket, he set out on the first of his many long travels. He went first to Holland but fell ill there. His money was exhausted so he returned home on foot, which was the way he most often journeyed.

Two years later he made it to London. From there he enrolled at Oxford; later he said that the sight of all the books in the university's library was what first inspired his bid for authorship. Back in Copenhagen, he lectured at its university and later taught at Leipzig, Halle and Hamburg, keeping up his travels during free intervals. Attaining the rank of professor with a travel grant, he took full advantage of his renewed opportunity. He went everywhere in Europe, still covering long distances on foot – and sometimes on roller-skates! In his wanderings he endured frequent physical hardships.

He rose higher and higher in teaching posts, which ended his money troubles. He wrote constantly on law, philology and history. He suddenly won fame with a long satiric poem, but it also created such serious enemies for him that his life was put in danger.

This most famous and respected of Danish playwrights was actually Norwegian. His travels – especially in Germany, Italy, France and England – exposed him to the best theatres in those more sophisticated countries, before he began his own playwriting, a profession that was more or less pressed on him.

In 1720 a troupe of French actors had won favour at Copenhagen's royal court. Encouraged by the friendly reception, two years later a Frenchman named René Montaigu gained a patent to establish a Danish National Theatre with a company of native Danes. This makes it Europe's second oldest national theatre after the Comédie Française. The first season was launched with a translation of Molière's *The Miser*. Montaigu was anxious to obtain Danish plays using the vernacular, and urged Holberg, now known as a poet, to provide him some. The mock-epic poem that had brought Holberg a large measure of recognition three years earlier was *Peder Paars*; in it, he poked fun at a good many aspects of Danish life. Obviously he had a rich talent for genre humour. Holberg now used his long poem as a source for much of his comic dramatic material; his stage works, though, are recast in "simple, homely prose".

In 1722 he obliged Montaigu by furnishing him with no less than five scripts, all of which were promptly mounted for the stage. Over the next two years, with excited haste, he added ten more, in a feat not equal but comparable to that of Goldoni. What is more, Holberg's first five scripts are counted as among his finest. He was thirty-seven when he was enlisted into the theatre; by the time a decade had elapsed and he was forty-seven he had turned out twenty-six plays, the major part of his output. The feverish pitch with which he turned out scripts caused him to fall ill again, this time from exhaustion. He recuperated by travelling once more.

His final group of scripts came after a silent hiatus, when Montaigu's theatre was closed; this occurred in 1728. Frederick IV had succeeded to the throne, and a fire had taken a devastating toll on Copenhagen. Pious counsellors persuaded the King that the blaze was a judgement from heaven upon the wicked citizens, and the suggestible monarch halted the players' subsidy. Christian VI, who ruled next, was a religious zealot; all during his reign the theatre remained shut.

In 1747 Frederick V inherited the sceptre. He was a patron of the arts and issued a patent to reopen the playhouse, appointing Holberg as its director. The year before, in 1746, the King had also given him the title of Baron in recognition of his having endowed a college. Shortly after the theatre opened, in response to the demand for more works, Holberg resumed playwriting. He added six more to his earlier twenty-six, but this last group shows his intense creative power in decline. He was sixty-five.

Holberg's plays draw not only on his serio-comic poem, but also on the works of Aristophanes, Molière and Calderón. His satire is broad. He infused little of his own temperament into his work, and seldom betrayed personal convictions about the moral issues his plots sometimes raise. What one does see reflected in the characters and the handling of his themes is the confusion brought on by a society in transition, which Denmark was at the time. He presents, like a genre painter, lively Danish bourgeois types and places them in often effective scenes that evoke the life of the period with almost documentary fidelity. A good example of this is his *Jeppe of the Hill* (1722), in which Jeppe, a poor drunken peasant, is taken up by an aristocrat who disdains stupid people and amuses himself by convincing his victim that he is in fact a man of riches and rank. Any belief Jeppe might have that he was once impoverished and humble is a hallucination. In his new role the erstwhile peasant displays many bad traits, including cruelty, despotism and rudeness. This piece is invariably linked to Calderón's *Life Is a Dream*, though it is manifestly inferior in scope and originality, and does not have Calderón's inherent poetry. In its purposeful confusion of reality and illusion it also echoes Shakespeare's prologue to *The Taming of the Shrew*. None the less, many consider *Jeppe of the Hill* to be Holberg's masterpiece.

In *Jean de France* (1772) a young man – who at his doting mother's insistence has been briefly educated in Paris – returns home with an inflated sense of self-importance. His name is really Hans, but he has Gallicized it to the more elegant Jean. His extravagance and pretentiousness infuriate his middle-class father and further alienate his fiancée, who because of his vanity and fickleness was never too fond of him. He even becomes the despair of his indulgent mother. Finally the heroine's clever Danish maidservant masquerades as a sophisticated Parisian lady of fashion, and succeeds in getting rid of Hans-known-as-Jean by leading him to make an even greater fool of himself. The moral of the play is that good Danes should place a higher value than they did on their own homespun customs and virtues.

In Holberg's farces the characters of the *commedia dell'arte* reappear, but more and more they are given Danish names and acquire new traits. For the most part, too, his people do not change after they escape from their dilemmas. Like the figures in Jonson and Molière they are not reformed or regenerated but cling to their obsessive folly. Thus Jeppe learns nothing from his maddening experience, nor does the posturing Jean (Hans). Essentially they are caricatures.

The hero of *Master Gert, or The Very Talkative Barber* (1722), who is from Westphalia, belongs in the same category. He is ready to hold forth at extreme length on every conceivable subject; his neighbours think him an intolerable bore, but he looks on them with contempt as dull and uncouth. An innkeeper, who complains that Gert's lengthy discourses are driving away customers, sues him. A rascally lawyer tries to collect fees from both parties in the suit. When Gert is sentenced to keep three days of total silence, he suffers exceedingly. The girl he wishes to marry rejects him. He leaves Denmark to find a more receptive audience elsewhere. Like Molière, Holberg is preaching that excess in any phase of life should be curbed.

So run his thirty-two plays, which include *The Political Pewterer* and *The Fickle Woman* (both 1722). In the first, a pewterer with political ambitions becomes the butt of a practical joke. He is told – and believes – that he has been elected Mayor of Hamburg and soon discovers himself so beset with problems that he prepares to hang himself. His wife is seduced by her self-image as the Mayor's wife, and though she has previously scorned her husband's interest in politics she now outdoes him in putting on unseemly airs. When the pewterer learns that he is not the chief official of Hamburg after all, he is delighted. He renounces all future political aims and lets his daughter marry the young man of her choice.

Lucretia, in *The Fickle Woman*, is so capricious that she baffles everyone. Her lovers abandon her because of her vagaries. This play still holds the boards.

Erasmus Montanus (1723) is similar to the earlier *Jean de France*. A peasant, Erasmus, having been sent by his parents to the university, comes home a pedant. The villagers take a dislike to him; they resent his obnoxious parade of Latin, geography and absurd logic. Some are jealous of him, too. By contrast, he has a brother, Jacob, who is full of shrewd common sense. Jacob concentrates on tilling the soil and making money. Erasmus, overreaching himself, is impressed into the army by a recruiting officer who chides him for showing off, saying, "A learned man ought chiefly to be distinguished from others by being more temperate, modest and accommodating in his speech than an unlearned man."

These amusing plays offer good-natured vignettes of mostly rural Denmark. Another constant theme is that social change should not occur too rapidly. Holberg ridiculed the still backward Danes but did not advocate major reforms. As he continued to write, some of his characterizations grow more rounded. Outstanding is Vielgeshrey in *The Bustling Man* (also known as *The Fidget*; 1723), who is forever trying to save time by his ingenuity and, ironically, is terribly rushed as a result.

The structure of Holberg's plays is often rambling, diffuse and overly episodic. For all their faults, they are usually lively and nicely detailed and sharply satirize the same long roster of social ills and foibles – greed, lust, affectation, hypocrisy and credulity – that are the immemorial objects of the scorn of comedy writers.

Holberg almost single-handedly brought into being a Danish literature; before his advent Danes of the nobility or educated upper classes spoke French or other languages. For this reason he is perhaps more highly honoured than he might be if one measured him only for his artistic accomplishments. A statue of his likeness, standing on a pedestal amid the swirling traffic in Copenhagen, pays him tribute today. His popularity extended from Scandinavia to Germany, but he is little known elsewhere.

His most ambitious work, perhaps, is a tragicomedy, *Don Ranudo de Colibrados* (1723), which is a study of an ageing man and his wife, decaying aristocrats whose pathetic respect for titles and gentility betray them. Uncharacteristically it is laid in Spain, and in many ways is less successful.

Three lesser writers followed Holberg: Johann Herman Wessel (1742–85), Johannes Ewald (1743–81) and Nordahl Brun (1745–1816). Beyond Denmark their names connote too little to grant them space here.

Both Goldoni and Holberg had a pervasive influence on the leading German dramatist of the eighteenth century, Gotthold Ephraim Lessing (1729–81). Theatre in Germany had scarcely flourished before his arrival. From the time of Hans Sachs on – that is, from the sixteenth century to the middle of the eighteenth – stage-fare consisted mostly of crude if vigorous "Hanswurst" farces. Hans Wurst ("Sausage") has been described as a coarse, debased German "harlequin", that is, a fat and drunken Teutonic buffoon. He is somewhat akin, too, to a popular Dutch comic figure, Mr Pickle-Herring. The noisy, vulgar Wurst farces were scarcely more than knockabout clown plays larded with acrobatics and juggling of a sort long since outgrown elsewhere. None of them has survived, which is probably a comment on their utter lack of quality. Audiences, on the whole, were too unlettered to welcome anything but what appealed to the risibility of peasants.

Even when alien players brought serious material, it had to be cheapened. Comic vaudeville elements were added – this happened with performances of opera, Shakespeare, Corneille and Racine brought by foreign troupes. German actors were mostly members of families that had toured about for generations; they were ignorant and socially untrained. Again, since none are remembered by name, probably they were not too skilled at their craft. The fact that native companies frequently advertised themselves as "English comedians" reflects the greater prestige of players from abroad.

If Germany was this laggard, it was partly because of the wars that endlessly wracked the countryside, and partly because the German people did not yet comprise a nation but were a fragmented collection of small duchies, city-states and principalities, with only a few centres of culture and art. In such places opera was a favourite long before serious drama was accepted; the invasion of musical drama was evident at courts in relatively southern cities nearest to Italy, like Vienna and Munich. Another place where the arts were somewhat advanced was Salzburg, also in the south and open to Italian influence.

In Germany during much of this time there were no permanent theatres. Outdoor platforms and booths were utilized, as well as town halls and large rooms in castles or palaces. Italian, English, Dutch and French companies regularly visited the larger towns, but that was hardly enough to constitute a "theatre". German professors and students produced the only plays that had any pretension to style; these were modest adaptations of classics, perhaps a comedy by Plautus or Terence, or translations of scripts acclaimed in London or Paris. Attempts at a native dramatic literature carefully followed Italian or French models. Tragic writers of the day slavishly imitated Voltaire and obeyed the rules as to how a play should be structured, as well as what subject matter should be chosen.

During the latter part of the seventeenth century and the first half of the eighteenth, some earnest if not too able efforts had been made at literate drama. One early playwright is the Silesian-born and much-honoured poet Andreas Gryphius (1616–64), who was a clergyman's son. (The family name was Greif, but the son Latinized it.)

Gryphius was left an orphan when he was very young and was driven from home by the chaos and enduring troubles that accompanied the Thirty Years' War. His difficult childhood and adolescence left permanent scars that caused him to develop a morbid temperament.

While he was yet a schoolboy he was singled out for his aptitude for scholarship and skill with Latin verses. At twenty he found a patron who bestowed on him "a poet's laurel crown, the title of doctor of philosophy and a patent of nobility". Later he travelled, lectured in Holland, visited France and Italy and came back to Germany to teach.

He composed a series of tragedies, more or less as an avocation. The plays, five in all, are in Alexandrine verse. He was particularly influenced by Vondel, the Dutch dramatist. *Leo Armenius* tells of an emperor deposed and executed by conspirators. *Katherine of Georgia* portrays a Christian Queen who chooses martyrdom rather than apostasy. *Cardenio and Celinde* is a compilation of horrors based on a story Gryphius heard during his stay in Italy. *Murdered Majesty, or Carolus Stuardus* was unusual in that it dealt with an event that was very recent, the beheading of Charles I. "Seeing that our whole fatherland is now buried in its own ashes and converted into a theatre of vanity, my aim is to represent the mutability of human affairs," he wrote. Gryphius accomplished this all too well in these Senecan works that present the ugly aspects of life and man's ineluctable misery. But the plays are far-fetched and bombastic. They show their author possessing little sense of the dramatic.

What is surprising, for one of his grim outlook, is that he does far better with comedy. He wrote three, the best of which is *Horribilicribrifax*. In this an old friend reappears, the *miles gloriosus* Horribilicribrifax, though here he is doubled – that is, there are two braggart captains, both of them thorough cowards at heart. There is also a foolish pedant, Sempronius, who addresses people in Latin and Greek though they cannot understand him. The characters are hardly original, but they have more life than the author's tragic heroes. In one comedy Gryphius uses Silesian dialect, and in another instance he freely borrows from Shakespeare's incident of Pyramus and Thisbe from *A Midsummer Night's Dream*.

A contemporary of Gryphius was Johann von Rist (1607–67), also the son of a Lutheran pastor, and later himself in the pulpit of that faith. A poet, he began his playwriting career with *Perseus* (1634). His two most interesting works are *Das Friedewünschende Teutschland* (*Germany Wishing Peace*; 1647) and *Das Friedejauchzende Teutschland* (*Germany Rejoicing in Our Peace*; 1653). He was crowned laureate by Ferdinand III in recognition of his poetic ability. Today Rist is better remembered as a composer of church hymns than as a dramatist. Historical interest in him, as in Gryphius, is largely academic so far as the theatre is concerned.

Vienna had its Burgtheater, and in Stockholm a similar project, the Royal Swedish Theatre, was launched in 1737; a second National Theatre was built in 1773. Some of Germany's leading stage artists were drawn to a like enterprise in Hamburg, principally Konrad Ekhof and Friedrich Ludwig Schröder, two actors of legendary stature in German history.

The first important sign that conditions in Germany's theatre might improve was the advent of an indomitable woman, Carolina Neuber, who headed an acting troupe. By all accounts she was beautiful and talented, and her thinking was progressive. She dreamed of raising the level of stage art in Germany. In 1717 she had run away from an uncongenial home to join a touring group. She had been accompanied by a young man who became her husband. Her dream was to popularize a new and more subdued style of acting and acquire better plays.

In 1727, after a decade of hard experience, she encountered a remarkable man, Johann Christoph Gottsched (1700–1766), who was the dominant literary figure in Leipzig. He was charming and persuasive, or seemed so to the aspiring Carolina Neuber. He talked, as she did initially, of a more exalted German theatre not only in Leipzig but everywhere else in the country. She joined forces with him to attain that goal.

Gottsched was highly ambitious. His firm aim was to make himself the cultural dictator of all Germany. Leipzig was already a centre of literary and other artistic activity. He agreed to furnish Neuber with fresh scripts, promising that together they would drive out the degraded Hans Wurst kind of theatrical fare.

He kept his word. He translated French tragedies, including one by Pradon, and made them available to the Neuber company. He also wrote dramas in the same pseudo-classical style. Unfortunately these were more stilted and lifeless. His poetic gifts were limited. He had no theatre-sense or stage experience, so that the Neuber company hardly prospered. In fact they had to restore their finances regularly by providing the loathed Hans Wurst slapstick.

Gottsched, venturing a play of his own, modelled it on Addison's enormously successful

Cato. The Neubers put it on some time later, but it was a disaster. One reason was that Gottsched insisted that the costumes be authentically Roman. Neuber conceded to his demand though she doubted that the spectators were ready to accept the bold innovation. Her instinct was right. Because his concepts were soon outdated, the actors' simple but archaic dress was much condemned. In all Gottsched has perhaps been defamed more than he should be, as he did strive to bring shape and decorum to the stage.

The once hopeful alliance between the courageous Neuber and Gottsched constantly worsened. It did not help when he insisted that she use a new version of *Alzire*, a script by Voltaire, translated by his wife, even though the troupe already had a better one by another hand. Gottsched and the Neubers broke off the relationship and he became their enemy, and as the leading critic in Leipzig his pen was destructive. Eventually, after a series of failures, the Neubers fell on hard times.

Before this sad event, though, Carolina had discovered a young genius who was really to inaugurate the reforms of which she dreamed. His name was Gotthold Ephraim Lessing. She recognized a gift and generously helped to start his amazing career.

Born in Kamenz in Upper Saxony, and destined to be one of the great minds in German literature, Lessing was the son of a pastor who was, in addition, a serious theologian. But this educated family was poor and sometimes knew hunger. From age twelve to age seventeen the boy studied at Meissen, where supposedly he initiated his effort at playwriting. He was drawn towards the theatre, and his meeting with his "free-thinking" cousin Carolina Neuber was a lucky event that led him to submit to her a script, *The Young Scholar* (1748), which he had just revised from an earlier draft. The Neuber troupe produced it successfully.

The Young Scholar, another satire on pedantry, went over well. Lessing was a precocious nineteen, and Frau Neuber hailed him as the "German Molière". He tried to justify this appellation by hurriedly writing four more comedies during the next two years, *The Woman Hater*, *The Old Maid*, *The Jews* and *The Free Thinker*. Actually they show little or no trace of Molière but rather evoke Regnard, Marivaux, Destouches, Congreve, Vanbrugh and Holberg.

As a whole, these, and two subsequent scripts, one of them (an adaptation of Plautus) still derivative, are the work of a very young man. Their most original aspect is his attitude towards religion and foreigners. Both his one-act *The Jews* and *The Free Thinker* contain pleas for tolerance. In all his works, too, the dialogue is decidedly lively, an effective mixture of good humour and good sense. Increasingly the characters become more human, and there is an infusion of sentiment that remains above sentimentality.

As an artist Lessing had an innate sophistication and refinement and avoided many of the errors that waylay other neophytes. The chief fault in these early scripts is structural, and this is the weakness of virtually every young playwright, as Aristotle long ago observed.

From Lessing's close association with the Neubers and their company, however, he got a first-hand look at a theatre and was able to analyse some of its essential dynamics. He had also wisely taken some acting lessons.

His parents, hearing of his theatre connections, strongly disapproved. He was summoned home; he obeyed and agreed to study medicine. When the Neuber company ran into financial trouble and temporarily broke up, Lessing himself was much in danger of being arrested for debt because he had stood surety for some of its members. He fled from Leipzig to Berlin where over the next few years he worked as a freelance critic and writer, paying special heed to matters theatrical.

The post of theatre poet was offered to Lessing, who modestly refused it; he chose instead to become the official critic. This led to his epochal series of play reviews, later gathered into a volume called *Hamburg Dramaturgy* (1769), often described as second only to Aristotle's *Poetics* for their impact on people's thinking about the theatre.

The German National Theatre lasted a mere two years. Among other factors, extremely bad management and excessive intrigue among the actors brought about its untimely end. Lessing, writing its epitaph, said ruefully, "What a naïve idea to give the Germans a national theatre, when we Germans are not yet a nation."

At least, however, his developing concepts of drama were now accessible in a book. In *Hamburg Dramaturgy* Lessing builds up his assault on what he calls French pseudo-classicism. He asserts that the Racine–Voltaire type of play was not really Greek, but the opposite of what Athenian playwrights achieved. Corneille and Voltaire are subjected to withering scrutiny. Lessing pays high tribute to Shakespeare and ranks him with Sophocles, which may strike some readers as heretical. He dismisses the compressed unities that those who claimed to be disciples of Aristotle embrace, arguing that they have misinterpreted what the Greek philosopher said.

Lessing's essay was just the polemic the German theatre needed to become free from decades of slavish imitation of French models. He cleared the stage for Romanticism and realism, stating as he did in his oft-quoted rallying cry, "The one thing we can never forgive in a tragic poet is coldness: if he arouses our interest it does not matter what he does with the petty mechanical rules." That was deliverance from the academic pedants.

All form should be organic, Lessing said: it should spring from the circumstances and inspiration that lead to a work of art, and what might have been of consequence to an Athenian play-maker or French Baroque tragic poet might not apply with the same force to a dramatist whose purpose is different, or who writes in a new time and social context.

To give examples of what he meant, Lessing himself wrote a comedy and a tragedy. *Minna von Barnhelm* (1767) was so original that it has been called the first work of its kind in any European language. A new form of comedy came into existence. The plot was not wholly fresh, but it could hardly be expected that by now any comic plot could be: minute critical studies have inevitably brought to light other literary influences. Yet in sum *Minna von Barnhelm* marks the creation of a truly novel genre, a contribution the stage badly needed, that answered to the changing times.

The principal figure is not really Minna but her lover Tellheim, a Prussian army officer. At the end of the Seven Years War, with the victory going to Saxony, Tellheim is penniless and in disgrace. He reveals his generous nature when he refuses payment of money by the widow of a man indebted to him. In much the same spirit, he no longer considers that he has the right, in his impoverished state, to claim the hand of Minna, daughter of a wealthy Saxon landowner. He cannot bear the thought of being financially inferior and dependent on her.

The lovers are separated not only because Minna is rich and Tellheim is overly proud but poor, but also because she is a Saxon and he is a Prussian, and bitter feeling still prevails between these two German peoples. The play bespeaks the need for reconciliation between enemies who are of the same stock and speak the same language. The unification of Germany was one of Lessing's most fervent hopes.

The affectionate portrait of Tellheim is a result of Lessing's strong friendship with a Major Ewald von Kleist, also a poet, who perished from a wound he received at the Battle of Kunnersdorf. Tellheim is idealistic and thoroughly impractical, as instanced by his firm adherence to the Prussian officer's outmoded code of honour. Lessing saw the urgent need for many social reforms in the Germany of his day. He was also able to handle the conflicting attitudes of Saxons and Prussians with subtle tact, giving offence to neither side, criticizing both.

At the same time, a minor plot brings in Riccaut de la Marlinière, an exiled French adventurer who is dishonest, who is made an object of ridicule by the patriotic Lessing. The playwright decried the then current German infatuation with all things Gallic and held French culture in some contempt.

Minna has been searching for Tellheim. When she overtakes him but he refuses to marry her, she resorts to several bits of guile to learn his true feeling for her and then to recapture him. She is finally able to persuade him by telling him that she has been disinherited; if she is poor, he feels that he can wed her. Tellheim optimistically plans to make a new fortune for them both.

Next, word comes that Tellheim is once more in the good graces of the Prussian King, Frederick the Great, so that his prospects are brighter. Lessing admired Frederick, who is fulsomely praised in the play because he promises to be the one who might yet lead the Germans to nationhood.

The humour of the play arises from a series of embarrassments and misunderstandings, as well as from the light dialogue. The character portrayals are shrewdly authentic, as they are prone to carry things too far. Tellheim is often irrational and Minna has a streak of obstinacy and is occasionally mischievous, though these traits are at odds with her essential practicality.

A second sub-plot concerns Franziska, Minna's maidservant, who is in love with Paul Werner, an ambitious sergeant-major who has served with Tellheim. This love intrigue is treated as seriously as Minna's and Tellheim's, a democratic touch that forecasts the increasing humanization of modern comedy. These are not literary or stock characters. Simpler and more traditional farce types are present, however, in the person of Tellheim's fanatically loyal manservant, and the mercenary landlord of the inn that provides a setting for most of the action. The plot is excellently structured, and Lessing anticipates Ibsen in his apt use of distributed exposition in revealing Tellheim's artistic background by scattering brief allusions to past events throughout the play.

Outside Germany, the worth of *Minna von Barnhelm* is somewhat debated today. In places the dialogue is too sentimental for modern taste, and its piety and patriotism seem too naïve. But it was a far better comic work than any being produced not only in Germany but in England at that time, and it gave the local stage its first classic, one still revived endlessly. This is a new kind of domestic comedy; the language in it is everyday speech, and everyone in it acts plausibly.

The tragedy *Emilia Galotti* (1772) is now more highly esteemed. The Roman tale of Virginia, whose stern father stabs her to death to spare her the clutches of a lecherous tyrant, furnished Lessing with the outline of his plot. He gave it a contemporary setting, though it is still an Italian one. The theme had obsessed Lessing for a long while, and he had at first intended to give it political overtones. But it finally became the story of an art-loving nobleman who has wearied of his mistress and become infatuated with the virginal beauty of Emilia Galotti. Lessing alters the plot-line by having Emilia consciously respond to the lascivious Prince's seduction and then beg her father to kill her lest she succumb to her seducer's advances; her father finally obliges her.

The story is *au fond* an unlikely one; it is hard to make it believable, and Lessing, despite a display of masterly technique, does not succeed in making it wholly credible. But the characters are alive, the pace is swift, and the script's many telling lines and close-knit structure have earned it much admiration. What is more, this play about a dissolute aristocrat was seen as a comment on the depravity of contemporary German princelings. As such, it was a contribution to a revolutionary sentiment that had begun to stir and grow. Indeed it was not without political significance, however muted that element in it might be.

In the final issue of the *Hamburg Dramaturgy* Lessing openly renounced the name of poet. He felt that his chief talent was that of critic, and he attributed any poetic success he might have had to his critical rather than poetic faculties. He defended his chief gift, however: "They say it stifles genius, and I thought I had got from it something that comes very close to genius." He did not like to hear the critical sense belittled. "I am a lame man," he continued, "who cannot be edified by a lampoon against crutches." Both of these famous and influential plays, *Minna von Barnhelm* and *Emilia Galotti*, might best be described as accomplishments not of a true and spontaneous poet but of a writer with a superbly disciplined and penetrating intellect that enabled him to achieve works not of greatness but of the highest distinction.

Lessing's most important drama was to be his last, however, after a lapse of seven years during which he had a post awarded him by the Duke of Brunswick. He badly needed an income. Here he chanced upon the unpublished manuscript of a lately demised scholar, H.S. Reimarus, that analysed and challenged the literal truth of the Bible. The author had laboured on his examination for years but had not dared to print it, aware that it would scandalize orthodox Lutherans.

Lessing, devoted to truth at any cost, was not as easily deterred. He found Reimarus's arguments to be impressive, though he did not always concur with them. He chose excerpts from the book, had them published and immediately was the focus of a furious controversy. He was roundly assailed as an "enemy of religion" and replied to his foes in brilliant pamphlets that championed what is now called the "higher criticism" of the scriptures. His contention was that religion predates the Bible and therefore need not depend solely on the scriptures for its warrant. His opponents persuaded the Duke of Brunswick to silence him by official decree.

At this point Lessing reminded himself that the stage was a means whereby to continue his struggle. "I must see whether they will at least let me preach undisturbed in my old pulpit, the theatre." In a few months he brought out *Nathan the Wise* (1779).

The setting of this dramatic poem is Jerusalem during the third Crusade. Nathan, a sage Jew, is a portrait of Lessing's own friend, the eminent philosopher Moses Mendelssohn. Recha, Nathan's adopted daughter, falls in love with a hot-headed German Templar who has been taken captive. Nathan is called before the Sultan Saladin and asked to declare which religion is best. The old man responds by reciting and reapplying the parable of the Three Rings (borrowed from Boccaccio's *Decameron* though it dates much earlier).

In Boccaccio's version the ring is a priceless jewel that each father bequeaths to a favourite son to designate him the successor as head of the family. It finally comes into the possession of a warm-hearted father with three sons whom he prizes equally. Not wishing to discriminate among them, he orders two new rings so like the original that he himself can hardly tell them apart. Before his death he gives a ring to each son. Though they quarrel among themselves, each asserting that he is the chosen one, there is no certain way of determining whose claim is best, and it is finally left unsettled until their future behaviour reveals the answer.

Lessing has his wise Nathan adapt this parable, enriching and deepening it. The ring has magical powers: both God and men cherish whoever possesses it, as long as it is worn "with faith in its efficacy". Also, the modest judge to whom the contentious sons appeal rebukes them for their debate. He tells them a thousand thousand years must pass, "when a wiser judge may be able to render a right decision". Even more, it is discovered that Nathan's adopted daughter is actually Saladin's niece – the child of the Muslim's brother by a German wife – and the Templar is her brother. Though no marriage follows, there is a happy family reunion. Muslims, Christians and Jews spontaneously embrace. All men are brothers, it would seem.

The play embodies fully the tolerant and rational spirit of the Age of Enlightenment as the "natural religion" of Diderot, a faith that is to be adjudged by its fruits, not by its historicity or the sway its dogmas have over people's minds. The test is an evolutionary one; the truth of any cult shall be tested by the long-term results its followers achieve in "good works". At the same time it is not anti-religious, as many views held by disciples of the Enlightenment tended to be.

But in another way *Nathan the Wise* anticipates the Romantic Age that is soon to ensue, for it is not written in Alexandrines that Lessing deemed ill-suited to German, but in blank verse like a Shakespearean play. He thus established – along with Herder and Klopstock – a precedent for Goethe and Schiller and the other exemplars of Germany's more lyric school of drama who were to succeed him. As he had frankly acknowledged, he himself was an indifferent poet, but his dialogue, nervous and terse, works well on the stage.

Nathan the Wise was not produced during Lessing's lifetime, when anti-Semitism was strong in Germany. It was first staged, with scant success, in Berlin in 1785, and then revived by Goethe and Schiller (with some changes by Schiller) in Weimar in 1801. Afterwards it became surprisingly popular.

Unlike Holberg, who had stayed a bachelor, Lessing belatedly married a widow, when he could afford to do so, in 1776. His venture was ill-starred; his wife died in childbirth in 1778. He himself had only three more years of life, and his crowded days closed with him weary, lonely and impoverished. But he had created the foundation of a vital German theatre.

— 10 —

THEATRE IN RUSSIA

By the beginning of the eighteenth century, in 1702, Russia had a state theatre built by Peter the Great. The Russian people might be said to have a genius for the theatrical, an instinct for ceremony and pageantry. They had long displayed it in wedding festivities and religious rituals that were first pagan, then Christian. It has been said the ancient and traditional wedding celebrations lasting two or three days are essentially many-act plays in which various stages of the groom's conquest of the bride are pantomimically dramatized, along with solo and choral chants and dances.

Funerals were similarly enlivened enactments by professional mourners. Elaborate festivities with masks and costumes also marked the arrival of spring, the New Year, and activities such as hunting, weaving and cattle breeding. After the advent of Christianity in the tenth century there were Lenten carnivals that involved magnificent costumes with participants disguised as animals, principally as goats and foxes. All through these early epochs, too, ballad singers recited the epic tales.

The Middle Ages (the tenth to the sixteenth centuries) saw the rise of *skomorokhi*, vagabond entertainers frowned on by priests and the nobility for incorporating indecent songs and dances in their performances. These exhibitions might also include trained bears and dogs in their cast. Puppet shows were also a frequent item on their programme. The antics of the bears were much appreciated by audiences, even by the rich boyars and aristocrats. Social criticism was also voiced in the songs and puppet plays in which the boyars and local officials were depicted as harsh, greedy and foolish. At court, jesters borrowed jokes and "business" from the pranks of the *skomorokhi.*

In the booths of the puppeteers, Pierrot in the Italian and French *commedia dell'arte* took on the identity of Petrushka. Gradually, in the sixteenth century, the humour of these plays ascended from the coarse and obscene to more tasteful works, partly as a result of Polish influence. The Church, too, intervened, substituting as entertainment a series of biblical incidents enacted by puppets. A programme might consist half of religious playlets and half of bawdy representations of everyday life.

Morality plays appeared as well, but had less appeal. The liturgy was already in the Slavonic vulgate, and consequently the Mass needed less interpretation. But such small dramas as *Jesus on the Donkey*, performed on Palm Sunday, and *The Last Judgement* and *The Drama of the Burning Furnace*, enacted on the Saturday before Christmas, were popular. Significantly, they were staged at the altar, or at least in the church, and not in the street.

In the sixteenth century, too, students from the Kievan Theological Academy travelled about, bringing with them religious dramas, the texts based on evangelical themes or biblical incidents; at first, the plays were in Latin but later in Russian. These allegorical scripts often imitated Jesuit models, and had some literary merit. The best were written by St Dimitry of Rostov, known to have died in 709. The plays were staged at the Academy, but during the summer holidays they were performed elsewhere by students taking to the road. In return, wealthy landowners, in whose houses the students presented the pious dramas, gave the players clothing, food and drink.

Theatre of a far more professional sort reached Moscow in the reign of Tsar Alexei, during the second half of the seventeenth century. The Tsar was told of the marvels of the French stage, and also of occasional performances in the foreign embassies in the capital, especially at the home of the English ambassador. The ruler sent an envoy abroad to bring back a company of players. These were late in coming, however, because they were fearful of venturing into rumouredly barbaric Russia. Impatient, Alexei called upon Johann Gottfried Gregory, pastor of the Lutheran Church, to mount a biblical play at court. Gregory, an amateur poet, was eager to oblige. With the aid of some other foreigners of his acquaintance he put into rehearsal a dramatic version of the tale of Esther. Some months of preparation were needed, while he recruited a cast of sixty-four and improvised a theatre at the Tsar's palace. This description of it by Marc Slonim is vivid:

> It was lighted by tallow candles in wooden candelabra, the walls decorated with bright raspberry and green cloth, the benches and the Tsar's seat upholstered in red velvet, and the curtains slid along a thick iron rod to which were attached sixty brass rings. The stage, decorated by fir trees on both sides, had a red carpet and a bright blue background which represented the sky. Costumes were sprinkled with gold; Esther wore a magnificent white dress with golden stripes, the warriors had real swords, and Haman was hanged on a real gallows. Music was played between the scenes. The day of the first performance, October 7, 1672, the Tsar came alone, without his family, and was first stunned and then so enchanted that he stayed in the theatre for ten consecutive hours. The succeeding officials came from the capital in a long procession; those who showed little desire to attend "foreigners' tricks" were summoned by the Tsar's messengers. The new entertainment had great success, and the Tsar's whole family was allowed to enjoy it from a special box endowed with sliding gratings and curtains.

Before long, the performances were shifted to Moscow. A comedy and interludes were added to the programme.

Encouraged, though his knowledge must have been limited, Pastor Gregory began a theatre school the next year, the expenses covered by a royal grant. He enrolled twenty-six students.

Thus, from its start, the theatre in Russia was under court control, supported by the state treasury. Soon it took on a frankly political colouring: it aimed to bolster the monarchy. The plays habitually contained fulsome praise of the Tsar. It also became the subject of controversy, incurring the approval of progressives and criticism by conservatives.

Pastor Gregory's theatre flourished for several years; most of its scripts came from the Kievan Academy. When Tsar Alexei died in 1676 the theatre's public career was suspended; but his daughter, Sophia, was fond of writing plays and acting in them with courtiers. Under her auspices a private theatre continued in the palace.

Peter the Great, that energetic Westernizer, restored a state theatre and appointed another German, Johann Kunst, to direct it. To Kunst was entrusted a task similar to that given to his predecessor, Gregory. As is often told, Peter was determined to bring his people up to date. He decreed that native actors must be trained and dress in modern garb. Once more, his aim was to use the theatre as a political tool. Peter had erected a theatre in Moscow; in 1709 he opened a second in St Petersburg, the new city to which he was transferring his seat of rule. The theatre in Moscow was a wooden structure not far from the Kremlin. It had a gallery, benches and a lofty decorated ceiling almost 50 feet high. The auditorium was of moderate size, approximately 140 by 105 feet.

Peter called on Kunst to provide secular dramas popular elsewhere in Europe. Performances were given thrice weekly and consisted of both tragedies and farces. The Tsar's purpose was to wean the Russian intelligentsia away from a clerical, Byzantine tradition to which he attributed much of his people's backwardness. Accordingly, Kunst staged works by Corneille as well as successful Italian writers and even sought to introduce opera, though with little luck.

When Kunst died in 1703 another German, Otto Furst, an ex-jeweller, replaced him. The company that acted in both theatres was made up largely of students of Kunst and Furst. One of the Tsar's sisters, Natalia, developed a personal zeal for theatre and had a wooden pavilion built at court for more performances, mounting thirteen plays there.

To further Peter's agenda, the newly formed Slavonic Greek and Latin Academy in Moscow also staged works lauding him for his reforms and military triumphs. When Peter divorced his Greek Orthodox Queen and wed Catherine, a German Lutheran, the story-line of Esther was obligingly altered: the biblical King was shown getting rid of his unpleasant mate and choosing in her place an attractive, virtuous foreigner. Feofan Prokopovich (1681–1736) wrote many of the scripts to Peter's orders.

Another lull followed Peter's demise in 1725. His successor, his niece the Empress Anna, had a taste for the more primitive, coarse, loud German farces. A troupe from Leipzig took over the Russian stage. It was during Anna's reign, however, that Italian opera reached St Petersburg, this time scoring a hit. In its invasion, this company directed by Francesco Araia brought *commedia dell'arte* mimes, actors and singers. Audiences were strongly impressed by the elaborate scenery and unfamiliar stage effects. Araia remained in St Petersburg for twenty-four years, from 1735 to 1759, and, with the help of his Bolognese designer, Giovanni Buon, greatly raised the state of stagecraft and production. Italian operas were given at least once weekly and often more frequently, alternating with plays of every sort, chiefly at the court theatre but sometimes in a hall now provided in the Summer Garden.

Very important was the arrival of another Italian, Antonio Fusano, who with his attractive wife Giulia introduced the Russians to ballet. Shortly after came Jean-Baptiste Landet (or Landé), who offered a school for dancers, creating a *corps de ballet* in which his students performed. He gained financial aid from the Empress. By making his student dancers available, he prepared the way for other foreign choreographers who were also invited to the court. Landet is often called the "father of Russian ballet".

Soon a conflict arose between Italian and French influences. Italians stressed leaps, jumps and other acrobatic tricks, while the French were more interested in showing plastic beauty, grace and elegance, in a style they developed at Versailles.

The next Empress, Elizabeth – Peter's daughter – was light-hearted and pleasure-loving. She sought to imitate the French monarchs, decorated her palace lavishly and entertained resplendently. Her courtiers, like those in France, took part in amateur theatricals; some were plays based on Russian folk tales, incorporating native dances.

Drawn in by rumours of the imperial largesse, more and more foreign troupes came to St Petersburg. Outstanding among them were the French, who presented works by Racine, Corneille and Molière. To compete, the Italians staged Metastasio's *opera seria La Clemenza di Tito* with great *éclat* on the occasion of Elizabeth's coronation.

In 1750 the Empress issued an edict permitting nobles to stage plays in their far-flung manors. Living in isolation on their estates, with many serfs, wealthy landowners soon organized private acting and dance companies. From these, talent was gradually recruited for the cities.

In the capital a national theatre was finally coming into being. The appearance of the poet Alexander Petrovich Sumarokov (1718–77) expanded this development; his tragedies were first acted by cadets of the Academy of the Nobility, of which he was an alumnus. The students greatly admired Sumarokov's scripts. The Empress, hearing them much praised, had them presented at court, beginning with *Khorev* (1749), followed by *Zemir* (1751) and a series of similar works. Sumarokov was also responsible for an adaptation of Shakespeare's *Hamlet* (1748), revised to have it conform more nearly to Voltaire's stilted precepts for serious drama.

A still more important factor in the development of Russian theatre was the arrival of Fyodor Volkov (1729–63). During two years in St Petersburg this merchant's son had become deeply enamoured of theatre. He returned to his native town, provincial Yaroslavl. Intent upon becoming an actor, he taught himself and his brothers and friends the art. Their activity began in a barn transformed into a theatre.

Volkov's range as an actor was wide. He assumed both tragic and comic, feminine as well as masculine roles. He fashioned himself after French models, too, adopting a "sing-song" mode of declaration. His interpretations were emotional, especially at the climax of a scene. He deserves credit as well for his contributions as a teacher, a director and a translator. He and his brother Gregory also took part in politics; they earned the gratitude of the Empress Elizabeth for their aid in the *coup d'état* that brought her to power.

His productions impressed the people of Yaroslavl so much that they enthusiastically put up a theatre to accommodate 1,000 persons. Word of this eventually reached the Empress, who sent for the company and had it perform at court. An ancient morality play, *The Repentance of a Sinner*, was their vehicle; it won Elizabeth's unstinted approval. She arranged for some of the cast members to enter the Academy of the Nobility to complete their training.

Following Sumarokov's example, other Russian writers were turning out plays. Even an opera, with libretto by Sumarokov and score by Araia, was attempted; the entire ensemble of singers and dancers was Russian. The Empress perceived that her country could now have a theatre of its own, like those in more progressive Western countries. On 30 August 1763 such a theatre was formally established. The director was to be Sumarokov. Curiously, the state subsidy went mostly to Italian productions – six times as large an annual sum as to Russian endeavours – and then the second largest amount to the French. German productions had lost favour by now. Some of the money was to provide the native actors with costumes of velvet, brocade and glittering stones, to satisfy the public fondness for such rich display. To encourage native Russian art even more, Elizabeth commissioned two noted Russian men of letters, Trediakovsky and Lomonossov, to furnish tragic scripts.

The theatre was housed in a stone building on Vassily Island, in St Petersburg. Its accomplishments scarcely matched those of the players still at court. Molière, in translation, proved to be exceedingly popular. The public was particularly drawn to a lavish production of *The Bourgeois Gentleman* (*Le Bourgeois gentilhomme*), done on a scale that led the company to double the price of tickets.

The ascent of Catherine II marked a further advance of Russian theatre. Volkov was knighted, as was his brother who had assisted him. With Sumarokov they staged a splendid festival to honour the new ruler. It was a mythological pageant entitled *Minerva's Progress*. While working outdoors on some details in Moscow's frigid winter, Volkov unfortunately caught cold and died shortly after. He was only thirty-four.

Through Sumarokov, who published a translation of Boileau's essay on poetic art, French classicism gained a firm foothold in Russia. Tragedies were modelled on those of Racine and Voltaire, as in Germany before Lessing. One of Sumarokov's prominent successors was Yakov B. Knyazhnin, whose best-known drama, *Vadim of Novgorod* (1789), was shaped along classical lines.

With the Empress's support the theatre flourished more than ever. Catherine was more than a passive spectator. With some help, she herself wrote more than a dozen comedies and dramas and five musical plays. Mostly members of her family and retinue took part in these and even danced in ballets, in a new Court Theatre she ordered erected at the Winter Palace.

More importantly, in 1773 Catherine had a huge public theatre constructed, to which was later given the name the Bolshoi (which means "the large"). To staff it, in 1779 she also founded an Imperial Theatrical School to educate young actors, singers and dancers. Both the theatre and the school were soon put in charge of an imperial administration whose control – reflecting the wishes of the sovereign – was absolute. During this time, too, provincial theatres had begun to spring up. They also were under governmental supervision. One quarter of their gross profits was taken in tax; the money collected was assigned to orphanages. For over a century this rule was enforced, and the tax on theatres was turned over to charities and scholarly institutions. Consequently the administrative stranglehold on stage activities, including opera, ballet and concerts, was imposed early in Russian's history. In practice, however, provincial theatres, if distant from the capital, had a measure of autonomy. Many did not have state financial aid. How much freedom they enjoyed often depended upon the provincial governor, since he knew best what was happening in his region.

Any description of the Russian stage at this period must include the private theatres, those belonging to the nobles and the richest landowners. Soon Russia was dotted with such stages. Many were very elaborate, designed by foreign architects and gave magnificent productions costing fortunes. An estate-owner might possess as many as 10,000 or 20,000 serfs. From these he would assemble or draft the most gifted actors, dancers and musicians. The training of these "artists" was sometimes extremely harsh: if they failed to perform well they might be flogged or publicly humiliated. The knout was frequently used when an actor failed to please a cruel master. Concubinage was also a feature of the still barbaric system. Some of the autocratic landowners had two and even three theatres, perhaps one or more on separate estates in the country and one in town. The actors could be bought or exchanged: companies were sometimes put on the block by an owner. Agents sometimes purchased unusual talent on behalf of the official theatre companies in the capital. Once these serfs became government property they might purchase their freedom or be emancipated in acknowledgement of their outstanding accomplishments.

A wealthy landowner might have a correspondent in Paris who sent word of the latest stage successes there and obtain the scripts. Count Peter Sheremetyev, who had three theatres, had a principal company of 230 members. Royalty and foreign dignitaries attended and extravagantly applauded his productions. As a climax to the Count's infatuation with theatre, he fell in love with one of his low-born actresses. He finally obtained permission from the Tsar to marry her, and her early death in childbirth left him heartbroken.

Foreign plays, predominantly the works of the French including Racine, Corneille, Molière, Beaumarchais, Destouches and Voltaire, flooded the Russian stage through the first half of the century – but also the plays of Shakespeare, Holberg, Goldoni and Goethe. The second half of the century saw a rise in the number of original Russian contributions. One record shows that at least 250 plays by native authors comprised the dramatic library in print or manuscript. Over a hundred were comedies. As might be expected, these drew more directly on everyday life and hence were more realistic and authentic. The tragedies, as has been noted, borrowed heavily from literary models. They adhered strictly to the three unities. The aristocrats were by now oriented to looking westwards in all matters cultural; they despised their own folklore as primitive and coarse, as indeed it often was. Even though tragic heroes might have Russian names, and the theme of the drama was taken from Russian history, they talked and acted like figures in the works of Corneille and Racine. The plays were still largely dedicated to glorifying the monarchy and exalting the bonds of loyalty between the nobles and their sovereign. As long as the theatre contributed to a nationalistic feeling and fervour, it continued to have generous imperial support.

Besides those by Sumarokov and the tragedy *Rosslav* by Knyazhnin, tragedies of this sort were written by Mikhail Kheraskov (1733–1807) and Vladislav Ozerov (1769–1816), in his rousingly patriotic *Dmitry Donskoy*. Though they had contemporary success (Ozerov especially), neither of these last two authors was destined to win immortality.

Both Sumarokov and Knyazhnin were not above producing "low" comedies. Those by Sumarokov were more than a little didactic. Knyazhnin turned out satirical portraits of social climbers, fortune-hunters and title-seekers in such pieces as *The Braggart* and *The Queer Fellow*. Those plays and other comedies by Knyazhnin have a down-to-earth quality. Tearful comedy found its proponent in V. Lukin, with *The Spendthrift, Reformed by Love* (1765) and *Rewarded Constancy*. Another with a pen for lachrymose humour was the actor Peter Plavilschikov (1760–1812), who wrote *The Wretched and Solitary One* and *The Store Clerk*; he also used it for published articles calling for more plays that pictured the national scene more fully.

By far the most able comic author of this epoch is Denis Fonvizin (1743–92), whose two masterworks are *The Brigadier-General* (1766) and *The Minor* (1781). These are pieces of permanent vitality. In the first, the son of a retired military officer is engaged to marry a councillor's daughter. But both he and his father are rivals for the favours of the elderly and dishonest councillor's wife, who visits Paris and is a devoted reader of French novels. The plot is slight and secondary; what counts most is the clear image of social manners of the time. The atmosphere of the period is vividly summoned up. Fun is poked, as in Holberg, at the affectations of those who superficially assume a Gallic style of life. They are contrasted to the rude behaviour of those unenlightened Russians who have not yet embraced foreign customs. Both the determination to remain backward and the attempt to be "advanced" are satirized as extremes that should take moderation into account.

The Minor is even more highly estimated. The Prostakovs are a wealthy family of simpletons. The father is weak; the mother is mean and bossy, the brother-in-law boorish, the sixteen-year-old son completely spoiled. In contrast to this motley crew are representatives of the more high-minded of the *ancien régime*: the courageous hero, a soldier, the earnest-souled heroine, her virtuous uncle, and a government inspector who eventually has the Pros takovs evicted from their estate.

The dialogue is heavily didactic: the uncle, Stavrodum, is forever comparing present-day manners and morals to those of the past, the better days of Peter the Great. Now he declares that all is corruption, that French literature brings demoralizing ideas. The true ideal is for an aristocrat to serve his country and his fellow men. The Tsar ought to be above flattery and care for his subjects' well-being.

Prostakov's wife has hired a trio of tutors for her pampered son Mitrophan. The Tsarina had ordered that all the children of the aristocracy be educated, a notion that the mother – herself dull-witted – dismisses as nonsensical. Nevertheless she complies. The boy is ignorant and wishes to remain so. This leads to amusing scenes in which pedagogy is discussed, tested and defeated. Sophia, the heroine, resists her guardian Prostakova's efforts to make a match between her and the idiot son. The brother-in-law, a crude pig-lover, enters the competition for Sophia's hand. Finally Sophia regains her legacy – unlawfully appropriated by Prostakov's wife – and weds a military officer of her choice. The play abounds in rich minor as well as major characters, evokes it era vividly and is full of racy speech. It is an unquestioned Russian classic.

Education is also the theme of a shorter piece by Fonvizin, *The Choice of a Tutor* (1792). Here a good teacher and a bad teacher are presented. The latter is a manicurist. The good teacher very much resembles the very French uncle, Stavrodum, in *The Minor*. By this time the French Revolution had occurred, and the good teacher – a Russian scholar – is of the opinion that "equality" is a dangerous concept. An earlier, hilarious farce by Fonvizin is *The Booby* (1782). The fatuous young hero of this script wishes to be married "this very night"; he does not care who the bride might be.

Other effective practitioners of comedy are a former serf, Mikhail Matinsky (1750–*c.* 1820), and Vasili Yakovlevich (1757–*c.* 1824). Both take off the unscrupulousness of local magistrates, the former in his *St Petersburg's Gostiny Dvor* (1782) and the latter in *Chicanery* (1798). These are lively satires.

A play by Vasily Kapnist (1758–1823), *Chicane* (1798), has a remarkable history. Because the author disrespectfully portrayed a bureaucracy that was out to grab all it could, the infuriated Emperor Pavel decreed that the author be packed off to Siberia. On the day set for the luckless Kapnist's departure the Tsar viewed a performance of the work in the palace theatre; he was the only spectator. The play charmed him so much that he instantly revoked his sentence and instead of sending him into exile he appointed Kapnist a State Councillor. The play, however, waited another seven years before it was staged again, only to be proscribed once more. Not until another forty-eight years had passed was it at last performed without hindrance, in 1853.

Comic opera also established itself as a popular form. Two long-lasting works in this genre were *Aniutu* (1772), a tale of peasant life, and Matinsky's *St Petersburg's Gostiny Dvor*. Matinsky also wrote *The Pasha of Tunis* (1782), which continues to amuse after more than two hundred years. Even more acclaimed was *The Miller, the Witch-doctor, the Cheater and the Matchmaker* (1779), which was much in demand for many ensuing decades. This piece with the long name, often shortened to *The Miller*, was by Alexander Ablesimov.

A notable stage figure of the era was the long-lived actor Ivan Dmitrevsky (1734–1821). Over his lengthy span of years he served as stage interpreter, teacher, director, translator and historian of his art. Following Volkov's untimely death, Dmitrevsky became the star of the Russian stage. He sharpened his craft by study in Paris with the famed Talma. Handsome and gracious, he had the poise and dignity of a courtier or envoy. An intellectual, he was the familiar of the foremost writers of the day. Like Volkov he sometimes played feminine roles; but after a few years actresses gradually appeared on the stage. He excelled in tragedy but was also noted for his interpretation of Stavrodum in *The Minor*. He was finally elected to the Imperial Academy, a rare achievement for an actor; that honour did much to affirm the steadily rising estimation with which the profession was held.

A century ahead came Russia's Golden Age, bringing such geniuses as Pushkin, Ostrov sky, the two Tolstoys, Chekhov, Gorky, Stanislavsky, Turgenev, Yesenin and Meyerhold. The once-backward theatre was now foremost in Romantic, Realistic, Symbolist, and Constructivist, agit-prop and other experimental and innovative genres of drama and staging.

. . . AND IN CONCLUSION

If today's ticket-buyer attended a play in the eighteenth century, he or she would see much that was unfamiliar. The style of acting – with its semaphoric gestures, its reliance on asides to reveal the character's well-hidden and perhaps devious motives – would seem strange.

Soliloquies and lengthy *tirades* allowed even more direct expression of a character's strong beliefs and feelings. Most of the dialogue was poetic, in rhymed couplets or blank verse. Some lesser characters, especially in the comedies, might bear names that identified their occupations and personality traits – Manly, Tattle, Cook and Foible, for example. This practice dates back to Greek New Comedy and Menander's day; it was strengthened during the Middle Ages in the oft-performed religious allegories, and Shakespeare even used it sparingly in his farces. Giving such names to characters tends to flatten them to caricatures, but at the same time it universalizes them.

A historical drama that lacked appropriate period costumes would be disconcerting to a twenty-first-century play-goer, as all the characters would be in eighteenth-century attire. Julius Caesar would be dressed looking like a newly elected Parliamentarian or a fastidiously suited member of an exclusive London club or daily parader in St James's Park – nary a glimpse of a toga.

In France, Racine asked for plausible apparel for his players, but in vain. In Germany, Gottshed daringly experimented with archaic-style garments for his cast of *Cato*, but critics and the public denounced him and the production closed. Only at the end of the nineteenth century had the charismatic duo Sir Henry Irving and Ellen Terry sent their costume designers to libraries and museums to study old paintings and learn how people dressed in past epochs. This time their venture was acceptable, but the quest for authentic details raised the cost of putting on historical dramas.

One significant development, which originated at this time, was that it became possible for women to have prosperous careers as playwrights, because of Aphra Behn. Congreve and Goldoni also helped the cause of feminism by creating independent young women characters who were cleverer and more practised than their suitors. The men were mostly involved in the pursuit of facile sexual gratification and a match with a pretty young heiress who had a substantial dowry.

Neoclassicism was pervasive during this time. A disproportionate number of scripts in the French and English repertoires of this period dealt with events and people – military leaders, statesmen, poets, philosophers – from ancient Rome, as might be expected when Pierre

Corneille turned to that past epoch, as did Dryden with *All for Love* and Addison with *Cato*. There was little originality, and most things Graeco-Roman were idealized. The minds of intellectuals in the eighteenth century compulsively referred to them. What better code of conduct existed, they asked themselves, that could offer itself for guidance?

The earliest plays borrowed from classical and Renaissance sources, as did Shakespeare, and the later ones from one another. There were frequent revivals of Shakespeare, with changed endings, such as ones that had Hamlet triumphantly restored to his throne and spared Desdemona's life. The titles of many plays, lost or forgotten, also suggest a passing attraction of works with exotic Turkish, Middle Eastern or Oriental settings and colour.

Advances in stagecraft came with increasing aptitude in achieving perspective on the painted canvas flats and with more facility in lighting them.

The audience was limited in size. There were few theatres, since they needed royal or ministerial licences. The runs tended to be very short. In France and England the spectators were likely to be ever more conformist. They believed in the divine right of Kings. The monarchs were often theatre producers; that is, they licensed scripts sent to them for approval and paid for them to be staged. They provided pensions and grants to the authors and troupes and decided what was to be enacted at the palace and at the public playhouses as well. So, though it was not yet institutionalized, a royal and ministerial censorship existed. (In England official oversight began in Fielding's day and continued into the twentieth century.) Religion was not discussed on stage; this did not trouble the Puritans. They disapproved of any theatre and simply stayed away.

Only in England did comedy become blatantly bawdy and there only for a brief time. Afterwards the outrageous Restoration farces almost vanished. As late as 1895, near the end of Victoria's reign, Frederick Hawkins in his *Annals of the French Stage* defended Parisian playwrights from the intimation that the rampant eroticism of the Restoration theatre had been due to the Cavaliers' exile and residence in France. That country's light drama had been decorous and conventional then and at all subsequent times. But he exulted that the disgraceful Restoration period was past and almost forgotten, and a London theatre-goer, after an evening out, could rest his head on his pillow without a feeling of shame for having sought entertainment at a gross display of lust and impropriety. The shunning of Restoration theatre was long lasting.

If the Age of Baroque yielded less than a dozen major authors of poetic tragedies, it did contribute many interesting and effective plays that are of enduring interest for the graphic pictures they give of life, social customs and moral values during a century and a half, recreating a past world that has been absorbed into this age. And, fortunately, it was an age that saw the rise of sophisticated comedy, an accomplishment that has still not been surpassed.

INDEX

Notes: Titles of plays and other works which receive frequent mention or detailed analysis have independent main headings; works receiving only passing reference appear as subheadings under the author's name. Detailed analysis is indicated by **bold** type.